CONTENT AREA LITERACY
A Framework for Reading-Based Instruction

Fifth Edition

ULA C. MANZO

ANTHONY V. MANZO

MATTHEW M. THOMAS

WILEY

JOHN WILEY & SONS, INC.

VICE PRESIDENT AND EXECUTIVE PUBLISHER *Jay O'Callaghan*
ACQUISITIONS EDITOR *Robert Johnston*
PRODUCTION SERVICES MANAGER *Dorothy Sinclair*
PRODUCTION EDITOR *Janet Foxman*
MARKETING MANAGER *Danielle Torio*
CREATIVE DIRECTOR *Harry Nolan*
DESIGNER *Jim O'Shea*
PHOTO EDITOR *Sheena Goldstein*
EDITORIAL ASSISTANT *Carrie Tupa*
SENIOR MEDIA EDITOR *Lynn Pearlman*
PRODUCTION SERVICES *Sunitha Arun Bhaskar/Pine Tree Composition*
COVER IMAGE *Bix Burkhart/Getty Images*

This book was set in New Caledonia by Laserwords Private Limited, Chennai, India and printed and bound by Courier/Westford. The cover was printed by Courier/Westford.

This book is printed on acid-free paper. ♾

ISBN: 978-0470-12909-8

Printed in the United States of America

10 9 8 7 6 5 4 3 2 1

DEDICATION

To our children: Maria, Lisa, Anthony, Byron, Maggie, Emma, and Claire
and
To teachers everywhere–guardians of the past and trustees of the future.

"Bear in mind that the wonderful things you learn in your schools are the work of many generations. All this is put in your hands as your inheritance in order that you may receive it, honor it, add to it, and one day faithfully hand it on to your children."

—Albert Einstein

PREFACE

What we become depends on what we read after all of the professors have finished with us. The greatest university of all is a collection of books.

Thomas Carlyle (1795–1881)

Let this book be your companion—As far as learning is concerned, it is not about how many books you get to as it is about how many books get to you. The contents of this book span more than 100 years of accumulated experience, knowledge, and wisdom about the science and art of productive pedagogy. It is a reference book and ongoing story as much as a textbook. Its focus is the high art and science of teaching most any content subject in ways crafted to meet historical and current school challenges, such as accommodation for struggling readers, high achievers, and English Language Learners.

The chapters in Section I provide the conceptual foundations of Content Area Literacy, including a brief history of the emergence of this field of study, common misconceptions about reading-to-learn, a metaphor for understanding the process of reading-to-learn, and a framework for structuring reading-based instruction. Each chapter in this section concludes with a description and example of a teaching method to illustrate how theory can be translated into practice. Section II takes a close look at each of the three stages of the study-reading process—prereading, reading, and postreading—and offers descriptions and examples of teaching methods for each stage. Section III elaborates on the basic instructional framework with chapters on vocabulary, critical and creative reading, Emergent Content Area Literacy, assessment, and study strategies. Included in Section IV are chapters that focus on discipline-specific methods, provisions for the special literacy needs of adolescents, and the schoolwide Content Area Literacy program.

To allow this book to get to you, you must get into it. Read actively, write in the margins, and highlight critical passages that aid your grasp of this highly evolved science. Keep a copy close by when you teach. Rarely is it possible to study all the instructions for a game before beginning to play or to memorize a manual before turning on the computer. Learning *about* something and learning how to *do* something most often must unfold as a recurring act of doing and checking back, and then doing again. In the end, mastery of any system rests upon thorough understanding of its purpose and intended result. Our hope is that this book will enhance your understanding of the study-reading process, and content area teachers' potential roles as day-to-day, lesson-to-lesson models of this process, for students to observe and emulate, to try out and refine from grade to grade and across the disciplines.

CONTENTS

SECTION

I

FOUNDATIONS OF CONTENT AREA LITERACY

The first three chapters introduce some of the basic concepts that structure the field of Content Area Literacy (CAL). Chapter 1 addresses how CAL came to be a formal field of study, and why it should be a common strand of knowledge across all subject areas. Chapter 2 takes a close look at current research-based understandings of the cognitive processes involved in "reading-to-learn," as the basis for guiding students' acquisition of effective study-reading strategies. Chapter 3 outlines a framework for planning and implementing text-based instruction in ways that align with and reinforce these reading-to-learn strategies. Each of these chapters concludes with an example of a CAL teaching method that illustrates how teaching reading-to-learn is, essentially, a more informed means of teaching anything.

CHAPTER 1

CONTENT AREA LITERACY
Why and What Teachers Should Know

One who learns from someone who is learning drinks from a running stream.
—Native American proverb

This chapter encourages all teachers to reflect on their potential roles as facilitators of reading, writing, and thinking across disciplines and in a multicultural and multimedia world. The chapter opens with an overview of the historical emergence of the Content Area *Reading* movement—the questions that impelled it and its evolution into its current form, which is now more accurately referred to as Content Area *Literacy*.

The underlying theme of this chapter is that teaching students to be *self-teaching* moves them toward becoming truly literate more than simply not being illiterate. Some of the issues that have tended to cause content area teachers to resist wholehearted participation in a schoolwide implementation of a Content Area Literacy program are presented next, and the chapter concludes with a description and example of a Content Area Literacy method called Listen-Read-Discuss. This teacher-friendly and broadly applicable method illustrates a basic theme of the chapter: Content Area Literacy isn't an additional thing to teach, but simply a source of knowledge and skills that can inform and fine-tune the teaching of any subject.

▶ SOMEONE WHO IS LEARNING

The best content area teachers strive to be masters of their subjects, and *also* masters of teaching and learning. They consider what content needs to be taught and in what order and to what depth, *and* how it can best be learned. They reflect upon what it is about a topic of study that is engaging, and how a sense of this engagement can be communicated to novice learners. The field of Content Area Literacy offers a wealth of research-based insight into the learning process, and of practical and effective methods for teaching in ways that help students "see" how to learn.

Current research in learning psychology informs us that all learning, including reading-to-learn, requires

- focusing upon the topic and searching prior knowledge and experience for any means of connecting the new information with the known.
- maintaining engagement with the new information, and noticing when the meaning becomes unclear.
- questioning the new information by comparing it to relevant prior knowledge and experience.
- categorizing and further connecting the new information—which may require reevaluating and revising what previously was "known".

This view of learning as a *constructive* process is a theme throughout this text. In many ways, the history of Content Area Literacy parallels the journey of individual teachers as they move from subject area mastery toward subject area teaching mastery.

▶ BACKSTORY: FROM CONTENT AREA READING TO CONTENT AREA LITERACY

The field of Content Area Reading evolved from an idea sparked in the 1920s into a movement that swept the nation by the 1960s. In recent years, the field has continued to evolve into the broader dimensions suggested by the label "Content Area Literacy." Before the 1920s, education tended to follow a "survival of the fittest" model. Those who fell behind were simply permitted to drop from the system. A growing awareness of the need for an educated citizenry led to mandatory schooling legislation. It quickly became clear, however, that equal access to education meant more than merely requiring all students to stay in school until a certain age. If all students were to profit from staying in school, then schools would need to find ways to help them learn while they were there.

In this context, educators began to believe that instead of simply presenting information, we could and should find ways to help students *learn how to learn*—and especially how to learn through reading. This was a dramatic role change for schools and for teachers. It raised a host of questions. Just who was supposed to be responsible for figuring out why some students learn to learn and others do not? Who was supposed to help those who fell behind? And how could this be done? Some educators still question whether it really *can* be done or even really *should* be done, given spiraling costs and competing priorities.

Nevertheless, this new concept of public education was an idea whose time had come. The need to equalize opportunities for all citizens was growing into a national priority that was fueled by the civil rights movement and the increasing skill demands of the job market. Today, most schools and teachers understand that they are not merely responsible for teaching a subject but for teaching all students to be flexible and independent learners. It is this shift in perspective that has driven the continued development of the Content Area Reading movement.

Early proponents of this movement laid the foundations for extending the definition and practices of reading instruction from an elementary grade focus on merely learning to read to a new and broader focus on reading-to-learn, as summarized by Moore, Readence, and Rickleman in 1983:

> The specialty of content area reading instruction came about in recognition of the fact that readers require various strategies when they study particular subject areas and read many kinds of materials for different purposes. Content area reading instruction is designed to deliver those strategies. To date, the primary mission of this instruction is to develop student reading-to-learn strategies. (p. 420)

To meet this expectation, schools and teachers needed answers to immediate and pressing questions about how students learn and about how to help students become better learners. Many found and welcomed the answers that the field of study known as Content Area Reading was beginning to offer. In recent years, Content Area Reading specialists and researchers have advocated renaming this field of study. The name *Content Area Literacy*, many believe, more appropriately designates the evolution from a time when the purpose of education was merely to reduce the level of illiteracy to the more lofty purpose of increasing the number of students who are truly literate.

It still is the case, however, that the answers that Content Area Literacy offers conflict with some teachers' attitudes and expectations. Some teachers, both practicing and beginning teachers, view their role as that of an information dispenser.

Changing teachers' views of their roles and responsibilities, like most change, has not been easy. It has been an ongoing process that continues to unfold within one teacher at a time, among both practicing and beginning teachers.

▶ READING-TO-LEARN: WHOSE JOB IS IT?

In its early years, the slogan of the fledgling field of Content Area Reading was "Every Teacher a Teacher of Reading." This slogan probably did the field more harm than good, since most middle school and high school teachers saw themselves as teachers of their subject areas and thought of reading as a basic skill that should have been mastered in the elementary grades. The following line of questioning represents the major points in the reasoning process that many experienced middle and high school teachers have worked through.

1. *Haven't students learned to read by the time they finish grade school?* The answer to this question must begin with a basic definition of *reading.* Many people think of learning to read as learning to *decode,* or translate, the little squiggles we call letters into the sounds we call words. Reading, however, means much more than this simple translation process. It means constructively comprehending, or making meaning from, print. Reading comprehension generally is defined as follows:

- *Understanding* the author's intended message (reading the lines).
- *Interpreting* the message's meaning and implications (reading between the lines).
- *Applying* the message in meaningful ways (reading beyond the lines).

Most children do master the decoding aspects of reading by about the fourth grade. At each higher grade level, however, the reading materials become more difficult. To express increasingly complex ideas and information, authors must use more technical vocabulary and more complex language forms. Thus, learning to read is a process that continues as long as one continues to learn.

Even children who master beginning reading in elementary school must continue to develop effective strategies for learning from more difficult materials and about increasingly specialized subjects. Some students acquire these strategies rather effortlessly, but many others do not. Even in elementary school, some children begin to fall behind their peers in comprehending what they read. As middle and high school teachers' expectations increase, these children begin to have more frequent unsuccessful experiences in attempting to learn from reading. And, of course, a few children fail to master even basic decoding.

For these reasons, content area teachers can expect to have several categories of students in their classes. A few students will still have basic decoding problems. Some will have fairly serious comprehension problems. Many will simply need assistance in acquiring the comprehension strategies appropriate to each higher grade and subject area. Finally, some students will continue to read and develop the needed comprehension strategies on their own. In the past, teachers could concern themselves primarily with presenting information and materials to the latter category of students. Learning to read content materials was treated as a "sink-or-swim" challenge: You figured out how to do it, or you failed to learn the subject.

Today, most teachers are willing to accept more responsibility for helping *all* children learn to read and think. As they do so, they are accepting the challenge to teach in ways that don't simply *require* but that help students *acquire* the thinking strategies they need to actively construct meaning from print.

2. *If some students acquire reading–thinking strategies naturally, simply by reading increasingly difficult materials, why do others fail to do so?*
The fundamental premise of this book, and a large sector of the Content Area Literacy movement, is that if all students did spend time reading and working at understanding in every subject through the grades, they all might continue to develop the reading–thinking strategies they need. However, for a variety of reasons, this does not always happen.

One simple reason why some students do not spend sufficient time reading and working at understanding every subject is that at each higher grade level, students' personal interests begin to influence how much reading they do in different subjects. They read more in subjects they prefer and often avoid reading in subjects they do not like. Thus, they may continue to acquire the specialized vocabulary, language, and thinking strategies needed in some subjects but not in others.

Another reason why some students do not do enough reading to make expected levels of progress is related to their early experiences with being taught to read. Reading instruction, even in the elementary grades, often is structured and conducted in ways that cause some children to see themselves as poor readers. For example, when children are grouped for reading, children placed in the low group know that they are seen as poor readers by their teacher and their peers and learn to see themselves as poor readers. The strength of this learning is evidenced in the fact that they seldom advance to a higher group. When children begin to view themselves as poor readers, for whatever reason, they read less and progress at a slower rate. By the time these struggling readers reach secondary school, they have had years of negative experiences with reading.

Thus, at each higher grade, in any given subject, there are students who have fallen behind in acquiring the necessary natural reading–thinking strategies: some simply because of stronger interest in other areas, and some because prior failures have caused them to stop trying. Secondary teachers, faced with increasing numbers of students who cannot or will not learn from reading, sometimes make the well-meaning but ironic attempt to present information in other ways that involve little or no reading. The irony in this approach is that it removes any possibility of students' acquiring greater ease and self-confidence in reading. Even those students who might have developed grade-level reading strategies through continued reading may fail to do so if no reading is required. The better alternative, and one of the most influential things a secondary teacher can do, is to use teaching methods that structure reading-based lessons in ways that enable more students to have more successful experiences with reading. It is only through repeated successful reading experiences that appropriate thinking strategies are acquired, and the effects of years of negative experiences can be counteracted.

3. *Aren't there some students who just can't be taught to read better?*
Since reading comprehension is almost synonymous with thinking, many educators once believed that there was a simple, one-to-one relationship between general intelligence and reading comprehension. It was assumed that intelligent students would acquire the ability to read and comprehend well and that some less intelligent ones would not and could not be taught to do so. Today, few educators hold this simplistic view. We now know, for example, that intelligence is much more multifaceted than is measured by most conventional tests of intelligence. Several aspects of critical and creative thinking, in fact, appear to be only minimally related to conventional IQ test scores. In fact, some educators have proposed that poor reading comprehension may be a causal factor in low IQ scores rather than the reverse. In recent years, educational researchers have provided convincing evidence that thinking can be improved and that the methods for doing so are not terribly complex. Content Area Literacy is based on the premise that all students can be taught to read, learn, and think better, and that all teachers can share the challenges and rewards of helping them to do so.

4. *Why can't reading be taught in a separate pull-out class?*
Reading *should* be taught in a separate class by a reading specialist for those few students at middle and high school grade levels who have not acquired basic decoding strategies. Severe reading disabilities usually have multiple causes and may be accompanied by emotional and behavioral disorders. (You may have heard the media statements about how our prisons are filled with nonreaders, who, presumably, if they could read would not be there. These are exaggerations. Most people who can't read are decent and, by some estimates, quite able in many other ways [Manzo, 2003]. It is best not to overstate an already serious situation. Professionals think and ideally speak in more balanced terms.)

Students who can decode adequately but simply do not seem to understand what they read are a different matter. At the beginning of the Content Area Reading movement, and sometimes still today, separate reading classes were designed for these students. The problem with the separate-class approach is that even though it seems to be the most logical solution, it simply doesn't work very well. Why it doesn't work seems to be related to at least three conditions. First, whenever students are grouped by ability, a multitude of negative factors tend to outweigh the logical advantage that might be gained by offering them instruction that is geared to their achievement level. Second, as discussed previously, most secondary students are stronger readers in some subjects than in others. Identifying which students are lagging in which subjects and trying to provide this level of individualized assistance is practically impossible. Finally, the pull-out approach assumes that students will be taught general reading–thinking strategies that they will then modify and apply when reading their various subject area assignments. This kind of transfer of training is a higher-order thinking process that is, almost by definition, what poor readers have difficulty doing.

Gradually, after years of trying various approaches, two things have become clear: (1) Pull-out programs are necessary for those students who have not mastered basic decoding. (2) However, all students, including those receiving separate remediation, need specific coaching in the particular grade-appropriate reading–thinking strategies of each subject. And who are more experienced in reading, thinking, talking, and questioning in the respective subject fields than the content teachers themselves?

5. *How can content teachers be expected to find time to teach reading and thinking?*

The fact that content teachers are being held responsible for the learning of *all* students is the strongest argument for all teachers to be prepared to coach students in the particular reading strategies relevant to their subject areas. Coaching reading and thinking need not be done *in addition to* teaching content. In fact, it is best done *while* teaching content. When such coaching accompanies the teaching of content, students (including mainstreamed students with learning disabilities) become more able to learn independently. Thus, in the big picture, teachers who help students read on their own are able to teach more content rather than less.

Teaching methods that result in effective coaching of subject area reading and thinking have two important characteristics that make them appropriate for subject area teachers. These methods tend to be concurrent and interactive. *Concurrent* methods permit the teacher to teach toward several objectives at the same time. *Interactive* methods are designed to encourage what is called the *constructivist* side of education—that is, increasing student involvement in instructional exchanges and supporting the use of thinking strategies for making, or constructing, meaning. Many good teachers teach some reading without labeling, or even realizing, it as such. Teachers are teaching reading, for example, when they introduce a reading selection in a way that engages students' interest, or when they invite meaningful discussion following reading, or even when they just ask some questions to check comprehension following reading. Teachers who do these things naturally will want to know more; those who do not do so naturally need to know more.

6. *Why should all subject areas be included in the schoolwide reading program?*

Some content areas, such as English, science, and social studies, have an obvious connection with reading. Some content areas, such as foreign language, vocational and industrial technology, theatre, business education, and family and consumer science, require moderate amounts of reading. Others, such as physical education, art, music, and mathematics, traditionally involve less reading. Yet most states require that all teacher certification programs include at least one course in the teaching of reading. This consensus is in part due to two concepts that are central to effective schools. First, schools are more effective when *all teachers accept responsibility for the overall goals of the school,* not simply for those of their own discipline and classes. Accordingly, every teacher is expected to contribute to the schoolwide literacy program. In some subject areas, this contribution may be as simple as including just a few reading-based lessons that are carefully designed to permit even poor readers to have more successful experiences as readers in that subject. Second, effective schools are organized not merely to teach a given body of information but also to develop interests and abilities that will allow students to continue to be reasonably well versed in their subjects in the future. In this information age, it is not enough to merely acquire information; students must know how to acquire it and, more important, to interpret and use it.

7. *What level of reading achievement can content teachers expect students to have, and how can they evaluate their students' reading?*

Naturally, the higher the grade, the higher the overall average reading level you can expect of a class. However, this fact tends to mask another more important one: the higher the grade, the wider the *range* of students' reading abilities from lowest to highest. This is because children who encounter difficulty in beginning reading often make far less than a year's progress for each year in school. Others, however, make more than a year's progress in a school year. Thus, a typical seventh-grade class may be expected to have reading levels ranging from the third- to the tenth-grade level, while a tenth-grade class is likely to range from the fourth-grade to the college level.

Some basic information about students' reading levels usually can be gathered from standardized test scores that are on file. Students with particularly low scores can be noted and observed during the first weeks of school to verify this test-based information. As discussed previously, however, students' reading abilities are likely to vary from subject to subject according to their personal interests, experiences, and prior knowledge. Subject area teachers can use a variety of techniques to cross-verify standardized test score information. These include observation, informal assessment procedures, and systems for portfolio collection, all of which are detailed in Chapter 10.

8. *How can students of varying reading achievement levels learn from a single textbook or supplementary material that is written more or less on grade level?*

Over the years, the field of Content Area Reading has proposed and explored many solutions to this logistical question. Most of the early solutions were logical but not very practical. One popular suggestion, for example, was to collect a variety of reading materials on the same topic but at different difficulty levels and to match these with student reading levels. Individual students, or groups of students, could then explore the topic of study by reading at their own levels. Another suggestion was to prepare reading guides at different difficulty levels and to assign these based on student reading level. For example, lower-achieving readers were guided through acquiring the basic information, and more advanced students were asked questions that required more complex analysis of the information. These early attempts, while reasonable and still viable in some situations, tend to require an extraordinary amount of preparation and continuous monitoring. They also raise troublesome questions about how to evaluate students' work on these differentiated assignments and about whether lower-achieving students would be penalized rather than assisted by a steady diet of literal-level questions and easy material.

Content Area Literacy has moved to simpler, more manageable, and more equitable solutions. The basic approach is based on *interactive methods* for teaching reading–thinking *concurrently* with subject area knowledge and applications. Regular use of such methods from grade to grade and across subject areas supports student development of independent reading–learning strategies and empowers even relatively poor readers to read and learn from materials that they otherwise would find difficult.

▶ CONTENT AREA LITERACY: A SCHOOLWIDE GOAL

Information versus Knowledge

The research-supported answers and perspectives that have evolved in response to the preceding questions represent a fairly complete picture of the traditional field of Content Area Reading. A substantial body of research now supports the propositions that teachers *can* teach reading–thinking strategies, that they *can* meet the needs of a fairly wide range of student reading levels in a single classroom, and that the most effective schoolwide reading programs are those that enlist the participation of *every* educator in the school. With that groundwork established, the field has begun to broaden its focus, viewing reading within the broader context of literacy. Whereas the term *reading* connotes acquisition of strategies needed to successfully complete schooling, the term *literacy* speaks more to the breadth of education needed to function in modern life, where ordinary citizens are given the executive power of the vote but also must live in a milieu of rapid technological change and job displacement.

In today's world, the acquisition of large amounts of information is less important than the acquisition of effective strategies for accessing and evaluating information, problem solving, and communicating and interacting with interested parties. Wisdom is now clearly more challenging to find than information. We once assumed that learners must first acquire information before they could be challenged to critically analyze and apply it. Many frustrating hours have been spent in trying to teach/learn isolated history facts, math facts, grammar rules, and the like. These required so many hours that teachers often despaired of students ever acquiring sufficient information to enable them to operate at higher levels of evaluation and application. Research in the field of learning theory is refocusing our attention on what many effective teachers have long intuited: If students are initially engaged in an authentic, relevant problem, situation, or challenge, the relevant information is acquired almost effortlessly and in a fraction of the time.

Similarly, reading and subject area specialists are redirecting their attention toward creating educational environments in which students are challenged to analyze, reflect, communicate, and create. In such environments, effective strategies for reading, writing, speaking, listening, and thinking are likely to develop more naturally and easily than when these are addressed as isolated elements. Thus, there is a growing trend to refer to this emerging field as *Content Area Literacy*. This reorientation shifts the emphasis from reading as a somewhat isolated function toward its role in overall communication and higher-order thinking. Ironically, the need to write and to read highly technical information has been greatly intensified by telecomputing and related technologies that once were expected to reduce the demand for every citizen to be highly literate.

CAL—Enlightened Instruction, Every Teacher's Goal

So who, in conclusion, should have knowledge about Content Area Literacy? In our judgment, everyone who teaches, and certainly anyone who will teach in a conventional school setting, should know about Content Area Literacy. The interactive and strategic teaching methods of Content Area Literacy permit students with a wide range of reading levels to learn from the same reading materials and in the same classroom. These methods offer practical ways to satisfy today's expectation that students of varied learning aptitudes and even those with special learning needs and from diverse cultural backgrounds should have the opportunity to learn in the traditional class setting. And, given the additions of new, electronic communication and computing systems, traditional class settings are now anything but traditional. Nonetheless, all teachers, including those who might think they have the least need for content literacy methodology, have the obligation to be informed about what constitutes enlightened instruction so that they can participate in the school's primary mission.

On a more personal career level, an understanding of Content Area Literacy precepts and practices prepares all who work in a school setting to be ready to step in for their colleagues and to have sufficient flexibility and preparation in their education to be able to take on other related jobs, as often as is required over a typical lifelong career. It is not unusual today for those who originally prepared to teach in a conventional classroom to find themselves teaching in other settings: in adult basic and high school equivalency programs; in one of the burgeoning educational programs within business and industry; or extending their certification to work as school-based consultants or central office administrators.

▶ LISTEN-READ-DISCUSS: A TEACHER-FRIENDLY CAL METHOD

The Listen-Read-Discuss (L-R-D) method was created as a "starter" method for bridging from traditional instruction to a more interactive approach. Traditional reading-based instruction typically begins by having students read the assignment, then listen to a brief lecture or overview by the teacher, and then discuss their responses to questions. The L-R-D simply inverts the first two steps.

Effective learning, including learning how to be an effective teacher, needs something to get it started, something to keep it going, and something to keep it from becoming random or misguided (Bruner, 1966). The L-R-D method (Manzo & Casale, 1985) tends to meet these requirements for both teachers and students. It is a simple lesson design that can be tried almost immediately and offers several variations that can be phased in as a personal program of professional development. The L-R-D is a heuristic, or hands-on, activity designed to induce self-discovery about effective teaching by teachers and about effective learning by students. It is, in other words, a way to self-improve teaching that ideally helps students self-teach in all the ways that their environments will allow.

Steps in Listen-Read-Discuss

Step 1. Review the reading selection, and prepare a brief, organized overview that points out the basic structure of the material, relevant background information, and important information to look for and generates interest in the topic.

Step 2. Present the summary orally to students. (See Figure 1.1.)

Step 3. Have students read the textbook version of the same material. Students will then be empowered to read material with which they have some familiarity.

Step 4. Discuss the material students have heard and read. Begin the discussion with the information and ideas students were directed to look for.

Less Than Obvious Benefits of the Use of the L-R-D

Use of the L-R-D tends to benefit teachers, students, and the school program in ways that are not always immediately apparent. One such value emerges almost immediately in the lesson-planning stage. When teachers select textual material for use in an L-R-D lesson, they find themselves looking at the textbook more carefully and from more points of view than they might otherwise. They begin, quite naturally, to sense where students' comprehension is likely to falter and to better align the phrasing, facts, and organization of the lecture material they are preparing with the textbook material that students will read. This amounts to a new level of teacher empathy and a growing belief that they *can* teach content to struggling readers using the course textbook. With better alignment and organization, teachers automatically begin to heed a basic dictum of effective reading instruction: to stimulate active reading by preteaching key terms, pivotal questions, and new concepts before reading. Better organization and alignment also are likely to raise teachers' levels of tolerance for reasonable digressions in the form of comments about how the new information relates to real-life events and experiences. In so doing, teachers help students to better recall and develop relevant background information and appropriate anticipation, both of which have been shown to be natural to proficient readers and of great value in effective comprehension (Crafton, 1983; Harste, 1978; Stevens, 1982).

Careful preparation of L-R-D lessons actually raises students' ability to read a particular piece beyond their typical reading and thinking levels. This can be a positive and enabling experience for students and teachers. It tends to become a new benchmark for students to strive for in learning from text and for teachers to strive for in helping students learn from text.

The following sample Prereading script is based on the article"Dance and Sport: The Elusive Connection," which follows in this figure.

Did you know that football coaches sometimes have their players take ballet lessons? Can you see Frank over there in a tutu? (Frank is one of the school's star football players.) Well, this article tells about where this idea came from, and why it seems to work. Look for seven things dancers learn, and think about why these would be useful for football players. Write these down when you come to them—they're listed in one of the first paragraphs. Then, the author tells how some sports are more like dance than others. In dance, it is the mastery over one's movement that is important. In sport, it is the result *of mastery over one's movement that is important. Look for the difference between "open skill" sports and "closed skill" sport, and how one type is more like dance than the other. The title of the article is "Dance and Sport: The Elusive Connection."* Elusive *means something that seems to keep slipping away. Read to see why the connection between dance and sport might keep slipping away.*

Students then read the following article, from the *Journal of Physical Education, Recreation, and Dance*.

DANCE AND SPORT: THE ELUSIVE CONNECTION

Techniques and principles effectively used in teaching dance can be applied to teaching sport.

Sandra Minton
Bradford Beckwith

(1) What are the functional connections between dance and sport and the benefits that are derived from participation in both pursuits? This article presents ideas which are applied to both dance and sport in order to enhance performance and reduce injury.

(2) Many well-known people have recognized a connection between dance and sport skills. It may have been this kinship that convinced Knute Rockne, famed football coach at Notre Dame, to require his players to enroll in dance classes. Maybe it was the similarity between dance and sport that caused Woody Hayes, former Ohio State head coach, to expect his players to take dance as part of their practice procedures (Lance, 1981). Lynn Swan, three-time Pro Bowl wide receiver while playing with the four-time World Champion Pittsburgh Steelers, studied dance for 14 years and attributed his graceful athletic abilities to dance.

Figure 1.1 Example of an L-R-D Prereading Script.

(3) It is possible that each of these individuals witnessed movement competencies shared by dance and sports. Some of these shared abilities include centering, balance, focus, breathing, transfer of weight, relaxation and the ability to use space, time, and energy with mastery. Such abilities are taught specifically in dance classes, while in athletics they are only alluded to as a part of skill instruction.

(4) The basic difference between dance and sport is that sport takes place within the conditions of a game, while dance is performed in other contexts. A game is a contest in which opposing interests are given specific information and are then allowed a choice of moves with the object of maximizing wins and minimizing losses. A game entails dominance over an opponent and the acquisition of some mutually coveted symbol. The athlete, by improving his or her movement abilities, will then improve sport skills.

(5) Dancers, on the other hand, are process-oriented rather than product-oriented. The goal in dance is the improvement of movement quality.

(6) Similarities between dance and sport outweigh their differences. Participants in both areas train to go faster and farther, while moving with increased control. The dancer and the sport participant both work to expand their movement vocabulary so they can use a particular action when the situation demands. Biomechanical analysis has been used for many years by physical educators to help their students learn. In recent years, dancers have also begun to use biomechanics to analyze movement with the goals of sharpening perception of movement, decreasing learning time, and enhancing performance (Laws, 1984). Dance and sport are similar in another respect. While some would say a dance was choreographed but a sport contest was not planned, further examination indicates that all the X's and O's used in game strategy simply represent another form of choreography.

(7) Some sport activities are more similar to dance training than others. The concept of open and closed skills helps explain this point. In a closed skill, one strives to master an effective and efficient motor program with the goal of being able to duplicate this program with each repetition. Environmental conditions remain relatively constant, and the performer attempts to be consistent in the execution of the skill. Sports such as the shot put, diving, and gymnastics are closed skills. Open skills exist in a changing environment, and the selection of appropriate movement responses is as variable as the environment itself. Baseball, football, soccer, and basketball are open skill activities (Sage, 1977). Both open and closed skill athletes can benefit from dance training. The abilities which are taught in dance classes used by both kinds of athletes are different, but are not less applicable to their sports' requirements.

Figure 1.1 *(continued)*

(8) The principle of relaxation can be used as an example. Dancers frequently talk about using the right amount of tension in one part of the body while allowing other body areas to remain relaxed. The main idea is to use energy efficiently and only where needed to perform a movement. Efficient movement is characterized by using the appropriate muscle groups in proper sequence. The use of the wrong muscle group at the wrong time can be deleterious to the skill and possibly to the performer. Another common word heard in dance class is "centering." Centering is finding the body's center of weight and manipulating it effectively in relation to gravity. It also brings the mind and body together to produce better concentration. Achieving a heightened perception of and facility with space, time, and energy is another principle used in teaching dance. Dancers are asked to look at the direction or level of a movement, its speed in relation to an underlying pulse, or the quality of energy used to propel actions through space. Such movement descriptions are provided in dance classes to help students see movement more clearly and to enhance understanding of the expressive aspects of each action (Minton, 1984).

(9) The point is that these principles are used in teaching dance, but generally not in teaching sport. In dance, these ideas are singled out in the classroom and used as learning tools. The examples given here are several of the techniques used in teaching dance that could be applied profitably to the teaching of sport.

REFERENCES

Lance, J. (1981). Practicing for touchdowns. *Journal of Physical Education, Recreation, and Dance, 5,* 38.

Laws, K. (1984). *The Physics of Dance.* New York: Macmillan, Inc.

Minton, S.C. (1984). *Modern Dance: Body and Mind.* Englewood, CO: Morton.

Sage, G.H. (1977). *Introduction to Motor Behavior: A Neuropsychological Approach* (2nd. ed.). Reading, MA: Addison-Wesley.

This article is reprinted with permission of the *Journal of Physical Education, Recreation and Dance,* May/June 1986, pp. 26 and 54. JOPERD is a publication of the American Alliance for Health, Physical Education, Recreation and Dance, 1900 Association Drive, Reston, VA 20191.

Sandra Minton is coordinator of the Dance Program at the University of Northern Colorado, Greeley, CO 80639. Bradford E. Beckwith is a doctoral candidate, psychological kinesiology, at the same school.

Figure 1.1 *(continued)*

Following the lecture and empowered reading, the lesson design calls for discussion, providing a third repetition and elaboration of the material. This built-in redundancy factor is a most basic—and often overlooked—practice of effective teachers and principle of effective learning.

Finally, a teacher who follows the L-R-D guidelines will have begun to restructure class time and expectations from the typical 90% lecture format to one containing greatly increased proportions of purposeful reading and informed discussion. This achieves yet another important practice of effective teachers and precept of effective learning: increased time on task. Some have argued that the simple lack of attention to reading in typical content classes accounts for a great part of the current higher-literacy crisis in the schools. This conclusion seems justified by the fact that several observational studies of subject teaching at the postelementary levels reveal that virtually no purposeful reading goes on during class time (Feathers & Smith, 1987; Greenewald & Wolf, 1980; Mikulecky, 1982; Ratekin, Simpson, Alvermann, & Dishner, 1985).

Overall, the greatest value of the L-R-D seems to be its ability to provide a simple, hands-on way to introduce and initiate oneself to the principles and practices of Content Area Literacy. The reapportioning of class time offers teachers with defensive teaching styles—who overuse either lecture or seatwork—an opportunity to experiment with reasonable alternatives. This tends to leave teachers with more energy and a greater willingness to try more sophisticated teaching methods and potentially benefit more fully from in-service workshops, consultations, and graduate coursework (Watkins, McKenna, Manzo, & Manzo, 1995).

1. Have students reread the information covered in the L-R-D format rapidly to increase their speed of reading and thought processing. Reading speed tends to rise as a result of increases in prior knowledge although it also can be easily improved simply by systematic attention and practice.
2. Inform the class that you will lecture, intentionally omitting a few important details that they will need to read their texts to discover. This gives practice in recognizing what is not yet known and experience in careful reading and knowledge seeking.
3. Inform the class that your lecture will cover all the details of a lesson but that they will need to read to discover what questions these details answer. This is one way to teach students to actively seek an understanding of the concept base, or central question, around which an area of study is focused.
4. Inform the class that a quiz will follow the L-R-D sequence. Allow a short study period. This is recommended to activate a high level of focused attention, give practice in test taking, and set the stage for questions and discussion about how to study effectively.
5. Invert the core process occasionally by having the class R-L-D, or read (for about 15 minutes), then listen, and finally discuss. This variation tends to focus and improve listening attention and the ability to learn from an effective lecture. This effect can be further heightened when joined with the other listening training and note-taking techniques covered ahead.

Figure 1.2 Ladder of variations and elaborations on Listen-Read-Discuss.

6. Watch a videoclip, educational film, or other multimedia presentation on a text topic *before* reading about it in the text. Such visual representations are compatible with the habits of contemporary students and can help build new bridges to print. (See Figure 1.3.)
7. Ask students which portions of the text struck them as inconsiderate, that is, poorly written, poorly organized, or presuming too much prior knowledge. This activity can help students learn when to ask for help with textual and class material. It also helps the teacher become more aware of students' learning needs. Analysis of the writing in texts is also a good way to informally teach some of the basics of effective writing.
8. Provide the class with a definitive purpose for reading and discussing that will require critical and/or creative expression or application. State that purpose clearly on the board for easy reference; for example, "As you read this section on the steam engine, try to determine why it was bound to be replaced by the gasoline engine." This will serve as a reminder to read actively and with reference to real-life problem solving.
9. Hold Postreading discussions on teaching and learning strategies. Make the discussion positive by asking students what they or you may have done that resulted in solid learning. Such discussion gives credit to student intuition, develops reciprocity, and furthers metacognitive processing, or thinking about thinking.
10. Create research teams, and provide time for students to delve into a topic in greater depth. One group could simply see what other textbooks say on the topic. Another could check with other authoritative references—persons, books, and the internet. Another could write a best estimate of which real-life problems the information learned might help solve or answer. Still another group, when appropriate, could try to identify and discuss theme-related stories, poetry, music, or art. Activities such as these provide links between text topics and nonprint resources and among school learning, artistic expression, multicultural perspectives, and the rest of the real world.

Figure 1.2 *(continued)*

Variations on the L-R-D

To help content area teachers ease their way into the use of more sophisticated, interactive teaching methods, and to provide alternatives for different learning styles, we have developed a ladder of variations on the basic L-R-D procedure (see Figures 1.2 and 1.3). You can use L-R-D variations and elaborations to develop your sophistication as an interactive teacher and to explore possible diverse student learning style needs. Try working through this sequence as your own readiness and students' needs suggest. It's a good idea to keep notes of your thoughts and questions as you try different variations. Your notes and thoughts will be useful

Purposes for Viewing

Teacher: Today we are going to continue our study of Kenya by focusing on the Maisi tribe of Southern Kenya. First, we will watch a 20-minute National Geographic DVD on this most unusual tribe of people. Listen carefully as you watch for two things, which you will then read about: the diet of the Maisi and the names of three other tribes of the north which few people know of but that figure in Kenyan life in a big way.

Brief Review Following Viewing

Teacher: Okay, what were the two points we listened for?

Student: The Maisi basically live off their cattle, eating meat and drinking their blood and raw milk.

Teacher: And?

Student: Well, there were three other tribes mentioned, but I can't remember any of them.

Teacher: Okay, read pages 66 to 71 in your text now to learn more about the Maisi diet, and let's get the names of those tribes. If you happen to finish reading early, there are a few copies of a recent magazine report on cholesterol here on my desk that might help answer the question, "Why aren't the Maisi dying of clogged arteries and heart failure from their high-fat diet?"

Postreading Discussion

Teacher: What did you understand best from what you watched and read about?

Student: The names of the three other tribes.

Teacher: Say and spell them, and I'll write them on the board.

Student: Samburu, Turkana, and Hamitic.

Teacher: What did you understand least from what you watched and read about? [When students have understood what they have viewed and read, they will take this question to mean pretty much the same thing as the next one: What questions or thoughts did this lesson raise in your mind?]

Student: I pretty much understood what was said, but I don't understand why the Maisi don't raise things the way the other tribes do.

Teacher: The land they live on is not arable. There is poor topsoil and little water. But that really doesn't explain why they don't move to where there is arable land.

Student: I was wondering about their high-fat diet, so I read fast to get to the article you talked about. It seems that there are at least two reasons why they don't have high blood cholesterol. The raw milk has enzymes that break down fat in the blood. Also, they lead very active lives. They burn off the fat as fast as they put it on.

Teacher: If raw milk is so good for you, why do we homogenize and pasteurize ours, I wonder? Why don't you ask Mrs. Shell in science today if she can help us out with this?

Figure 1.3 Example of L-R-D elaboration 6: Viewing a videoclip or film before reading in a world geography class.

in discussions with your instructor and coursemates and in processing your own teaching experiences.

▶ CONCEPT SUMMARY

The field of Content Area Reading grew out of societal needs for a more literate citizenry and more egalitarian educational practices. It has grown into the study of theories and methods for teaching students to grow in wisdom as well as acquiring information and skills, better and more broadly labeled Content Area Literacy. Several key questions have impelled the development of the field, and of individual teachers. The question "Shouldn't students be able to read by the time they leave elementary school?" leads to the distinction between learning-to-read and reading-to-learn, which in turn draws attention to students' need to continue to acquire study strategies through the grades and across the disciplines. The question "Aren't there some students who just can't learn to read better?" uncovers a common assumption that reading comprehension is a function of intelligence: if one can decode, one should be able to understand. Content Area Literacy's response to this assumption is that intelligence is a function of the same learning strategies that produce reading comprehension, and that although these can be acquired through trial and error, they also can and should be taught. The Listen-Read-Discuss (L-R-D) method is an example of a teacher-friendly method for teaching the powerful effect on comprehension of "frontloading" learners by simply inverting the typical *sequence* of text-based instruction. Use of the L-R-D, and any of the suggested or other variations on this method, tends to awaken both students and their teachers to the possibility that they are more capable than they had believed of reading and learning from text.

CHAPTER 2

THE SCIENCE OF READING-TO-LEARN

"Everyone who teaches has a theory of teaching, even if they don't realize that they do."
—Harry Singer

This chapter opens with an important distinction between reading-to-learn and either very easy reading on the one hand or very difficult reading on the other. These difficulty levels are referred to as *Independent* level (easy reading), *Instructional* level (reading-to-learn, or study reading), and *Frustration* level (very difficult reading). Over the past half century, theories about the process of reading-to-learn have developed alongside psychological theories of learning and within distinct social and cultural contexts. Early views of the reading process drew from *behaviorist* perspectives and tended to focus on the outcomes of reading. Current views draw from *constructivist* theories that focus on study-reading processes and thus offer greater insight into how these can be taught in order to effect improvement in comprehension. The Oral Reading Strategy is offered as a straightforward approach to translating understandings about the reading process into practice.

- THE SCIENTIFIC STUDY OF READING
- DIFFICULTY LEVELS OF READING: INDEPENDENT, INSTRUCTIONAL, FRUSTRATION

- THE READING PROCESS: FIVE ERAS OF THEORY
- CLASSROOM EXAMPLES OF THEORY
- A METAPHOR FOR THE STUDY READING PROCESS
- THEORY INTO PRACTICE: CAL METHODS
- THE ORAL READING STRATEGY: A STRAIGHTFORWARD "HOW-TO" METHOD
- CONCEPT SUMMARY

THE SCIENTIFIC STUDY OF READING

Reading can be defined, simply, in terms of its product: unlocking and constructing literal, interpretive, and applied meanings from a coded message. The next level of explanation is far from simple. For example, why is it that one student can accurately decode a page of print and comprehend 95% of the information, while another student also accurately decodes the same page but comprehends only 60%? To answer this question, it is necessary to consider the reading process—the cognitive events that occur from the moment the eyes perceive print to the time one is asked to respond to the meanings represented in that print. Since these cognitive processes are unobservable, our knowledge about them exists in theories and the findings from research designed to test the accuracy of these theories.

The scientific basis for the study of the comprehension process began around the time of World War I with a study designed to demonstrate that acquiring understanding from reading was far more than the simple act of reading words. Edward L. Thorndike (1917), one of the most eminent educational psychologists of the twentieth century, made the following observation:

> Understanding a paragraph is like solving a problem in mathematics. It consists in selecting the right elements of the situation and putting them together in the right relations, and also with the right amount of weight or influence or force for each. The mind is assailed as it were by every word in the paragraph. It must select, repress, soften, emphasize, correlate and organize, all under the influence of the right mental set or purpose or demand. (pp. 327–328)

In this single paragraph, Thorndike makes it clear that reading comprehension is a process of actively engaging text. It requires that the reader be attentive, analytical, purposeful, flexible, self-aware, world aware, and emotionally sound.

Even as readers ourselves, it is difficult to identify the cognitive processes that yield such a complex product. Reading remains an unobservable act. We can see what goes in and test what comes out, but what goes on in between is a mystery wrapped in theory. Ahead, we provide a brief overview of the historical development of theories about the reading process that have led to current understandings that inform this text.

First, however, it is important to note that there is one aspect of reading that is easily observable: For each of us, some things are easy to read, other things are more difficult, and still others are next to impossible. Although this may seem obvious, it is important to distinguish among these *difficulty levels of reading* in order to clearly focus on what reading-to-learn *is*, and as important, what it is *not*.

▶ DIFFICULTY LEVELS OF READING: INDEPENDENT, INSTRUCTIONAL, FRUSTRATION

The level at which materials are easy to read is technically referred to as the *Independent* level. Reading feels effortless at this level, because we often know something about the topic and are familiar with the language, style, and vocabulary used. All we need to do is fit the new information into existing categories. At this level, we are able to read and comprehend without assistance. The Independent level typically is defined as the highest level at which we can accurately decode 99% of the words and comprehend with 90% accuracy. (It should be noted that these percentage criteria, and the criteria for Instructional and Frustration levels ahead, assume that the material is read through once, and then questions of several types—such as main idea, details, vocabulary, and inference—are answered without looking back at the material read.) For most people, Independent-level reading—whether it is nonfiction, news, or novels—is enjoyable, relaxing, and entertaining. When a reading selection is at our Independent level, we can begin at the beginning and read straight through without stopping. We literally can absorb the information without much active effort at all.

Most of us occasionally have had the experience of reading and suddenly realizing that we have not understood the last sentences, paragraphs, or even pages. What usually has happened is that we have been trying to read something that is somewhat difficult for us, using the same passive reading process that works for Independent-level reading. When the topic, language, style, and/or the vocabulary are less familiar to us, we reach what is referred to as our *Instructional* level of reading. To comprehend material at this level, we often need to create new categories or stop to decipher the meanings of unfamiliar words and/or language patterns. This is the level at which we probably would be able to read and comprehend with the type of assistance a teacher might provide in a classroom setting or by using a study-reading strategy we have internalized. Instructional-level reading is defined as the highest level at which we can accurately decode 95% of the words and comprehend with 75% accuracy. Instructional-level reading cannot be done by reading straight through, passively, from beginning to end. It requires an active stance. It can be painstakingly slow because it is more than reading—it is learning. The terms *reading-to-learn*, *study reading*, and *Instructional-level reading* are used interchangeably throughout the remainder of this text. It is important to note for both formal and informal assessment purposes, this type of reading is not an abstract concept but has specific and easily quantifiable components. See Figure 2.1 for a diagram of the distinctions between Independent- and Instructional-level reading processes.

When decoding falls to 90% accuracy or lower, or comprehension falls below 50% accuracy, the material is at the *Frustration* level in difficulty. Material at this level for a given reader is so difficult that it is next to impossible to understand without an extraordinary level of effort and assistance.

Considering the reading process in this way, essentially as three *different* processes, helps explain why many teachers fail to see the need for providing guidance in reading strategies. One reason is the frequent misinterpretation of the

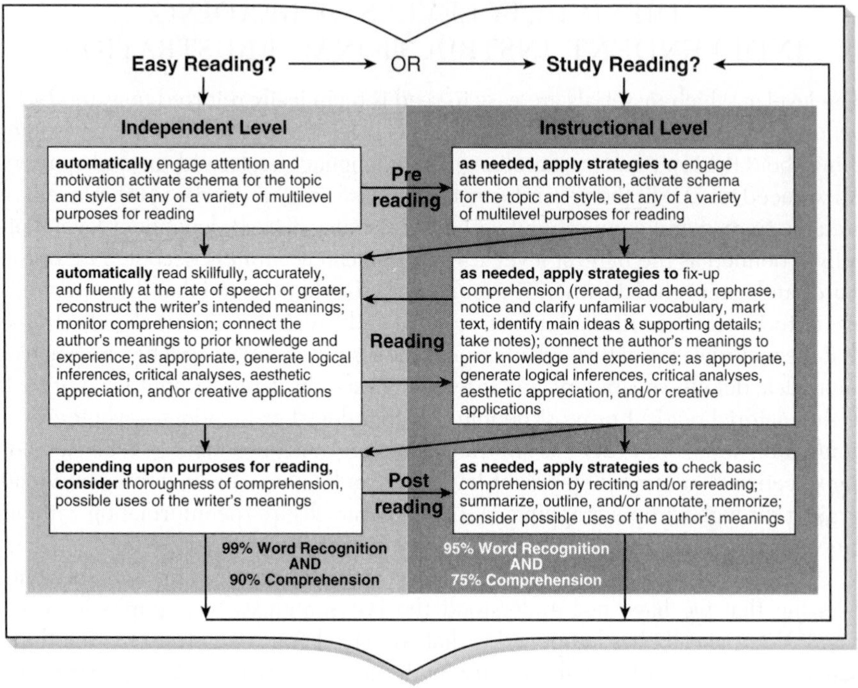

Figure 2.1 A Diagram of Instructional versus Independent–Level Reading

grade-level designation of textbooks. We tend to assume that this designation means that students at that grade should be able to use the book for independent study. In fact, it means that the book is intended to match the *Instructional* level of the students' grade. It should be manageable for them, but only with a reasonable degree of guidance from the teacher. A second reason why teachers sometimes fail to provide reading strategy instruction is that they simply are uninformed about these levels and about the dramatic difference between passive, Independent-level reading and active, Instructional-level reading. Textbooks that are written at students' Instructional level require the use of active thinking strategies for constructing meaning. Since these same textbooks will likely be at the teacher's Independent level, the teacher can read them easily and passively and may be puzzled as to why students are not understanding what seems perfectly clear. This misunderstanding is probably the reason for the fact that some middle and high school teachers still rely on "round-robin" reading. In this familiar activity, students take turns reading aloud, a paragraph or two at a time. For this kind of straight-through reading to be comprehensible, it must be at the readers' Independent level. Since this is seldom the case, few students gain much that is profitable from this activity. Better readers are bored, most others are occupied with looking ahead to the section they will be reading, and struggling readers are dreading the humiliation of reading aloud.

Teachers' ability to provide guidance in Instructional-level reading strategies depends largely on their understanding of the nature of the study-reading process.

What do teachers think when *they* engage in study reading? Recent research related to the reading process suggests that many of our intuitive assumptions about the reading process may be inaccurate. This research is changing not only the way beginning reading is taught but also how it is guided through the upper grades and even through professional-school levels.

THE READING PROCESS: FIVE ERAS OF THEORY

Most reading professionals today subscribe to theories of the reading process that describe study reading as actively, intentionally, and flexibly using sets of cognitive strategies, usually in the form of questions, to accurately reconstruct a writer's meanings and to construct personal connections and responses to those meanings. This view is fairly recent; in fact, researchers have identified five distinct "eras" of reading process theory over the past half century. Each theory has sharply different implications for how schools should be designed and how instruction should be delivered.

An introductory chapter entitled "A Historical Perspective on Reading Research and Practice" by Alexander and Fox in the current, fifth edition of *Theoretical Models and Processes of Reading* (2004) offers useful labels for these eras and discusses not only the nature of the prevailing theories of each era, but also the social, cultural, and political contexts that influenced the sciences of the time period, as well as other noteworthy coexisting rival views. In the brief summaries that follow, we have summarized our own take on the main points of the reading process theories in each of the eras that Alexander and Fox so aptly labeled, and we highly recommend the full chapter as an excellent resource for further study.*

The Era of Conditioned Learning (1950–1965)

Learning theory during this period was dominated by *behaviorist* theory, which viewed all learning as conditioned behavior. Reading with comprehension, in this view, is a complex behavior that can be broken down into subskill components, and the primary job of educators is to identify and sequence these subskills and to design techniques and materials to teach them at an appropriate pace. Behaviorists insisted that the only way to *scientifically* study learning is to describe and research it apart from any possible effects of the learner's interests, motivation, or other innate characteristics. The job of the reading educator was to break down the complex behavior of comprehension into subskills that could be observed and measured: answering different types of questions after reading, including main idea, detail, vocabulary (from the selection), and simple inference questions. Comprehension instruction focused on drill in reading and answering these types of questions. Whether the learner was able to evaluate what was read or to form an opinion based on reading was a matter of the *behaviorist* educator's interest

*Adapted with permission from: Alexander, P.A. & Fox, E. (2004). A historical perspective on reading research and practice. In R.B. Ruddell & N.J. Unrau (Eds.), *Theoretical models and processes of reading* (5th ed., pp. 33–68). Copyright 2004 by the International Reading Association.

only after the prerequisite subskills had been "passively drilled and practiced until reflexively demonstrated" (Alexander & Fox, 2004, p. 37).

The Era of Natural Learning (1966–1975)

Research in language learning, led primarily by linguists and psycholinguists studying, respectively, the interface of language and learning and the interface of language, psychology, and learning led to dramatically different views about reading comprehension and how it should be taught. A fundamental tenet of these theories was that learning is an innate and natural process that needs only a favorable environment in order to unfold and develop. In this view, humans have the inborn capacity to read with comprehension, just as they have the inborn capacity to understand spoken language and to learn to speak. The branch of this research that had the greatest effect on educational practice was that of the psycholinguistics, who "felt that the attention to discrete aspects of reading advocated in behaviorism destroyed the natural communicative power and inherent aesthetic of reading" (Goodman & Goodman, 1980; Smith, 1973, 1978, Alexander & Fox, 2004, p. 38). The main job of the reading educator was to structure learning environments and challenges conducive to the natural unfolding of the learner's inherent ability to think and to learn.

The Era of Information Processing (1976–1985)

Bruer (1993) identified the origins of the next major change in the field of learning psychology:

> In 1956, a group of psychologists, linguists, and computer scientists met at the Massachusetts Institute of Technology for a symposium on information science (Gardner, 1985). This three-day meeting was the beginning of a cognitive revolution in psychology. . . . That scientific revolution became a movement, and eventually a discipline, called cognitive science. Cognitive scientists study how our minds work—how we think, remember, and learn. Their studies have profound implications for restructuring schools and improving learning environments. Cognitive science—the science of mind—can give us an applied science of learning and instruction. (pp. 1–2)

The study of mind in this era came to focus primarily upon information-processing theory, seeking "processes or 'laws' that explained human language as an interaction between symbol system and mind" (Alexander & Fox, 2004, p. 42). The study of reading comprehension focused on the cognitive processes that enable an individual to learn from text and demonstrated that teaching processes such as predicting and summarizing improved reading comprehension.

The Era of Sociocultural Learning (1986–1995)

This era of research was strongly influenced by writers outside of education, who argued that understanding schooling in general and the individual learner in particular were less important than an understanding of learning as a sociocultural experience. One strong focus in this era was on the development of instructional techniques for creating inclusive and interactive classroom environments that invited collaborative learning. The job of the reading educator was to find ways and means of involving all learners in the educational journey and to help them translate the unschooled knowledge acquired in social and cultural interactions outside of school into the more formal knowledge objectives of the classroom.

The Era of Engaged Learning (1996–Present)

The current era has seen a renewed focus on learning as the active construction of knowledge and, relatedly, increased interest in the study of motivation and the developmental nature of learning. The influence of motivation on learning is important because in order to actively construct knowledge, the learner must not only know how to use strategies, but also must voluntarily and selectively use them when and to whatever extent is appropriate in a given learning situation. The influence of the learner's psychological development on ability to construct knowledge is important because the ability to strategically construct knowledge is a process that is never "mastered," but one that continues to develop throughout the grades and across subject area domains.

▶ CLASSROOM EXAMPLES OF THEORY

Of the five eras of reading process theory, those that have had the strongest impact on classroom practice have been the era of conditioned learning, the era of natural learning, and the current era of engaged learning. The implications of these theories for teaching can be illustrated in how each would translate into teaching a foreign language.

A behaviorist (conditioned learning) teacher would begin an introductory-level class by requiring students to learn the alphabet and sound system of the new language and several sets of high-utility words, such as days of the week, months of the year, numbers, and colors. Learning would be reinforced through a variety of drill-and-practice activities. Subsequent instruction would introduce the rules governing basic sentence structure, verb tense, and the like while continuing to practice vocabulary and would add practice with short phrases. Most of the class would be conducted in the students' first language.

A psycholinguistic (natural learning) teacher would begin an introductory-level class differently from the bottom-up teacher described previously. This teacher would enter the classroom speaking the new language, call the roll in the new language, begin to make simple requests and communications supported by reference to concrete objects and supported by gestures and expressions and would continue to conduct the class almost entirely without use of the students' first language.

While a natural learning approach clearly aligns more closely with natural learning processes than does a conditioned learning approach, its limitation is that it tends to align with how learning would occur under ideal circumstances and without the physical and temporal constraints of classroom teaching and learning.

A teacher representative of the era of engaged learning would begin by considering the essential elements of the learning task—elements that might be acquired naturally over time but that given the realities of classroom instruction and diverse student needs, would more efficiently be directly taught. These essential elements often appear to be similar to the subskills that might be identified in a conditioned learning approach. However, the intent here is not to teach these elements in sequential subskill fashion, but to teach them directly within a larger and meaningful context. Rather than drilling students on basic vocabulary, like the behaviorist teacher, or speaking only in the target language, like the psycholinguistic teacher, the cognitivist teacher might enter the classroom on the first day speaking only the target language and continue to do so for much of the class period. However, the topic of the lesson might be an interesting cultural holiday, illustrated in pictures or videoclips, and some portion of most class sessions would focus on direct instruction in the essential elements the teacher (or curriculum guide) has identified—such as high-utility words for things such as days of the week, months of the year, colors, and numbers, as well as basic rules of grammar and syntax explained in the students' first language.

▶ A METAPHOR FOR THE STUDY-READING PROCESS

The diagram of Instructional vs. Independent reading in Figure 2.1 outlined the reading process as it is understood in the era of engaged learning. The reading process, and the Instructional-level, study-reading process in particular, is viewed as a three-stage process of initiating the reading act, applying strategies to read actively, and checking and building comprehension after reading. A useful metaphor for this process is the construction of a large and intricate net, such as might be used in fishing.

Prereading: Locating the Appropriate Section of the Schema Net

Effective reading begins with readers quickly scanning some or all of the material to be read, consciously calling to mind what they know about the topic and making some initial predictions about the content and the difficulty level of the selection. This process, in general, is called *schema activation.*

Schema is a term used in learning psychology to refer to an individual's personal organization of information and experiences about a topic. A reader's schema for a topic can be thought of as a large fishing net, composed of information and experiences represented by the fibers of the net. Learning, then, is catching new bits of information and experience and attaching these to appropriate sections in the net. New bits also can be added most easily when the relevant section of the schema net is finely woven with many cross-strands. Thus, the more information and experience readers have related to a topic, the better able they will be to learn, or catch and integrate, the new information (see Figure 2.2). It is important to note,

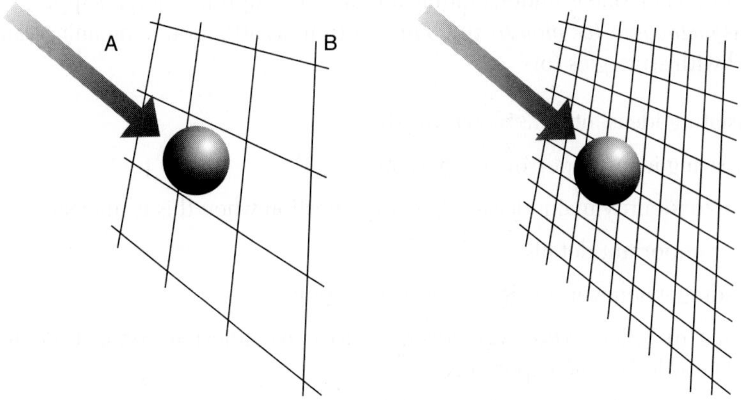

Figure 2.2 Schema theory

Source: From MANZO. *Teaching Children to Be Literate,* 1E. © 1996 Wadsworth, a part of Cengage Learning, Inc. Reproduced by permission. www.cengage.com/permissions

however, that prior knowledge and experience may not facilitate study-reading comprehension unless these are actively called to mind. Figuratively, new bits can be added most easily to one's schema net when the appropriate section is located, picked up, and held in front of one's face. This *Prereading* work is called schema activation: consciously calling to mind one's knowledge and experience about a topic.

Sometimes reading simply involves adding to and refining information and categories within an already well-developed section of the net. This can be done fairly effortlessly and can be used as a metaphor for Independent-level reading.

When readers have an undeveloped schema for a particular topic (very few strands in the net), it is more difficult for them to read and to learn. At this Instructional level, reading requires active construction of the major cross-strands of the section of net, or even undoing and reweaving strands in order to categorize, accommodate, and retain new information or experiences.

Schema activation is the essence of the Prereading stage of study reading. It can be prompted with several types of strategies, such as:

- Deciding how easy or difficulty the reading selection is likely to be.
- Recalling related information, experiences, attitudes, and feelings.
- Looking for organizing concepts.
- Trying to develop a personal interest.
- Setting a purpose for reading.

During Reading: Keeping a Grip on the Schema Net

Once readers have the appropriate section of the schema net in place, they have comparison points for checking that what they are reading is making sense. Actively keeping track of when one is understanding and when comprehension is slipping is referred to as *metacognitive monitoring*. This continuous attention to meaning can be prompted with strategies for

- translating ideas into one's own words.
- comparing ideas to personal experience.
- trying to identify main ideas—stop and question when this is unclear.
- noting important details.
- rereading whenever necessary for clarification.
- pausing to reflect whenever necessary to make relevant connections to prior knowledge and experience.
- consolidating ideas into meaningful groups.
- noticing unfamiliar vocabulary and predicting meanings based on context when possible.
- forming mental pictures.
- evaluating the author's purpose, motive, or authority when appropriate.
- inventing study strategies as needed.
- managing time to sustain concentration.

Metacognitive monitoring helps the reader keep a firm grip on the schema net and thereby avoid lapsing into a passive, unproductive mode. When comprehension does begin to falter—as it often does during study reading—when the net begins to slip, good study readers use a variety of fix-up strategies to maintain their grip on the net and follow or discover the writer's meaning (Baker & Brown, 1984). *Fix-up strategies* are actions taken during study reading to regain the thread of comprehension. Depending upon the situation, fix-up strategies may include simply pausing to reflect and refocus, rereading, reading aloud, identifying problematic terms and using context to predict or confirm possible meanings, paraphrasing difficult sections, forming mental images, or even asking for help.

Postreading:
Fine-tuning Schema Net Additions

In the final stage of active Instructional-level reading, readers check basic comprehension and interpretations and decide on relevant applications of the new information and ideas. To do so, they may use any of a variety of strategies for *schema enhancement*, *schema-structure building*, or *schema restructuring*. These terms correspond to the learning processes that developmental psychologist Jean Piaget called "assimilation" and "accommodation." The reader consciously compares the new information to existing schema categories and either adds it or constructs a new category or categorization system to incorporate it (two forms of assimilation) or alters existing schema structures to fit the new information (accommodation). Strategies to prompt Postreading schema building include:

- Checking basic comprehension by reciting.
- Organizing information into chunks of manageable size.
- Deciding what is important.
- Trying to clarify ambiguous ideas.
- Evaluating new information in terms of previous knowledge and experience.
- Developing study strategies according to class demands or personal purposes.
- Reviewing material periodically.
- Relating what has been learned from reading back to real-life experiences and related learning.

▶ THEORY INTO PRACTICE: CAL METHODS

The organization and contents of this text are based on the assumption that students will be most successful at using, personalizing, and internalizing study-reading strategies when teachers make a point of systematically demonstrating their own favored strategies for prompting Prereading schema activation, for metacognitive monitoring and comprehension fix-up during reading, and for Postreading schema building. Most often, these strategy prompts take the form of questions. Content Area Literacy methods offer a variety of contexts for demonstrating good strategic questions to prompt active study reading.

In the illustration of the Listen-Read-Discuss method presented in Chapter 1, for example, the Prereading script for the article, "Dance and Sport—the Elusive Connection," includes several schema-activating prompts:

- Did you know that [main point from the selection]?
- Read to find out [why the title was selected].

The L-R-D script also includes comprehension monitoring prompts:

- Can you see [someone you know] doing [something from the selection]?
- Look for [list of key ideas] and write these down.
- Look for the difference between [key idea] and [key idea].

Every career stage has developmental problems to face and resolve in working toward new levels of proficiency. For new and experienced teachers alike, it is more comfortable to teach in the traditional manner they most likely experienced as students than it is to acquire a more strategy-based interactive/intervention teaching style. Most of us have had far fewer personal experiences with interactive/intervention teaching than with traditional methods. Furthermore, for new teachers who have been successful students, it can be difficult to realize the problems that many of their peers experienced in those more familiar instructional settings. These obstacles are magnified by the fact that teachers attempting to try out new methods and approaches must do so while standing before a class of students who have their own preoccupations, unique histories, and concerns. No "lesson plan" ever unfolds in exactly the same way twice. In a typical classroom setting, teachers must continually evaluate progress toward instructional goals and make many complex "in-flight" decisions based on their perception of a given situation (Padak, 1986).

As a result of obstacles such as these, Content Area Literacy methods typically are designed to meet several criteria:

- CAL methods are general and flexible enough in nature to be easily applied across grade levels, subject areas, and types of teaching materials.
- CAL methods are aligned with research-based understandings of the reading process, offering routines to structure Prereading instruction during reading instruction and Postreading instruction.
- CAL methods offer specific structures for lesson design, which often reduces lesson planning time.
- CAL methods are step-by-step guides, but not strict rules or scripts. They can be used to create a lively interaction in virtually any teaching-learning situation, freeing teachers to add as much creativity as time and physical and mental resources permit.
- CAL methods help keep instruction and learning on course through most student disruptions as well as during teacher lapses resulting from inexperience or distraction. This structure helps create a classroom environment that is conducive to the kind of cognitive and social risk taking that is essential to effective teaching and learning.
- CAL methods are designed to encourage greater student participation. Teaching and learning become more interesting and engaging for both students and teachers.
- In sum, CAL methods are designed to produce a well-thought-out, but not confining, teaching-learning environment in which students can observe and try out a variety of thinking strategies.

▶ THE ORAL READING STRATEGY: A STRAIGHTFORWARD "HOW-TO" METHOD

The Oral Reading Strategy (Manzo, 1980) is a simple, direct way to model thinking strategies for Prereading and active Silent Reading. The teacher reads a brief portion of the selection aloud to students while they follow along on their copies of the selection. While reading, the teacher makes a conscious attempt to think aloud—that is, to model the thinking strategies that proficient readers might use to focus attention, develop and maintain interest, and monitor comprehension. A similar method is called "Think Aloud" (Davey, 1983). The Oral Reading Strategy calls for the teacher's oral reading to be *brief* so that students can maintain attention and have an immediate opportunity to emulate the model as they continue to read silently. (The literacy specialist or teacher with opportunity for individual tutoring may wish to have students attempt a "think aloud" while reading to get a sense of what students may or may not be saying to themselves while reading.)

Steps in the Oral Reading Strategy

Step 1. *Teacher preparation.* Preview the reading selection, trying to "see" it from your students' perspectives. On a photocopy of the first page or so (depending on print formatting), make notes of the thinking strategies that would be useful to model for students as you read the first few paragraphs aloud just before students' independent Silent Reading of the assignment. The Prereading and active Silent Reading strategies listed in Figure 2.1 are a good place to start.

Step 2. *Teacher oral reading.* Tell students that you will read a little of the beginning of the reading assignment aloud to show them how to read actively when they are reading silently. Using the notes you have prepared, read and think aloud. Encourage students to answer your think-aloud questions.

Step 3. *Release responsibility to students.* At a reasonable stopping point (after no more than about three to five minutes), tell students to continue immediately to read silently, trying to use the same active thinking strategies you have just demonstrated. See the example in Figure 2.3 to get a sense of how the teacher can use this think-aloud process to demonstrate active reading strategies in a direct and interactive way.

The Oral Reading Strategy was used toward the end of class to scaffold students' independent reading of a supplementary reading selection. In this example, the teacher has used the Oral Reading Strategy with this class several times before.

After distributing copies of the article, the teacher begins the interaction by stating, "Before you start to read this article, I will read the first part out loud to remind you of some of the ways we have to think actively when we're reading to learn something new."

The teacher then reads the first three paragraphs aloud (the boldface portions that follow), with the think-alouds inviting student responses as shown in parentheses.

Figure 2.3 Example of the Oral Reading Strategy with "Dance and Sport—The Elusive Connection."

Source: This article is reprinted with permission from the *Journal of Physical Education, Recreation and Dance,* May/June 1986, pp. 26 and 54. *JOPERD* is a publication of the American Alliance for Health, Physical Education, Recreation and Dance, 1900 Association Dr., Reston, VA 20191.

DANCE AND SPORT—THE ELUSIVE CONNECTION

(*T:* Okay, when we read to learn something new, we start right off to do what?)
(*S:* Talk to ourselves.)
(*T:* Great, so, then, let's stop and think about the title, dance and sport—how *might* they be connected?)
(*S:* You have to learn to move in both.)
(*S:* You have to practice both.)
(*T:* Okay. Let's think some more about the title. If dance and sport are connected, how might the connection be *elusive*?)
(*S:* What does *elusive* mean?)
(*T:* That's a good strategy question—what's the word culprit? *Elusive* means hard to hold on to or hard to pin down—in this case, it probably means hard to hold on to.)
(*T:* So, how might the connection be *elusive*?) (*after no immediate response*, *T:* Well, if we're not getting it, we could ...?)
(*S:* Read on a little bit.)
(*T:* Okay.)

Techniques and Principles Effectively Used in Teaching Dance Can Be Applied to Teaching Sport

(*T:* Let's stop and think about the rest of the title. Does this remind you of anything you've heard about?)
(*S:* I've seen how some football coaches make their players do ballet.)
(*T:* And how might that connection be elusive?)
(*S:* The guys probably feel kind of dumb doing it.)
(*T:* I think we've got a prediction about where the title is leading us; let's read on a little.)

1 **What are the functional connections between dance and sport and the benefits that are derived from participation in both pursuits? This article presents ideas which are applied to both dance and sport in order to enhance performance and reduce injury.**

(*T:* Let's stop for a second and boil that down.)
(*S:* By doing both dance and sport, you can do your own thing better and not get hurt.)
(*T:* Any questions about this?)
(*S:* Do ballet dancers benefit from learning to play football?)
(*T:* Good question. Let's read on a little.)

2 **Many well-known people have recognized a connection between dance and sport skills. It may have been this kinship that convinced Knute Rockne, famed football coach at Notre Dame, to require his players to enroll in dance classes.**

Figure 2.3 *(continued)*

(*T:* There's your football/ballet connection.)

Maybe it was the similarity between dance and sport that caused Woody Hayes, former Ohio state head coach, to expect his players to take dance as part of their practice procedures (Lance, 1981). Lynn Swan, three-time Pro Bowl wide receiver while playing with the four-time World Champion Pittsburgh Steelers, studied dance for 14 years and attributed his graceful athletic abilities to dance.

(*T:* What's the point of this paragraph?)
(*S:* Examples of people who have seen the connection between football and dance.)
(*T:* Let's read on a little bit.)

3 **It is possible that each of these individuals witnessed movement competencies shared by dance and sports. Some of these shared abilities include centering, balance, focus, breathing, transfer of weight, relaxation and the ability to use space, time, and energy with mastery. Such abilities are taught specifically in dance classes, while in athletics they are only alluded to as a part of skill instruction.**

(*T:* What's important here?)
(*S:* Those look like the things that people need for both dance and sport.)
(*T:* The *functional connections?*) (*after nods,T:* Can we predict where this is going?)
(*S:* Maybe it's going to tell more about these things, like centering, and balance? Or tell about some other things that are the same in both?)
[Teacher writes on the chalkboard: "What are the functional connections between dance and sport?"]
(*T:* Any questions about this?)
(*S:* I still wonder whether any ballet dancers have tried to play football.)
[Teacher adds to the chalkboard; "Do the connections go both ways, or only from sport to dance?"]
(*T:* Do you have any other questions before you continue reading by yourselves?)
[No questions are raised.]
(*T:* Okay, continue reading to find answers to these questions. Remember to use the strategy phrases as you go.)

4 The basic difference between dance and sport is that sport takes place within the conditions of a game, while dance is performed in other contexts. A game is a contest in which opposing

Figure 2.3 *(continued)*

interests are given specific information and are then allowed a choice of moves with the object of maximizing wins and minimizing losses. A game entails dominance over an opponent and the acquisition of some mutually coveted symbol. The athlete, by improving his or her movement abilities, will then improve sport skills.

5 Dancers, on the other hand, are process-oriented rather than product-oriented. The goal in dance is the improvement of movement quality.

6 Similarities between dance and sport outweigh their differences. Participants in both areas train to go faster and farther, while moving with increased control. The dancer and the sport participant both work to expand their movement vocabulary so they can use a particular action when the situation demands. Biomechanical analysis has been used for many years by physical educators to help their students learn. In recent years, dancers have also begun to use biomechanics to analyze movement with the goals of sharpening perception of movement, decreasing learning time, and enhancing performance (Laws, 1984). Dance and sport are similar in another respect. While some would say a dance was choreographed but a sport contest was not planned, further examination indicates that all the X's and O's used in game strategy simply represent another form of choreography.

7 Some sport activities are more similar to dance training than others. The concept of open and closed skills helps explain this point. In a closed skill, one strives to master an effective and efficient motor program with the goal of being able to duplicate this program with each repetition. Environmental conditions remain relatively constant, and the performer attempts to be consistent in the execution of the skill. Sports such as the shot put, diving, and gymnastics are closed skills. Open skills exist in a changing environment, and the selection of appropriate movement responses is as variable as the environment itself. Baseball, football, soccer, and basketball are open skill activities (Sage, 1977). Both open and closed skill athletes can benefit from dance training. The abilities which are taught in dance classes used by both kinds of athletes are different, but are not less applicable to their sports' requirements.

8 The principle of relaxation can be used as an example. Dancers frequently talk about using the right amount of tension in one part of the body while allowing other body areas to remain relaxed. The main idea is to use energy efficiently and only where needed to perform a movement. Efficient movement is character-

Figure 2.3 *(continued)*

ized by using the appropriate muscle groups in proper sequence. The use of the wrong muscle group at the wrong time can be deleterious to the skill and possibly to the performer. Another common word heard in dance class is "centering." Centering is finding the body's center of weight and manipulating it effectively in relation to gravity. It also brings the mind and body together to produce better concentration. Achieving a heightened perception of and facility with space, time, and energy is another principle used in teaching dance. Dancers are asked to look at the direction or level of a movement, its speed in relation to an underlying pulse, or the quality of energy used to propel actions through space. Such movement descriptions are provided in dance classes to help students see movement more clearly and to enhance understanding of the expressive aspects of each action (Minton, 1984).

9 The point is that these principles are used in teaching dance, but generally not in teaching sport. In dance, these ideas are singled out in the classroom and used as learning tools. The examples given here are several of the techniques used in teaching dance that could be applied profitably to the teaching of sport.

References

Lance, J. (1981). Practicing for touchdowns. *Journal of Physical Education, Recreation, and Dance,* 5, 38.

Laws, K. (1984). *The Physics of Dance.* New York: Macmillan.

Minton, S. C. (1984). *Modern Dance: Body and Mind.* Englewood, CO: Morton.

Sage, G. H. (1977). *Introduction to Motor Behavior: A Neuropsychological Approach* (2nd ed.). Reading, MA: Addison-Wesley.

Sandra Minton is coordinator of the Dance Program at the University of Northern Colorado, Greeley, CO 80639. Bradford E. Beckwith is a doctoral candidate, psychological kinesiology, at the same school.

Figure 2.3 *(continued)*

► CONCEPT SUMMARY

The first concept in this chapter is the distinction between Independent and Instructional reading. This is one of the most important concepts in thinking about and implementing Content Area Literacy. Many content teachers tend to think of reading as what *they* do when they read class textbooks—which makes it difficult for them to understand why students need the kind of assistance that Content Area Literacy methods offer. Most students also think that "reading is reading" and become discouraged when they encounter difficulty in reading increasingly difficult textbooks. The idea that study reading is a completely different process than easy reading, but a process that can be taught and learned, is important for both teachers and students.

The chapter next summarized the major trends in theoretical views of the reading process over the past half century and illustrated how these have markedly different implications for classroom practice. Current understandings of the study-reading process as engaged learning focus on identifying sets of strategies for Prereading schema activation and metacognitive monitoring and fix-up strategies for reading and Postreading schema building. The metaphor of a large fishing net is a useful one for this three-stage process. The Oral Reading Strategy is a straightforward method for teaching Prereading schema activation strategies. The Content Area Literacy methods in the next chapters offer a variety of structures for teaching these strategy sets.

CHAPTER 3

A FRAMEWORK FOR READING-BASED INSTRUCTION IN THE INTERACTIVE CLASSROOM

We have to change the way teachers interact with students in the classroom—and the changes must be grounded in an understanding of how children learn.

—John T. Bruer (1993, p. 7)

This chapter provides an overview of the instructional elements that distinguish interactive teaching/learning from more traditional approaches. These elements are then translated into a Framework for Text-Based Instruction that can be used to guide planning and teaching any reading-based lesson in any subject at any level. The Framework described is rooted in the stages of the reading process described in Chapter 2: (1) *Prereading* for schema activation, (2) *Guided Silent Reading* to encourage metacognitive monitoring and comprehension fix-up, and (3) *Postreading* for schema building and possible restructuring. Initial planning elements include preassessment of students' readiness to read the given material, possible selection of supplementary reading materials, and selection of methods to be used for modeling thinking strategies for study reading. Additional elements to be considered—in terms of whether or how much to incorporate in a given lesson—are engagement, scaffolding and fading of supports, reciprocity, and structured peer interactions. An example is given of how this three-step Framework can be implemented using a method referred to as the Three-Phase Graphic Organizer. The goal of the Framework is to have *more* students have *more* successful experiences with reading and learning from text.

THE MORE THINGS CHANGE...

In many cities, middle and high school buildings built in the early 1900s are still in use. Wide hallways, marble floors, high ceilings, and architectural detail are a testament to society's belief in the value of education. On the other hand, these schools are a reminder of the somewhat elitist nature of school in those days, with a far lower percentage of the population even attending high school. Today, schools are charged with serving the entire population; yet if we were to visit classrooms in those historic buildings, we would find that instruction hasn't changed a great deal since they first opened their doors. The same is true in today's more functional buildings. Students have changed, society has changed, and our understanding of the learning process has changed; yet life in many classrooms goes on much the same. A recent study of internet access in K-12 classrooms found that today, almost all schools have internet in at least some classrooms, as compared to only 14% of those schools in 1997 (Technology counts 2007: A digital decade, March 2007). The same study found that while new technologies and software programs are less expensive and more user-friendly, and while students of all ages text, wiki, blog, youtube, and podcast, very little has changed in the way teachers organize and deliver instruction. This is partly explainable by the fact that technological innovations are appearing at such a dizzying rate. Teachers who used instructional software that was cutting edge in 2000 find it hopelessly outdated today.

As technology continues to make its way into the "traditional" classroom, students will encounter instructional text on liquid crystal display screens, on their classroom laptops, and on their phones. Regardless of the medium, many, if not all, parts necessary for robust, interactive teaching and learning seem to be in place now–most importantly, a better understanding of the nature of study reading provides insight into just what it is that we should be teaching. This understanding is translated into a Framework for Reading-Based Instruction in the next section.

▶ A FRAMEWORK FOR READING-BASED INSTRUCTION IN THE INTERACTIVE CLASSROOM

Most middle and high school students need some guidance in reading to learn from text, and some need a great deal. Bintz (1997) lists some of the problems that teachers typically face with reading-based instruction. They face students who

- experience daily difficulties learning from text materials.
- regularly refuse to do required reading outside of class.
- do read but fail to comprehend the most important information.
- are bored or uninterested in much of what they read.

Content teachers often address such problems by providing guidance without labeling it as "reading"—when they provide specific questions for students to answer when they read or for example, guide students in creating graphic organizers for the material read. Such guidance is most effective when it aligns with the study-reading process described in Chapter 2 and as illustrated in Figure 3.1, which also summarizes key planning elements for reading-based instruction.

A fundamental premise of this Framework is that "thinking" is not completely, or even primarily, a function of intelligence. Rather, it is a constellation of strategies

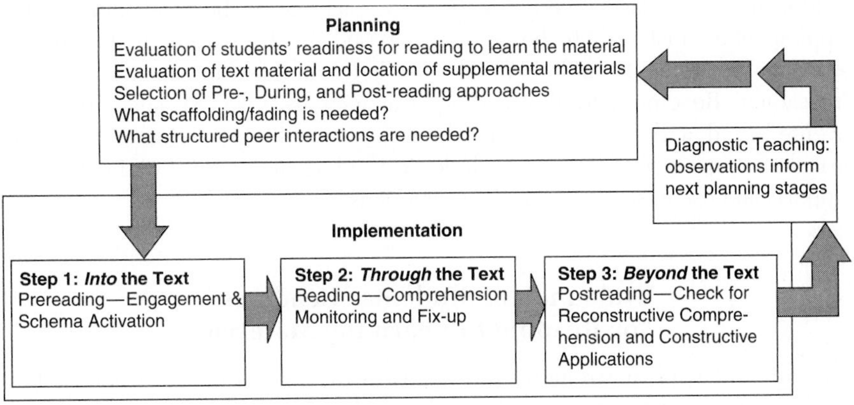

Figure 3.1 A Framework for Reading-Based Instruction

and cognitive habits, or "habits of mind," that can be identified and taught through cognitive modeling. *Cognitive modeling* is thinking aloud to demonstrate a particular thinking strategy. Although modeling has long been used to teach complex manual procedures, as in art and craft apprenticeships and in athletic coaching, it is only in relatively recent times that it has been intentionally applied to teaching thinking strategies that facilitate learning and that are otherwise unobservable. *Thinking strategies*, in this context, *are phrases, usually in the form of questions, used intentionally and flexibly in study reading to prompt one's accurate reconstruction of an author's meanings and to construct personal connections with and uses of these meanings.* The purpose and nature of these strategies differ from Prereading to Silent Reading to Postreading. The next three chapters, 4, 5 and 6, provide research-based approaches, techniques, and methods for structuring each of these steps in reading-based instruction.

An important value of cognitive modeling is that "more is caught than can be explicitly taught." That is, when thinking strategies are modeled in the context of reading-based instruction, students acquire not just the strategy, but a host of other behaviors, such as body language, attitude, and social poise.

The essence of strategy instruction is the intentional, frequent repetition of the strategy phrases, and the intentional, frequent cueing of students to use the strategy phrases. The goal is to help students internalize the phrases to the point that they automatically use the phrases in independent study-reading situations.

Modeling and direct instruction in thinking strategies enables at-risk students while simultaneously building self-awareness and confidence in developmental and advanced students as well. Intentional, structured use of cognitive modeling may be one of the great discoveries of modern pedagogy—it is, or has the power to be, to education what the polio vaccine and penicillin were to public health.

▶ PLANNING

Planning for reading-based instruction in the interactive classroom begins with understanding of students' abilities, knowledge, interests, and attitudes. This understanding is placed alongside the text material to be read and possible supplementary materials to be acquired. Based on the nature of the "match" between the students and materials, methods and techniques for modeling Prereading, Reading, and Postreading strategies are selected, adapted, and/or invented, and a decision is made about how much instruction needs to be provided. Final considerations include scaffolding and fading of instructional supports and use of structured peer interactions.

Evaluation of Students "Readiness" for Reading to Learn the Material

Evaluation of student strengths and needs in the interactive classroom is both wider, in terms of the range of factors considered, and more frequent than in traditional instructional approaches. It draws upon many sources of knowledge about students' strengths and needs. If available, standardized test scores and other records provide some initial information about students' general achievement records. Daily interactions with students and observations of students' interactions with one another help teachers accumulate information about the nature and extent of students' prior knowledge and experiences, as well as an understanding of their personal interests, attitudes, talents, and possible areas of learning difficulty and social-emotional needs. As instruction progresses, each lesson provides assessment information for the next. This process of planning and implementing instruction in ways that intentionally provide ongoing informal assessment is referred to as *diagnostic teaching.*

Student evaluation is a daily, ongoing, problem-solving component of diagnostic teaching that differs sharply from the assessment component of more traditional instructional approaches. In traditional mastery learning approaches, for example, lesson planning begins with a "pretest" of the content to be learned, typically at the beginning of a unit rather than a daily lesson. Initial presentation of the unit content focuses on weaknesses identified by the pretest and is followed with a test to check for mastery, and then with provisions for reteaching students who failed to demonstrate mastery. The assumption underlying such approaches is that the teacher's primary job is to sequence and pace the presentation of content to be learned and monitor students' acquisition of the content.

In diagnostic teaching, each day's lesson is designed with students' responses to previous instruction in mind. Observations of attitudes, behaviors, and interests are taken into consideration along with content knowledge and achievement. More specific and objective assessment information for diagnostic teaching can be collected from a variety of informal assessment techniques. Several of these are described in Chapter 10.

Evaluation of Textbook Material and Location of Supplemental Materials

In the traditional classroom, most of the "text" that students are required to read is in the form of textbooks. The assumption is that at each higher grade level, the difficulty level of the textbooks, or their *readability,* increases to a degree that equals students' increasing reading ability. This is, of course, far from an exact science. In any classroom, students' reading abilities vary widely, and any individual student's ability may vary from subject to subject, as a result of prior instruction, experience, and interests. In lesson preplanning, the teacher places student strengths and needs alongside the difficulty of the text to be read and learned to determine how to best structure the lesson, and how much support to provide.

There are a number of reasons for periodically supplementing the textbook with materials from other sources. One is a growing recognition of the *multiple literacies* needed to function in today's complex society, and acknowledgment that traditional school-based definitions of literacy represent a narrow strand of this broader picture. Students who struggle with the abstract and often isolated learning requirements of school may be masterful users of other real-world literacies. Today's students check movie schedules online and click to read and evaluate reviews in order to choose which movie to see. They communicate via cell phones, text messages, e-mail, instant messages, blogs, discussion boards, and chat rooms. They individually and collaboratively engage in complex and rapid problem solving in video games. They engage in virtual social activities, simulated stock trading, and real-world buying and selling on websites. They selectively gather information from television, movies, magazines, and the internet and post information, art, photos, and music to websites. Using supplementary materials can sanction some of these areas of expertise and help students discover connections between school curricula and their wider life experiences.

The narrow focus of traditional school literacy may even have the effect of driving many students' discovery of and interest in literacy activities "underground." In an article with the captivating title, "On Every Page Someone Gets Killed! Book Conversations You Don't Hear in School," Worthy (1998) describes her study of her middle school son and his friend, as "renegade readers." The study begins with a familiar scenario:

> Both Chase and Jared had followed a typical course of development in all academic and social areas and had been average to above-average students during their earlier school years. Each had grown up in homes in which literacy was valued and reading materials were abundant, and in which they had rich access to books, magazines, and comics of their choice. Both had enjoyed reading in their preschool and primary years, and both had begun to resist school reading in their upper elementary years and continued to do so. (p. 510)
>
> *Source:* Worthy, J. (1998). On every page someone gets killed! Book conversations you don't hear in school. *Journal of Adolescent and Adult Literacy, 41,* 508–517. © International Reading Association.

The author goes on to describe the animated conversations that Chase and Jared had about self-selected books they were reading outside of school (as suggested in the title of the article), in contrast to their resistance to reading school-required books, and their lack of participation in class discussion of these. She describes her son and his friend as "renegade readers" and suggests that one solution is to supplement the school curriculum with materials that are more representative of students' lives and interests.

Another literacy researcher undertook a study with his two adolescent daughters to document the girls' various real-life literacy activities. Not unexpectedly, the report coauthored by father and daughters revealed differing patterns related to the girls' different ages and interests but very little overlap between in-school and out-of-school literacy involvement (Bean, Bean, & Bean, 1999).

Until recently, it was difficult to imagine an alternative to teacher-selected classroom reading materials: a single textbook or class sets of novels and supplementary books. Newspaper and magazine articles could not be reproduced easily until the cost of copying came down to practical levels. Simply locating materials related to an instructional unit was difficult. As schools and classrooms go online, these financial and logistical restrictions are dissolving. Search engines facilitate location of information on virtually any topic, by the teacher and/or students themselves. The use of high-interest, real-world online supplementary readings on unit topics has a number of benefits (Figure 3.2).

Selection of "Pre-, During, and Post-" Reading Approaches

Based on the match between students and materials and consideration of supplementary resources, the next planning decisions are how to structure the Prereading, Guided Silent Reading, and Postreading stages of instruction. Chapters 4, 5 and 6 provide many options for this instructional decision making. Two Prereading methods have been presented in Chapters 1 and 2: Listen-Read-Discuss and the Oral Reading Strategy. Ahead in this chapter is an example of how any type of graphic organizer can be used to structure Pre-, During, and Post-reading instruction.

1. High-interest non-textbook-type short readings are an ideal way to generate interest in any topic prior to reading a textbook treatment at any level.
2. For classes with traditional textbooks, supplementary online readings can be selected to parallel, correspond to, or contrast with the textbook author's treatment of the topic to stimulate critical analysis.
3. Supplementary online readings can provide a simpler version, or a more detailed version, depending on the students' interest and prior knowledge of the topic.
4. Supplementary readings can add currency in rapidly changing subject areas.
5. Supplementary readings can link abstract new concepts to familiar real-world events.
6. When textbooks are not available, occasional reading-based activities with materials located online can introduce students to sources for pursuing their interests outside of and beyond the classroom.
7. WebQuest sites (*http://webquest.sdsu.edu*, for example) make it easy for students to select from a wide range of potential sources of information on a given topic and to access these at their own pace.
8. The online world is coming to be more "real world" than the regular classrooms for some students. Use of supplementary materials and online resources may help these students see that the curriculum does not reside solely in classrooms and textbooks, but is a vibrant and real part of their actual and virtual lives as well as.

Figure 3.2 Advantages to using supplementary resources

Any approach to Pre-, During, and Post-reading instruction can be implemented with varying degrees of instructional support, or *scaffolding.* Structured peer interactions also can be built in to a greater or lesser degree. These two final planning considerations are discussed next.

What Scaffolding/Fading Is Needed?

Scaffolding refers to elements of instruction that support the learner during the early stages of learning. Any new learning involves the building of new schema structures. This takes much more time than all subsequent learning and is characterized by a high-risk trial-and-error period that, in the social context of a classroom, can threaten the learner's self-esteem. One of the best ways to build internal motivation and strengthen self-esteem is to design lessons with sufficient scaffolding to build students' sense of their own competence as learners. For interactive instruction to occur, learning situations must be structured in ways that reduce the social risks of active participation and encourage the learner to experiment with new ways of thinking and communicating. One important function of cognitive modeling is to externalize thinking in ways that honestly portray the initial awkwardness and increasing competence in acquiring new knowledge and skill.

As students gain confidence and automaticity in using a set of strategies with a particular content, the teacher *gradually removes the scaffolding,* a process referred to as *fading.* This happens to some extent within each lesson, and more obviously over the course of a semester or year. It is during this fading process that learners internalize new learning strategies by adjusting them into forms and formats for personal use.

What Structured Peer Interactions Are Needed?

In the traditional classroom, any active participation can be a risky proposition. Yet genuine learning is virtually defined by active participation. By talking to others, we discover what we think and feel; by listening to others, we learn to consider other points of view. In recent years, the early, complex versions of cooperative learning have evolved into more fluid, flexible cooperative structures for managing the complex social dynamics of the classroom. A *cooperative structure* is *an activity intended to produce active interactions among participants and create a sense of classroom community.* Kagan (1994) uses the acronym "PIES" to represent the elements of an effective cooperative structure:

*P*ositive interdependence	Interactions are structured in ways that students come to rely on their peers in positive ways.
*I*ndividual accountability	Each student is, however, responsible for his or her own learning.
*E*qual participation	All students are actively involved in the interactions for the same amount of time.
*S*imultaneous interaction	A number of interactions occur at the same time.

▶ IMPLEMENTATION

The Pre-, During and Post- stages of the reading process and reading instruction often are referred to as *Into* the text, *Through* the text, and *Beyond* the text. These are useful terms to share with students in discussions of study reading.

Step 1: Into the Text
Engagement and Schema Activation

Engagement is *focused attention on the learning task at hand.* It is the single most essential element in teaching/learning: If the learner is not paying active attention to the learning task, none of the subsequent elements can be achieved. While traditional instruction tended to rely on external sources of motivation (such as grades) to encourage engagement, the interactive approach emphasizes building internal motivation by directing attention to the larger context, importance, and relevance of the learning task, as illustrated in the following poem:

Points to Ponder
What! No star, and you are going out to sea?
Marching, and you have no music?
Traveling, and you have no book?
What! No love and you are going out to live?

Translated from the French
(Author unknown)

This poem represents the intent of engagement. In traditional instruction, it is the teacher who presumably has the larger vision: the "star," the "music." The students' job is to be patient, cooperate, practice the parts as presented, and trust that at some point it will all come together. Failing to provide for engagement is somewhat like trying to teach a child to speak without ever letting her or him hear spoken language or experience its value. Some children will accept the teacher's authority and attempt seemingly aimless activities. But learning becomes more focused, animated, and rapid when students can see the "stars" before they begin. It is not always easy to work backward to the driving questions and fundamental issues of a discipline and then to translate these into classroom experiences. However, online activities and resources like WebQuests (pioneered by Bernie Dodge and Tom March at San Diego State University—see http://webquest.sdsu.edu) are offering a rapidly growing collection of interactive resources for providing engagement.

Effective, engaged study readers use a variety of strategies to consciously call to mind relevant schema for the general topic, including personal prior knowledge, experiences, and attitudes. This schema activation permits the reader to anticipate the structure, organization, and general content of the selection. Approaches to teaching Prereading anticipation strategies may involve brainstorming, inquiry training, and/or guided prediction. The Listen-Read-Discuss method described in Chapter 1 is one simple approach to providing engagement and modeling schema activation strategies. In the L-R-D, the teacher delivers a "mini lecture" just before having students begin to read. The lecture tells why the material to be read is important, what is especially interesting about it, how it might connect with students' prior knowledge and experience, how it is structured, and what important things students should look for as they read.

General guidelines for prereading instruction include the following:

- Model schema activation strategies, such as
  "What does the title tell me?"
  "What do I know about this already?"
- Provide low-risk, scaffolded opportunities for students to practice these strategies.
- Preview the material, including pictures and graphics, and make predictions.
- Generate clear purpose questions to focus student reading.
- Preteach any vocabulary terms that might be unfamiliar to most students and important to the meaning of the reading material. Vocabulary for a larger unit of study may be introduced at the beginning of the unit and reinforced over the course of the unit.
- Consider structured peer interactions to elicit students' background knowledge, experiences, and attitudes prior to reading.
- Consider visual and auditory prompts to aid in schema activation.
- Consider activities that might serve as Prereading engagement and schema activation for a series of reading assignments over the period of a larger unit. Many textbook teachers' manuals provide ideas for this type of unit introduction.

Step 2: Through the Text
Comprehension Monitoring and Fix-up

In Independent-level reading, the *Through* stage can be an almost automatic process of moving the eyes across the print and passively and correctly absorbing the author's meanings. In more difficult Instructional-level materials, the reader must monitor comprehension more consciously. In more difficult, Instructional-level materials, the reader must monitor comprehension more consciously and more continuously. Silent Reading can be guided by asking students to do various things as they read. One traditional approach is to provide students with a reading guide—a set of questions to consider and answer as they read. In various think-aloud approaches, such as the Oral Reading Strategy described in Chapter 2, Silent Reading strategies can be modeled by the teacher and practiced aloud by students before they begin to read—students then are encouraged to use these strategies as they continue to read.

Guidelines for helping students acquire strategies for monitoring and fixing up comprehension as they move *Through* reading include the following:

- Model comprehension-monitoring strategies, such as
  "How could I say that in my own words?"

"What part of this isn't making sense?"

- Model fix-up strategies, such as
  "I should reread that last part, more slowly this time."
  "I should stop and think about that for a minute."
- Use class time periodically for Silent Reading of core assignments: The goal is to increasingly expect students to complete reading assignments as homework. When reading is assigned as homework, reinforce the expectation that students will *do* it by rewarding those who do rather than punishing those who don't. Several structured peer interactions for doing this are described in Chapter 6.
- Provide traditional reading guides with questions to be answered as students read.
- Remind students that study reading cannot be done "straight through" as easy reading can be done by suggesting "stopping points" for checking and clarifying comprehension, such as each paragraph, or each subtopic section in a chapter.
- Provide a "strategy guide" by combining the previous two suggestions: Construct a reading guide that directs students to read a given portion of text and then respond to a strategy question, rather than a traditional question at each stopping point.
- Consider structured peer interactions in which pairs or small groups of students work *Through* a reading assignment collaboratively, using a traditional reading guide or a strategy guide.
- Consider ways to occasionally ask students to "think aloud" as they read short sections of text, reminding them to do this in the way the teacher has modeled using the Oral Reading Strategy.

Step 3: Beyond the Text Postreading Check for Reconstructive Comprehension and Constructive Applications

Postreading strategies for connecting what has just been read with existing schema begin with questions to check basic comprehension and include additional Postreading strategies for analyzing and interpreting the author's message to add new schema structures or alter existing ones. Approaches to helping students think *Beyond* the text include peer discussion, writing, and traditional teacher-directed discussion. Peer discussion and writing activities help students process and formulate their responses to reading in preparation for a larger group discussion. Guidelines for structuring the Postreading stage of reading-based instruction include the following:

- Model strategies for checking basic comprehension, such as
  "Did I get the answer to the purpose question(s)?"
  "What were the main points?"
  "Should I reread any sections?"

- Model strategies for reaching higher levels of comprehension, such as
  "What would be an example of this in my own experience?"
  "Does this confirm or change anything that I knew or believed before?"
- Emphasize to students the difference between basic comprehension and higher-order responses to reading such as connection with personal experience, interpretation, application, and evaluation. In fact-dense subject areas, the emphasis may be on basic comprehension across several lessons in a unit, with greater emphasis on higher-order responses to conclude the unit.
- At the end of reading guides constructed to direct students *Through* the reading, add a question or two to prompt them to think *Beyond* the author's meanings. See the Three-Level Guide in Chapter 6, for example.
- Consider structured peer interactions for basic comprehension checking and for discussion of higher-order responses.
- Consider various uses of writing in response to reading for both comprehension checking and prompting higher-order responses. See Write-Pair-Share in Chapter 6, which combines these last two suggestions.

This three-step Framework is not terribly different, on the surface, from one of the first published Content Area Reading frameworks: Russell Stauffer's (1969) *Directed Reading-Thinking Activity* (DR-TA). Intuition and good sense often outrun theory and research. Stauffer's DR-TA recommended five steps for a reading–based content area lesson: Preparation for Reading, Reading the Material Silently, Developing Comprehension, Rereading, and Follow-Up. We have translated this generic framework into the version described in this chapter primarily to place stronger emphasis on the elements of thinking-strategy instruction that have evolved, along with a clearer understanding of the study-reading process, into a powerful technology over the 40 years since Stauffer's groundbreaking publication. A multitude of methods and approaches now are available for the Pre-, During, and Post- steps of the Framework for Reading-Based Instruction. One such method, using a graphic organizer to structure each step, is described next.

Using a Graphic Organizer to Plan and Teach a Reading-Based Lesson

A *graphic organizer* is *a two-dimensional picture of the logical organization of textual material.* In one standard format, called a *structured overview*, the main topic is placed in the center, subtopics are arranged around it, and details related to each subtopic are noted alongside it. Other forms of graphic organizers include Venn diagrams, flowcharts, pyramid charts, and "herringbone charts" (see Figure 3.3 for examples).

Graphic organizers can be used in many ways to help students make concrete connections with abstract ideas and relationships. They can be used to structure brainstorming, to encourage active Silent Reading, or to prompt Postreading

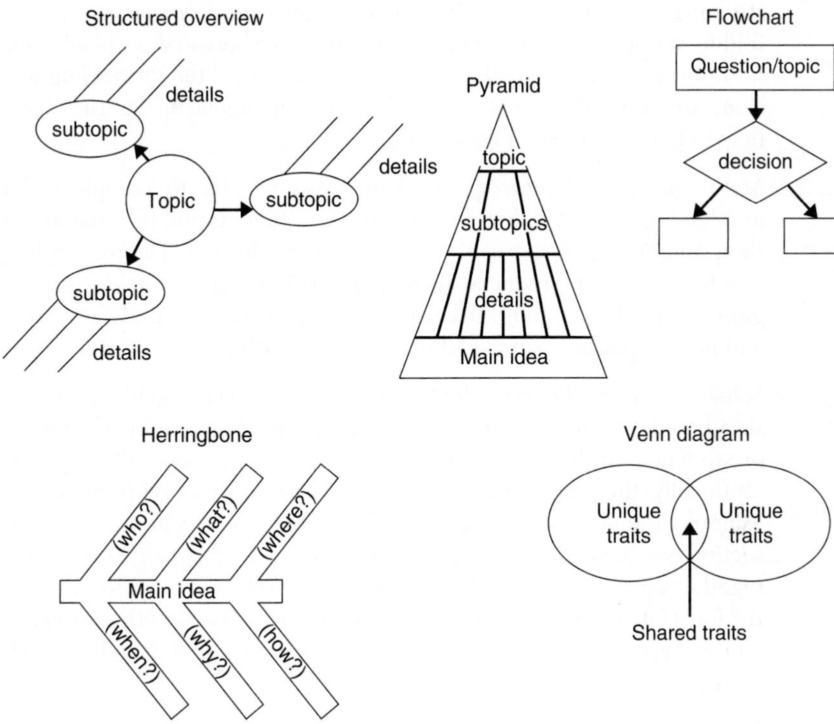

Figure 3.3 Graphic organizer formats

reflective discussion or writing. In the following method, a graphic organizer is used to do all of these tasks.

Steps in the Three-Phase Graphic Organizer

Preparation: Analyze the reading selection to determine a graphic organizer format that illustrates its organization. Prepare a graphic organizer that includes all important information in the selection.

Step 1. *Prereading Schema Activation.* Without showing the prepared graphic organizer to the class, announce the topic, and ask students what they think they will read about in the selection. As students make suggestions, begin a rough construction of the graphic organizer on the board or overhead while students copy it on their papers. Typically, the first suggestions made will be details rather than major subtopics. For example, in a selection about spiders, one of the students' first suggestions would likely be that "they have eight legs" rather than the subtopic "body parts." For some selections, students will be able to generate the needed subtopics or anchor information; for other selections, the teacher will need to supply some if not most of these. During this interaction, the teacher should be open to modifying the planned structure of the graphic organizer if students make reasonable alternative suggestions. For maximum scaffolding support, the teacher may show students where to draw blank lines for information to find in their reading. By the end of the Prereading session, students will have an incomplete graphic organizer that they have helped to develop (see Figure 3.4).

Step 2. *Metacogniztive Monitoring.* Students read silently to complete the graphic organizer. While they read silently, students add information to their graphic organizers as they find it in the selection. The incomplete graphic organizer produced in Step 1 provides a ready-made reading guide, reminding students to read actively; question their understanding; and note important points, details, and relationships.

Step 3. *Schema Building.* Once students have read, the teacher guides a discussion based on students' additions to the Prereading graphic organizer, or students are directed to compare their work in cooperative groups. Optionally, the graphic organizer may be used as a writing prompt. For example, the graphic organizer may be divided into sections, with each section assigned to a small group of students. Each group then works together on their portion of the organizer to "retranslate" it from pictorial form into a connected paragraph (see Figure 3.4 for another variation on this idea) or to add some deeper level of understanding and research on the topic.

Implementation Notes on Graphic Organizers

Many content textbooks now include graphic organizers at the beginning or end of each chapter. Recent research indicates, however, that graphic organizers have little influence on reading comprehension if they are simply *given* to students before or after reading. Their effectiveness lies in students' participation in creating them. For this reason, in the Prereading portion of the Three-Phase Graphic Organizer, the teacher uses the prepared graphic merely as a reference for guiding a brainstorming session on students' background knowledge about the topic.

Graphic organizers have been found to be especially useful in helping readers deal with what has been called *inconsiderate text*—that is, textual material that is too difficult because of poor writing and/or faulty assumptions about the reader's level of familiarity with the topic (Alvermann & Boothby, 1983). They do this by visually highlighting important ideas and playing down irrelevant and potentially distracting points. In the example shown in Figure 3.4, the description of creativity is not clearly laid out in the article: Part of the description is toward the beginning, and part at the end.

Notice that in the Three-Phase Graphic Organizer lesson example, students spend a good deal of time speaking, listening, and writing, as well as reading. Structured peer interactions are used to encourage students to talk about what they have read and to develop points for an argument. After they have predicted, read, taken notes, compared notes with peers, and discussed an arguable position, they are asked to write a summary of what they have discussed. This intermingling of

This example is based on a short article entitled, "How Do I Know if I Am, or Could Be, Creative?" as used by high school art teacher, Jeanette. Working from notes for a complete graphic organizer (GO), Jeanette wrote the topic "*Are Some People More Creative Than Others*?" in the center of the chalkboard. She told the class, "I found an interesting article on the internet about creativity. Before I have you read it, let's think together about some of the ideas you have about creativity—who is creative and who isn't." As I put your ideas on the chalkboard, each of you should copy them onto your own paper. This will make a kind of worksheet for you to use as you read the article. Now, what is something you would expect to find in an article on this topic?" [Note: Jeanette reworded the topic for the graphic organizer because she thought that the title of the article would lead the Prereading brainstorming down the wrong paths.] The next interactions went something like this:

Student: Well, sure. Look at Sheila. She always comes up with ideas for her projects that no one else would have thought of. [Sheila jokingly replies, "Maybe I'm just weird."]

Jeanette: So, one answer could be "yes." Creativity is something you're born with—something innate. [Jeanette adds the word "yes," followed by the phrase "Creativity is innate" to the GO, indicating that students should copy these terms and their placement on their papers.] Is that what you think?

Student: Yes. [Several students nod.]

Jeanette: Okay, then, think about creativity: What kind of mental process is it? How do you know it when you see it? [She adds "Define creativity" to the GO.]

Student: I don't know about that, but some people might be kind of creative but not, like, show it—because they don't want to be different or something.

Jeanette: Ah, so there may be people who are *potentially* creative? [adds the word "*no*" and the phrase "Some just have unrealized potential?" to the GO]. Anyone could be creative, but for some reason some people just don't use their potential. Maybe because they don't want to be different [adds the phrase "looking different" to the GO]—can you think of any other reasons why someone might not realize his or her creative potential?

Student: Well, like you said, what do you mean by "creative"? Some people might be creative in some things that they're interested in, but not in other things that don't interest them as much.

Figure 3.4 Example of a Three-Phase Graphic Organizer

Source: Am I Creative? © 1999, Creativity Web http://www.ozemail.com.au/~caveman/creative, e-mail: charles@mpx.com.au. Reprinted by permission.

Jeanette: Good, so, "motivation" would be a reason for not realizing creative potential [adds "motivation" to the GO], and we're back to trying to define "creativity." Let's stop here and go to the article. Add a few lines to your graphic organizers to show where there is information to look for [adds lines]. While you're reading, look for how the author describes creativity—be sure to put these into your own words—and two other reasons why some people may have unrealized creative potential. Also look for what the author says about testing creativity.

By the end of these exchanges, Jeanette and the students had created the following incomplete graphic organizer. Its structure and contents follow the one Jeanette had prepared, with one point ("looking different") added from a student's contribution. Jeanette also added a few points to direct students to key points in the article.

Prereading Incomplete Graphic Organizer:

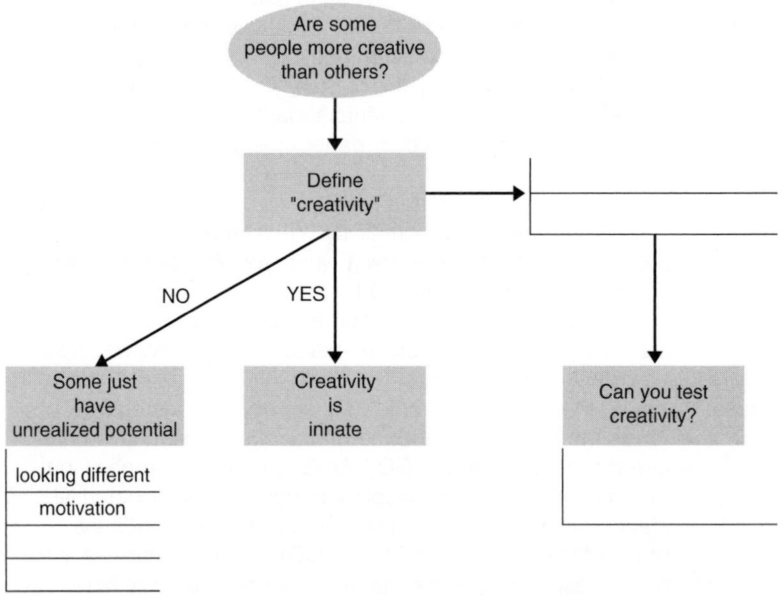

Students now were instructed to read the article to complete their graphic organizers:

HOW DO I KNOW IF I AM, OR COULD BE, CREATIVE?

Every living, breathing human being has the potential to be creative. Each of us is a unique individual capable of creating . . .

Figure 3.4 *(continued)*

it comes with the human territory. We are, simply, quite a creative species.

All people can be creative but those who are recognized as being creative have an awareness that others don't. Creative people seem to be able to tune in more to their thought patterns and glean great ideas. People who do not use their creative potential don't know how to do this or aren't even aware it is possible. Creative people can start thinking about something, then forget it.

Meanwhile, their brains are still thinking about it. Later on, the person will start thinking about whatever it was again and their brain will say, "Excuse me, I've been thinking about this while you were off doing other things and I have a few ideas. Care to hear them?" Noncreative people don't know that their brains are working for them off-shift—they don't know what they don't know!

This is not to say that people tremendously fluctuate in their creativity day to day and hour to hour; the opposite is often believed—that some individuals are generally more creative most of the time than others. The reasons why some people are more creative, however, are many.

1. Without the abilities needed to do the creative act, it is highly unlikely the individual will do the act. Just because a person has the ability to do something, however, does not necessarily mean that the person will do it. This is why researchers examine people's motives.
2. Without the motivation to do so, it is unlikely that a person would complete an act, regardless of the person's abilities.
3. Lastly, opportunities in the environment can affect the creativeness of individuals and groups of individuals.

If you've ever generated a novel response to a problem or challenge then congratulate yourself as being creative. If you do this on a regular basis, say every day, then put the "creative person" badge on yourself. With practice, your ability to generate novel and useful responses to problems and challenges will greatly improve.

One aspect of a creative personality is the fluency with which he/she generates a number of new ideas. Not only does the creative person think of good ideas, but he/she can think of many ideas, explore them, and record them. If you feel a need to quantify your creative ability, go to a local psychologist and ask about taking a test to measure your creative ability. If you live near a college or university approach their psychology department with this request. But recognize that creative ability can be learned, improved upon, and increased over time.

Source: Am I Creative? © 1999, Creativity Web http://www.ozemail.com.au/~caveman/creative. E-Mail:charles©mpx.com.au. Reprinted by permission.

Figure 3.4 *(continued)*

After students have read the article and completed their graphic organizers, they are directed to go to their home groups (four students each), compare what they have written, and make corrections or additions as needed. They are then asked to number off within groups. Student 1 and 2 are directed to develop the strongest arguments they can for the position that some people are naturally more creative than others. Students 3 and 4 are directed to develop their strongest arguments for the alternate position. They are given about 5 minutes to complete this discussion, and then students 1 and 3 are asked to relate their arguments to the other pair in their group. As a final step, students are asked to write on the back of their graphic organizer one paragraph stating and defending the position of their own choice.

Figure 3.4 *(continued)*

listening, speaking, reading, and writing is a key characteristic of interactive teaching and learning.

It also should be noted that computers, personal digital assistants (PDAs), and tablet PCs in the classroom can be used in new ways to facilitate the process of using Three-Phase Graphic Organizers. For instance, many word-processing and common drawing software programs can be used to build sophisticated and visually pleasing graphic organizers that the students design themselves. Specialty software such as Inspiration (*www.inspiration.com*) is getting enthusiastic reviews from teachers for the ways it helps facilitate visual learning and graphic organizer creation. Finally, assigning online discussion board responses as a Three-Phase Graphic Organizer Postreading activity could be another way to encourage student thinking, writing, and interaction regarding the content area material they have read (cf. Thomas & Hofmeister, 2003).

▶ A QUICK WORD ABOUT WRITING IN THE READING FRAMEWORK

The process of simply writing something down—a note while reading, an item on a "to-do" list, a message to a friend, or an answer to a study guide question—adds a slight but significant element of commitment to that thought that it previously did not have. It becomes more real, more concrete, more likely to be remembered. Any form of writing before, during, or after reading heightens engagement, connections between the new and the known, critical analysis, and constructive applications. It increases sensitivity to the content, logic, and organization of the text, as language and thought trigger one another to discover the value and/or shortcomings of the "inchoate lump of meanings" (Henry, 1974, p. 17) that we often are left with following typical passive reading. Many of the methods and approaches in the next chapters use writing of one form or another to build comprehension strategies. A section in Chapter 9, called "Writing to Learn," lists a number of additional ways to use writing for these purposes. It is important to note that not everything students write needs to be graded, or even *read* by the teacher, just as not everything students say needs to be graded or even heard. In short, writing is not the English teachers' "job": It is a tool that can be turned to many advantages in developing active readers across the curriculum.

▶ CONCEPT SUMMARY

Instructional-level reading is, by definition, difficult. Many students give up on even *attempting* to read textbook assignments. Worse, many teachers give up on *expecting* their students to read. When teachers combine content instruction with concurrent strategy instruction, *more* students have *more* success in study reading. The Framework for Reading-Based Instruction provides a template for lesson planning that aligns instruction with current understandings about the study-reading process. Diagnostic teaching helps evaluate the match between students and materials. Occasionally, supplementing core reading assignments with additional materials and resources located online validates students' multiple literacies and facilitates engagement. Many methods and approaches are available to model Pre-, During, and Post-reading strategies, with the reminder to consider how much scaffolding/fading and structured peer interaction to build into these. A good number of these involve directing students to "write to learn" before, during, and/or after reading—in informal ways that are more like speaking than formal composition. As computers and internet connections are increasingly available in classrooms, it is hoped that these resources will be used to facilitate a different *kind* of content area instruction than has been the norm, effecting genuine changes of the type envisioned by cognitive psychologists half a century ago.

SECTION

II

PUTTING WINGS UNDER READING AND LEARNING FROM TEXT AND MEDIA

The first three chapters introduced the fundamental concepts, principles, and sampling of CAL practices. The next three chapters contain the research-based and experiential core of Content Area Literacy instruction. Knowledge of these methods will place you among the most technically competent of teachers. Skill in *delivering* a representative group of the methods in these chapters will cause you to be among the most competent and influential of teachers. Read now about the best means available by which to guide reading and learning before, during, and following encounters with content-rich textual material.

CHAPTER 4

INTO—METHODS FOR PREREADING SCHEMA ACTIVATION

The whole art of teaching is only the art of awaking the natural curiosity of young minds for the purpose of satisfying it afterwards.

—Anatole France

This chapter explains the importance of Prereading instruction and sets out the primary goals of this essential *Into* phase of study reading. It discusses the principles of mental modeling as the most efficient means of teaching these active, focused habits of mind. Research-supported methods that employ these principles in various ways are presented, along with options for alternating teacher-directed instruction with cooperative structures that provide opportunities for students to try out questioning techniques that set the stage for effective comprehension.

- IMPORTANCE OF PREREADING
- GOALS OF PREREADING INSTRUCTION: READER ENGAGEMENT, SCHEMA ACTIVATION, AND PURPOSEFUL INQUIRY
- MENTAL MODELING: A FORM OF APPRENTICESHIP TRAINING

▶ IMPORTANCE OF PREREADING

In a survey of teaching practices, professors specializing in Content Area Literacy ranked the use of Prereading methods as the most important action content teachers could take to help students learn from textbook reading (Gee & Rakow, 1987). Prereading instruction helps students establish an appropriate orientation to the reading task at hand. Regular Prereading instruction in the classroom also helps students acquire and refine the tools they need to be strategic, independent learners (cf. Pressley 2000). An effective orientation to a given study-reading task has three dimensions: *attitude, background,* and *reading strategies.*

Taking Aim: Prereading Orientation

Attitude Orientation: For Reader Engagement

- Focus attention and reduce distractions.
- Generate interest in the topic and the task.
- Motivate for sustained effort.

Background Orientation: For Activation of Relevant Schema

- Activate appropriate schema: relevant background knowledge and experiences.
- Preteach key concept terms and unfamiliar allusions.
- Correct possible misunderstandings.
- Provide necessary new ideas and information.
- Establish a sense of the organization and sequence of the reading selection.

Reading Strategies Orientation: For Active Meaning Making

- Preview the text to establish a sense of the larger context, structural organization, and sequence of the selection.
- Identify reading aids such as headings, graphics, pictures, and terms in italics.
- Predict possible outcomes based on prior knowledge and experience.
- Raise both factual *and* evaluative-type questions that can serve as purposes for reading and thinking.

Of course, these components are not taken up in a tedious, step-by-step fashion. Rather, they should be addressed selectively, depending on the particular needs of students and the challenges presented by the material to be read. Each method in this chapter addresses some combination of these elements, but in a focused, brisk, and interactive manner.

▶ GOALS OF PREREADING INSTRUCTION: READER ENGAGEMENT, SCHEMA ACTIVATION, AND PURPOSEFUL INQUIRY

Reader Engagement

Successful reading begins with genuine attention to the task: The reader must be actively *engaged* in the process (Rosenshine, 1984). Thus, one goal of Prereading instruction is to help students develop the attitudes and interests that build the habit of quick and lively engagement as an initial step in study-type reading.

Schema Activation

In a previous chapter, schema was defined as the sum of one's prior knowledge and experience about a given topic. Schema provides the "net" for receiving and organizing new information and experiences. A broad background of information and experience about a topic may not ensure effective comprehension. To read with comprehension, the reader must consciously recall the schema structures that are relevant to the particular reading selection so that he or she can actively form connections between this personalized organization of facts, perspectives, and experiences and the new information from the text. Thus, schema activation, or how readers *use* what they know, can be as important as how *much* they know.

Purposeful Inquiry

A final goal of Prereading instruction is to demonstrate and build Prereading strategies that readers can use flexibly and effectively in independent study reading. Most such strategies, beginning with setting appropriate purposes for reading, take the form of purposeful questioning. Interest and motivation are driven by, expressed in, and organized around questions. New knowledge is built by discovering the questions that cannot be answered without further study. Nonetheless, students in most traditional content classrooms ask very few lesson-related questions. One of the primary reasons for teacher burnout, in fact, is teachers' perception that students lack interest and motivation. For the most part, however, lack of interest and motivation is only a secondary symptom. Inquiry and learning are natural human inclinations. The primary cause of what appears to be apathy, in most cases, is that students simply do not know *what* they don't know and do not know *how* to ask questions in the classroom environment, which can be layered with subtle inhibitions to student questioning. Noting the inhibitions to inquiry is one way to begin to remedy this common problem.

Why Don't Students Ask More Questions?

One layer of inhibitions to student questioning is composed of peer-related issues. Asking a question in class amounts to making a public admission of ignorance. It also is a public acknowledgment of the teacher's expertise and authority—something many adolescents tend to resent having to state, even implicitly. Another layer of inhibitions is composed of the cognitive aspects of inquiry. Each subject area is, in a way, a foreign language, with its own vocabulary and "grammatical" styles of thinking that need to be used in order to formulate useful questions. Moreover, research and intuition suggest that rather than encouraging and supporting student questioning, teachers too often behave in ways that inadvertently teach students to avoid asking questions. See Figure 4.1 for elaborations on some of the ways in which teachers may be teaching students *not* to ask questions. See if these sound familiar.

Teaching students to ask as well as answer questions is what Aristotle was explaining when he said, "these, then are the . . . kinds of questions we ask and *it is in the answers to these questions that our knowledge consists*" (McKeon, 1947, p.73, as quoted by Ciardiello, 1998). The simple goal of teaching students to engage in active questioning is to put them into an intelligent, ongoing, and *purposeful* search

The Squelch.
Teachers sometimes respond to questions with sarcastic replies. Often, the questions that receive these replies are the kind of passive-aggressive questions that students raise when they are fearful or defensive. Before a test, for example, teachers often hear this flurry of questions: "Do we have to skip a line after every answer?"; "Do you want last names first?"; "Can we use notebook paper?"; "Can we use pencil?" Faced with these irrelevant, time-consuming questions, teachers sometimes get *too* skilled at squelching student questions with responses such as, "Is today any different from yesterday?"or "Are you new here?" Students, however, don't always see the distinction between relevant and irrelevant questions. If they come to expect sarcastic replies, they will be less likely to raise genuine, on-task questions. Overuse of the squelch is partly a matter of personal style, in which case it should still be used sparingly and in good humor. In general, we find that when a good rapport is established in a classroom, the passive-aggressive questions that deserve a squelch seldom occur.

The Sting.
As teachers, we occasionally use questions as a kind of "weapon" against student misbehavior. When we suspect that a student is unprepared or is not paying attention, we may call on him or her to answer a question. Or when a student persists in talking while we are trying to explain a point to the class, we might use a punishing question like, "John, will you please explain this to the class?" When students feel and observe the sting of punishing questions, they often overgeneralize and become fearful of asking and being asked any question. They fear that to ask a question is to challenge the teacher, and that to be asked a question is to be suspected of some misdeed. Even worse, more aggressive students begin to intentionally use questions to undermine the teacher's authority.

Figure 4.1 Why students stop asking questions

The Void.
"Any questions?" is a popular teacher tool for encouraging students to raise clarifying inquiries. When students are asked this question in an inappropriate context, however, they quickly lose confidence in their ability to ask good questions. They often don't know what it is that they don't know and/or, don't know how to articulate a vague thought into a clear question, and/or are unsure of how to frame the question so as not to annoy the teacher or alienate their classmates. Ironically, the more one knows about a topic, the easier it is to ask questions about it. With this in mind, it is important for the teacher to anticipate points of the lesson that may be unclear and to guide student questioning into those areas: "Can someone ask a good question to clarify when we need to change signs in an equation?" Then "What other questions could be asked about signs?" And finally, the more general question, "Any other questions about anything discussed today?"

The Volley.
Teachers too often fall into the habit of answering a question with a question, like the classic approach of indirect psychiatry. Although there is a place and a time for this technique, if students expect that they will be put on the spot with a return question, they will grow reluctant to ask questions. Admittedly, this technique can be useful in "buying time" to think of an answer to a question that has come seemingly out of the blue. However, even in these instances, the more helpful teaching strategy is to think aloud through the processes needed to come up with an answer. This provides a perfect opportunity to demonstrate the teacher's role as a coach, rather than an encyclopedia.

Figure 4.1 *(continued)*

mode. In this way, the quest to learn is more likely to continue after a particular lesson is over, the book is closed, and the classroom lights are dimmed.

Questions to Prompt Schema Activation, Engagement, and Purposeful Inquiry

The most effective way to help students develop the complex cognitive and affective elements of effective questioning is *not* simply to teach them about questioning, although arguably there could be some small benefit to this as well (Ciardiello, 1998). In general, questioning may be too complex, both cognitively and affectively, to be guided by a set of simplified rules. It appears best to address questioning as *inquiry training* and to provide opportunities for students to interact with models of effective questioning in real and simulated reading-thinking situations.

Questions for prompting Prereading engagement, schema activation, and purposeful inquiry include the following:

Translate: "What do the title and first few sentences seem to *mean*?"

Recall Prior Knowledge: "What do I know about this already?"

Recall Prior Experience: "What experiences does this remind me of?"

Engage: "What *might* be really interesting about this?"

Predict: "What are the main things I might learn from this?"

Set Purposes: "After I read this, what should I be able to do or say about it?"

Categorize: "What are some categories that might fall under this topic?"

Inquiry training is done in an apprenticeship setting that is suitably matched to the complexity of the task. The demonstration of purposeful questioning in such settings to guide study-type reading has come to be called "mental modeling" (Manzo & Manzo, 2002), and although it may now seem obvious, it was not until the late 1960s that it became an explicit and intentional educational practice.

▶ MENTAL MODELING: A FORM OF APPRENTICESHIP TRAINING

Modeling of a certain act or skill is a form of teaching in which the instructor demonstrates a desired outcome and encourages the learner to imitate it. It is the traditional means of apprenticeship training in trades and crafts, in which the objective is to teach complex motor skills. It is only fairly recently that learning psychologists and educators have begun to recognize and explore the power of this form of teaching when applied to cognitive, rather than motor, learning (see Figure 4.2).

The human inclination to observe and imitate another person is the most familiar and frequently used mode of human learning outside of school. A good example of its use is in natural language acquisition. Only a very small percentage of the words and language forms we know were acquired as a result of direct instruction. A mother may teach her child to say some important words such as "mommy," "hot," "chair," and so on, but the child picks up an enormous number of other words on his or her own. A parent or teacher may remind the child to say "he ran" instead of "he runned," but the majority of what the child learns about word order and language structures is learned incidentally and through imitation. This does not mean that it isn't intentional. On the contrary, children actively decide much of what they will learn based in great measure on who appears to be doing best in that environment.

Model Selection

The way we speak, the words we use, and the way we feel when using these words are the direct result of the speech patterns and concerns of the models to whom we were exposed and with whom we have interacted. From the models we select to emulate, we learn motives and attitudes, as well as words and actions. Thus, *inquiring minds beget inquiring minds.*

In any situation, however, there are various models available from which to choose. Selection of the model to be emulated is based on subconscious and subjective assessments of the degree to which those around us appear to have mastery

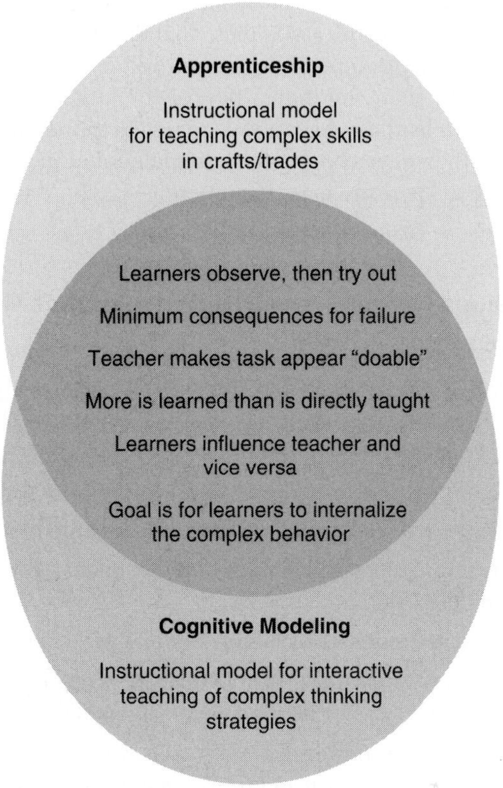
Apprenticeship
Instructional model for teaching complex skills in crafts/trades
Learners observe, then try out
Minimum consequences for failure
Teacher makes task appear "doable"
More is learned than is directly taught
Learners influence teacher and vice versa
Goal is for learners to internalize the complex behavior
Cognitive Modeling
Instructional model for interactive teaching of complex thinking strategies

Figure 4.2 Cognitive modeling and apprenticeship training

over a given environment or situation. In school settings, the student does not automatically choose the teacher or the good student as a model. There is an ongoing competition with other influential peers and adults in the home and community. *Instructional strategies that employ modeling must include devices for winning students' attention to the desired models and behaviors.*

Social and Imitation Learning Theory

Modeling of mental operations has its rational basis in *social and imitation learning theory* (Bandura & Walters, 1963; Miller & Dollard, 1941; Vygotsky, 1978). Simply put, the idea is that we tend to copy and internalize a *larger* array of a model's character and behaviors than merely those traits that are essential to the task at hand. By taking advantage of this additional, (seemingly) incidental learning dimension, it becomes possible to teach complex and subtle behaviors along with key target behaviors, and in a much shorter period of time. For example, young sports fans may say they look up to sports stars for their jump shots or swings, but they often also imitate the way the stars wear their sweat bands or even how they talk to those who ask them questions. Similarly, the mental image of the teacher who has regularly used mental modeling in the classroom serves as a mental template, or set of guidelines, that the novice can use to monitor and evaluate subsequent attempts to apply and refine a new thinking strategy in different situations. In short, internalization of the target strategy is most likely to occur only after individuals have used a cognitive operation in situations in which adults and other peer experts have modeled and given them some form of feedback on their performance (Camperell, 1982; Manzo, 1969a, 1969b; Vygotsky, 1978).

Conditions Conducive to Effective Mental Modeling

Modeling is an efficient means of teaching complex tasks; however, its effectiveness is likely to vary depending on the management of certain conditions. Seven conditions that have been identified (Camperell, 1982, Manzo, 1969a, 1969b; Manzo & Manzo, 1997a; Vygotsky, 1978) seem to be particularly relevant to the content area classroom:

1. When the student's attention is drawn to a desired model.
2. When the impression can be made that the model is doing something masterful and desirable.
3. When there is a reduced social risk in imitating a desired behavior.
4. When the new behavior appears "doable," as when a student observes someone from his or her peer group engaged in the behavior.
5. When students are permitted to interact with the model in an affective (feeling) manner as well as in purely cognitive or "school-like" ways.
6. When students have the opportunity to receive feedback of some form from the teacher and from peers.
7. When *reciprocity* is used to help students develop a sense of *agency* or the feeling that they have some reasonable level of influence over the instructional environment.

Together, these conditions tend to raise student competence in identifying and imitating effective and purposeful questioning strategies. Initially, the mental model is likely to be the teacher, but eventually other students will be noticed as models as they internalize, personalize, and use strategies initially modeled by the teacher.

As you study the teaching methods ahead that feature mental modeling, remember to look for the specific action(s) of the teacher that might attract students' attention and desire to emulate available models of question asking, reflecting, and answering. *How* does the teacher, using a particular method, meet the conditions listed here? Ideally, the use of methods to teach Prereading purposeful questioning will invite students' individuality to emerge and will establish habits that will guide effective reading and learning both in and outside of the classroom.

▶ PREREADING METHODS FOR READER ENGAGEMENT, SCHEMA ACTIVATION, AND PURPOSEFUL QUESTIONING

The short article, "Vaulting Vampires," in Figure 4.3 is used for examples of the prereading methods in this section. Skim through the article before beginning to read about the ReQuest Procedure.

(1) On most nights a vampire bat tries to drink about half its body weight in blood. After feasting, the blood-bloated bat launches itself into the air. But unlike other bats, which simply drop from their perches to initiate flight, vampire bats jump from the ground into the air. How do they manage their takeoffs?

(2) "They can't run to get up a head of steam like a swan or a goose does," says William Schutt, a zoologist at Bloomfield College in New Jersey. Schutt recently managed to give biologists their first detailed look at the dynamics of a vampire bat takeoff.

(3) Of the world's 900 or so bat species, only the common vampire bat, Desmodus rotundus, is able to maneuver as well on the ground as it does in the air. "They can hop, move backward, side to side—like little spiders," says Schutt.

(4) To study how the bats launch themselves, Schutt put them on a force-measuring platform and recorded their movements with a high–speed camera. The animal begins with all four limbs on the ground. Then it extends its hind knees and tips itself forward, so the center of mass is over the forelimbs. For the actual jump, it extends the forelimbs and pushes itself off the ground with the tremendously large pectoral muscles," he says. Schutt found that the pectorals are the major flight muscles in bats, just as in birds. The triceps muscle and the bat's very long thumb also generate some force. The thumb is the last part of the body to leave the ground and helps steer the bat's takeoff.

(5) The entire jump lasts a mere 30 milliseconds, but during that time the bat catapults itself three to four feet off the ground. The transition from jump to flight is almost seamless, says Schutt. At the end of the jump "all the limbs are pointed toward the ground, which is the equivalent of a downstroke. So now it just has to bring the forelimbs into an upstroke position and it can begin to power itself in flight."

(6) Since vampire bats do most of their feeding on level surfaces, their deftness is a definite advantage. "If they are feeding on a cow's foot, and the cow takes a step back, they need to be quick to get out of the way," Schutt says, "and they also need to be fast on the ground to get away from predators."

Figure 4.3 Sample Reading Selection "Vaulting Vampires" (*Discover*, March 1998, 19:3)

ReQuest Procedure

The Reciprocal Questioning or ReQuest Procedure (Manzo, 1969b) is a well-proven method that introduced the idea of mental modeling to educators in literacy and learning. It is a constructivist method designed to permit the teacher to model good questioning and question answering (Ciardiello, 1998). It encourages students to *focus on the teacher and competent peers* as effective models of question asking and answering. ReQuest emphasizes *strategy* more than mere *skill* learning by teaching students how to set their own purposes for reading. Just as important, the *reciprocal* structure of the method gives students a good deal of control and makes a learner of the teacher as he or she grows in understanding of students' different constructions of what they have read.

ReQuest can be used to introduce an in-class reading activity or at the end of a class period for a home reading assignment. It has been used from the primary grades to the graduate school levels.

Steps in the ReQuest Procedure

Preparation: Teacher and students should have copies of the reading selection. ReQuest is best used by directing students to look at only one sentence at a time, without reading ahead. When possible, it is useful to have the first portion of the selection on a PowerPoint slide or an overhead transparency, so that it can be shown one sentence at a time (title and first sentence together first, then the second sentence, the third, etc., to about the fifth sentence). Ideally, the teacher should prepare at least four questions—one each for the title and first sentence and the second through about the fourth sentences. These should be questions that students would probably *not* ask, since students are given the chance to ask questions first.

Step 1. The first time the method is used the teacher should explain its purpose; for example, "Before you read this selection, we will look at the first few sentences together and ask each other some questions. The purpose of this activity is to improve your ability to set a sound purpose for reading."

Step 2. The teacher guides the students through as many sentences of the selection as necessary to formulate a logical purpose to guide Silent Reading. This is done in the following way:

a. Students and teacher read the title and first sentence. Students are told that they may ask the teacher as many questions as they wish about the title and first sentence only (see Figure 4.4). Students are told that they should try to ask the kinds of questions a teacher might ask, *in the way a teacher might ask them* (this is one way to subtly urge students to mentally note the teacher's mental processes).

b. The teacher answers each question fully, but without excessive elaboration and without asking questions back. How much to "tell" in answering a question will be a judgment call in any lesson. The objectives at this stage of the lesson are to encourage and reinforce questions that activate relevant schema, to fill in needed background information (but only in answer to questions), to stay focused on setting a sound purpose for reading, and to *model good question-answering behaviors.*

c. Once students have asked all their questions about the title and first sentence, the teacher follows up with a few additional questions. Some question types to consider include basic information, translation, inference, personal experience, and evaluation. The purpose in this follow-up questioning is to model the kinds of prereading questions that activate schema and to help set good purposes for reading.

d. The pattern used to review the first sentence—Silent Reading, followed by student questions, followed by teacher questions—is continued through the second, third, and fourth sentences, and/or continuing until enough information has been generated to form a sound purpose for reading.

Step 3. After *about* the fourth sentence, the teacher should conclude his or her questions on the sentence by asking students what they think the rest of the selection will *mostly* be about (few things are written with only one focus and one solitary purpose). Briefly note student responses on the board, and then ask students to form one or more of these ideas into a question. Write the purpose question(s) on the board. If students are to read the remainder of the selection outside class, have them copy the purpose question(s).

Step 4. Following Silent Reading, the teacher's first question should be, "Did we set a good purpose for reading this selection?" If so, discussion can begin with what was learned in answer to this question; if not, a better purpose question should be stated and then answered (Manzo, 1985).

Implementation Tips for ReQuest

- **Overcoming "blank stares."** The first time you use ReQuest with a group, it is likely that when you direct them to ask questions over the title and first sentence, they will respond with blank stares. Be calm. Count to 10. Take confidence from the fact that you know *why* you are making this seemingly strange request, and you know *where* the lesson is going. You know that the purpose of spending time at the beginning of a difficult reading selection is like initializing a computer disk: It helps the brain recognize and process the information that is coming. You also know that while there are only a handful of fact questions that can be asked about a single sentence, there are many more inference and beyond-the-lines questions that would be helpful in recalling prior knowledge and experience in order to set a good purpose for reading. Most important, you know that students have been unintentionally conditioned *not* to ask questions in the classroom and that you are willing to try to counter this conditioning. Much of this counterconditioning is accomplished simply by setting up the gamelike ReQuest situation, in which students are *procedurally rotated* to the position of asking as many questions as they can over a single sentence at a time. So don't despair in waiting for that first question. If wait time isn't enough, you can say something like, "This is a different kind of lesson, I know. Any question you can come up with is fine. It will help to try to think of the type of questions teachers might ask. You've heard a few questions asked, I take it." When the first question or two come, answer them respectfully: Another important element in counterconditioning students' reluctance to ask questions is the way the teacher *responds* to the questions that are raised—discussed next.

- **Be prepared for unexpected questions.** When students take you up on your offer to answer any questions on a sentence, in ReQuest, you can expect a few unexpected questions: ones for which you do not know or cannot quickly formulate answers. Be ready for this. It's your chance to show students that you *aren't* threatened or frightened by questions you can't answer and that you won't respond with sarcasm or by asking a question back. Instead, you will give the question a thoughtful, measured response. If it is a relevant, schema-activating question, you will say so and give an honest explanation as to why you can't answer it, if only to say you just can't remember: "That's exactly the kind of question we're trying to bring up here. It is information the author assumes the reader knows. And, do you know, I can't remember that fact myself." At this point, another student may know the answer. Since it's not your turn to ask questions, turn to the person who asked the question and tell him or her that another student is willing to help you out . . . a wonderful and practical way to build toward the ideal of a *community of learners*. If, on the other hand, the question that stumped you is clearly off the subject, you might say something like, "Because of the way the title was worded, I didn't think the author was going in that direction, so I haven't tried to remember what I might know about that. It's an interesting point, but I don't think I'll get myself off the subject with it right now." This too can demonstrate the concept of a *community of learners*.
- **Encourage shy students.** When calling on students to *ask* you questions, keep an eye on students who typically do not participate in discussion. With the ReQuest structure, you've given all students, even the most shy and reticient, a much more possible situation for involvement. They don't have to answer a question—they only have to ask one. Call on them, and be supportive in your answers.
- **Prepare your model questions in advance.** When it is your turn to ask questions, you will need to have several questions prepared for each sentence that students probably won't ask. Prepare four or five such questions for each sentence, even though you may not use them all. How many questions you ask on each sentence will depend on how many and what kind of questions the students ask. In general, you should ask at least two questions when it is your turn, trying to ask questions of different types than the

students have asked. Basic facts will probably be covered by student questions. In fact, the reason ReQuest uses single sentences for questioning is that this places a natural limit on the number of fact questions that can reasonably be asked. Once these are covered, both teacher and students are challenged to ask schema-connecting beyond-the-lines questions.

- **Avoid "competition."** Although it is somewhat gamelike in the back-and-forth rotation of questioning, ReQuest shouldn't take on a *stump-the-teacher/stump-the class* tone, which tends to get off the track of a clear focus on setting a sound and sensible purpose for reading a specific selection. This can happen if the teacher asks questions that the class clearly cannot answer—students will begin to ask the same types of questions back. Be careful to ask questions that *can* be answered by prediction, inference, judgment, evaluation, and experience.
- **Keep it moving.** ReQuest should move along briskly, taking no more than about 15 minutes. If it is extended too long, it can become tedious and lose focus. This can be difficult to keep in mind. Even though student questions can be intimidating at times, it also can feel satisfying to be asked the very questions you want students to be able to answer. Be careful not to go into too much detail.
- **The goal is a good purpose question—have one in mind.** The questions generated from the first three or four sentences usually yield enough context for students to form a sound purpose question or two. When preparing your own questions, you usually can predict a good stopping point. You should have a possible purpose question in mind in order to help guide students' suggestions.

See Figure 4.4 for an example of the ReQuest Procedure with "Vaulting Vampires," from *Discover* magazine.

Further Backstory and Wider Uses of ReQuest

ReQuest has played an important part in advancing several different areas of social learning and cognitive psychology and in translating constructivist theories into practice, before they were known as such. Again, ReQuest pioneered the use of cognitive modeling to teach mental processes. It first was developed for one-on-one teaching. However, it proved equally effective in content classrooms with heterogeneous groups (Manzo, 1973), in programs to promote personal-social adjustment in juvenile delinquents (Kay, Young, & Mottley, 1986), in mainstreaming learning-disabled students (Alley & Deshler, 1980; Hori, 1977), with second-language students (McKenzie, Ericson, & Hunter, 1988), and as a significant part of an instructional program to improve social studies education (Ciardiello, 1998; Ciardiello & Cicchelli, 1994). It also has become the basis for a larger movement in education called Reciprocal Teaching (Palincsar & Brown, 1984). A survey of more than 450 teachers revealed that based on descriptions of 10 leading comprehension improvement methods, teachers would most like further information and training on ReQuest (Spor & Schneider, 1999).

The teacher prepared the following questions for the lesson.

Title & Sentence 1: *Vaulting Vampires: On most nights a vampire bat tries to drink about half its body weight in blood.*

What are two other words for "vaulting"?

How big is a vampire bat?

What type of creatures feed at night?

Who has ever seen one?

Does anyone know where their natural habitats are?

Sentence 2: *After feasting, the blood-bloated bat launches itself into the air.*

Why is "feast" a good word to use here?

Where do you think the vampire bat launches from?

Does this sound like any other animal you know?

Sentence 3: *But unlike other bats, which simply drop from their perches to initiate flight, vampire bats jump from the ground into the air.*

Why might it be important for vampire bats to be able to jump into flight from the ground?

What would it take to be able to do this?

How many kinds of bats do you think there are?

Sentence 4: *How do they manage their takeoffs?*

How do you think they manage?

How might a scientist study this question?

Possible purpose questions:

How do vampire bats launch into flight from the ground?

How have scientists studied this ability?

Why is it important for vampire bats to have this ability?

The short selection was distributed to students familiar with the ReQuest procedure. Students were asked to keep their papers face down, while they used ReQuest to set a relevant purpose for reading. The title and first sentence were shown on the overhead:

Title & Sentence 1: *Vaulting Vampires: On most nights a vampire bat tries to drink about half its body weight in blood.*

Figure 4.4 Example of the ReQuest Procedure with "Vaulting Vampires"

Teacher: Who has a question about just the title and first selection of this article?
Student 1: What does "vaulting" mean?
Teacher: Good vocabulary question. It means leaping. Springing or jumping high.
Student 2: How much do vampire bats weigh?
Teacher: Hum, I'm just guessing here, maybe 3 pounds.
Student 3: Whose blood do they drink?
Teacher: Large animals, like cows. That's a good question, because it gets at why it's important for them to be able to vault.
Student 3: Why is that?
Teacher: To get out of the way if their prey tries to shoo them off.
Teacher: No other questions? Okay, my turn.
Has anyone ever seen a live vampire bat?
[Several students raise their hands]
Jake, you have? Where was it?
Student 4: At the zoo, they make a big show out of the vampire bats' "feeding time."
Teacher: Has anyone seen them in the wild?
[No hands]
Why does it say "on most *nights*"?
Student 4: Bats sleep during the day and feed at night.
Teacher: Yes, and what's another name for creatures that do this?
Student 2: Nocturnal animals.
Teacher: Good. Let's go on to the next sentence. After you've read it, you can ask me questions.

Sentence 2: *After feasting, the blood-bloated bat launches itself into the air.*

Student 5: Do they jump off the cows' backs?
Teacher: Not usually.
Student 5: What do they jump off?
Teacher: The ground.
Student 2: Can they fly?
Teacher: Yes.
Student 6: Can they walk on the ground?
Teacher: Yes, they can move very easily and quickly on the ground.
No more questions? Okay, my turn.
Why is "feasting" an especially good word to use here?
Student 1: Because they eat or drink I guess (yuck) so much.
Teacher: If you picture yourself as a bat, what muscles do you think you would use to launch yourself into flight?
Student 7: My leg muscles.
Teacher: Maybe. Do you think other kinds of bats launch into the air in this way?

Figure 4.4 *(continued)*

Student 5: Maybe other ones just drop off the branches they're hanging from.
Teacher: Okay, let's look at the next sentence.

Sentence 3: *But unlike other bats, which simply drop from their perches to initiate flight, vampire bats jump from the ground into the air.*

Teacher: So that was a good prediction, John. What questions could we ask now? Remember, we're trying to predict what the rest of this article is about, and write a purpose question.
Student 8: How many kinds of bats are there?
Teacher: Actually, this article says that there are over 900.
Student 1: So they have to jump into the air to get out of the cows', or whatever's, way. Is this going to explain how they do that?
Teacher: That's a good prediction. Let's put it up here.
[Writes "How vampire bats vault" on the board]
Student 7: Is it about what muscles they use?
Teacher: Another good prediction.
[Writes "What muscles?" on the board]
Any others?
[No hands]
Teacher: Okay, well, how do you think a scientist might try to find out how the vampire bat launches itself from the ground?
Student 9: Take a video?
Teacher: Good idea. What if it's too fast to really see on the tape?
Student 9: Put it in slow motion.
Teacher: Good prediction. [At the risk of creating a digression, the teacher may occasionally wish to add other sidebar information, such as "By the way, when something is filmed for slow motion, the film/tape often needs to move much faster, except if it is 'time-lapse' photography."] In any case, how can you tell how hard it has to push off?
Student 6: What if you put a scale, like you weigh yourself on, under it. Would that show how hard it was pushing down to jump?
Teacher: Good idea. Let's see what we have.
[Writes "Use videotape & scales to study?" on board]
Can we put these predictions into one or two purpose questions?
Student 2: What muscles do vampire bats use to vault, and how did scientists find out?
Teacher: Terrific.
[Writes prediction question on board:
"What muscles do vampire bats use to vault, and how did scientists find out?"]
Teacher: Okay, turn your papers over, and let's go ahead and read to see if we find answers to this question.

Figure 4.4 *(continued)*

[Students read article]

Teacher:	Was this a good purpose question for the article?
Student 2:	Yes, it told what muscles, and how scientists found out.
Student 3:	But it seemed like the point of the article was the part at the end, about why it was important for this kind of bat to be able to do this.
Teacher:	To get out of the way if the cow started kicking! That came up in our discussion before we read. So, just from the title, we might have added another purpose question:

[Writes, "Why is it important for them to vault?"]

Discussion continues with what students learned about how one scientist studied these bats, and what he learned.

Figure 4.4 (*continued*)

Special Benefits for English as a Foreign Language (EFL)

Special benefits of ReQuest for EFL students were documented by El-Koumy (1996) in a research study involving 86 first-year EFL students at Suez Canal University in Egypt. Students were randomly assigned to three treatment groups. The group using ReQuest scored significantly higher on comprehension measures than either the group using teacher questioning or the group using student-generated questions. The following stipulations and adaptations were carefully followed and were considered to have contributed to the effectiveness of ReQuest in this study:

1. Asking questions that trigger probative thinking.
2. Distributing the questions in terms of students' abilities.
3. Presenting questions to the class before calling upon someone to answer.
4. Accepting correct answers sincerely and correcting wrong ones only.
5. Displaying the correct answer when students failed to provide it.
6. Giving students the opportunity to raise their own questions.
7. Handling students' questions with appropriate consideration, no matter how silly they may seem.
8. Asking students to rephrase "wrong" questions due to poor syntax and/or incorrect logic (El-Koumy, 1996, p. 11).

Effect of ReQuest on Self-Regulation

Mason (2004) reported comparing the effects of two rigorous approaches to teaching strategies for reading comprehension to 32 fifth-grade students who were struggling readers. One method was ReQuest, and the other was TWA: *Think* before reading, think *while* reading and think *after* reading), which was taught following explicit self-regulated strategy-development procedures. ReQuest was taught following the guidelines for the Cooperative ReQuest Procedure (Manzo, Manzo, & Estes, 2001). There were no significant differences between groups on three written comprehension measures or on self-efficacy or motivation. There was a significant result in favor of the TWA approach on oral reading comprehension measures. Students were positive about both methods. In most other studies over the past 45 years, the ReQuest procedure has proven to be as effective or more effective than any other comprehension instruction method.

Cooperative ReQuest

Even with ideal participation, if four different students asked a question about each of the first four sentences of a selection, only 16 students, a little more than half of a traditional classroom, would have actively participated. Once students have become familiar with the method, try this cooperative structure variation to increase active involvement of more students. Our sense is that it increases active involvement of more students. Several of these suggestions also add more of the elements of what Ciardiello (1998) calls TeachQuest, or explicit teaching about and cueing of question types to students.

Preparation

- Prepare an overhead transparency or PowerPoint presentation with the title and first four sentences or so of the selection, or write these on the board, with strips of paper taped over each sentence to be removed to uncover one sentence at a time; for even more cueing of the type recommended by Ciardiello (1998), prepare a worksheet for each group, with space after each sentence for questions to be written.
- The teacher should prepare questions over the title and first four sentences, as described for ReQuest (personal experience, translation, inference, background information, evaluation, and prediction questions).
- Form groups of four. A good way to form heterogeneous groups for the topic of a given reading selection is to have students form a "lineup" from "no knowledge or experience with the topic of xxx" at one end to "lots of knowledge and/or experience with the topic of xxx" at the opposite end. Then count off by the number of groups needed to form groups of four. Have students, in groups, number off or self-select roles such as recorder, speaker, discussion starter, and encourager. Roles can be rotated for each sentence.
- Have copies of the reading selection available for each student.

Step 1. Assuming that students are familiar with ReQuest, show the title and first sentence, and tell students that they have two minutes in their groups to come up with as many questions as they can over that portion of the reading. Tell students that even though they may not use all of their questions, you will collect all of them at the end of the lesson.

Step 2. Proceed as with ReQuest, calling on the speaker in one of the groups to begin. Not every group needs to be called on for each sentence.

Step 3. At a reasonable point, have groups write possible purpose questions for the selection. Have the writer from each group write his or her group's purpose question(s) on a designated spot on the board. Review these together with the class and select from or combine these to form the best collaborative purpose question(s).

Step 4. Have students read silently to answer the purpose question(s).

Step 5. Ask whether a good purpose was set, and continue discussion based on what students learned in answer to the question(s).

Now let's gather some details about another *rotation* and modeling teaching method. It, too, has been carefully researched.

Reciprocal Teaching

Reciprocal Teaching (RT) (Palincsar & Brown, 1984) is an attempt to amplify and elaborate the fundamental elements of the ReQuest Procedure into a more broadly based educational approach (Gipe, 1998). To raise students' sense of *agency*, or involvement in the process, RT begins, as does Ciardiello's (1998) TeachQuest, with a class discussion of why we sometimes experience difficulties in reading text. The processes of *questioning, summarizing, clarifying*, and *predicting* are introduced as helpful strategies for attending, understanding, and remembering.

The next phase in Reciprocal Teaching is direct instruction in each of these four seminal processes. This is done in isolation but through teacher modeling and examples based on a meaningful text. When students are comfortable with the four processes of questioning, summarizing, predicting, and clarifying, they and the teacher begin to take turns assuming the role of teacher. The one playing the role of teacher is responsible for leading the dialog examining the reading selection. Figure 4.5 presents an example of the questioning, summarizing, and predicting aspects of Reciprocal Teaching. This script is taken from an actual classroom dialog with a group of students that Palincsar and Brown trained in this strategy.

In this content area version of Reciprocal Teaching, students are grouped by twos in "peer dyads" and are instructed to ask each other questions about the material to be read. The content area variation has the following steps:

1. Students convert subheadings in the text into two written predictions of what they think they will read about.
2. The class discusses these.
3. Following reading of a segment of material (usually four paragraphs), students write two questions and a summary reflecting the information in that segment.
4. Students write examples of any information that requires clarification.
5. Students discuss their written questions, summaries, and clarifications.

Positive outcomes have been reported from studies using Reciprocal Teaching with students who were classified as good decoders but poor comprehenders (Reeve, Palincsar, & Brown, 1985). *Time* magazine (circa 1988) called Reciprocal Teaching the most important development in instructional theory in the twentieth

Student 1 [in role of "teacher"]:	My question is, what does the aquanaut need when he goes under water?
Student 2:	A watch.
Student 3:	Flippers.
Student 4:	A belt.
Student 1:	Those are all good answers.
Teacher:	Nice job! I have a question too. Why does the aquanaut wear a belt? What is so special about it?
Student 3:	It's a heavy belt and keeps him from floating up to the top again.
Teacher:	Good for you.
Student 1:	For my summary now: This paragraph was about what aquanauts need to take when they go under the water.
Student 5:	And also about why they need those things.
Student 3:	I think we need to clarify *gear.*
Student 6:	That's the special thing they need.
Teacher:	Another word for *gear* in this story might be *equipment*—the equipment that makes it easier for the aquanauts to do their job.
Student 1:	I don't think I have a prediction to make.
Teacher:	Well, in the story, they tell us that there are "many strange and wonderful creatures" that the aquanauts see as they do their work. My prediction is that they'll describe some of these creatures. What are some of the strange creatures you already know about that live in the ocean?
Student 6:	Octopuses.
Student 3:	Whales?
Student 5:	Sharks!
Teacher:	Let's listen and find out. Who would like to be our teacher?

Figure 4.5 Illustration of Reciprocal Teaching

century. Bruer (1993) further referred to it as a primary example of the cognitive psychology revolution that has taken place in instruction and that few outside education are aware of. Ironically, Reciprocal Teaching has appeared in fewer and fewer textbooks for teachers in recent times. A possible reason for this diminished interest may be found in the fact that Reciprocal Teaching requires considerable teacher and student training prior to use, whereas its predecessor ReQuest, which Palincsar and Brown (1984) credit as RT's theoretical platform, ideally is used by uninitiated students and teachers to learn how to interact reciprocally. The only other reservation that we once had about RT was that findings on its efficacy were based exclusively on investigator-made tests based on the subject matter read. Now, however, there are findings to suggest that overall reading comprehension can show improvement on standardized tests as well (King & Parent Johnson, 1999), as is the case with primary research on the ReQuest Procedure (Manzo, 1969a, 1969b). In other words, if you are looking for *evidenced-based methods,* both of these qualify.

The next few methods have the simplicity of a straight piece of wire twisted into the now ubiquitous paper clip: evident once seen and said, but apparently not so easy to imagine without prompting. See if any of these instructional ideas have ever occurred to you in some form. The first such method for facilitating the prereading stage of comprehension arose from earlier studies on the rise and decline of curiosity in school-age children. The method that evolved from these studies is robust and slightly unorthodox.

Question-Only

To follow this simple instructional idea, it is useful to review some prior points on inhibitions to questioning. Whenever students read or listen in school, questions are being answered. The problem is that students often don't know what those questions are and hence cannot read or listen actively. Even when they have some level of awareness of an important organizing question, students tend to be inexperienced in framing their question in such a way as to allow focused reading, or to invite appropriate help from a speaker/teacher when they are listening. In due course, natural curiosity begins to suffer and soon most inquiry grinds to a halt. Question-Only (Manzo, 1985) can almost instantly reverse this trend.

Question-Only is designed for nonfiction materials and does not work particularly well with fiction or poetry. It can be used for a selection to be read in class or as preparation for an outside reading assignment.

Steps in the Question-Only Method

Preparation Review the reading selection to write several quiz questions covering important information and including at least two questions that students are not likely to ask about before they read. Decide whether to use the title of the selection to introduce the lesson or a more general statement of the topic.

Step 1. The teacher announces the title or topic of the reading assignment to the class and explains that *before reading* the selection, they will have a chance to learn about it by asking questions. Then, still *before reading* the assignment, they will be given a quiz over the content of the selection. Students are told that the quiz will cover all the information the teacher considers important, whether or not the students actually acquire the information with their questions. (The first time Question-Only is used, students may be intimidated by the prospect of a test over material they have not yet read; by the time of the test, and in subsequent uses of the method, they will understand that the questions they ask in this step will provide them with the answers to most of the test questions.)

Step 2. The class asks questions and the teacher answers fully but without going beyond the answer to the question as asked. The teacher records, in brief form, on the board or overhead, all information acquired during the question-asking step.

Step 3. The teacher gives the quiz, selecting from preprepared questions all but one or two that students have acquired answers for by questioning.

Step 4. Do *not* "grade" the quiz yet. Simply ask students to raise their hands if they think they got most of the questions right. Ask which question(s) they had trouble with—the question(s) they did not ask. These become the purpose questions for reading the assignment.

Step 5. Have students read silently to double check their answers to the quiz questions and to find the answer(s) to the question(s) they did not ask. If the selection is to be read as a homework assignment, write the purpose question(s) on the board or overhead for students to copy.

Step 6. After students have read, begin discussion or other follow-up with their answers to the purpose question(s).

Implementation Tips for Question-Only

- **Always give the quiz orally.** If the quiz is prepared on a handout ahead of time, you can't adjust it based on the questions students asked. Remember, the objective is to have as many students as possible get the correct answers to all but one or two questions. Therefore, you should prepare more quiz questions than you probably will use.
- **Make students' questions/answers available during the "test."** When answering student questions during Step 2, write a *brief form* of each question and a *brief form* of the answer on the board and leave this in view during the quiz. When students ask why you are leaving it up, you have the perfect opportunity to explain that the object of the lesson isn't really to get the quiz questions right but to learn to ask good questions. All the information students got from questioning, therefore, is theirs to use during the quiz. It is very important, though, to use abbreviated forms and write quickly, or the lesson can get bogged down and tedious.
- **Encourage shy students.** Keep an eye on students who did not typically participate in class discussion. Question-Only gives them an excellent opportunity to participate. They don't have to answer a question, only to ask one.
- **Keep the questioning on track.** Many questions are likely to be about information not covered in the reading selection. To keep the lesson on track, simply tell students when this is the case. Say something like, "That's not included in this selection, but you're using good logical thinking processes to eliminate possibilities." You can also answer in ways that subtly direct students toward important questions and follow-up questions (see the example in Figure 4.6).
- **Be prepared to move quickly.** Ironically, the only time this highly analytical activity may go stale is when the teacher becomes overwhelmed by the rapid pace with which material is covered. The teacher may react by slowing down the lesson and, in the process, take the winds of enthusiasm out of the students' sails; therefore, be prepared to cover a good deal of information quickly and in considerable depth.

The teacher prepared the following topic and quiz questions:

Topic: Vaulting vampire bats

Quiz Questions:
[Underlined questions are questions the teacher expects that students may not *ask—one should be included in the quiz to serve as a purpose for reading]*

- Do vampire bats really drink blood? (yes)
- How much blood do vampire bats drink? (half their weight per night)
- How do vampire bats launch themselves into flight? (jump from the ground)
- How high do they jump? (3–4 feet)
- How many types of bats are there? (about 900)
- What is unusual about the vampire bat's ability to move on the ground? (It is the only bat that can move as well on the ground as in the air.)
- What is the major muscle the vampire bat uses to launch itself from the ground? (the pectorals)
- How have scientists studied the vampire bat's vaulting? (force measuring platform and high-speed camera)
- Why is "vaulting" an important ability for vampire bats? (They do most of their feeding on level ground.)
- What are two ways in which other creatures launch themselves? (dropping from branches and running to build up speed)

Teacher: For tomorrow, your assignment will be to read an article called "Vaulting Vampires." Right now, I'll give you a chance to find out everything you can about it just by asking me questions. Then, I'll give you a quiz over what's in the actual article.
Student 1: You mean, we have a quiz before we read it?
Teacher: Yes, but you have a chance right now, to get all the answers you can.

[Writes "Vaulting vampire bats" on the board—see below for information eventually written on the board]
Student 2: Oh, vampire *bats*. You didn't say that before.
Teacher: Yes, *vaulting* vampire bats.
Student 3: Why do they vault?
Teacher: They vault, or jump, to launch themselves into flight.
Student 1: Will that be on the quiz?

Figure 4.6 Example of the Question-Only with "Vaulting Vampires"

Teacher:	The questions can only be about what might be in the *article*.
Student 1:	Can they really fly?
Teacher:	Yes.
Student 4:	Are there other kinds of bats?
Teacher:	Yes, and the article tells how many other kinds.
Student 1:	How many?
Teacher:	About 900.
Student 2:	Where do they live?
Teacher:	Good question—about a whole category of information—but the category of their habitat isn't included in this article. Now you've narrowed it down a lot. I'm going to use the abbreviation "NI" to mean that there's no information about the vampire bat's habitat in this particular article.
Student 5:	Do all bats vault?
Teacher:	Good question! No, vampire bats are the only ones that launch themselves into flight from the ground.
Student 6:	How do the others do it?
Teacher:	They begin their flight by dropping down from a tree branch.
Student 7:	How high does the branch have to be?
Teacher:	Ha. Good detail question, but this article is about the vampire bats, remember.
Student 8:	Do vampire bats really drink blood?
Teacher:	Yes, they certainly do; you might be surprised at how much.
Student 8:	How much do they drink?
Teacher:	They try to drink half their body weight every night.
Student 9:	How much is that?
Teacher:	Well, they're kind of small. The article doesn't say how small, but I'll guess about 3 pounds. So that would be a pound and a half of blood a night.
Student 4:	What kinds of animals do they drink blood from?
Teacher:	The article mentions cows, as one of their prey.
Student 1:	How do they hang onto the cow's neck?
Teacher:	The article doesn't mention the bats drinking from the cow's *neck*.
Student 4:	Where, then?
Teacher:	It mentions the bats drinking from the cow's *foot*.
Student 7:	Don't they get kicked?
Teacher:	They would, if they couldn't move around pretty well on the ground.
Student 9:	Can they?
Teacher:	Can they what?
Student 9:	Can they move around pretty well on the ground?

Figure 4.6 *(continued)*

Teacher:	Yes, in fact they're the only kind of bat that can maneuver as easily on the ground as in the air. You've asked some good questions: Take out a sheet of paper now, and number from 1 to 7. You can use the information you got from your questions [on the board].

Information recorded on the board:

Vaulting Vampire Bats

Why do they vault?	To launch into flight
Really fly?	Yes
Habitat?	NI
Other kinds?	Yes, about 900
Do all vault into flight?	No—drop from branches to launch
Drink blood?	Yes—½ body wt.—about 1½ lbs.? a night
Prey?	Ex: cows
How?	Not from the neck—from the foot
Move on the ground	Yes—only kind of bat that can

The teacher then gives this oral quiz:

1. Do vampire bats really drink blood? (yes)
2. How much blood do vampire bats drink? (half their weight per night)
3. How do vampire bats launch themselves into flight? (by jumping)
4. How many types of bat are there? (about 900)
5. What is the major muscle the vampire bat uses to launch itself from the ground? (the pectorals)
6. How have scientists studied the vampire bat's vaulting? (using a high-speed camera)
7. What is unusual about the vampire bat's ability to move on the ground? (It is the only bat that can move as well on the ground as in the air.)

Teacher:	How many of you think you answered at least 5 questions correctly?
[Most students raise their hands]	
	Which ones did you have trouble with?
Students:	Numbers 5 and 6.
Teacher:	Okay, copy these two questions on the back of the article, to read for tomorrow:
[Teacher writes questions 5 and 6 on the board.]	

Figure 4.6 (*continued*)

Support for Question-Only

Research and field experience have revealed that Question-Only helps students at all levels raise incisive and systematic questions (Legenza, 1978; Manzo & Legenza, 1975). The enthusiasm students have shown for this method probably arises from the upbeat and ego-protective atmosphere it creates, while illustrating the power of asking purposeful questions before reading.

Cooperative Question-Only

To increase opportunity for student participation in Question-Only, try this variation. King and Rosenshine (1993) found that students' knowledge construction has been significantly enhanced by guided cooperative questioning.

Preparation

- Prepare the quiz questions as for the regular Question-Only lesson and decide whether to use the title of the selection or a reworded version.
- Form heterogeneous groups of four students each. Assign roles such as recorder, speaker, clarifier, and encourager.

Step 1. Introduce Question-Only in the same way as previously, but tell students that they will have three minutes, in groups, to write as many questions as they can to get the information in the reading assignment.

Step 2. Call on each group in turn to ask one question, continuing around the groups until all questions have been asked. A group may ask a question only if they have it written down. If all their questions have been asked, they must "pass." Tell students that they will have one more opportunity to compose follow-up questions, so each group's writer may want to make some notes of ideas for these.

Step 3. Give groups an additional two minutes to form and write as many follow-up questions as they can.

Step 4. Call on groups in turn to ask their follow-up questions, again accepting only questions they have written, and continuing until all have been asked.

Step 5. Give the quiz.

Step 6. Have students read silently to check their answers to the quiz questions and look especially for the question or questions they did not ask.

Anticipation-Reaction Guide

The Anticipation-Reaction Guide (A-R Guide) (Duffelmeyer, 1994; Duffelmeyer, Baum, & Merkley, 1987) is a teacher-prepared worksheet that students use to respond to carefully crafted statements before reading and again after reading.* The primary purpose of an A-R Guide is to alert students to currently held ideas and attitudes, which may differ, from those presented in the reading selection.

*Excerpt from "Maximizing reader-text confrontation with an Extended Anticipation Guide" by F. Duffelmeyer, D. Baum, and D. Merkley, *Journal of Reading, 31.* © 1987 by the International Reading Association.

Thus, the effectiveness of the method depends on the teacher's knowledge of the particular group of students' background of information and experience.

Steps in the Anticipation-Reaction Guide

Preparation Review the reading selection to identify information or attitudes that may differ from what students might expect to read based on prior knowledge and experience. Write statements to which students will be asked to agree or disagree with before they read, and again after they have read. Use these statements to create an A-R Guide worksheet such as the one shown in Figure 4.7.

Step 1. Distribute the A-R Guide to students, with directions to write their responses (agree or disagree) to each statement.

Step 2. Students then are directed to read and, after reading, to respond again to the A-R Guide statements.

Step 3. Begin discussion by asking whether anyone changed his or her responses to any of the A-R Guide statements after reading the selection.

Implementation Tips for Anticipation-Reaction Guides

- A-R Guide statements must be written so that students have a reasonable basis for agreeing or disagreeing with each statement.
- Statements can be based on facts that can be verified in the selection; however, consider attitude-type questions as well, since these are more likely to elicit experience-based schema connections with the new information.
- As a variation on the basic A-R Guide, have students write the page number on which they found confirmation for or a difference from their Prereading belief, or have students select one of the statements as the topic for a brief Postreading essay.
- A-R Guides can be used with fiction as well as nonfiction.

Cooperative Anticipation-Reaction Guides

Anticipation-Reaction Guides can be used as the content for a number of cooperative structures, after students have individually completed the Postreading step. For example in "home groups" of four students, appoint these roles: Writer, Pro, Con, and Arbitrator. Distribute an extra copy of the A-R Guide to the Writer in each group. Give students a time limit of about two minutes, in which Pro attempts to convince the Arbitrator that one should agree with the statement, Con attempts to convince him or her to disagree with it, and the Arbitrator attempts to document "proof" for one position or the other or to state a compromise position. The Writer records the Arbitrator's conclusion. Continue in the same way with each statement, *shifting roles* one person to the right each time.

Prereading Graphic Organizer

The Prereading Graphic Organizer described in Chapter 3 is another way to help students activate schema prior to reading. See Figure 4.8 for a Prereading Graphic Organizer a teacher might help students create for the "Vaulting Vampires" article.

Name: ______________________ Date: __________

Hour: ____________

Directions: Read each statement below, and in the left-hand column labeled "Before Reading," write an "A" if you Agree with the statement, or a "D" if you Disagree. After you have read today's assignment, you will be asked to re-read each statement, and respond in the right-hand column labeled "After Reading."

Before Reading		*After Reading*
______	1. Vampire bats really drink blood.	______
______	2. Bats can jump very long distances, but they don't really fly.	______
______	3. Bats are unable to move easily on the ground.	______
______	4. Studying animal behavior would be an interesting and challenging occupation.	______

Figure 4.7 Example of an Anticipation-Reaction Guide for "Vaulting Vampires"

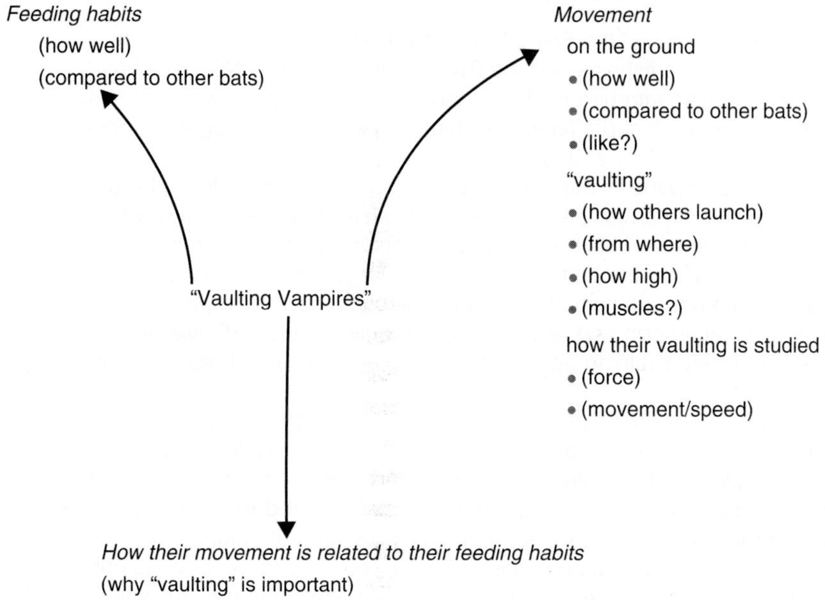

Figure 4.8 Prereading Graphic Organizer for "Vaulting Vampires"

Reading-Before-Reading

The idea of *reading-before-reading* started as a popular movement in the 1950s with *Cliffs Notes*, or book digests. In due course, comic-book versions of the classics became familiar underground means of making the classics more palatable and giving readers a head start on reading unabridged versions. Not surprisingly, these mechanisms received a black eye when many students began using them as substitutes for, rather than supplements to, the original books. Open resentment against digests and abridged materials was reversed shortly thereafter, however, when a theory called *Advance Ideational Organizers* restored credibility to the intuitive value of some type of reading-before-reading.

Advance Organizers

In a now classic study, learning theorist David Ausubel (1960) had college students read a "prestructured" statement (500 words), or Advance Ideational Organizer, before reading a longer (2,500-word) selection in science. The Advance Ideational Organizers significantly improved student comprehension. Subsequent studies by several other researchers produced results that sometimes replicated this finding but at other times did not. The difference in these outcomes was traced primarily to the quality of the Prereading passage. Ideally, an organizer had to impart a sense of structure but not be too abstract. There also were some findings to indicate that short literal accounts, usually used as the "control group" treatment, had a positive effect on comprehension as well.

The Old Man and the Sea tells of an extremely poor old fisherman, SANTIAGO, who fishes along the Gulf Stream, and of MANOLIN, a boy who had fished with him until the man's luck had gone bad. The boy still had deep respect and affection for him, however, and brought him food and other things he needed.

The book opens in September as the old man decides to go far out into the Gulf Stream to take advantage of a strong current. He rowed out in the dark, lowered his bait, and began drifting with the current. When the sun was high, the bait was taken by a large fish. The man tried to pull the fish up, but it was too big and simply began towing the boat out to sea. All afternoon and all night the fish pulled the SKIFF, with the old man resolutely straining against the line to ensure that the fish did not break it.

About sunrise, the fish gave a lurch, which cut the man's hand. Santiago ate strips of raw tuna to keep up his strength, and he wished the boy were with him. Finally, the fish surfaced, and it was the biggest fish the man had ever seen—longer than the skiff. But it dove again and continued towing the boat the rest of that day and into the night.

The old man was suffering greatly by now but was still resolved to bring the fish in. He tried to sleep, still standing and holding the line, but woke as the fish again surfaced and pulled him down into the boat, where the line cut into his hands and his back. He got up and fought the fish to try and tire it. As the sun rose on the old man's third day at sea, the fish began to circle, and the man was able to pull in some line. After several hours, feeling dizzy and faint, the old man pulled the fish near enough to the boat to harpoon it. Since the fish was larger than the boat, the man lashed it alongside, rigged the sail, and, exhausted, set sail for home.

But it was too good to last. Sharks had caught the scent. From sunset until after midnight, the old man fought the sharks, first with his harpoon, then his knife, and finally a club. But it was no use—they had cleaned his fish, and he was beaten.

He arrived in the harbor and managed to reach his shack before he collapsed with fatigue. In the morning, the fishermen were astounded at the 19-foot skeleton lashed to the boat. When the old man awakened, the boy heard of his ordeal and tried to console him.

Figure 4.9 *The Old Man and the Sea*: Literal organizer

Accordingly, we recommend using *both* abstract and literal organizers. Prepare the organizers as a handout to distribute to students to read before they read the longer assignment and to refer to as needed as they read. Figures 4.9 and 4.10 provide examples of a literal and an abstract organizer for Hemmingway's *The Old Man and the Sea*.

Reiterative Reading

Reiterative Reading (Crafton, 1983) is based on the proposition that students can independently acquire relevant background information through the reading

> *The Old Man and the Sea* tells of a fisherman's struggle with the elements while trying to hook and kill a huge fish, only to have it eaten by sharks.
>
> The story is a testament to humankind's unconquerable spirit—to our ability to achieve dignity in the face of defeat. Humans are shown to be noble because of their willingness to struggle and persevere against the hardships in life. The man tells the fish, "I will show him what a man can do and what a man endures" [p. 66] and "Man is not made for defeat . . . a man can be destroyed, but not defeated" [p. 103].
>
> The book also shows the author's view of humankind in relation to the physical universe. The fisherman refers to both the stars and the fish as "my brother." This is taken to mean that we should respect and love our natural environment even as we strive to carve existence out of it and conquer it.

Figure 4.10 *The Old Man and the Sea:* Abstract organizer

process itself.* In one study of this approach, it was found that simply having eleventh graders read two different articles on the same topic "dramatically improved students' comprehension of the second article and the cognitive level at which they processed it" (Crafton, 1983, p. 587). This researcher's work supported three assertions: (1) "the common view of reading as a natural knowledge-generating activity"; (2) the belief that "text on an unfamiliar topic can serve as cognitive preparation for the next"; and (3) the observation that experimental subjects who read two forms of the same material "were more *active* during the reading process and personalized information to a greater degree than did subjects who read unrelated materials" (1983, p. 590). Figure 4.11 offers anecdotal validation for Reiterative Reading.

Translating the value of Reiterative Reading into practice was difficult at the time Crafton's research was published, since it was not always easy to find two selections on the same topic at appropriate levels of difficulty. Internet search engines have given this research-based approach a new level of viability, with an ever-present supply of content-rich electronic text on any topic. As more and more classrooms have at least one computer in them, using the internet for reading-before-reading is not only much easier than ever before but also becomes one more simple, quick, and effective way to use technology to enhance instruction. Without very much preparation time, teachers can use computers (or assign students) to quickly search the internet for material relating to core topics for the day. In your own classroom, you will probably find some favorite portals or search engines that can be called up regularly to search for reiterative reading materials. Online encyclopedias and even Wikipedia.com can also be useful

*Excerpt from "Learning from reading: What happens when students generate their own background information?" by L. K. Crafton, *Journal of Reading, 26.* © 1983 by the International Reading Association.

> The second author once taught world geography to a difficult, sometimes unruly class of low-achieving ninth graders. We had a new, slick, black-covered text that was impossible in almost every way: the print was small, information was dense, and sentence structures were complex beyond reason. In short order, we found 20 copies of a very old geography text in the district's attic. We read both books, alternating the order according to fancy more than to any deep analysis of textual value. In addition to the obvious benefits of seeing most things twice, and in different words, we often were challenged and amused by diverse perspectives, sometimes contrary information, and changing and often bewildering facts. For example, we puzzled over how a then-obscure and backward Iran could have been the seat of the great Persian Empire. There were many times when we wished we had a third or fourth text to explain some things in even greater detail. We never could quite get a conceptual fix, for example, on how maps were made in times past when map makers could not get up high enough to see.

Figure 4.11 Anecdotal evidence for reading-before-reading

starting points in a search for these types of materials. As a variation, public and cable television offer numerous opportunities for nontextual Prereading through *viewing* films, documentaries, and programs on topics in literature, science, social studies, and the arts.

▶ CONCEPT SUMMARY

Prereading schema activation is the first stage in effective study reading, when the reader quickly surveys the reading material to see what it is generally about and consciously tries to recall what he or she knows, believes, feels, and has experienced related to that topic. Schema activation effectively raises the reader's ability to comprehend and learn from a given selection. As such, it is an important first *instructional* step in the Framework for Text-Based Instruction presented in Chapter 3. Schema activation usually is done by asking questions in order to set good purposes for reading; thus, Prereading instruction largely is a form of inquiry training. Methods such as Reciprocal Questioning and Question-Only provide opportunities for students to hear and imitate many models of purposeful Prereading questioning. Anticipation-Reaction Guides, Prereading Graphic Organizers, and Reading-Before-Reading challenge students to raise their own questions about their knowledge and experience-based connections with the new material. Pairing prereading methods with Cooperative Structures, as in Cooperative ReQuest and Cooperative Question-Only, increases students' opportunities to try out the questioning strategies modeled and illustrated—at first as simple imitation, and eventually as personalized, habitual prereading strategies.

CHAPTER 5

THROUGH—METHODS FOR GUIDING SILENT READING

Reading taste and ability are always tethered to past experience. But reading itself is one way of increasing this capital fund of past experience.
—Edgar Dale

Of the three phases of reading instruction referred to as *Into*, *Through*, and *Beyond*, it is the *Through*—guiding students while they read silently—that we know least about. Pre- and Postreading strategies can be modeled and practiced in various ways before and after students read; how, though, can we model and ensure that students try out the "during reading" strategies for monitoring and "fixing" comprehension *while* they are engaged in study reading? Even with the best Prereading instruction, at some point each student goes into the printed page alone. The teacher cannot physically follow students on their silent incursion into print. They can, however, provide support in the form of various types of reminders to read actively and purposefully. This chapter presents the techniques, prompts, and methods now available for doing so. These range from methods for teaching readers to internalize strategies that prompt self-questioning to various types of reading guides, to restructured or reformatted text to better meet readers' needs.

- TEACHING STUDENTS TO THINK WHILE THEY READ
- TECHNIQUES FOR COMPREHENSION MONITORING AND FIX-UP
- READING GUIDES
- COOPERATIVE COMPREHENSION MONITORING TO SUPPORT STRATEGY ACQUISITION
- BUILT-IN GUIDES TO SILENT READING
- TEXT STRUCTURE: HISTORICAL FOOTNOTE AND LUKEWARM SUPPORT
- CONCEPT SUMMARY

TEACHING STUDENTS TO THINK WHILE THEY READ

The aim of effective Content Area Literacy instruction is not so much to teach *reading skills* as to build the habit of *skilled reading*. This is not just a play on words. It is the difference between teaching how to use a skill and teaching understanding of a skill's purpose and role and then offering the supportive scaffolding needed as a learner struggles through the process of trying it out, adjusting, and mastering it as an intentional and flexibly applied strategy.

In one study, students were interviewed about their understanding of this metacognitive process:

> When Susan, a seventh grade student, was asked to talk about what she had been thinking as she read a portion of text she responded: "Oh, I don't usually think while I read." Clearly, Susan misunderstands the purpose of reading and cannot be successful. (Lipson & Wixson, 1997, p. 581)

For Susan, like many students, all reading is the same. She makes no distinction between the easy, passive process of Independent-level reading and the challenging, active process of Instructional-level *study reading*. Helping students make that distinction is an important aspect of the Guided Silent Reading step in the Framework for Text-Based Instruction.

In Instructional-level study-reading, students must sustain attention, draw on prior knowledge and experiences, translate new information into familiar terms, identify main ideas and relevant details, monitor comprehension, use fix-up strategies when they are not understanding, and, most of all, sustain these efforts in a sea of other competing interests, needs, and distractions.

Metacognitive Monitoring and Fix-Up Strategies

Most people, adults and students alike, do more reading of Independent-level than Instructional-level materials. Therefore, passive reading becomes a strongly imbedded habit, and we tend to enter any reading act as if it were easy, Independent-level reading. When Instructional-level study reading is undertaken

Metacognitive Monitoring Strategies

Summarization: "How would I say that simply, in my own words?"

Clarification: "What part of this isn't making sense?"

Identifying main ideas and/or themes: "What is the point of this part?"

Clustering important details: "What details support this point?"

Prediction: "Where is this going next?"

Evaluation: "Is this important/accurate/interesting?"

Visualizing: "Can I picture what is going on here?"

Fix-Up Strategies

Rereading: "I'd better reread that part."

Identifying unfamiliar vocabulary: "Is there a word or phrase here that is unclear?"

Reading ahead: "I should read ahead a little bit and see if that helps."

Pausing to reflect: "I should stop and think about that point."

Asking for help: "Who could I ask about this?"

Figure 5.1 Review of metacognitive monitoring and fix-up strategies

in the habitual, passive way that Independent-level reading can be done, several paragraphs or even pages may be "read" with little to no understanding or recall. Effective study readers know that this does not mean that the reading is "too difficult," but simply that they need to switch gears. When reading *this* material, they understand that they need to consciously and continuously keep track of when they are understanding and when they are *not* understanding. This metacognitive monitoring process sends up a red warning flag when comprehension is shaky: "Uh oh, I don't think I'm getting this," prompting the realization that something more needs to be done here. The "something more" is any of a number of *fix-up* strategies: *actions the reader can take to actively build comprehension during study reading.* See Figure 5.1 for a review of the metacognitive monitoring and fix-up strategies introduced in Chapter 3.

The short newspaper article reprinted in Figure 5.2 was used by a Kansas City social studies teacher to introduce a unit on the internment of Japanese citizens early in World War II. It is used for the examples of the methods discussed in this chapter.

TECHNIQUES FOR PROMPTING COMPREHENSION MONITORING AND FIX-UP

Impulsivity, distractibility and unreflective reading are comprehension killers. The wise teacher is always on the lookout for ways to counter such unseen and unheard

(1) Early in 1942, amid the mood of rage and fear following the Japanese attack on Pearl Harbor, the U.S. government interned more than 110,000 Japanese-Americans living on the West Coast. The great majority of those internees, some of whom were held as long as three years, were native-born American citizens.

(2) At the time, few outside the Japanese-American community had the courage or foresight to protest what many now consider one of the most shameful acts in American history. But one man who did speak out was a Presbyterian minister named William Lindsay Young, then president of Park College in Parkville, just across the river from Kansas City.

(3) Young happened to be in Los Angeles when the internment process began. And he was horrified to see thousands of people herded into a holding area behind barbed wire at the Santa Anita Racetrack. He was even more distressed to discover that the internees, rounded up solely because of their ancestry, were being shipped off to hastily constructed internment camps in Wyoming, Colorado, Arizona, Arkansas, and other states. What he was witnessing, Young thought, was frighteningly similar to fascist doctrines espoused by the nations that the United States was fighting in the name of democracy. "If we are not careful," Young said in a speech to Park students, "we are apt to do damage to those very values which we are now anxious to preserve."

(4) When he learned of a government program allowing some interned students to attend colleges away from the West Coast, he immediately set out to recruit as many as possible. "Would you like to study at Park College? All expenses provided?" he wired to prospective students. In all, he enrolled nine second-generation Japanese-Americans, or Nisei, each of whom had to be cleared by six federal agencies, including the FBI, before they could travel to Missouri.

(5) But the federal bureaucracy was not the only obstacle facing Young. His recruitment policy aroused an anti-Japanese furor in the community around his school. The response grew so intense that local newspapers called the debate the "Battle of Parkville." And into that heated atmosphere came the nine Nisei students, already traumatized by the sudden upheaval in their lives.

Dreadful Journey

(6) One of them was Masaye Nagao Nakamura, who came from East Los Angeles. She left for Park College as her family was being sent to an internment camp in Wyoming. She began her college journey

Figure 5.2 Sample supplementary reading selection: "Embracing the Persecuted: Park College Kept Japanese-Americans out of Detention Camps during War," by Joe Popper
Source: Kansas City Star, Saturday, February 20, 1999. Metropolitan Edition, page A1. Reprinted by permission of the *Kansas City Star*.

in an Army truck. "I sat on my suitcase in the back of that open truck surrounded by three soldiers," she said. "I was going to Union Station in Los Angeles, but I felt like I was going to the guillotine." After boarding the eastbound train, she was denied a seat and forced to crouch on her suitcase in the front of the passenger car among the baggage. "You could hear a pin drop when I got on," she said. "And then, behind me, all I could hear were whispers of 'Jap, Jap'." After the conductor disdainfully snatched her ticket, he leaned down and spit in her face. "I was so shocked, I couldn't raise my arm to wipe it off," she said. "I felt his spit running down my face. I wanted a hole to open up so that I could drop through and vanish."

(7) For two days she sat alone and terrified. She did not move. She did not eat. She did not go to the lavatory. Arriving in Kansas City, though, she was encouraged by Young's warm greeting. "The students and faculty of Park College all welcome you," he said. But then he added a warning. "You must be careful when you leave the campus," he said. "Some people in Parkville have threatened to lynch any Japanese-American student they catch."

A Hostile Town

(8) Young had good reason to be wary. The mood in Parkville, already hostile to the Park College Nisei program, was further fueled by the Mayor, Herbert Dyer. "If the FBI is so sure that these Japs are loyal citizens, why didn't it let them remain on the West Coast instead of sending them to a concentration camp?" Dyer told the *Kansas City Star*. It was outrageous, he added, that the government chose to "dump them" on Parkville. He threatened legal action. Anonymous calls to the college threatened worse.

(9) Dyer was supported by the City Council and by local chapters of the American War Mothers and the American Legion. Two Parkville merchants, saying they spoke for many others, announced they would not serve any Japanese-Americans.

(10) But Young stood his ground with calm dignity. The opponents of his plan, he told the *Kansas City Times*, "apparently have lost sight of exactly those things for which this nation is now fighting." He sent a letter to 1,000 residents of Parkville and adjacent towns pointing out the irrational and racist nature of the internment policy. "What about the thousands and thousands of young men and women already in our colleges whose parents were born in Germany?" he wrote, "Is war hysteria making us lose sight of our democratic ideals?"

(11) In September 1942, at the college's opening convocation, Young addressed the student body. "The Axis (powers) are not the only danger to our liberties as we know them," he said. "There are

Figure 5.2 *(continued)*

those who, because of their intolerance and bigotry, would deny to a fellow American citizen his just rights. . . . What makes this spurious loyalty so dangerous is that it is cloaked in the garb of patriotism."

(12) His words inspired students and alumni alike. "I am proud of you and proud to be a graduate of your school," wrote one alumnus living in Chicago who had read a news report about the Battle of Parkville. "What a stirring speech it was," said Harold Smith, who graduated from Park College in 1944. He later became the college's librarian, and his research was a major source for this article.

(13) "Dr. Young had already met with us in small groups," Smith said. "He told us that when the Nisei students arrived, they would need our help. And we were all receptive to the idea. I don't think there was a doubt in our minds that what was being done to the Japanese-Americans was wrong." Echoing Young, a headline in the campus newspaper proclaimed: "Welcome Nisei."

(14) But off campus, Nisei students faced threats of violence several times that year. When Nagao Nakamura walked into Parkville alone, she was harassed by a crowd that followed her through the streets. Two other Japanese-American students were chased by a mob brandishing a rope. In response, the Park College students formed groups to escort and protect their classmates. Gradually, the mood in Parkville changed. Within two years, the town, having seen reality rather than stereotypes, had embraced the Nisei students.

"You took me in"

(15) After she graduated in 1945, Nakamura returned to California, where she became an honored teacher in the Oakland school system. Retired now, she often speaks to student groups about the internment period. "It was a long time ago, but it is vivid to me yet," she said recently. "And I will remember Dr. Young's courage until the day I die."

(16) One of her classmates, William Yamamoto, became a physician and a professor at the University of Pennsylvania Medical School. In 1991, he sent a large contribution to his alma mater along with a letter. "I was declared a stranger in my own land, and you took me in . . . from behind the barbed wire that surrounded the Santa Anita Racetrack," he wrote. "At Park, many befriended me and became my campus family. All the modest success I have enjoyed, and the fullness of my days since, I owe them, the people who made up Park College."

Figure 5.2 *(continued)*

debilitating habits. One way to help students build effective habits of comprehension monitoring and fix-up is simply to require them to pause periodically while reading and use one of several types of self-monitoring strategies. These techniques can be highly structured at first, fading to greater student independence as they gain familiarity with the technique. Three variations on this quintessential *prompting* technique are described next; other possible variations are limited only by the individual teacher's imagination and creativity.

Strategic Guiding Questions

Several research findings suggest that students can easily be taught to ask strategic questions while they read (Baker & Brown, 1984; Meichenbaum & Asarnow, 1979; Singer & Dolan, 1980). For example, there are three simple questions that have been shown to guide students in story-type reading:

1. What is the main idea?
2. What are the important details?
3. How do the characters feel, and why? (Meichenbaum & Asarnow, 1979)

The first two questions also can be used to guide the reading of expository textbook material. This simple approach can be structured initially by having students pause after a few minutes of Silent Reading and asking them these questions aloud. Depending on the content of the reading material, other strategic questions might be added, such as:

1. Where is the author going next with this?
2. How might you organize the information you have read so far?

Students reading the newspaper article in Figure 5.2, for example, might be given about a minute and a half to read silently. This should put most students up to about the first subheading, "Dreadful Journey," a good point to pause and model strategic questioning: "Turn your papers over for a few minutes. A good first *strategic question* to ask about anything we read is, 'so far, what seems to be the main idea here?' Can someone say, in your own words, the main idea of what you have just read?" Students should be encouraged to respond with more than single words or facts and helped to shape a main-idea statement that the teacher records on the board or overhead. They should not look back to the article while trying to recall the information. The main-idea statement might eventually read something like this:

> The president of a college near Kansas City saved Japanese-Americans from being put in detention camps during World War II by offering them a special full scholarship and helping them qualify for a government program that would allow them to attend a college away from the West Coast.

As students suggest ideas for the main-idea statement, the teacher should ask, when necessary, "Is that part of the main idea, or is it a supporting detail?" Ideas that students decide are supporting details can be written to the side of the main idea statement. After the main idea has been formulated, the teacher might permit students to look back at the article for a very brief, timed, period—in this case about 10 seconds—in order to locate the more important details to add to the list that has been started on the board or overhead. The list for the opening section of this article would reasonably include the following:

1. This happened in 1942, after the Japanese attack on Pearl Harbor.
2. More than 110,000 Japanese-Americans on the West Coast were interned.
3. The camps were in Wyoming, Colorado, Arizona, Arkansas, and other states.
4. Few other Americans protested.
5. The college president's name was Lindsay Young.
6. The college was Park College.
7. Young enrolled nine Japanese-American students.
8. To qualify for the special program, prospective students had to be cleared by six federal agencies.
9. The local community was against the students coming to the college.

Then the teacher might say, "Now, before you turn your papers back over, where do you think the author is going next with this?" Likely responses might include the following:

1. Real stories about some of the Japanese-Americans who went to Park College.
2. How the town responded.
3. How the college responded.
4. What eventually happened to those students.

Finally, the teacher might ask whether the five-W's of a newspaper article (*who, what, where, when,* and *why*) have all been answered. In this example, the teacher might emphasize what they have learned so far about the "why" question: "Why did President Young put himself and his college on the line to go against public opinion?" Students may recall reading in the introductory section that Young had been in Los Angeles when the internment began and had seen people herded into one of the camps. But this doesn't fully explain why he decided to personally undertake to do something to change what was happening. Urged to consider this question further, students will be more likely to take note of the message of Young's speech, which is quoted later in the article.

After several lessons in which Silent Reading questioning has been modeled in this way, the teacher can begin to fade out the supportive scaffolding. For example,

1. Direct students to make small pencil checks on the reading assignment at given points. When they come to these points during reading, they are

instructed to write out a clarifying question of any type and briefly record their answers.

2. Direct students to select three points on their own, while reading, and to stop and write clarifying questions and answers.

Each of these variations also is ideal for structuring student collaboration in pairs or groups of four.

About-Point

About-Point (Martin, Lorton, Blanc, & Evans, 1977) is an easy-to-remember formula for strategic reading. Students are taught to pause at logical points, such as at the ends of paragraphs or text subsections, and complete the following two phrases:

This section is about ____; and the point is ____.

The simple About-Point prompt reminds readers to translate the basic meaning of the section and then to ratchet up their comprehension to the interpretive level in order to state the author's probable intent for presenting just this information in just this way. Teach students the basic About-Point format using several short sample paragraphs. Explain that an *about* statement should be more than a single key word but less than a summary. A *point* statement should include the most important elements of the section. It is useful to demonstrate a few examples and talk through the process of expressing good *about* and *point* statements. Here are two possible About-Point statements from the newspaper article in Figure 5.2:

Paragraph 6

This paragraph is about one Japanese-American woman's trip from Los Angeles to Park College, and the point is that having done nothing wrong, she was treated worse than a criminal.

Paragraph 11

This paragraph is about President Young's opening-of-school speech in September 1942, and the point is that bigotry is a greater threat to freedom than an invading army.

Once students have the idea, the simple format can be used in at least two ways.

1. For a structured beginning, have students put pencil checks beside particular paragraphs in a reading assignment. Direct students to write About-Point statements on these paragraphs.
2. For decreased structure (fading), instruct students to select their own paragraphs for About-Point statements.

Like the Guiding Questions technique described earlier, About-Point statement writing is an ideal activity for student pairs or cooperative groups.

Comprehension Monitoring System

The *Comprehension Monitoring System* was field tested with high school teachers in home economics, social studies, and biology (Smith & Dauer, 1984). In this self-prompting technique, teachers create a coding system for students to use to record their *cognitive* and *affective* responses while they read. The code will vary according to the characteristics of the material and the curriculum objectives. A coding system for social studies reading might be as follows:

B = Bored
C = Confused
D = Disagree
MI = Main idea
Q = I've got a question about this (Note the question, because you are not likely to remember it.)

A coding system for science reading might be:

C = Clear
D = Difficult
I* = Important
S! = Surprising

Not every paragraph needs to be marked, but initially, the teacher should assign a minimum number of paragraphs for marked responses. If students are permitted to write in their reading materials, they can note the letter codes in the margins while reading. If not, 2-inch-wide strips of paper (or sticky-notes) can be distributed to insert in the assigned pages for recording responses.

Sample markings for the article in Figure 5.2 might be as follows:

Coding System:

ID = Important detail(s)
R = Reminds me of something
MI = Main idea
S = Surprising

Paragraph 1	ID	(Sets out the basic newspaper requirements for "who, what, when, where".)
Paragraph 2	R	(Reminds me of how people don't have the courage not to laugh at crude ethnic jokes.)
Paragraph 3	MI	(We were doing the same thing the Nazis were doing to the Jews.)
Paragraph 4	S	(Nine students doesn't sound like many, when 110,000 were arrested.)
Paragraph 6	R	(Reminds me of movies I've seen about the time when African Americans were supposed to sit in the back of the bus.)
Paragraph 11	MI	(This seems to be the main point so far—that we were doing the same thing to these people that the Nazis were doing to the Jewish people.)
Paragraphs 15 & 16	ID	(Important to note what became of these two people)

After students have been introduced to the basic technique of coding their responses to sections of a reading selection, they can work together in cooperative groups to compare their responses and/or to create their own custom and self-prompting coding systems.

K-W-L Plus

Know-Want to Know-Learned, Plus (Carr & Ogle, 1987; Ogle, 1989, 1996) is a popular method for implementing the full three-step Framework for Reading-Based Instruction. It is placed in this chapter on *Silent* Reading because of the unique way in which it facilitates this step of the Framework. In K-W-L Plus, students are guided in generating their own anticipation-based reading guides to prompt active Silent Reading. This helps them read with greater awareness of what they already knew, what they need to know, and *with the charge to carefully process and restate what they learn from reading.*

Steps in K-W-L Plus

Step 1. *Know.* Students make or are given a three-column worksheet with the columns headed *Know, Want to Know,* and *Learned.* The teacher leads a brainstorming session on what students already know about the topic. As ideas are given, students write them in the *Know* column of their individual worksheets. (See Figure 5.3 for an example of a worksheet that might be generated with a class for the reading selection on World War II Japanese-Americans that we have been using for illustrations in this chapter.)

Step 2. *Want to Know.* The teacher then moves the discussion toward aspects of the topic that students do not know. Students are helped to state these as questions and write them in the *Want to Know* column of their worksheets.

Step 3. *Learned.* As they read, students locate and write their answers to the *Want to Know* questions in the *Learned* column of their worksheets. New questions and answers can be added as they read and find information they did not anticipate. The teacher leads a discussion of what was learned in answer to the original questions and what additional information was learned.

Step 4. *Plus.* The teacher leads students in categorizing the information that was learned and in creating a graphic organizer to represent this. (See Figure 5.7, p. 109, for a graphic organizer format that might be used for this article in the *Plus* step.)

Notes on K-W-L Plus

The early version of a K-W-L that did not contain the *Plus* step of creating a graphic organizer did not fare well in research comparisons with other methods. The Plus version, however, has been uniformly supported; it is a tail that now wags the dog.

Know	Want to Know	Learned
Japanese-Americans were imprisoned during World War II even if they were American citizens. Some of the prison camps were in California. There was a lot of negative public opinion about German Americans at that time, too.	How did a *college* keep them out of the camps? How many people did the college help in this way? Was everyone in favor of this, or did some object? How did those who were helped feel about it?	

Figure 5.3 Example of a K-W-L Plus worksheet for the article "Embracing the Persecuted: Park College Kept Japanese-Americans out of Detention Camps during War."

Teachers especially like this method because it is well structured and students respond well to reading to answer questions that they themselves have raised.

The next section describes several types of guides that teachers can prepare for students to complete while they read. Teachers' understanding of the specific active reading processes they are attempting to encourage significantly enhances this fairly traditional form of reading assistance.

▶ READING GUIDES

When coaches shout commands during an athletic event, they are attempting to remind the athletes of what has been taught and practiced in a less competitive situation. Such coaching from the sidelines would be distracting were it not for extensive prior training. The same general principle applies to written aids to text comprehension or adjunct aids. These aids work best when students have been explicitly taught to use them and are given ample opportunity for guided practice. This specific Plus practice step has been missing from prior uses and research evaluations of the effectiveness of reading/study guides. Its addition is analogous to a "coach's game"—when a basketball coach comes on the court during a scrimmage for the purposes of prompting strategic moves and critiquing live play.

The idea of *reading guides*, according to Herber (1978), an early proponent, is to simplify difficult material. Reading guides are designed to teach reading processes as well as to improve information acquisition. Students are expected to refer to the guide while reading, then back to the text, then back again to the guide (Manzo & Garber, 1995). Often, a guide amounts to an attempt to create a written-out version of the *three-step Framework*—or *Into, Through,* and *Beyond*—described in Chapter 3. It can contain vocabulary and concept preparation as well as guiding purpose questions. Ideally, reading guides serve as supplementary aids in the independent processing of heavily content-dense text. The most significant advantages of guides, in our judgment, are that (1) they permit the teacher to focus student attention on key information and concepts in a passage and (2) they require *every* student to attempt some type of active and reflective response to at least the points referenced.

Despite mixed findings on guides, (we suspect for lack of the Plus step noted earlier), their popularity is evident in the numerous versions that have been developed. Some of the most traditionally used formats for reading guides and some innovations are described next.

Three-Level Guides

A *Three-Level Guide* is designed to lead students from basic to more advanced levels of comprehension of textual material (Herber, 1978). Part 1 of a Three-Level Guide contains questions at a literal level: What did the author say? Part 2 contains interpretive questions: What did the author mean? Part 3 contains application questions: How can you *use* this information?

Guidelines for Constructing a Three-Level Guide

1. The Guide should alert readers to the information and ideas needed to respond to the questions or activities in Part 3. Therefore, begin by deciding which Part 3 *applications* are appropriate to the material. This will help you select the details and inferences to focus on in writing Parts 1 and 2 of the Guide.
2. Next, determine what information is needed to make these applications and whether it is explicitly stated in the text or must be inferred. Information that must be inferred to make the level-three applications is used to develop questions for Part 2 of the Guide.
3. Finally, write questions for Part 1 of the Guide, directing attention to the necessary literal information in the reading selection (Vacca & Vacca, 1986).

Typically, students are directed to answer the literal questions in Part 1 while they are reading and to complete the interpretive and applied questions in Parts 2 and 3 after reading. A useful variation is to have students complete Part 1 independently and then form cooperative learning groups to complete Parts 2 and 3. See Figure 5.4 for a simple example of a Three-Level Guide for the short article used for examples in this chapter.

Process Guides

Typical teacher-made reading guides focus on product or fact identification and basic inference. A *Process Guide* is intended to teach the active thinking strategies needed to construct meaning by combining text with experiences and learnings beyond the text. There is no single format for a Process Guide. The sections and questions need to be matched to students' background information and experience related to the topic and the difficulty of the particular reading selection. The best

Directions: Answer questions in Part 1 as you read. After you have read, go on to Parts 2 and 3.

Part 1: Literal Understanding

1. Who did the U.S. government imprison early in 1942?
2. Who protested this, and why?
3. What did President Young do to help some of the Japanese-Americans?
4. What was the response of the townspeople?
5. What was the response of the college students?

Part 2: Interpretive Understanding

6. Why did Parkville merchants refuse to serve the Japanese students?
7. What did President Young mean by his statement that "what makes this spurious loyalty so dangerous is that it is cloaked in the garb of patriotism"?

Part 3: Applying your Understanding

8. You are a Park College student in September 1942. You have just listened to President Young's opening-of-school address. Write a one-page script in which you and a friend argue about the President's decision to offer scholarships for Japanese-American students to attend your college.

Figure 5.4 Example of a Three-Level Guide

way to learn how to construct one is simply to try it. Following are a few suggestions for preparing this type of guide. See an example of a simple Process Guide in Figure 5.5.

Guidelines for Constructing a Process Guide

1. Pick an important selection. Process Guides are time consuming to construct, so you will want to spend your efforts on something of conceptual value.
2. Read the selection carefully, putting yourself in the students' place: "If I didn't know much about this, what would I need to do?"
3. Construct questions that engage the reader in setting a purpose for reading and in reading actively to reconstruct information and examples.
4. Construct questions that engage students in considering possible interpretations, implications, and applications of new information.

The next type of reading guide breaks with traditional routines. It departs from the usual expectation that students need to begin at the beginning and read every word through to the end.

1. Read paragraphs 1 and 2. Record as briefly as possible the answers to the 5-W questions:

   Who?
   What?
   Where?
   When?
   Why?

2. Imagine that you are a Japanese-American in 1942, and have just learned that your family is to be sent to one of the internment camps. Write five words to describe your feeling.
3. As you read the remainder of the article, jot down your thoughts about these two general questions:
   a. What was the mood of the country that permitted this to happen?
   b. What can one person do to change the minds of an entire campus, or town, or country?
4. What more current examples of discrimination came to mind as you read or reflected on this article?
5. What parallel did President Young see between internment of Japanese-Americans and the events leading to U.S. involvement in World War II?

Figure 5.5 Example of a Process Guide

Nonlinear Guides

A Nonlinear Guide, originally called "Reading Guide-O-Rama," (Cunningham & Shablak, 1975) is a set of written prompts to students as to the best way to read and think about a given reading selection. To construct items for the Guide, teachers should determine which concepts and information they expect students to learn from the reading. Next, teachers should consider how they, as an expert reader, would approach the selection. As its name suggests, the Nonlinear Guide directs students to sections of a reading assignment out of sequence. A particularly compelling section might be addressed first, for purposes of engagement, or students may be directed to read a well-written summary first. The Guide might point out unimportant as well as important information and/or instruct the student to read a short section of the assignment and then summarize the key points presented. See Figure 5.6 for an example of a Nonlinear Guide.

Graphic Organizers as Reading Guides

As described in Chapter 3, graphic organizers provide another way to guide Silent Reading comprehension. These may be partially constructed through a whole-class brainstorming session as described in Chapter 3, or included as part of a structured Reading Guide. See Figure 5.7 for an example of a graphic organizer used to guide fact acquisition, interpretation, and application.

Directions: Reading for information is not like reading a story. In study reading, it often helps to skip around, looking for a "hook," instead of reading straight through from beginning to end. Use this Guide to show you how this process works. Notice that you are to read paragraphs 6 and 7 first.

Read paragraphs 6 & 7	Write some brief predictions about *why* this might be happening. Briefly describe something this reminds you of.
Read paragraphs 1–5	Stop and put in your own words why the young woman in paragraphs 6 and 7 was traveling to Park College.
Read paragraphs 15 & 16	How does the story turn out?
Read paragraphs 8, 9, & 14	Briefly describe ways in which the Japanese-Americans faced "a hostile town" in 1942.
Read paragraphs 10–13	Briefly describe the strategies used by President Young to encourage acceptance of the new students.

Figure 5.6 Example of a Nonlinear Guide

Additional Notes on Creating and Using Reading Guides

Composing any type of Reading Guide can be a powerful *heuristic,* or insightful experience for teachers. It draws one into a careful analysis of the textual material and a deeper understanding of the processes that students must call on to read in a given discipline. It also can get the creative juices flowing; teachers often are surprised at the insights into students' reading and learning needs that can be gained in this way. Furthermore, former limitations related to producing, revising, and storing guides have been virtually eliminated with the increasing availability of computers with word-processing, graphics, and storage capabilities.

▶ COOPERATIVE COMPREHENSION MONITORING TO SUPPORT STRATEGY ACQUISITION

Frequent use of Cooperative Structures is an important element in the Framework for Reading-Based Instruction. Paired Reading is a Cooperative Structure that teams easily with any of the comprehension-prompting techniques in this chapter, and with any type of Reading Guide. The basic steps in Paired Reading are outlined next, followed by suggestions for several "during reading" variations.

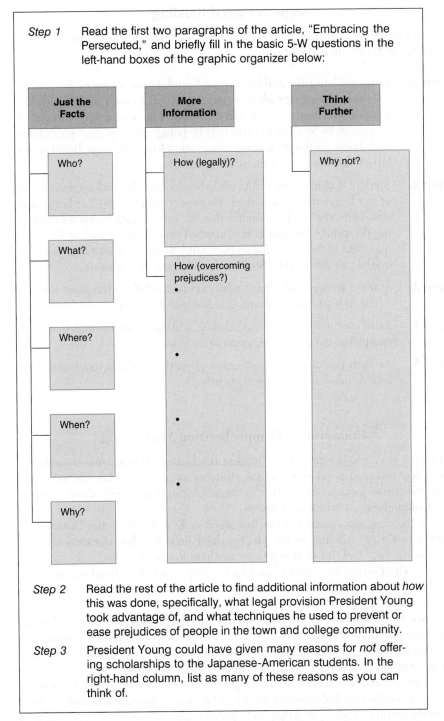

Step 1 Read the first two paragraphs of the article, "Embracing the Persecuted," and briefly fill in the basic 5-W questions in the left-hand boxes of the graphic organizer below:

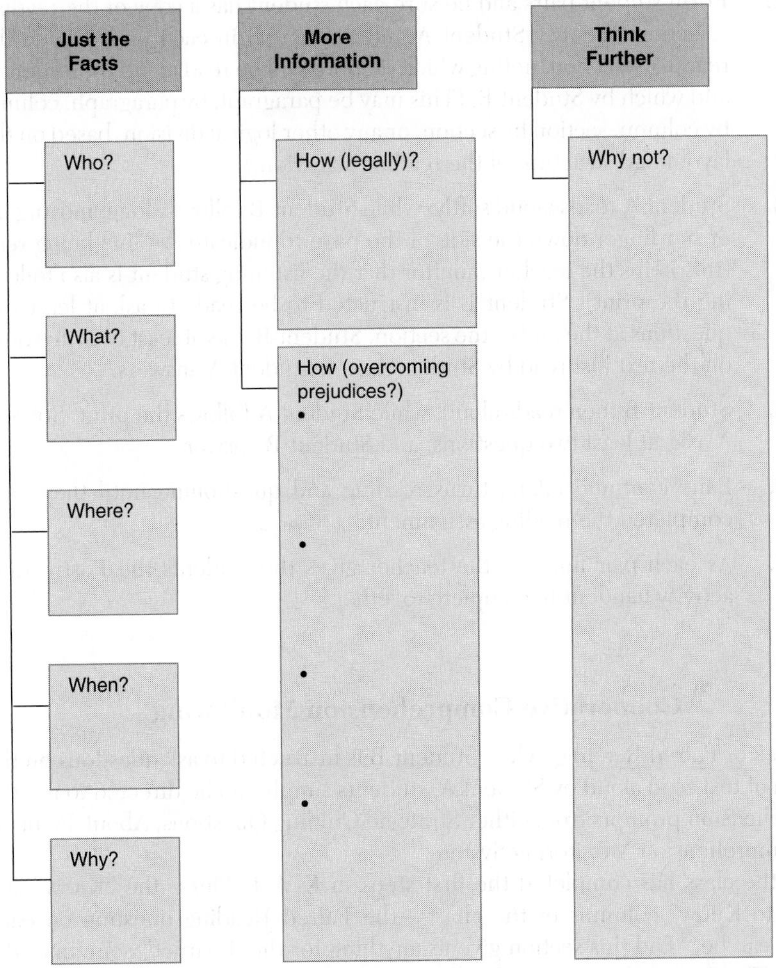

Step 2 Read the rest of the article to find additional information about *how* this was done, specifically, what legal provision President Young took advantage of, and what techniques he used to prevent or ease prejudices of people in the town and college community.

Step 3 President Young could have given many reasons for *not* offering scholarships to the Japanese-American students. In the right-hand column, list as many of these reasons as you can think of.

Figure 5.7 Example of a graphic organizer for guiding Silent Reading

Steps in Paired Reading

Preparation: Copies of a reading selection for all students (or textbooks), and a Postreading activity in handout form.

Step 1. Form student pairs and be sure each student has a copy of the reading selection. Identify Student A and Student B in each pair. Divide the reading selection, noting which sections will be read aloud by Student A and which by Student B. (This may be paragraph by paragraph, column by column, section by section, or any other logical division, based on the layout and structure of the reading selection.)

Step 2. Student A reads aloud softly, while Student B follows along, moving his or her finger down the side of the page to indicate the line being read (this helps the teacher monitor that the listening student is also following the print). Student B is instructed to be ready to ask at least two questions at the end of the section. Student B asks at least two questions on the text just read by Student A, and Student A answers.

Step 3. Student B then reads aloud, while Student A follows the print. Student A asks at least two questions, and Student B answers.

Step 4. Pairs continue taking turns reading and questioning until they have completed the reading assignment.

Step 5. As each pair finishes, the teacher gives the students the Postreading activity handout to complete together.

Cooperative Comprehension Monitoring

In Step 2 of Paired Reading, when Student B is instructed to ask questions on the portion of text read aloud by Student A, students simply can be directed to use the comprehension prompts from either Strategic Guiding Questions, About-Point, or the Comprehension Monitoring System.

If the class has completed the first steps in K-W-L Plus—the "Know" and "Want to Know" columns of the chart—the Paired Reading question on each section can be, "Did this section give us anything for the 'Learned' column of the chart?" The Postreading activity handout for Step 5 in Paired Reading can direct student pairs to use the information just recorded in the "Learned" column to complete the "Plus" step together.

Any type of Reading Guide can also be tweaked to work well with Paired Reading. One portion of the Guide can be structured to be completed as student pairs take turns reading sections of the text. A final portion of the Guide can be designed to serve as the Postreading activity for Step 5 in Paired Reading.

The next and final section of this chapter describes a way to give students ready access to another kind of guidance for Silent Reading. These are aids that are built directly into the reading selection and optimistically are a harbinger of things to come.

▶ BUILT-IN GUIDES TO SILENT READING

A logical alternative to teacher-prepared Reading Guides is a textbook with *built-in* comprehension aids. These may be electronic or hard copy versions of what now is called *hypertext.* These internal aids have been called *imbedded aids* (Manzo, 1977) and *marginal gloss* (Otto & Hayes, 1982). Both typically include help with word analysis, word meaning, basic comprehension, remembering, and even thinking beyond the text to greater depth, elaboration, and critical analysis. Aids can lend timely prompts and assistance at all levels of reading and to readers at all levels.

The idea of built-in aids is that they are woven into the actual textbook itself during the production stage. A. V. Manzo produced the "imbedded aids" prototype shown in Figure 5.8 for a chapter from a high school world history text, *Man's Unfinished Journey* (Perry, 1971), as part of a research and development project more than three decades ago.

Despite the high marks that the built-in aids received from teachers and students, it was a hard sell to publishers at the time to assume the additional costs involved in producing such books on a regular basis. However, books with imbedded aids are beginning to appear quite regularly now (note how similar many news magazines and new high school textbooks are to Figure 5.8). This may be due to significant advancements in desktop publishing software and to our growing collective exposure to hypertext. This latter software innovation, which provides additional explanatory detail when one clicks on an idea or sentence, seems to be increasing our expectation that such things can be achieved in some measure with conventional print. Relatedly, a field of study called *text technology* (Jonassen, 1982, 1985a, 1985b) first grew rapidly but now seems to have stalled out. It seems that the delight that many of us are having in accessing vast amounts of information through intelligent search engines on the internet has at least temporarily distracted efforts to help people better read, process, and critique the content of this new medium. It is our hope (and anticipation) that improvements will be made in this area soon. Such progress in support of cross-disciplinary comprehension seems assured with the growth in popularity of e-textbooks increasing, along with other student-friendly computer tools like the Tablet PC, which are starting to be integrated into literacy research studies and classroom practices (cf. Murry, 2003; Thomas, 1998; Thomas, King, & Cetinguc, 2004).

▶ TEXT STRUCTURE: HISTORICAL FOOTNOTE AND LUKEWARM SUPPORT

Some reading educators contend that teaching students to identify text structure and expository patterns is an effective way to improve Silent Reading comprehension (see Figure 5.9 for a listing of the 12 most common paragraph patterns). This belief is based on a frequent research finding that there is a strong *correlation* between reading comprehension and knowledge of text structure (Meyer, 1975). This was thought to imply that teaching poorer readers about the structure

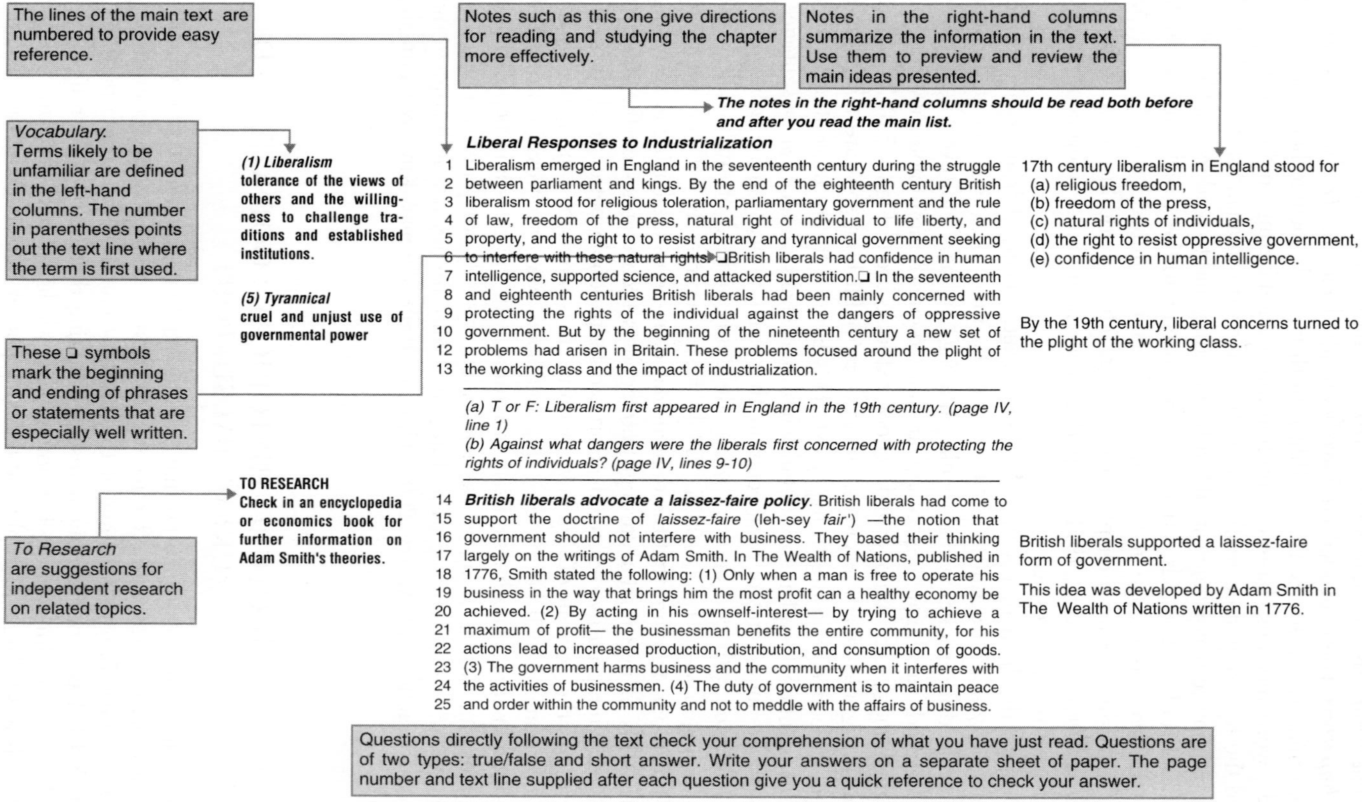
The lines of the main text are numbered to provide easy reference.

Notes such as this one give directions for reading and studying the chapter more effectively.

Notes in the right-hand columns summarize the information in the text. Use them to preview and review the main ideas presented.

The notes in the right-hand columns should be read both before and after you read the main list.

Vocabulary.
Terms likely to be unfamiliar are defined in the left-hand columns. The number in parentheses points out the text line where the term is first used.

(1) *Liberalism*
tolerance of the views of others and the willingness to challenge traditions and established institutions.

(5) *Tyrannical*
cruel and unjust use of governmental power

These ❑ symbols mark the beginning and ending of phrases or statements that are especially well written.

Liberal Responses to Industrialization

1 Liberalism emerged in England in the seventeenth century during the struggle
2 between parliament and kings. By the end of the eighteenth century British
3 liberalism stood for religious toleration, parliamentary government and the rule
4 of law, freedom of the press, natural right of individual to life liberty, and
5 property, and the right to to resist arbitrary and tyrannical government seeking
6 to interfere with these natural rights. ❑British liberals had confidence in human
7 intelligence, supported science, and attacked superstition.❑ In the seventeenth
8 and eighteenth centuries British liberals had been mainly concerned with
9 protecting the rights of the individual against the dangers of oppressive
10 government. But by the beginning of the nineteenth century a new set of
12 problems had arisen in Britain. These problems focused around the plight of
13 the working class and the impact of industrialization.

17th century liberalism in England stood for
(a) religious freedom,
(b) freedom of the press,
(c) natural rights of individuals,
(d) the right to resist oppressive government,
(e) confidence in human intelligence.

By the 19th century, liberal concerns turned to the plight of the working class.

(a) T or F: Liberalism first appeared in England in the 19th century. (page IV, line 1)

(b) Against what dangers were the liberals first concerned with protecting the rights of individuals? (page IV, lines 9-10)

TO RESEARCH
Check in an encyclopedia or economics book for further information on Adam Smith's theories.

To Research
are suggestions for independent research on related topics.

14 ***British liberals advocate a laissez-faire policy***. British liberals had come to
15 support the doctrine of *laissez-faire* (leh-sey *fair*') —the notion that
16 government should not interfere with business. They based their thinking
17 largely on the writings of Adam Smith. In The Wealth of Nations, published in
18 1776, Smith stated the following: (1) Only when a man is free to operate his
19 business in the way that brings him the most profit can a healthy economy be
20 achieved. (2) By acting in his ownself-interest— by trying to achieve a
21 maximum of profit— the businessman benefits the entire community, for his
22 actions lead to increased production, distribution, and consumption of goods.
23 (3) The government harms business and the community when it interferes with
24 the activities of businessmen. (4) The duty of government is to maintain peace
25 and order within the community and not to meddle with the affairs of business.

British liberals supported a laissez-faire form of government.

This idea was developed by Adam Smith in The Wealth of Nations written in 1776.

Questions directly following the text check your comprehension of what you have just read. Questions are of two types: true/false and short answer. Write your answers on a separate sheet of paper. The page number and text line supplied after each question give you a quick reference to check your answer.

Figure 5.8 Sample textbook passage with imbedded aids

Reader Helper Notes: stimulate you to think beyond the basic information covered in the text. Notes at the end of the chapter (pages 32-34) provide additional information and suggest possible answers to the questions raised.

To Think About: are questions which have no correct answer. They are intended to raise broad generalizations or to provide topics for discussion and debate.

Mini Notes: provide enrichment information related to the text.

Occasionally a word is missing from the text. You should be able to fill in the missing word with little trouble. Failure to do so may mean your attention is drifting. The correct word can be found in the lower left-hand margin.

Was the liberal idea of laissez faire limited to business? See reader helper Note 78.

TO THINK ABOUT
What possible connections can you see between the growth of liberal thinking in Britain and the success of the American Revolution?

MINI NOTE
Adam Smith and T. R. Malthus each had the ability to see things differently from others around them. This is called divergent thinking.

(3) laissez faire

The supporters of ________ insisted that poverty is natural. Since some are meant to be wealthy and some poor, government can do nothing about poverty. Any governmental reforms might hurt business and make things worse.

Malthus blames poverty on overpopulation. Another English thinker who helped shape the liberal attitude in the early days of the industrial revolution was T. A. Malthus. In his Essay on the Principle of Population (1789), Malthus declared that the population always increases faster than the food supply. As a result mankind is always threatened with starvation. The real cause of poverty, according to Malthus, is overpopulation. Until the poor learn to keep down the size of their families, poverty will never be eliminated, Malthus concludes:

When the wages of labor are hardly sufficient to maintain two children, a man marries and has five or six. He, of course, finds himself miserably distressed. . . He accuses the greed of the rich. . .He accuses the [prejudiced] and unjust institutions of society. . . The last person that he would think of accusing is himself.

Malthus had also argued that as the population increases, the supply of workers becomes greater than the demand. This leads to unemployment, low wages and perpetual poverty. For Malthus lowering the birth rate was the only effective way to combat poverty.

In effect Malthus was saying that, since the misery of the worker is his own doing, no law passed by the state can eliminate poverty. Factory owners were delighted with Malthus' view. It soothed their consciences to be told that they were not responsible for the suffering of workers.

Democratic liberals propose reform legislation. The problems of the working class persisted. Convinced that a laissez-faire policy was not acceptable, a growing number of liberals in England and elsewhere urged the government to introduce reforms to aid the working man. They wanted legislation that would improve conditions of work in the factory, allow the growth of labor unions, eliminate property requirements for voting, and increase educational opportunities for the poor. Whereas the older liberals

Another idea popular with British liberals came from T. R. Malthus in Essay on the Principle of Population (1798).

Malthus said excessive population growth was the real cause of poverty, not greedy business practices.

Figure 5.8 *(continued)*

1. Introductory
2. Definition
3. Transitional
4. Illustrative
5. Summary
6. Main ideas supported by details or examples
7. Chronological order
8. Comparison/contrast
9. Cause and effect
10. Problem/solution
11. Descriptive
12. Narrative

Figure 5.9 Paragraph patterns

of writing would result in improved comprehension. Those who interpret the research in this way propose that recognizing the form and format of a communication are integral parts of understanding its message. However, a study of the views of reading specialists had them ranking text structure instruction 14th of 23 teaching practices for comprehension improvement (Gee & Rakow, 1987), a very lukewarm level of support. Recent research in related fields, such as grammar and phonics, has concluded that elaborate instruction in classification schemes is not only unnecessary but potentially counterproductive. The reason is simple: In human learning, applications generally are acquired *before* rules. In short, when students are taught to read for meaning, their awareness of text structure increases, but when they are taught to identify text structures, comprehension growth does not follow to the same extent. That said, there is a difference between belabored isolated instruction in any system of rules and incidental teaching of these rules as they apply in a given meaningful context. Teachers of beginning reading should know phonics rules; all teachers should know something of English grammar; and all teachers should know something of the basic paragraph patterns that lend both variety and predictability to written language.

▶ CONCEPT SUMMARY

Effective readers understand that study reading must be undertaken in a different manner than easy reading. When study reading, they use metacognitive monitoring strategies continuously, and when they sense a weakening of comprehension, they draw on a variety of fix-up strategies. Teachers cannot observe what students "do" as they read silently, but they can provide guidance to help students build good study-reading habits. Techniques like Strategic Guiding Questions, About-Point,

Comprehension Monitoring, and K-W-L Plus teach students to pause regularly while reading to raise questions that prompt them to clarify and fix-up understanding. Teacher-prepared Reading Guides, such as Three-Level Guides, Process Guides, and Nonlinear Guides, are another means of modeling "during reading" strategies. Frequent use of Cooperative Structures such as Paired Reading to implement these Guided Silent Reading approaches greatly increases the number of times students see and hear these strategies used by peers, as well as the number of opportunities to try them out and become comfortable with using them themselves. Research also supports the effectiveness of various types of comprehension aids that can be built directly into text. Historically, these have been costly to create and produce, but rapidly developing technologies such as hypertext are making electronic comprehension instruction increasingly feasible.

CHAPTER 6

BEYOND—METHODS FOR POSTREADING SCHEMA BUILDING

Great discoveries and improvements invariably involve the cooperation of many minds.

—Alexander Graham Bell

Successful Silent Reading sets the stage for reflective verifying, clarifying, exploring, and elaborating on the information and ideas encountered in print. Teachers can help students develop active Postreading habits in a variety of ways. Traditional class "discussion" is probably the most familiar way, but orchestrating a "good" discussion—one with high participation and that rises above factual recitation—is an acquired skill. Discussion, by nature, is an unpredictable and sometimes unwieldy event. It depends on the group's willingness to pursue unplanned avenues of thought and the leader's accompanying ability to bring those avenues together toward some meaningful hub of conclusions and insights. This chapter begins with an analysis of discussion and then lays out a variety of whole class and small group methods that can help both students and teachers increase their competence and grace in this artful and sometimes elusive form of interacting, reflecting and transforming.

▶ CLASS DISCUSSION: WHAT IT IS AND HOW TO GET THERE

In Postreading, prior knowledge is combined with recently encountered information and transformed into usable new knowledge and opened thoughts that are likely to allow the process to continue in students' minds and in class. The Postreading, or *Beyond*, step of the Framework for Text-Based Instruction is the point at which teachers help students (1) check basic comprehension, (2) develop concepts, (3) connect new ideas with existing schema, and/or (4) identify misconceptions to restructure existing schema. The most familiar means of doing this is through teacher- directed class discussion. You can probably recall class discussions that helped you see an idea more clearly or caused you to look at something in a different way or perhaps even transformed your entire outlook on a topic. There is little done in school that is quite as "mind moving" as a good discussion, but there also is little that can be quite as numbing as a really dull one. Good, revelationary discussions are always going to be few and far between. Think how few you have heard on television or even on radio discussion programs. This is because conducting a memorable discussion is more like leading an improvisational music group than it is like conducting an orchestra that has great music on a stand. Of course, even improvisation only *appears* to be unplanned. Much unseen work has gone into "jamming." Keeping this in mind, let's take a closer look at some of the elements of an effective teacher-led class discussion. In this analysis, it becomes evident that teacher-directed discussion is more a culminating achievement than an inspirational moment.

Analysis of a Memorable Class Discussion

In a memorable class discussion, the teacher takes and releases control through several classical moves that are rooted in cognitive and social psychology—that is, in the way the mind works in learning and the way people feel while they are learning and thinking out loud. Here is a quick summary of this byplay.

- The teacher usually begins by asking questions to determine whether students have basic comprehension of the topic.
- The teacher maintains a low-risk environment by rephrasing questions that students cannot answer and through skillful handling of students' incorrect responses.
- The teacher uses various strategies to ensure that most students are engaged and following the discussion most of the time.

- Once it appears that most students have a basic understanding of the information, the teacher's questions become less literal and more conjectural. It is the degree to which these questions are compelling and evocative that moves the interaction to the next levels.
- At some point, the lines of communication shift from the pattern of teacher asks/student answers to a much looser pattern resembling informal conversations. Students interact with each other as well as with the teacher.
- Different points of view are welcomed, but there is a soft press to keep them relevant.
- Responses are longer and more elaborate than in recitation.
- The teacher encourages students to explore different avenues of thought but again tries to ensure that the discussion does not wander too far astray of intended educational objectives.
- As conflicting perspectives emerge, a dynamic tension is created within as well as among individuals.
- Discussants, including the teacher, are expected to be willing to change their minds or be transformed in response to points made.
- Passions are allowed to find expression, but incivility is not permitted.

Good class discussion tends to externalize the thinking strategies that characterize the internal conversations of effective learners of a given subject area. Students hear and find themselves trying out new ways of questioning and commenting that they ideally will internalize and independently employ (Calfee, Dunlop, & Wat, 1994; Tharp & Gallimore, 1989). This is more likely to happen in classrooms with rapport among students and between student and teacher. And to be realistic, just one constitutionally grouchy or conflicting-agenda student can be disquieting and disruptive . . . which is one of the reasons why teachers shy away from this format.

Clearly, leading a "common" class discussion is a worthy goal but an uncommonly difficult one to achieve. Consider now some of the guidelines and methods for providing quality discussion and a developmental plan for achieving greater mastery of these as a teacher.

A Developmental Plan for Fruitful Class Discussion

Following is a sequence of guidelines for emphasis and practice as you plan and implement Postreading instruction.

- Begin on safe ground with conventional recitation-based approaches. Students have all done this before and will recognize the drill.
- When you anticipate that students will *not* need a great deal of review of literal meaning after reading, use teacher-directed recitation, taking these opportunities to practice pacing, questioning techniques, and tactful handling of incorrect responses.

- When you expect a greater need for basic understanding, heighten the impact of recitation-based activities by implementing them through cooperative structures in which more students are more actively involved more of the time.
- Use writing-based methods to engage students in reflective thinking, building schema connections, and self-evaluation.
- Use cooperative structures to engage students in activities that raise higher-order comprehension and build students' confidence in offering and accepting constructive criticism.
- Teach students explicit listening strategies, including the subtle nonverbal signals that indicate listening involvement (Barton, 1995).
- Use teacher-directed class discussion sparingly at first, selecting topics and crafting questions that are likely to engage student interest and lead to lively interactions.
- Use known and tested methods and strategies designed to teach students *how* to engage in "instructional conversation" discussion.
- Alter the class discussion routine occasionally, using the guidelines for a Socratic Seminar (described later in this chapter).

▶ TEACHER-DIRECTED RECITATION FOR CHECKING COMPREHENSION

Traditional teacher-directed recitation, or old-fashioned drill, has gone from being overvalued and overused to being undervalued and occasionally derided. Some educators believe that Postreading drill should not be thought of as teaching at all but simply as another form of testing (Durkin, 1978–1979). We respectfully disagree. Simple literal-level questioning following reading is a reasonable way to reinforce and model several essential elements of effective reading, most particularly the following:

- The need to quickly check basic comprehension of what has just been read.
- The specific *kinds* of recitation questions that are useful for a given type of material.

Haven (1999) describes the importance of Postreading recitation even as it applies to reading fiction:

> The heart of student learning comes after the story is over and they have a chance to review and assess why the story was structured as it was and how the story achieved its effect. Before real analytical work can begin, however, it is important to cement each student's experience and version of the story in his head. Once they take full ownership of their images and interpretation of the story, evaluation and dissection of the story and of the associated writing techniques will be easier and more beneficial. (p. 12)

With nonfiction, there is even less room for variance in basic comprehension. After reading a nonfiction selection, it is not "each reader's experience and version of the story" that must be fixed in mind, but the basic facts and information the author has presented. This does not exclude challenges to material presented, but it does presuppose a certain amount of clarity of understanding of what has been presented.

Implementation Tips for Teacher-Directed Postreading Recitation

Postreading recitation as defined here, consists of three general types of literal-level questions: *recognition*, *recall*, and *translation*. Recognition questions require *finding* information; recall questions require *remembering* information; and translation questions require *paraphrasing*, or putting the new information into one's own words. When recitation is used as a Postreading comprehension check, it typically is not an end unto itself but a bridge to further, less fact-based explorations, reflections and applications of the new information.

There are several variations on the basic teacher-led recitation routine. Here are a few reminders for conducting this segment of Postreading in the most effective way:

1. *Help students differentiate recitation from discussion* by telling them that the object of the recitation is to check and encourage their basic understanding.
2. *Keep it short.* About 10 to 12 minutes is a good rule of thumb for most classes.
3. *Keep it moving.* The point is to review the facts, not to overly elaborate on them.
4. *Don't forget "wait time."* Students need to process the question and formulate a response; yet, the typical "wait time" is one second or less (Rowe, 1974, 1986). Try counting to 5 after asking a fact question, and to 10 after a translation question.
5. *Watch whom you call on.* Try to call on all students as equally as possible.
6. *Model active listening.* Modeling effective listening for your students goes a long way toward teaching them to listen to one another. Barton (1995) suggests these techniques for doing so: move toward students as they speak, occasionally write students' ideas on the board in their own words, and return to something someone said earlier.
7. *Avoid using recitation as punishment.* Rather than calling on students who clearly are unprepared or not attending, try calling on them to answer a question you're fairly sure they can answer. This will have the effect of pulling them in rather than pushing them out.
8. *Try versions of "Every Pupil Responds."* For example, ask yes/no questions to which, at a given signal, all students respond with thumbs up or thumbs down.

9. *Don't forget verification-level recitation.* Ask students to find and point to the place in the text that answers the question raised. Try using a timer; students like to race the clock.
10. *Don't forget translation (including vocabulary).* Read aloud a short section, phrase, or key term, and ask students to put it into their own words.
11. *Try open-ended recitation.* Following reading, call on a student to tell any *one* thing he or she remembers from what was read. Continue to call on students to offer information, in any sequence, but without repeating any item previously stated. A variation is to permit the student who offers an item to call on another student to offer the next item. This begins to build the habit of intrastudent interaction that will support discussion.

Teachers can use these recitation routines to build their own expertise in two important elements of group leadership: modeling listening behaviors and handling incorrect responses to questions. Think of different ways to say, "Sorry, that is incorrect." You will need all of them. Compare them to suggestions you will find in the next section.

Handling Incorrect Responses in Teacher-Led Recitation

Given that one of the primary purposes of recitation is to get things straight, it does present some nagging social problems in how to handle incorrect responses. There are several research-based means of turning incorrect answers into positive learning experiences (Collins, 1987; Rakes & Smith, 1987). You probably use or would use several of these techniques intuitively, but it is good to have your intuition validated when teaching is your profession.

1. *Think again.* The most common reason for an incorrect answer is a too-hasty or impulsive response. If you think this might be the case, simply ask the student to think again. Keep in mind that those moments between the time that the question is asked and an answer is given may be the most instructionally valuable time in the school day. These are the moments in which the students are engaged in active thinking, self-talk, and rehearsal for their public response.
2. *Give a prompt.* When a student gives an incomplete answer or needs you to provide more structure, offer a small piece of information—for example, "The person whose name we are looking for also died prematurely in a duel with Aaron Burr."
3. *Differential reinforcement.* Tell which part of the answer was correct: "You're right, bears are mammals. Do you recall whether mammals are warm blooded? Are human beings warm blooded?"
4. *Rephrase the question.* If no one seems to know the answer yet you think that they have learned the information, change the wording of the question: "When you go west, do you gain or lose time?" "Well, is it earlier on the East coast or the West coast?"

5. *Provide help but make students accountable.* If a student gives two incorrect answers to the same question or if two students answer incorrectly, give the answer and tell them they will need to remember it. Return to the student(s) again before the period is over, and ask the same question, "Now, before you go, who can tell me again one state that borders New Hampshire?"
6. *Permit clues.* Ask fellow students to give clues, or ask the student who missed the question to call on a classmate to help by giving either a clue or the answer, "Charlie, who would you like to ask for help in naming the other three Great Lakes?"
7. *Incorrect "if" statements.* If you recognize why the answer was wrong, supply the question for which the answer would have been correct. For example, if you asked, "What is the capital of New Zealand?" and the student answered "Canberra," you could respond, "Canberra would be the answer if someone asked what the capital of Australia was. How about the capital of New Zealand?"
8. *Examples of possibilities.* If students are drawing a blank, translate the question into a multiple-choice format: "Who was the first European to see the Pacific Ocean? Balboa, Cortez, or Cabeza de Vaca?"
9. *Nonexamples or opposites.* When students have difficulty answering, tell them what the answer is not: "Which country in South America has the oldest tradition of democracy?" "The answer is not Brazil or Chile."

Teacher-led recitation can raise attention and engagement and lay the foundation for further, more reflective discussion. This is no small accomplishment, since one of the biggest problems in any group discussion, at any level, is just getting everyone on the same page.

PEER RECITATION FOR INCREASED STUDENT INVOLVEMENT

To get more students more actively involved in checking their basic understanding of what they have read, it helps to add a certain measure of peer involvement. Several means of structuring these interactions are described here. These methods tend to support the important element of quality teaching that has been previously referred to as "fading," or withdrawing ancillary assistance so that students may assume more responsibility for guiding their own learning.

Recitation Led by Home Groups

Have "home groups" of four students each take turns leading Postreading recitation sessions, using structures such as the following:

- *Five-question format:* A team leads the class in filling out a "who, what, when, where, why" outline.

- *Peer questioning and the BUZZER!:* One team, designated as the answer team, tries to learn everything it can on a given section of text. The class then questions the answer team, and team members try to answer as best as they can, with a short time limit for conferring when necessary. For fun, a beeper or buzzer can be added. We observed one eighth-grade science teacher who gave the questioning group a child's toy that made a deep buzzing sound when a button was pushed. The class used it to signal a wrong answer. No one seemed disturbed by the competition, and several otherwise low-participating students were quite caught up in the "in-your-face" humor that young teens seem to enjoy.
- *Written questions:* Everyone prepares a few questions on the material. Going around the room in a certain order—up and down rows or across aisles—students read one of their questions that has not been asked and call on a volunteer to answer. The teacher might collect the questions and use some on a future test. This enhances students' motivation to write good questions and to listen carefully to the answers.
- *Have student groups work together to complete a graphic organizer,* on a large sheet of newsprint (or using a desktop computer, PDA, Tablet PC, or other such technology when available), based on the text material. This may be the final version of a graphic organizer generated as a Prereading activity and filled in individually by students as they read. Groups may be encouraged to use design elements that represent the content, or other creative twists. When finished, each group presents and explains its graphic organizer to the class.
- *Numbered Heads Together* (Kagan, 1994*): Have students number off within groups. The teacher asks a recitation-type question, and each group briefly confers to agree upon its answer. The teacher calls a number at random (1–4), and the student with that number in each group stands. The teacher calls on one of these students to answer, then asks the other standing students if they agree, students sit and the next question is asked.
- *Find the Fiction* (Kagan, 1994*): Seated in groups of four, students work individually at first to write three statements: two true statements, based on the reading, and one false or fiction. Within groups, students take turns reading their three statements and challenging their partners to "Find the Fiction." Optionally, each group may be asked to select the best set of its statements to challenge the rest of the class.
- *Act it out* (Haven, 1999): Developed by Kendall Haven for fiction and some nonfiction, this structure assigns a team to act out the story for the class. One team member tells the story as the other three enact each story element, providing sound effects, actions, and setting elements. Following the

*Adapted with peremission from Kagan Publishing. Kagan, Spencer. Cooperative Learning. 1 (800) 933-2667 EUR www.KaganOnline.com

group's presentation, discuss whether the enactment helped students picture scenes, events, and characters better, and whether it changed their first impressions of the story in any way.

Jigsaw

One of the most well-known cooperative learning activities, the Jigsaw approach (Aaronson, Blaney, Sikes, Stevan, & Snapp, 1975; Aaronson, Stephan, Sikes, Blaney, & Snapp, 1978) is particularly useful for Postreading recitation.

Steps in the Jigsaw Approach

Step 1. Divide a reading assignment into four numbered sections.

Step 2. Set up four-student groups, have students number off, one to four, and distribute the four-part reading assignment. Each group has the entire reading assignment, with each student having a different one of the four sections.

Step 3. Give students time to read their sections silently.

Step 4. Have all students who read the first section of the reading (one student from each group) meet in one corner of the room, all who read the second section meet in another corner, third section in another, fourth in another. In these groups, they are to check their recall and understanding of what they read, so they will be prepared to share it with their home group members. Depending on the nature of the reading selection, you may wish to have a worksheet for students to complete in these section groups.

Step 5. Students return to their four-member home groups and share, in order, the important information from their sections of the reading.

This method is especially useful for bridging to further analyses or applications in another cooperative group structure, since students already are in groups and each group member is an expert on some portion of the material.

Paired Recitation

Another popular approach to structuring peer recitation is to have students work in pairs. Kendall Haven (1999) suggests three "verbal-reprocessing activities" for fiction; these are reworded as follows to extend their usefulness to nonfiction material.

Steps in Paired Recitation

Step 1. Allow each student about one minute to tell their partner about what went through their mind while they read the assignment. What they were thinking about and picturing while reading? Hold a general class discussion in which students share with the class what they told to their partner (or each student summarizes what his or her partner said). Show students that most of their comments fall into the following three categories:

1. Evaluation of the reading assignment (form, content, style, etc.)
2. Comparison of the information to other versions
3. Relating the information to their own life and experience

Step 2. Give students about a minute to draw a quick sketch of the main point of the reading assignment. The time limit means that students can't worry about the quality of their drawing. Have student pairs compare and choose one of their drawings to share with the class. In the general discussion, help students categorize the text elements represented in their drawings.

Step 3. Have each student pair retell the information in the reading assignment. One student begins and speaks for 30 seconds. The other student continues for the next 30 seconds, then the first takes over again, and so forth. The teacher times the tellings and calls "Switch!" at 30-second intervals. If students can't remember what comes next, they are not excused from telling. Instead of moving forward, they repeat the last information told by their partner during their 30 seconds. If students are truly stuck, they can ask their partner for a hint. However, it is recommended that this be discouraged. Part of the value of this exercise is for each student to remember and claim his or her own version of the material.

▶ BRIDGING TO REFLECTIVE DISCUSSION AND APPLICATIONS

Examples of techniques and methods in this section are based on the short article, "Pollution of the Caesars," found in Figure 6.1. Take a moment now to read it, then study the original Guided Reading Procedure.

Guided Reading Procedure

The Guided Reading Procedure (GRP) (Manzo, 1975) is a highly structured method that begins with basic Postreading recitation and concludes with a test designed to convince students that they can read with much greater comprehension than they may have thought themselves capable of. This can be a transformative experience with a considerable impact on metacognitive monitoring and an increased feeling of empowerment and self-regulation. It teaches students how to harness their own will and self-determination to instantly improve comprehension. In the course of the GRP lesson, students retrace and restructure a reading assignment in several ways, thus providing a great deal of support for understanding, organizing, and recalling the information. See Figure 6.2 for an example of a GRP lesson.

The ancient Romans, for all their knowledge, didn't know that lead was poisonous. They used it to preserve food and to halt the fermentation of wines. Lead glazes coated drinking vessels and cookware. Some historians have speculated that the brain-damaging effects of lead poisoning contributed to Rome's downfall. Rome's leaden legacy survives in pottery, pipes, and other artifacts. It also survives, a physicist has now found, in Greenland's ice sheet. Kevin Rosman of the Curtin University of Technology in Perth, Australia, has detected traces of lead in Greenland's ice, evidence of large-scale pollution of Earth's atmosphere two millennia ago. And some 70 percent of that pollution can be pinned to Roman mining in one region: Rio Tinto in southwestern Spain.

Rosman wanted to trace the source of the lead found in a Greenland ice core studied by two of his colleagues. The lead concentrations in that 3,300-yard ice core peaked between 150 B.C. and A.D. 50. This matched historical records of Roman mining activity at Rio Tinto. Lead pollution levels during the Roman era were about four times greater than natural background levels of lead but were still low by modern standards. Between the 1930s and 1970s, the lead concentration in the ice was 25 to 50 times higher than during Roman times, due in large part to leaded gasoline.

Rosman was able to trace the Greenland lead to the Spanish mine because of the unique ratios of lead isotopes in the Rio Tinto ore. Lead and its isotopes form over billions of years from the decay of uranium and thorium. The ratio of two isotopes in particular—of lead 206 to lead 207—generally increases in crustal rocks over time. (The numbers refer to the total of protons and neutrons in lead nuclei.)

Unlike lead in crustal rocks, lead at Rio Tinto was trapped in a vein of silver ore and was isolated from uranium and thorium. So Rio Tinto's lead still has the lower ratio of lead 206 to 207 that it had when it became trapped in the ore billions of years ago. When Rosman found this low ratio in pieces of the Greenland ice sample dating from 600 B.C. to A.D. 300, he consulted historical records to determine which mines were active during ancient times and compared lead isotope fingerprints taken from them in recent years to isotope ratios from the Greenland core. Rio Tinto captured much of the blame.

"Greenland is quite a way from Spain, so the lead that went into the atmosphere affected the entire Northern Hemisphere," Rosman says. He also notes that hard scientific facts show the history books were right. "It's a beautiful example of the application of science using sophisticated instruments to really understand the past."

Figure 6.1 Sample reading selection: "Pollution of the Caesars" (*Discover*, March 1998, 19:3)

Source: Jessica Gorman © 1998. Reprinted with permission of *Discover Magazine.*

1. **Preparation**

   "Pollution of the Caesars" is used in a ninth-grade Physical Science class. Before the lesson, the teacher prepares the following test items:

   What is the effect of lead poisoning? (brain damage)

   Why have historians thought that lead poisoning was one of the reasons for the downfall of the Roman Empire? (evidence of lead in pottery they ate and drank from)

   Where was the Roman lead mine? (Rio Tinto, Spain)

   Where did Rosman find evidence of pollution from the Roman lead mine? (in the ice in Greenland)

   How did the Roman lead get to the place where Rosman found it? (in the air, as pollution)

   How did Rosman know the lead he found in the ancient ice was from the Roman mine? (it had a different chemical structure from most lead)

   Which two lead isotopes were compared to determine the type of lead Rosman found? (206 and 207)

   Which lead isotope is present in a higher proportion in most lead? (206)

   Why was the Roman lead different? (it had been trapped in a silver vein and not exposed to uranium and thorium)

   What was part of the cause of the lead pollution Rosman found in the ice dating from 1930–1970? (leaded gasoline)

2. **Purpose for Reading**

   A. "Read this article to find out how one scientist has used chemistry to find out about air pollution in ancient times."

   B. "Try to remember all that you can about this selection. You have 10 minutes to read, and then I'll ask you to turn your papers over and tell me everything you remember, so I can write it on the board."

3. **Recitation and Recalling (Following 15 Minutes of Silent Reading)**

   Teacher: Who can tell me one thing you read about?
   Student: A scientist found lead from a Roman mine in the ice in Greenland.
   Student: It's called "Pollution of the Caesars."
   Student: The lead mining in Rome caused major pollution.
   Student: No, the lead mine was in Spain.

   [Teacher records the information on the board or overhead and places a question mark above the words "in Rome."]

Figure 6.2 Guided reading procedure: sample dialogue

Student: The Romans used lead in the dishes they ate from.
Student: And drank from.
Student: The lead from the Roman mine had different kinds of isotopes.
Student: Not different ones, different amounts of them.
[Teacher places a question mark above the words "different kinds."]
Student: The lead he found was different because it came out of a vein of silver and didn't get exposed to the air.
Student: It had different amounts of the isotopes 206 and 207.
Student: They think lead makes you brain damaged.
Student: They know it does.
[Teacher places a question mark above the words "they think."]

[Interaction continues; teacher records information on board, putting question marks beside any items that are challenged.]

4. Self-Monitoring/Self-Correcting (Sample Student Responses)

Teacher: You remembered a lot. Now turn your papers over and reread the article to see if we need to change or add anything to what we have on the board.
Student: The mine was in Rio Tinto, Spain.
Student: The lead had the same isotopes, but more of the 206 than 207.
Student: Lead poisoning does cause brain damage, and more people than the Romans must have had it because the lead was in the air all the way to Greenland.
Student: We said what made the lead different was it wasn't exposed to the air, but this says it wasn't exposed to uranium and thorium.

[Interaction continues, with the teacher noting corrections and additions on the board.]

5. Restructuring

Teacher: Turn your papers face down again and let's organize our information into an outline. Take out a sheet of paper, and copy this down the way we reorganize it, so you'll have it for your notebooks. We have about 10 minutes to get this all down, and then I have a short test for you. Now, what would be a good title?
Student: It's called "Pollution of the Caesars." Maybe it should be called "Rosman Rats Out the Romans."
Teacher: Okay, that will be easy to remember; now, what's the first thing the author talks about?
Student: How they think lead poisoning made the Romans brain damaged.

Figure 6.2 *(continued)*

Teacher: Okay, the first topic will be "Lead poisoning in ancient Rome caused brain damage." Will that work?

Student: Then under that, they got it from their dishes.

Student: And it caused the downfall of the Empire.

[Teacher records the outline on the board:]

<u>*Rosman Rats Out the Romans*</u>

I. Lead poisoning in ancient Rome caused brain damage

A. Source

1. dishes

2. ?

[Teacher continues recording the outline for students to copy, leaving space where information or topics are missing.]

6. Teacher-Guided Correcting and Completing

Teacher: Turn your papers face up now, and reread quickly for the information that we are still missing, and let's fill it in.

[Teacher completes outline on board from students' contributions]

7. Evaluation

Teacher: Put away the articles and your notes, now, and I will pass out the test.

[Students complete the test.]

8. Introspection

Teacher: What did you learn from this lesson about how to "read smarter"?

Student: I remembered a lot more than the first time we did this, just by really trying to concentrate and remember.

Student: I still missed a lot the first time I read it, but then I knew what to look for the next time we got to look at it.

Student: Rereading and focusing really helps. I got 100% this time. I had only 40% the first time.

9. Optional Study Step (one week later)

Teacher: Today we're going to see how we are progressing in developing effective study habits. Take out your notes on *Rosman Rats Out the Romans,* and use the next five minutes to study them. Then I will put some questions on the board on that topic, and let's see how well you do. After our little quiz, we'll discuss how you studied and how to "study smarter."

Figure 6.2 *(continued)*

Steps in the Guided Reading Procedure

Step 1. *Preparation.* Select a reading assignment that is fairly short but information rich. Prepare a short-answer test of 10 to 20 items on the reading assignment. (As the lesson proceeds, make sure that the test items are given fair coverage.)

Step 2. *Purpose for reading.* Give the topic of the reading assignment, a brief purpose for reading, and tell students to read to remember *everything they can* about the reading assignment. Tell students that as soon as they have finished reading, you will write everything they remember on the board (or overhead, whiteboard, or SmartBoard). Tell them that if they finish reading early, they should reread to identify the most important information in the selection.

Step 3. *Reading and recalling.* Give students 10 to 15 minutes to complete their Silent Reading, and then ask them to tell anything they remember, without looking back at the reading selection. Record all information on the board in the order given. If students question the accuracy of anything that is offered, simply record the information, and place a question mark beside it.

Step 4. *Self-monitoring/self-correcting.* Instruct students to go back to the reading selection to correct any inconsistencies that arose in their attempts to recollect and/or to add information previously overlooked. Record all changes and/or additions on the board, overhead, or computer display.

Step 5. *Restructuring.* Guide students in organizing the information from the board into outline form to be recorded in their notebooks, again without referring back to the reading selection. The outline can be as simple or elaborate as age and grade level permit. Use nonspecific questions, such as "What was discussed first?" "What was brought up next?" and "What seems to be the main idea?" Avoid overly specific and leading questions.

Step 6. *Teacher monitoring and correcting.* If students appear to have overlooked any critical ideas or inappropriately equated them with other ideas, raise guiding questions about these points, such as "What do you suppose is the most important of these five points made by the author?" and "How does this information relate to what we studied last week?"

Step 7. *Evaluation.* Give the test prepared in Step 1. A score of 70% to 80% should be required to pass the test.

Step 8. *Introspection.* After the test, ask students whether they have learned anything about their own learning as a result of the GRP experience. *The point to be made is that accuracy in comprehension and recall can be greatly improved by an act of will.*

Step 9. *Optional study step.* Several days later, give a second test on the same material. Give students a few minutes before the test to review material from their notes.

Implementation Tips for the Guided Reading Procedure

1. In a typical GRP lesson, students may say little or nothing on the first invitation to recall and recite what they have read. As teachers, we tend to have great difficulty with silence. If you can force yourself to wait silently for a few (seemingly interminable) seconds, the flow of language and thought will begin. The first few, hesitant student responses will spark other recollections, which will lead to other connections, suggested corrections, and associations. This spiraling effect tends to draw in even the most reticent students. See the sample dialogue in Figure 6.2 for examples of this.
2. When writing on the board, take the opportunity to model good notetaking. Write as quickly as you can, and use as many logical abbreviations as you can. If you write slowly and painstakingly, the lesson loses its focus: While you're writing, students are forgetting. Depending on the age and level of the class, consider selecting one or two reliable students to do the writing in the first part of the lesson.

Efficacy of the Guided Reading Procedure

The GRP has been studied by several researchers and has collected strong empirical validation (Ankney & McClurg, 1981; Bean & Pardi, 1979). Its effectiveness has been most clearly demonstrated at upper elementary and middle school levels with science and social studies material. It also has been shown to be an effective way to improve active listening (Cunningham, Moore, Cunningham, & Moore, 1983) and a particularly effective method for adolescents students with special needs (Alley & Deshler, 1980; Maring & Furman, 1985).

Note Cue

Note Cue (Manzo & Manzo, 1987, 1990b) is another highly structured method to scaffold students' participation in a focused class discussion. It helps to *get* discussion going, *keep* it going, and keep it *on target.* It builds the behavioral and social learnings that come from actually doing something. More specifically, it teaches students to *ask* questions and, more important, to confidently *comment* on the text as well as simply *answering* questions. It does this by relieving students of the complex burden of having to think about what to say and how to say it, leaving them only to think about *when* to say it.

Note Cue, as its name suggests, provides *cues* to students, in the form of written *notes,* that guide them through participation in a *model* discussion—model because it is prescripted by the teacher. Initially, almost the entire discussion is prescripted. Enactment of these *early* Note Cue discussions is a form of *strategic parroting* in which students are paradoxically expected to participate with relatively little thinking. The potential value of strategic parroting was discovered separately by two sets of researchers working with reluctant learners (Manzo & Legenza, 1975; Palincsar & Brown, 1984). This opportunity for class participation through simple parroting provides a form of instructional scaffolding that can gradually be removed as students begin to internalize the many complex aspects of effective classroom discussion. As you read about Note Cue, notice its particular suitability for use with ELL (English Language Learners) students and others who may have underexposure to typical English sociocultural and language conventions. Note Cue is to discussion as T-ball is to baseball: Most everyone gets a hit, and some for the first time.

Steps in Note Cue Postreading Discussion

Preparation. Prepare a set of cue cards for discussion of the material. These should be prepared as follows:

- Write several questions on 3 × 5-inch index cards (one question per card), based on information from the reading selection. Include questions that go beyond the facts, such as translation, interpretation, inference, evaluation, and application questions.
- Write complete but brief answers to each question on *separate* cards (one answer per card). When writing answer cards, use complete sentences that include enough context to make it clear what question it answers (see sample provided).
- Write several comment cards (one comment per card)—relevant thoughts that might be sparked by the reading selection.
- Label each card at the top as appropriate: Question, Answer, or Comment.

Sample Note Cue cards for Postreading discussion.

Question	**Answer**	**Comment**
How did the lead from the Roman mine get to Greenland?	The lead from the Roman mine got to Greenland by getting into the air, as pollution.	I wonder what kind of brain damage lead poisoning causes.

Step 1. After students have read, the teacher places one or more of the prepared *Prereading* cards on each student's desk. *A few students may be given blank cards.*

Step 2. Students are instructed to read the card(s) they have been given and think about *when* they should read it (them) during the discussion; *students with blank cards are instructed to try to think of their own question or comment* related to the material they are surveying, and write it on the blank card.

Step 3. The teacher begins the discussion by asking who has a question or comment card to read that seems to be a good place to begin the discussion.

If a question is read, the teacher asks who has an answer that seems to fit it. This process continues until most or all students have had a chance to participate. At this point, the teacher should ask, "Who has other personal reactions or comments?" This last question is intended to encourage personal-evaluative thinking and responding apart from the statements on the cards but modeled after them in terms of relevance to the topic.

Step 4. (Optional) Within the same or the next class period, give a test of 5 to 10 questions that require brief written responses. Questions should be taken directly from the Note Cue cards and relevant comments made during the discussion. This builds appreciation of the value of reading one's card so that all might hear and learn, as well as respect for independent commenting.

Fading. As a group of students becomes familiar with Note Cue (as they quickly do), subsequent lessons should include *fewer teacher-prepared cards* and *more blank cards* for students to generate their own questions, answers, and comments. In this way, responsibility is gradually turned over to students as they become more equal to the expectation.

Implementation Tips for Note Cue Discussions

The Note Cue system can be used to structure Prereading as well as Postreading discussion, guiding students Into and Beyond the reading. For a Prereading discussion, questions should be written that will elicit students' background of information about the topic of the reading selection or that urge predictions that could be made from a quick preview of the selection. Similarly, write comment cards that contain relevant thoughts that might be sparked by previewing the reading selection.

The first author (U. Manzo) piloted Note Cue in an inner-city middle school with low-achieving minority youngsters who had an established pattern of low participation, poor oral reading, and ineffective participation in Pre- and Postreading discussions. Although these early trials of the strategy were not objectively measured, when these students' participation was prompted with Note Cue lessons, their behavior seemed to be more on task for longer periods of time, and their written responses on short tests showed higher levels of comprehension than they typically demonstrated. In a set of field-based studies for Education Specialist Degree projects at the University of Missouri–Kansas City three out of four teachers obtained similar results.

There are some other incidental benefits in using Note Cue. The cards students write offer insight into their thinking. Collections of student cards, and their placement in students' individual portfolios, can offer an overview of student progress in writing and oral communication.

A number of whole-class cooperative structures are useful for achieving optimal student involvement while checking and building on basic comprehension. Four such structures are described next: Inside-Outside Circle, Find Someone

Who, Stroll Pair Share, and Postreading Three-Minute Write. These structures can be implemented in a variety of ways. The descriptions are tailored from Kagan (1994) for use as Postreading recitation techniques.

Inside-Outside Circle*

Steps in the Inside-Outside Circle Cooperative Structure

Step 1. *Preparation.* Write half as many basic comprehension questions on cards as you have students in class (30 students = 15 question cards). The answer should also be included on the card. Opinion and evaluation questions may also be included.

Step 2. Move desks toward the walls to clear a large space in the center of the classroom. Have students count off by twos. Have the ones form a circle in the middle of the room, facing *out.* Have the twos form a circle *outside* the ones, facing *in.* There now should be a double circle, with student pairs facing one another. Students are asked to greet one another by name and shake hands.

Step 3. Distribute question cards to students in the inside circle. The inside student reads the question to his or her outside circle partner. The outside circle student answers, or attempts to answer. If the student cannot answer or gives an incorrect answer, the inside circle partner is to tell him or her the answer.

Step 4. At your signal (a switch of the lights, or a beeper), the outside circle students are to take a step or two to their left, so that they now are with a new partner. They are to shake hands and greet their new partner, who reads them a new question.

Step 5. The outside circle continues to shift to the left until students are back with their original partners. The inside/outside students then trade places, and the question card is traded to the new inside circle person. The new outside circle students take a few steps to the left to greet a new partner and continue until they are again back to their original partners.

Kagan (1994) recommends adding "gambits" to structures such as this. A gambit is a phrase students are instructed to say at a certain point in the interaction. For example, you might tell inside circle students that if their partner answers the question correctly, they are to say, "What a terrific answer!"—and sound like they mean it. Or outside circle students might be instructed that if they have to be given the answer, they are to tell their partner, "I appreciate your help with that!" Gambits sound awkward at first, and students say them jokingly, but don't be surprised to hear them again when you might least expect to, and spoken appropriately and sincerely.

*Adapted with peremission from Kagan Publishing. Kagan, Spencer. Cooperative Learning. 1 (800) 933-2667 EUR www.KaganOnline.com

Find Someone Who*

Steps in the Find Someone Who Cooperative Structure

Step 1. *Preparation:* Prepare any type of worksheet to check students' understanding of a reading assignment. The questions and worksheets in teacher's guides for textbooks are usually perfect for this.

Step 2. Have students clear their desks, keeping out only a pencil. Distribute the worksheets and give students 5 to 10 minutes to complete as much as they can individually (tell them they are not expected to complete the worksheet during this time, but to skim through the questions and answer those that seem "easiest" first).

Step 3. Have students stand, and tell them that they are to take their worksheets and pencils and walk around the classroom without talking until you give a signal. At the signal they are to stop where they are, find a partner, shake hands, greet one another by name, and find the nearest two seats together. They are to compare the information they have written on their worksheets, and each should try to give an answer to the other. They are to write their partner's initials beside information they got from him or her.

Step 4. At your next signal, students are to thank their partner, stand, and mill around again, quietly, until you signal again. They greet a new partner, find seats, and share information again.

Step 5. The milling and pairing continues until most students have completed their worksheets.

Stroll Pair Share*

Steps in the Stroll Pair Share Cooperative Structure

Step 1. *Preparation:* Write several discussion-type questions based on the reading assignment (again, teacher's guides usually provide questions of this type).

Step 2. Clear the outside perimeter of the classroom and have students form a double parade line—each student with a partner, facing forward.

Step 3. At the teacher's signal, students are to begin walking forward, casually, while talking to their partners. Beginning with the person on the inside, they are to tell everything they remember about what they have just read. After about two minutes, the teacher signals for the outside partners to speak. After about two more minutes, the teacher signals for the line to stop, and the inside partners to move up to a new partner in the outside line (the front person on the inside goes to the back).

Step 4. The process continues through several shifts of partners.

*Adapted with peremission from Kagan Publishing. Kagan, Spencer. Cooperative Learning. 1 (800) 933-2667 EUR www.KaganOnline.com

Postreading Three-Minute Write*

Several of the methods and techniques described earlier have included some form of writing. Writing is an especially useful ingredient in Postreading instruction for several reasons:

- It is another way to ensure involvement of more students.
- Writing something down forces it into a linear string of thought—this often helps students see when they may have been fooling themselves into thinking they know something they do not yet know.
- Writing induces a greater sense of agency or ownership and commitment that can be a useful lead-in to lively discussion.

The Postreading Three-Minute Write is a simple way to structure Postreading writing. After students have read, provide them with a prompt for writing about what they have read. The prompt may be as broad as "write everything you remember," or a specific question requiring analysis and/or evaluation. Let them know up front that their writing will not be collected or graded for spelling or other mechanics but that it will be useful to them later in the lesson. Some guidelines for this technique follow:

- It works best when everyone writes at the same time (ideally, including the teacher).
- The only rule is that everyone must be *writing something* for the entire three minutes, even if they are writing "I can't think of anything to write," over and over.

The three-minute write can also be structured as a "write-pair-share," in which, following writing, students are placed in pairs and take turns, within a specific time limit, telling (not reading to) their partner what they have written.

Group Reading Activity—A Cooperative Learning Method with Life Skill Values

The Group Reading Activity (GRA) (Manzo, 1974) predates most other cooperative structures, including the Jigsaw approach. Its goal is to structure Postreading recitation in a way that helps culturally and psychologically diverse students learn to collaboratively *offer and receive constructive criticism.* The GRA meets these fundamental requirements for effective learning as well as merely encouraging greater social interaction. It tends to be quite transformative of student classroom decorum and capacity to work toward common learning goals. It is ideal for today's heterogeneously grouped classrooms that mirror the diversity of the real world. The GRA teaches one of the softer life skill sides of the curriculum—how to critique and be critiqued.

*Adapted with peremission from Kagan Publishing. Kagan, Spencer. Cooperative Learning. 1 (800) 933-2667 EUR www.KaganOnline.com

Steps in the GRA

Step 1. The teacher selects the reading assignment and writes a purpose question on the board.

Step 2. The teacher divides the text into subsections of a few pages each and assigns each subsection to a small group.

Step 3. Students read silently and write their individual responses to the purpose question.

Step 4. Each group is given a worksheet to complete together. The worksheet should contain general, open-ended comprehension-check questions such as the following:

a. What question does this section answer?

b. Write a statement of the main idea(s) of this section. Support it with direct quotes or paraphrased facts and points found in the text.

c. Comment on the quality of the ideas and supporting statements: Do these seem true? Complete? Biased?

d. What other things, ideas, and facts have you learned in the past that seem to relate to what you have read here?

e. Using the information from the worksheet, the group works together to prepare a brief presentation for the rest of the class. Members should choose who should present what information, in what order, and in what way.

Step 5. As each group becomes ready, a student critic chosen by the teacher from one of the other groups is sent to see and hear the group's presentation. The student critic is expected to react with constructive criticism, such as "That sounds fine." "That doesn't seem to make much sense." "Perhaps you should have. . ."

Step 6. The group is given time to revise its presentation, drawing on the feedback provided by the student critic.

Step 7. The teacher consults briefly with each group to review its presentation plan.

Step 8. Presentations are made, and the class and teacher comment and question as relevant. The teacher or a designated student lists important information from each presentation on the board (or overhead, whiteboard, or SmartBoard).

Step 9. Finally, students are directed to "rapid-read" the *entire* reading assignment, watching for main points and important details.

Implementation Notes on the Group Reading Activity

Anecdotal reports (Manzo & Manzo, 1990a) indicate that students involved in the GRA tend to assume required roles in a surprisingly adult manner. Their language, thinking, and even social graces seem to rise to the occasion. Students tend to critique one another in constructive and intelligent ways, probably to reduce the likelihood of being treated sharply when they are critiqued in turn.

FULL CIRCLE TO DISCUSSION

The preceding sections presented a variety of teacher-directed and peer-group approaches to checking basic comprehension after reading. Structured experiences with these approaches help prepare students to participate in more sophisticated forms of classroom discussion. Before turning to the next methods for scaffolding discussion, however, let's further consider some of the ways in which teachers can anticipate and handle student questions, answers, and comments that can lead a discussion off track or otherwise diminish its impact.

Managing Difficult Discussion Situations

There are numerous ways for students to question, answer, and comment during classroom interactions. Some of these are facilitating and productive, and others are quirky and difficult to handle. Some typical problem situations that tend to arise, and some techniques we have seen veteran teachers use to deal with them, are described next. Consider starting a personal journal of "useful verbal protocols" or "things to say when. . ."

Problem: Irrepressible Talker
Students who can't seem to think without talking. They are not really disrespectful but garrulous or irrepressibly talkative. They begin to answer every question whether or not they know the answer.

Remedies

- Avoid eye contact with them.
- Occasionally turn your back to them and ask a question while walking away from them so that they can't quite hear it, thus preventing them from answering before others can.
- Call a name or a row before asking a question.
- Strictly enforce a rule of raising a hand before talking.
- Find a reason to talk about the different ways people think and talk. Be sympathetic, but point out that "compulsive talkers" tend to disrupt the teacher, dissuade others from speaking up, overly dominate a discussion, close out opportunities to listen and learn, appear boorish, and anger others. Stress that this is a problem that can plague a person for the rest of his or her life if not curtailed early.

Problem: "We Just Answered That!"
The student who raises the same question that has been raised and answered.

Remedy

Ask, "Does anyone recognize this question?" If no one responds, you have strong evidence that you need to raise and probably answer the question again. If the question or the answer has more than one part, write out key words on the board.

Problem: Low Talker

The student who characteristically speaks too low to be heard.

Remedy

Begin walking to the other side of the room so that the student must project to you, and in the process speak loudly enough for others to hear.

Problem: Distracting Noise

Disruptive sounds, such as heating or cooling systems, prevent class members from hearing one another.

Remedies

- Have students arrange desks so that they face one another.
- Repeat students' questions and answers (despite the usual prohibition against doing so).
- Explain the problem to the class, and say that you frequently will be calling on someone else to repeat questions and answers to ensure that everyone hears. This also can keep students more alert the first time.

Problem: Nonparticipants

Students who fail to participate in responding to recitation-type questions.

Remedies

- Examine your questions. You might be asking "guess what I'm thinking" questions. All teachers occasionally lapse into this routine.
- Provide more "wait time": Count to five mentally before saying another word, then ask students if they want the question repeated or explained further.

Problem: No Buy-In, Whatsoever

Students who do not pay attention or participate in discussions or other class activities.

Remedies

- Reassess what you are asking students to do. Is it meaningful, clear, and "doable" in the time you are allowing?

- Use a polling technique to warm up your audience and get them involved. The most popular method is to ask questions that require one of two choices, such as those asked in television polls in which one calls a given phone number for each choice. You can also offer more elaborate, content-related choices. Here is an example: "Some people think *The Merchant of Venice* is a put-down of Jews, others think it is a put-down of Christians. Who thinks it is a put-down of Jews? Christians? Who is undecided? Who has no idea? Let's continue to analyze this play and see whether Shakespeare tips his hand one way or the other."

Problem: Irrelevant Questions, Answers, and Comments
The student who asks a question, gives an answer, or makes a comment that is "out in left field."

Remedies

- Simply say, "I don't quite see the relevance of that. Can you explain further?" When such responses clearly are characteristic of a certain student and it is clear to the class that you are not being arbitrary, omit the request for further explanation.
- Ask if another student can help explain or clarify the question, answer, or comment.
- Try to get things going in another direction by simply accepting the response and saying, "OK, does anyone else have a different point of view or way of answering this question?"
- When such a response seems to be intentionally irrelevant, don't forget the power of a stare or simple silence in response.

The following techniques and methods provide further scaffolding to assist students in actively participating in more traditional forms of class discussion.

Fine-Tuning Discussion

When you are ready to further fine-tune your discussion strategies and techniques, you will want to consider some additionally effective gambits—or playful ways to elicit reflective discourse. It is wise not to try to master more than one or two of these methods at a time. Both you and the class will appreciate the orderliness of learned routines.

Fishbowl*

The Fishbowl technique (Baloche et al., 1993) is a useful way to raise students' awareness of their own and others' classroom discussion behaviors. Students are

*Baloche, L., Mauger, M. L., Willis, T. M., Filinuk, J. R., & Michalsky, B. V. (1993). "Fishbowls, creative controversy, talking chips: Exploring literature cooperatively." *English Journal*, 82. Copyright (1993) by the National Council of Teachers of English. Reprinted with permission.

seated in two concentric circles (both circles facing inward), with approximately the same number of students in each ring. Students in the inner circle are given a discussion topic and a time limit. Students in the outer circle are given an inner circle member to observe and a teacher-designed worksheet for recording their observations. When the discussion time is up, outer circle members give constructive feedback to their "fish." Feedback should focus on discussion behaviors rather than the topic of the discussion or specific points made.

This technique should be structured according to the sophistication level of the group. For optimal structure, assign students to one of the two circles; provide specific discussion prompts for the inner circle and very specific items on the observation worksheet provided to the outer circle. For more sophisticated groups, and as students become familiar with the technique, participants can be permitted to choose which circle they will be in, and discussion and observation prompts can be more open ended. Some ideas for structuring the observation checklist include the following:

- Place a check beside the appropriate item each time the person makes a verbal contribution to the discussion: states a new idea, paraphrases another person's idea, supports or agrees with another person, states an opposing or alternate point, summarizes, or makes a humorous remark.
- Place a check beside each nonverbal behavior observed: smile, laugh, nod, frown, or disinterested expression.

U-Debate*

Some Postreading discussion lends itself naturally to a debate-type format. The U-Debate (Athanses, 1988) is a useful structure for teaching students to engage in this type of discussion. The technique begins by the teacher stating two opposing ideas. Classroom seats are then moved into a "U" shape, with one side representing each opposing idea, and seats in the middle representing a neutral position. Students are directed to find a seat that best represents their opinion. The teacher facilitates the discussion in a typical way, with the difference that participants' views are readily observable to the teacher and one another. Students who select seats at the top of either side of the "U" usually are the most willing to begin the discussion. A lively camaraderie springs up among students seated in each of the opposing positions, and they begin to defer and/or appeal to one another as they attempt to express their points. As students change their opinions or the strength of their views, they are permitted to change their seating position.

Socratic Seminar

The Socratic Seminar is the primary instructional tool of Mortimer Adler's Paideia Proposals for educational reform (1982). Its intent is to engage students in meaningful Postreading discussion by minimizing the teacher's direction and maximizing student participation. This is done by laying out a set of specific guidelines for

*Athanses, S. (1988). "Developing a Classroom Community of Interpreters." *English Journal*, 77. Copyright (1988) by the National Council of Teachers of English. Reprinted with permission.

participants and by the teacher/discussion leader following another set of guidelines for opening the discussion and moving it along. Any text selection may be used, including standard textbook selections. It is helpful to number the lines in the text for easy reference. After everyone has completed the reading, the group is seated in a circle (or around a large table) and the basic ground rules for the discussion are explained (or reviewed). It is helpful to have students prepare name cards for themselves that they place in front of them so that during the seminar, participants can refer to each other politely by name.

Socratic Seminar: Guidelines for Participants

1. The purpose of the seminar is understanding the author's message and the group's interpretation and analysis of it.
2. Every comment or question must be based on a specific portion of the text. The discussion leader may open with a text section to respond to or may ask for a volunteer to identify a starting point.
3. You do not need to raise your hand; simply take turns as in a casual conversation.
4. Talk to each other, not the teacher.
5. You may make comments, ask questions of the group as a whole, or ask a question of a person by name.
6. You may "pass" when called on.
7. At any time, you may ask participants if they are ready to move to a different portion of the text. If they agree, identify the section you wish to respond to, read it aloud, and then ask your question or make your comment.
8. Stick to the point. Make notes of ideas you want to come back to.
9. Listen carefully, and ask for clarification when needed.

Socratic Seminar: Guidelines for Teacher/Discussion Leader

1. Identify a portion of the text to begin the discussion. Read the selection aloud, and ask a relevant clarifying question. With experienced groups, you may ask for a volunteer for this opening step. (For longer reading selections that may elicit more complex discussions, you may wish to assign the reading ahead of time and develop a plan for double-checking that the students have read and comprehended the basics of the text prior to class. For instance, you could require a "ticket" for admission to participate in the seminar (Zola, 1998). The ticket could be, as an example, a brief graphic organizer of the reading material that you could quickly scan from students as they take their seats in the seminar circle.)
2. Maintain an unintrusive role, communicating through body language the expectation that participants should share responsibility for moving the discussion along. It may help to avoid eye contact with the person speaking to encourage them to look at and speak to the other participants, rather than you.

3. Watch participants' body language to invite them in ("You don't seem to agree. Can you explain why?" "Can you give an example to support what he or she is saying?"). Remember that those who aren't speaking are thinking.
4. Correct all misreadings on the spot.
5. Supply key factual information when needed (but attempt to keep this to a minimum).
6. Coach students on seminar behaviors when needed.
7. Model effective discussion strategies, such as asking for clarification of a question or statement, paraphrasing the text, distinguishing between fact and opinion, identifying conflicting views, and drawing out the reasons for or implications of an answer or a comment.
8. If overly argumentative or nonparticipating members fail to respond to subtle approaches, speak with them privately after the discussion.
9. Conclude the seminar by going around the circle asking each participant to comment briefly on the seminar.

The final step in the Socratic Seminar is a writing prompt based on the text and the points raised in the discussion (steps and guidelines amalgamated from Gray, 1988; Paley, 1986; Sizer, 1984; and Zola, 1998).

In our view, "Socratic Seminar" is an unfortunate misnomer. The method just described bears scant resemblance to the method practiced by Socrates and his student, Plato, in which the teacher's role was that of a "grand inquisitor," posing a question and responding to questions and answers with ever more sharp and stinging questions intended to expose faulty assumptions and misinformation. This latter, more genuine version of the Socratic Method, as it has been most familiarly practiced in schools of law, has been referred to as "ritualized combat" (Guinier, Fine, & Balin, 1997).

▶ CONCEPT SUMMARY

Learning, remembering, and using what has been read is a process of adding to, building, and sometimes revising existing schema structures: connecting the new to the known. The most familiar Postreading tool is class discussion, but this often takes the form of teacher-directed rectitation in which the teacher asks all the questions and, unless these are limited to simple fact-based questions, little additional response is elicited. Teacher-direced recitation can be a useful tool for checking basic comprehension, as a bridge to more participatory, *Beyond the lines* discussion—the last step in the Framework for Text-Based Instruction. However, Cooperative Structures such as Numbered Heads Together, Find the Fiction, Act it Out, and Paired Recitation can serve the purpose of quick fact checking as well. The Guided Reading Procedure, Note Cue, and Cooperative Structrues such as Inside-Outside Circle, Find Someone Who, Stroll Pair Share, Postreading Three-Minute Write, and the Group Reading Activity effectively meet postreading puposes. Additional methods specifically designed to generate and focus in-depth participatory Postreading discussion include Fishbowl, U-Debate, and the Socratic Seminar.

SECTION

III

COMPLEMENTS TO CONTENT AREA READING: VOCABULARY, HIGHER-ORDER LITERACY, WRITING TO LEARN, ASSESSMENT, AND STUDY TECHNIQUES

This section addresses dimensions of planning for reading based instruction beyond the basic pre-, during and post-reading methods. Chapter 7 focuses on vocabulary development as an essential component of all learning and provides a variety of ways to assist students with their vocabulary development. Chapter 8 focuses on critical-constructive reading, writing, and thinking. Chapter 9 addresses the use of writing to enhance student learning. Chapter 10 introduces assessment technique for achieving the objectives of the previous chapters, and Chapter 11 offers a sampling of techniques that translate the principles of learning into guidelines for more efficient reading, listening, note taking and test preparation.

CHAPTER 7

METHODS FOR VOCABULARY AND CONCEPT DEVELOPMENT

The most powerful thing that can be done is to name something.

—Albert Einstein

From the first time you behold a beach at sunset to the next time your computer or your aspirations experience a "megaflop," new images get formed into clearer ideas, and ways to think, write, and speak. Improving students' access to this mental software does not merely facilitate learning, it is learning. This chapter is about increasing expertise in teaching the "software" language with which we organic computers process, feel, store, and express experiences, and in so doing, self-transform.

- WHAT'S IN A NAME?
- WHAT WE KNOW ABOUT VOCABULARY LEARNING AND TEACHING
- METHODS FOR PREREADING VOCABULARY INTRODUCTION
- METHODS TO TEACH WORD MEANING PREDICTION DURING SILENT READING AND GENERAL WORD CONSCIOUSNESS

- METHODS FOR POSTREADING AND GENERAL VOCABULARY/DEVELOPMENT
- CULTURAL-ACADEMIC TRIVIA
- CONCEPT SUMMARY

WHAT'S IN A NAME?

Einstein's comment invites one to consider the value of "naming something." Giving something a name—whether the thing is an object, a feeling, or a scientific theory—gives us the ability to think and speak about it, to evaluate and categorize it, and to *notice* it in the environment.

Learning a new word is, for the learner, analogous to creating a new word. Word learning improves one's capacity to learn: It is literally an IQ booster (Manzo, Manzo, & Albee, 2004). As children learn words that name the basic elements of their environment, they gain the power to express their needs and wishes. As we learn the words for increasingly abstract observations and feelings, we gain the power to reflect on these more subtle understandings and to incorporate these into our personal value systems and worldviews.

Words are the brain's shorthand system for *encoding* experience without having to turn its full attention to every item and nuance of sensory experience. Try looking around you, wherever you are at this moment. Imagine that you are experiencing (seeing, hearing, smelling, feeling) every aspect of your current environment for the first time, and try labeling everything you can. Would it be difficult to come up with 100 words? With 500? The brain doesn't have to be conscious of each of these things, because it has words for them. It is important to note that no matter how many words any one of us might have just listed, there are words we would *not* have listed—words we do not know. These represent objects, phenomena, or responses that we will not perceive, unless prompted to do so, because we have no words for seeing or feeling them. The words we know form a lens through which we see (and hear, and read, and sense) the world.

Vocabulary acquisition, like reading comprehension, is an ongoing, lifelong process. To teach someone effective vocabulary learning strategies is indeed a "gift that keeps on giving." Mastering the information and ideas of any discipline is largely a matter of mastering its vocabulary. This chapter opens with an overview of what we know about vocabulary learning and teaching. Approaches to vocabulary instruction include methods for introducing new words in ways that teach strategies, methods for building Silent Reading strategies for vocabulary development, and methods for Postreading and general vocabulary and concept development.

WHAT WE KNOW ABOUT VOCABULARY LEARNING AND TEACHING

A Metaphor for the Process

Earlier in this text, we introduced the image of a fishing net as a metaphor for schema—the intricate web of information and experience each person has constructed from his or her unique history of experience. Vocabulary can be thought of as the substance from which that net is constructed. Ideas, information, and experience are coded in words, represented by the knots in the fishing net, each connected to all the others by cords of meaning. This is a useful metaphor to keep in mind as we consider the following summary of what is known about the process of vocabulary acquisition.

Principles of Vocabulary Learning and Teaching

Estimates vary widely as to how many words we need to know at each grade level and, therefore, at what rate they should be learned. But a few things are clear: Children must learn at least 2,000 words per year through the fifth grade (Nagy, 1988), and many children learn more than 3,500 per year. There is an extensive body of research on how words are learned and how to best promote that learning. The following principles for vocabulary learning and teaching were derived from several reviews of this research (Baumann & Kameenui, 1991; Harmon, 2002; Kibby, 1995; Manzo & Manzo, 1990a; Manzo & Sherk, 1971–1972; Mountain, 2002; Nagy, 1988; Nilsen & Nilsen, 2003; Ruddell & Shearer, 2002; Stahl & Fairbanks, 1986).

1. Only about 20% of an average adult vocabulary of approximately 20,000 words is learned through direct instruction. The rest are learned incidentally through reading and listening. Therefore, it is more important to teach students strategies for learning word meanings than to require them to learn definitions of any given word lists. The most effective ways to teach vocabulary are those that most *resemble natural word learning strategies*.
2. Simply noticing unfamiliar words in print and oral language, or *word consciousness*, is a fundamental, natural word-learning strategy, and it is a habit that can be taught, practiced, and acquired. Teaching word consciousness should be a fundamental component of any effort to teach vocabulary.
3. When a student encounters a new word in print or everyday experience, he or she will remember the word in *association with the experience*—whether actual or vicarious—in which the word was encountered. Teaching strategies for associating new words and their meanings with personal experience and associations should be a key component of vocabulary instruction.
4. The meanings of many unfamiliar words can be predicted based on *knowledge of morphemes*—prefixes, suffixes, and roots. It is useful to teach students strategies for using what they know about word part meanings to unlock meanings of unfamiliar words.
5. There are levels of word knowledge, from simple understanding of a word's meaning when it is seen or heard in context, to ability to define it, to ability to use the word confidently in appropriate ways. Developing the higher levels of word knowledge requires multiple encounters with a new word in multiple contexts, and instruction in *use of context to analyze nuances of word meanings* in these varying contexts.

6. The reader's familiarity with the vocabulary in a given reading selection is one of the most important determinants of his or her ability to comprehend. *Preteaching difficult words* from a reading selection before students read greatly improves their comprehension of the material. This also is best done in ways that model strategies for effective word learning.

7. Students develop interest in learning new words primarily through observation and interaction with others. Intentionally or unintentionally, teachers communicate their personal attitudes about the importance of word learning and their interest in words. A teacher's interest in and knowledge of words are contagious and help a class become a community of learners in which word learning is a valued learning tool.

Do We Need to Do It Better?

Most content teachers would agree that vocabulary is an essential part of their curriculum. It could be that vocabulary instruction comes under the heading of "if it ain't broke, don't fix it." Research, however, suggests otherwise: The vocabulary level of college-bound 18-year-olds has dropped sharply in recent years. In 1940, these students typically knew the meanings of 80% of the words on a standardized reading test. By the mid-1990s, these students scored 30%, which is just a little better than random guessing (Johnson O'Connor Research Foundation, in Dortch, 1995). These figures are likely due in part to the fact that there are more college-bound students today than in 1940; however, it is still evident that students are not being well served by whatever approaches to vocabulary instruction they have experienced. While we are teaching vocabulary, a look at *how* we are teaching it suggests that we may not need to teach it *more*, but *differently*.

The teaching of vocabulary is one of the most consistent practices in schools. On Monday, a list of words appears on the board. Students copy the words, use a dictionary to look up and write the definition of each word and possibly write a sentence using it. Words are to be studied for a test on Friday. Although this approach does work for some students some of the time (Tan & Nicholson, 1997), better vocabulary instruction proves to be more effective for more students more of the time (cf. Rhoder & Huerster, 2002).

It is a well-known fact that regardless of education and training, it is difficult to get teachers to teach in ways that differ from those in which they were taught. This is especially the case with vocabulary instruction. Students who went on to become teachers most likely were among those few who did benefit from the traditional list-define-test approach when they were in middle and high school. They looked up and thought about the definition, rather than simply copying the first or shortest one. They worked to craft a sentence using the word appropriately, rather than superficial ones that ignore shades of meaning (e.g., *cascade* means "a shower." My father sings in the cascade).

Further comparison, in Figure 7.1, of the traditional approach to the principles of vocabulary learning and the more effective instruction based on vocabulary

Characteristics of Effective Vocabulary Instruction Based on Principles of Vocabulary Learning and Teaching	**Characteristics of the Traditional List-Define-Test Approach to Vocabulary Instruction**
Resembles natural word learning	People rarely learn vocabulary by studying a word list through the week for a test at the week's end.
Teaches the habit of *word consciousness*	The teacher provides the words for study—students are not taught to look for and recognize unfamiliar words.
Teaches the habit of *associating new words with prior experience*	Some students may make the effort to compose sensible sentences; many students' attempts to connect a new word meaning with personal experience are minimal.
Teaches *use of knowledge of morphemes to* predict word meanings	Although morpheme information is available in dictionaries, its use is generally not required.
Provides *multiple encounters with new words in multiple contexts*	Words are presented in isolation, with no opportunity to learn to make use of context.
Preteaches difficult words from assigned readings	Words on the list may be selected from reading assignments, but these are rarely referred to specifically before students read.
Models the teacher's interest in words and word learning	It relies primarily on the extrinsic motivation of the test, rather than building intrinsic motivation and interest in word learning.

Figure 7.1 Comparison of Principles of Vocabulary Teaching and Learning with the Traditional List-Define-Test Approach

teaching and learning reveals that the traditional approach does little to teach students how to learn words. Its purpose is to have students memorize definitions, and the expectation (usually unfulfilled) is that students will, on their own, make the comparisons, connections, evaluations, applications, and exclusions that will firmly affix the words as solid elements of operational schema—tight knots in their own personally connected net.

Selecting Words for Instruction

How many words should you teach each week/month/year? Which words should you teach? The answers, of course, depend partly on your students, partly on your subject, and partly on your instructional emphasis. In general, as they plan each course unit, teachers should identify key terms for concept development. Then, in previewing materials students will read during the unit, vocabulary for preteaching should be identified. Of course, there will be more words that *could* be taught than there will be time. Ruddell (1999, pp. 148–149) offers suggestions for selecting words for Prereading, Guided Reading, and Postreading instruction:

1. Select a word for Prereading instruction when it is central to the meaning of the selection and you anticipate that many of your students do not know

the meaning of the word as used in this context and the context does not convey the meaning.

2. Select a word for emphasis in a Silent Reading format when students are likely to know the word in general, but not in this specific context, or when the context clearly conveys the meaning.
3. Select a word for Postreading emphasis when it is central to the knowledge and concept base of the unit, and, because of students' limited background knowledge related to the word, small group and/or whole class discussion is needed to connect the new ideas to prior learning and experience.

▶ METHODS FOR PREREADING VOCABULARY INTRODUCTION

Introducing key terms from a particular reading selection often is an essential element of Prereading instruction. When a word is judged to be needed, vocabulary preteaching should meet three basic criteria:

1. Introduce students to words that are likely to be unfamiliar to them.
2. Do so in ways that not only provide the word meaning but permit the teacher to model strategies for learning new words (in doing so, the teacher also models an interest in words and word learning).
3. Establish a low-risk environment in which students can try out and experiment with these word-learning strategies.

We know of only a few methods that satisfy these criteria. Before we introduce these methods, consider some of the general components that they have in common.

1. They introduce a maximum of five words for a given reading selection.
2. They limit this part of the lesson to a maximum of 15 minutes.
3. Each method puts the words on display as each is introduced (not the entire list at once).
4. In each case, the word is spoken, written, and defined. This is a crucial component of vocabulary preteaching for several reasons. First, the meaning is given in the simplest terms possible. To see the importance of this translation step, look at the way dictionary definitions might be translated into "student" language:

vocabulary word	dictionary definition	translation
potential	*capable of being but not yet in existence; latent*	*a possible ability that has not been developed*
expansion	*the act or process of expanding*	*growing larger*

This step of providing students with a meaning (translated from a dictionary definition) is also crucial because it is contrary to one of the most basic teacher scripts we have internalized through years of traditional classroom experience: After the teacher writes a word on the board, she or he next asks, "can anyone tell me what this word means?" What this question does, in effect, is eliminate a large portion of the class—all those who don't have a clue as to the word's meaning. When the teacher says instead, "This word is ____, and it means ____," everyone is still able to participate.

5. The teacher then introduces a strategy for connecting the new word with its meaning and invites volunteers to try out the strategy. At this point, the teacher should watch for and encourage contributions from students who might not have known the meaning of the word and who might not otherwise have been able to participate.
6. As suggested, the teacher tries to keep the interactions brief and to the point.
7. When possible, time should be given for students to at least begin the reading immediately following the vocabulary preteaching. When it is not possible to have them do the entire reading in class, be sure to have students write the pretaught words and keep them with the reading assignment to be done later.

The word learning strategies used in the methods in this section offer several different ways of connecting the new word with some schema element that is related to the new word meaning. In the Keyword Method, the schema element is a visual image; in the Subjective Approach to Vocabulary, it is an image of a personal experience; and in Motor Imaging, it is a gestured pantomime that suggests the new word meaning.

Keyword Vocabulary Method

The Keyword Vocabulary Method is based on an ancient memory technique that dates back to the time when unschooled messengers had to recall long and explicit details. In this application, a new word is linked to a mental image that it suggests, and that in turn is connected in some logical way to the actual meaning of the word. The object is to create mental images that are easy to recall because they are easy to visualize, and even odd or amusing.

Steps in the Keyword Vocabulary Method

Step 1. Write the word on the board, pronounce it, and tell what it means.

Step 2. Ask students to use the *sound* of the word to come up with a visual image that will help them remember the word meaning. The visual image should link what the word sounds like to what it actually means. For example, *plateau* (a large grassy flatland) could be linked to the image of a huge upside-down green dinner plate. *Collage* (an artwork created by random combination of bits and pieces of other pictures and/or objects) could be linked to the image of a bulletin board filled with pictures of different colleges. *Amulet* (a charm worn around the neck to ward off evil forces) could be linked to the image of an arm bracelet with an odd charm on it.

Step 3. As an optional step, students can be directed to write each word and its meaning and draw a simple line drawing or stick figure to represent their visual image connector. Another option is to have students record the words in a form that can be used for later review by writing the word and drawing their picture representation on the front of a note card and writing the meaning on the back. This is a useful technique for studying lengthy word lists in preparation for standardized tests such as the SAT (Scholastic Aptitude Test).

Notes on Keyword Vocabulary

The Keyword Vocabulary Method has been reported to be effective in learning content material (Konopak & Williams, 1988; Levin et al., 1986) and with learning disabled students (Condus, Marshall, & Miller, 1986; Guthrie, 1984). Those who have studied Keyword the most extensively maintain that it helps students learn how to form connections and to develop elaborations on concepts (Pressley, Johnson, & Symons, 1987; Pressley, Levin, & MacDaniel, 1987; Pressley, Levin, & Miller, 1981).

A Keyword Vocabulary lesson usually sparks an interesting instructional conversation in which the teacher and students come to the "word workbench" together in an attempt to capture and represent word meanings in memorable ways. It also tends incidentally to reveal students' thought processes, thus making it a useful diagnostic teaching tool.

Subjective Approach to Vocabulary

The Subjective Approach to Vocabulary (SAV) (Manzo, 1983) builds on what students already know by urging them to find personal experiences or other associations with which to anchor the somewhat ethereal definitions of new terms found in dictionaries. The method helps students remember meanings of important content-related terms while illustrating how they might use the same strategy in self-directed word learning. In the Subjective Approach to Vocabulary, the teacher engages students in a highly interactive "talk-through" designed to have them learn how to use their *own and other students' experiences* and tales as a foundation for acquiring new word meanings. In this way, the biographies of individual lives become connected to the stories of the words and ideas offered in school. SAV can be particularly useful for providing multicultural outlooks and for working with second-language students. It gives teacher and students access to the alternative ways students may be processing and interpreting the world around and within them.

Steps in the Subjective Approach to Vocabulary

Step 1. Write the word on the board, pronounce it, and tell what it means. Direct students to write the word and its objective, dictionary-type meaning on their own paper.

Step 2. Ask students to try to think of a personal experience they are reminded of by the word meaning. (The teacher should have an example or two in mind for each word, in case students are especially slow in coming up with their own. Usually, once they have heard one example, they will quickly begin to come up with their own). Call on several volunteers to tell their "subjective" associations. Tell students to try to picture their association as clearly as they can and to think about how it connects to the new word meaning.

Step 3. Tell students to record their subjective association for the word underneath the objective meaning. They can record an association they volunteered in class, or one that they thought of but did not state, or one offered by another class member. See Figure 7.2 for a Sample SAV lesson.

Step 4. *Optional:* Distribute or guide students in preparing a worksheet consisting of a large square divided into four smaller squares. There should be one four-section square for each word introduced. Have students write the word in the top left section of a larger square, its objective definition in the top right section, their subjective association in the bottom left section, and a line drawing or stick figure illustration in the bottom right section.

The word "arboreal" was in a seventh-grade science text. The teacher wrote the word on the board and gave the meaning: "The word *arboreal* means 'having to do with trees or living in trees.'" A few examples were given: "Monkeys are arboreal animals; the word *arboreal* comes from the word *arbor,* as in Arbor Day, the day put aside to plant trees." The subjective-based aspect of the lesson began at this point. Explaining her question, the teacher added, "It will be easier for you to learn and remember this new term if you can think of some personal images or experiences that you can picture with it."

One student suggested, "The word reminds me of how my mother killed my peanut tree that we brought home from Georgia by overwatering it." To this, another student added, humorously, "That sounds like a 'tragic arboreal' experience." In that same humorous vein, another student asked, rhetorically, "Did you say that *arboreal* means 'living and swingin' in trees(?), 'cause I think my little brother is arboreal!"

The teacher then asked if any one had formed a new meaning for *arboreal.* "It sounds to me like 'anything to do with trees'," one student volunteered. The teacher then directed the students to record the word *arboreal* in their notebooks with the objective meaning she had provided and a parenthetical note on their initial and subsequent personal associations with the word.

Figure 7.2 Subjective Approach to Vocabulary—sample lesson

Implementation Notes on the Subjective Approach to Vocabulary

It is hard to tell how readily a class will take to an SAV lesson on its initial presentation. Group size may be an important factor. A large group sometimes may be necessary to increase the chance of at least one extrovert stirring the class's imagination and responding.

In a study with sixth-grade subjects (Casale & Manzo, 1983), SAV was found to be considerably better than traditional (dictionary "look-up" and sentence writing) approaches to vocabulary instruction. However, it was slightly less effective than the approach described next, which urges teacher and students to employ physical, or symbolic motor, associations to a greater extent than is usual in the sedentary context of schooling.

Motor Imaging

Motor Imaging (Casale [now Manzo], 1985) draws on the physical-sensory as well as the cognitive and affective domains of learning. The underlying principle of this method is akin to an expression that "Nothing is in the intellect that was not first in the senses."

Developmental psychologists have observed that infants learn to represent meaning with gross motor movements. Over time, these motoric representations, or "motor meanings," are increasingly refined until they are internalized as "symbolic meanings," in Piaget's terminology. Apparently our initial ways of learning consist almost exclusively of tactile and sensory-motor experiences. Although this is no great surprise, since that is all babies can do, we seem to have overlooked the fact that this aspect of learning may remain active and viable long into human development.

Steps in Motor Imaging

Step 1. Write the word on the board, pronounce it, and tell what it means.

Step 2. Tell students to imagine a simple gesture, or pantomime, for the word meaning that you might use to show the word meaning or that you might use when speaking the word in context.

Step 3. On the teacher's signal, students do their gestures, or pantomimes, simultaneously.

Step 4. While observing the students' pantomimes, choose one of the most common ones, show this gesture to all the students, and tell them that when you point to the word, they are to do the selected gesture while saying the word aloud.

Step 5. Introduce each of the words to be pretaught in this way. As words are added to the list, when you point to the word for students to say and pantomime, go back to earlier words to review these word/pantomime connections.

Step 6. Now that each of the new words has been connected to a pantomime, tell students that this time, when you point to a word, they are to do

New Word	Language Meaning	Motor Meaning
Appropriate	Right or fit for a certain purpose	Both palms together, matching perfectly
Convey	Take or carry from one place to another	Both hands together, palms upward, moving from one side to the other
Woe	Great sadness or trouble	One or both hands over the eyes, head tilted forward
Dazzle	Shine or reflect brightly	Palms close together, facing outward, fingers spread
Utmost	The very highest or most	One or both hands reaching up as far as possible
Abode	Place where you live	Hands meeting above the head in a triangular "roof" shape

Figure 7.3 Motor Imaging examples

the pantomime and say the meaning. Practice the words in this way, in mixed-up order, for several minutes.

Figure 7.3 presents some examples from a Motor Imaging lesson.

Notes on Motor Imaging

The same comparison study cited previously, of a cognitive (dictionary), affective (subjective association), and this physical-sensory motor approach to vocabulary, showed the Motor Imaging method to be significantly better on four of five vocabulary measures (Casale [now Manzo] & Manzo, 1983). It appears that the highest forms of learning have a most humble, if not primitive, foundation.

The promising implication of this point is that students at every level of intellectual ability seem to share a common capacity for physical-associative learning. This makes Motor Imaging, and possibly other motor-based methods yet to be devised, especially promising possibilities for heterogeneously grouped students.

▶ METHODS TO TEACH WORD MEANING PREDICTION DURING SILENT READING AND GENERAL WORD CONSCIOUSNESS

An important goal of vocabulary instruction is to teach students to predict possible meanings for unfamiliar words, and possibly more important, simply to *notice* an unfamiliar word when they are reading these words. One way to teach students to handle unfamiliar words encountered while reading is to teach them the straightforward steps in the Context, Structure, Sound, Reference method described first in this section. The next method, Contextual Redefinition, focuses on the process of using context to predict word meanings. Incidental Morpheme Analysis and Explicit Morpheme Analysis are two approaches to teaching students to draw upon word parts of *known* words to unlock meanings of unfamiliar words. The final three methods, the Community of Language Approach, the Vocabulary Secret Police, and the Vocabulary Self-Collection Strategy, focus on developing the habit of realizing that a word is unfamiliar when it is encountered in print or oral language.

Context, Structure, Sound, Reference: The Basic Strategy

Context, Structure, Sound, Reference is a good basic strategy for handling unfamiliar words encountered while reading (Gray, 1946; Ruddell, 1997).

Step 1. Read to the end of the sentence. Can you guess the meaning? Are there any clues in the surrounding sentences or paragraphs that help you? Now do you have a pretty good idea of the meaning? Does it make sense? If so, keep right on reading.
If not,

Step 2. Look at the parts of the word. Are there prefixes or roots that you know? Do the suffixes or inflections (plurals, past tense, etc.) help you? Combine this information with context information to arrive at a meaning. Does it make sense? If so, go right on reading.
If not,

Step 3. Try to pronounce the word. When you hear it, does it sound like a word you already know? If not, are there letters or letter combinations that help (e.g., the "ct" in "tract" as opposed to the "ck" in "track")? Combine this information with information from context. Does it make sense? If so, go right on reading.
If not,

Step 4. Look for footnotes or margin notes. Check the glossary or a dictionary. Ask someone for help: a friend, or me, or anyone else. Combine this information with information from context. Does it make sense?

Contextual Redefinition: Using Context to Predict Word Meanings

Typically, new words are encountered in the following sequence: context, isolation, context (Putnam, Bader, & Bean, 1988). This means that when readers encounter an unfamiliar word in context, they try to figure out its meaning from the context, and then, if unsuccessful, seek meaning from another source, such as a dictionary or another person. Finally, they return to the original context to make better sense of both the word and the context. Contextual Redefinition (Cunningham, Cunningham, & Arthur, 1981) applies this natural process to a simple format for classroom instruction (Tierney, Readence, & Dishner, 1990). Although this method is used before reading, its goal is to model and provide practice in an important during-reading vocabulary strategy.

Steps in Contextual Redefinition

To prepare for using this method, first select target words from the reading selection. Then, for each word, write one or more sentences that provide reasonable clues to the word meaning. The sentences may come from the selection itself, if these provide reasonable clues.

Step 1. Write each target word on the board or overhead and ask students to guess the word meaning. Students should be encouraged to discuss their ideas and to try to come to a reasonable consensus on their predicted meaning for each word.

Step 2. Present each target word in the context sentence(s) you have prepared. Have students revise their predictions for each word meaning, again encouraging them to provide the reasons for their ideas and building on one another's thoughts to come to a consensus.

Step 3. Ask a volunteer to look up the word in the dictionary and to compare the dictionary definition with students' predictions. This step can stir a productive instructional conversation, since dictionary definitions can sometimes be too abstract for easy interpretation, or the word could have been used in some unusual or ironic way.

Implementation Notes on Contextual Redefinition

This method teaches students that context can provide clues to word meaning (Gipe, 1978–1979), but it cannot be relied on to reveal word meanings in all cases. Teaching students to overrely on context clues is one of the most frequent errors that tends to be made in vocabulary strategy instruction. A less structured approach to calling student attention to context clues is to provide a list of words for students to watch for while reading an assignment. When they come to each of the words, they are to write a predicted meaning and tell what clues they used to make the prediction.

Incidental Morpheme Analysis: Using Known Word Parts to Unlock New Word Meanings

Eighty percent of the words in the English dictionary contain Greek or Latin prefixes, suffixes, or roots. The proportion probably is much higher for discipline-specific words, which tend to be more scientific and less likely to change with high frequency and casual language usage. These word parts, called morphemes, are units of language that cannot be further divided without losing meaning. Some morphemes have meanings only when attached to other word parts. Examples of such bound morphemes include *ed, ing, tele,* and *cide.* Other morphemes, such as *cover, graph,* and *stand,* called free morphemes, can stand alone, that is, are words in themselves.

Most expert readers and language users employ these word parts, or morphemes, to make sense out of and remember new words (cf. Nilsen & Nilsen, 2002). The Incidental Morpheme Method (Manzo & Manzo, 1990a) teaches students to apply existing knowledge of morphemes to new words encountered in content reading. It also offers a way to teach new morphemes by raising sensitivity to word parts and providing casual, or "on-the-spot," instruction in a set of morphemes with a high frequency of occurrence in "school" words.

Generally speaking, students with a weak orientation toward words, and therefore the greatest needs, are the ones least likely to warm to direct instruction in morphemic study. Hence, it is best to make these lessons brief, frequent, and spaced. A bulletin board display with space for adding examples can help keep the project ongoing and the students able to participate as they come across new words containing meaningful word parts. (A similar strategy is used at the elementary level very successfully for teaching children how to decode "new" words phonetically from a list of familiar "sight words.") This approach is especially recommended in classes with English Language Learners. Speakers of Romance languages, such as Spanish, actually could have a considerable advantage in learning and utilizing such word parts because Romance languages are derived in even greater measure from Latin root words that these students know from common native language usage.

Steps in Incidental Morpheme Analysis

As preparation for using the Incidental Morpheme Method, watch for words in reading assignments that probably are unfamiliar to students but contain familiar word parts, or morphemes. Use the following steps to *preteach* these terms.

Step 1. Write the term on the board or overhead, and underline meaningful word parts, or morphemic elements, that might help students understand the word's concept base.

Example:	*seis*	*mo*	*graph*

Step 2. Ask students if they can use the underlined parts to grasp the word meaning, and why. If the word meaning is predicted correctly, write the meaning under the word and proceed with Steps 3 and 4 as reinforcement.

Step 3. Tell students you will give them additional clues for predicting (or remembering) the word meaning. Beneath the underlined word parts, write "Level 1" clues, which are other, easier words using those morphemes. If students have not yet correctly predicted the word meaning, continue to ask for predictions.

Example:	*seis*	*mo*	*graph*
Level 1 clues:	*seizure*		*telegraph*
			graphic

Step 4. Beneath the "Level 1" clues, write "Level 2" clues, which are word part meanings, and continue to ask for predictions until the correct definition is reached and written below the clues.

Example:	*seis*	*mo*	*graph*
Level 1 clues:	*seizure*		*telegraph* *graphic*
Level 2 clues:	*to shake*		*written*

Meaning: An instrument that records the direction, time, and intensity of earthquakes.

See Figure 7.5 for a sample listing of common Latin roots. Many dictionaries will provide lists of Latin and Greek prefixes, suffixes, and roots.

Explicit Morpheme Analysis

Morphemes, again, are the smallest units of meaning within a word, and they are sometimes themselves a word, such as *auto.* In the Explicit Morpheme approach, a teacher identifies core concept words in the text—words such as *ecology* in science, *quadrangle* in math, *millennium* in social studies, *participle* in grammar, or *prologue* in literature—that are composed of elements likely to be familiar to students.

A graphic organizer for vocabulary acquisition such as that shown in Figure 7.4 is helpful for analyzing the morphemes from which unfamiliar words are constructed. The target word, correctly spelled, is written in the center of the graphic by the teacher and copied by the students. The teacher asks the students to use their knowledge to identify possible prefixes, roots, and suffixes that are embedded in the word. Students then define the target word as best they can, using clues from their knowledge of the parts of the word. Next, they share their definitions with a partner or in a small group. To conclude this first step, the pair or group composes one definition and writes it on the board. Groups compare their definitions and begin to discuss similarities and differences. When the root of the target word begins to emerge in the discussion, the teacher shares the dictionary etymology with the students, inserting this in the section of the graphic labeled "Root(s)."

Then the teacher writes the prime dictionary definition in the appropriate space on an overhead transparency copy of the graphic. The students compare their definitions with that written by the teacher. They discuss similarities between definitions, with emphasis on why the word means what it means and why it is spelled as it is. Often, the students are very close in their definitions, and since learning what something is *not* can be helpful in understanding what it *is,* the discussion of differences between the conventional and unconventional definitions helps everyone get closer to actually knowing the word.

The teacher and students create an exemplary sentence using the target word, based on what they've found together to that point. The teacher refers the students to the actual definition as the context of the discussion requires. This keeps the focus on the actual target of the lesson.

Next, students brainstorm synonyms for the target word. If a word can be substituted in the sentence and still make the same sense, it must be a synonym. Sometimes slight changes in the sentence are necessary to retain sense, but often the substitute word will not fit at all. Then the question becomes, "Is this a related

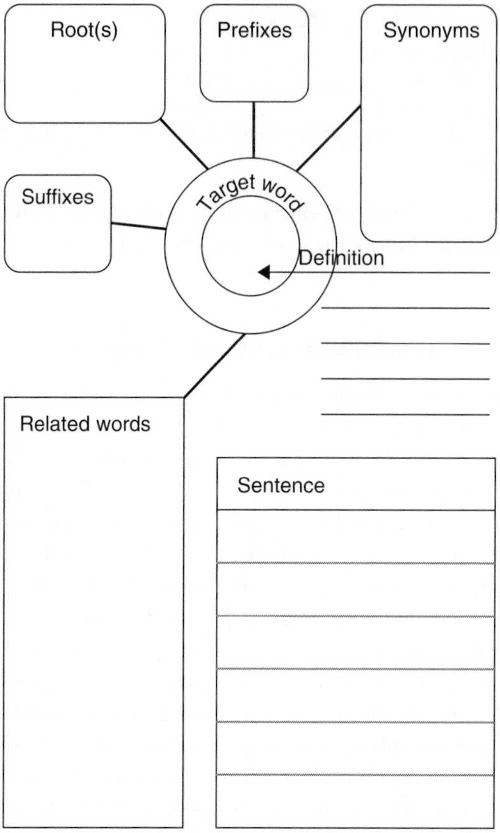

Figure 7.4 Graphic organizer for morpheme analysis

word or a discard?" (Related words are words similar in meaning, though not synonymous, or words with the same root.) When the morpheme graphic is complete, students have a picture of the meaning of a word and, more important, a clear idea of how the word means what it does.

Community of Language Approach Teaching Word Consciousness

Community of Language (Manzo & Manzo, 1990a) is an approach to teaching word consciousness that can be applied in a variety of ways. The basic formula is simple: The teacher identifies a set of vocabulary words that will be important to upcoming instruction and then intentionally *uses* these words as often as possible when interacting with the students. The approach may be implemented by a single teacher or any combination of teachers who have students in common. For example, an elementary teacher might identify three to five key vocabulary words from each of five subject areas from the content of the next three weeks' lessons. Or, a middle

Root	*Meaning*	*Derivatives*
-aud-, -audit-	hear	auditorium, audio
-avi-	bird	aviation, aviary
-caput-	head	capital
-ced-, -cess-	move, yield	recede
-clar-	clear	clarify
-clin-	lean	incline
-clud-, -claud-, -clus-	shut	seclude
-cord-	heart	cordial
-corp-	body	corporal, marine corp
-cred-	to believe	credible
-curr-, -curs-	run	current
-dic-, -dict-	say	predict
-domin-	master	dominate
-duc-, -duct-	lead	conduct
-fac-, -fic-, -fact-, -fect-	to make, do	factory
-fer-	bear, carry	transfer
-fin-	end	finish
-fort-	strong	fortitude
-jun-, -junct-	join	junction
-laud-, -laudat-	praise	applause
-let-, -lect-	gather, read	lecture, collect
-legis-, -lex-	law	legislate
-lux-, -luc-	light	elucidate
-magn-	great	magnificent, magnify
-mal-	bad	malevolent
-man-	hand	manual
-mit-, -miss-	send	missile
-mov-, -mot-	set in motion	motor
-nov-, -novus-	new	renovation
-pac-	peace	pacific, pacify
-pel-, -puls-	urge, drive	propel
-pend-, -pens-	hang, weigh	pensive
-plic-, -plex-	bend, fold	plexiglass
-pon-, -pos-	place, put	postpone
-sci-	know	science
-scrib-, -script-	write	describe
-solv-, -solut-	loosen	solution, solve
-spec-, -spect-	look	spectator
-sta-	stand firm	stable
-stru-, -struct-	build	construct
-tend-, -tens-	stretch	tendency
-tort-	to twist	distort
-ven-, -vent-	come	convention
-ver-	true	veritable
-vert-, -vers-	turn	reverse
-viv-, -vit-	live, life	vitality
-vid-, -vis-	see	evident
-voc-	call	vocation

Figure 7.5 Common Latin roots and derivative words

school interdisciplinary team of teachers might identify five vocabulary words each from the next few weeks of lesson plans and combine these words into one interdisciplinary list that each teacher then begins to use in interactions with the students they have in common. Teachers might tape the list to their desks or inside their lesson plan books for easy reference throughout the day.

The first time the approach is used, students are likely to notice the list at some point, and ask whether they will have to look up the words or whether they will have a test on the words. When these questions come up, the teacher should take advantage of the opportunity to call the rest of the class's attention to the list and explain the purpose of Community of Language: To help students develop the habit of (and strategies for) noticing new words around them, and to learn the meanings of new words by hearing them repeated in similar and differing contexts. Students should not be required to look up and define the words, and there should not be a test on the words, per se, other than as the words come up naturally in instructional materials and as part of the regular test on the material from which the words were drawn. An exception to this latter point might be to occasionally discuss the effectiveness of the Community of Language approach with students at the end of the time period in which it has been used, and follow this discussion with a test on the word list to permit students to discover for themselves how well they have learned.

The impact of this approach cannot be exaggerated. It builds student respect for teachers as models of language, reinforces reading vocabulary, raises word consciousness and precision in thinking, and boosts standardized test scores. This seemingly incidental approach can have an even more important and far-reaching effect: Students will take their new oral language home and, in turn, incidentally share it with their family and friends. This can elevate the levels of language and precision in thinking in students' families and in the community at large, *thereby reaching children who have not yet started school and parents who have long since left it.*

The Secret Language Police: Weaving New Words into the Environment

The Secret Language Police (Baines, 1998, pp. 209–210) is another approach to teaching students to pay attention to words around them.* It is compatible with the Community of Language approach and, in some ways, easier since it can be initiated with students with little prior commitment from others.

Steps in the Secret Language Police

Step 1. Designate two students in class to serve as the secret language police for a week.

*Baines, L. (1998). The future of the written word. In J. Simmons & L. Baines (Eds.), *Languages study in the middle school, high school, and beyond* (pp. 207–209). Copyright 1998 by the International Reading Association.

Step 2. The secret language police have the job of communicating the words and definitions of two bonus vocabulary words to other members of class.

Step 3. The secret language police cannot directly state, "These are the bonus words and they mean. . . , " but they should use the words in their own comments during class.

Step 4. The secret language police are encouraged to spread the words around to the principal and to other teachers. They can receive additional rewards, such as extra points on a test of their choice, by going beyond the basic requirement, for example, by having the word spoken in the school's morning public address system announcements, or locating, highlighting, and showing the class the word used in a newspaper, magazine, book, or website.

Vocabulary Self-Collection Strategy: Developing Independence in Identifying Unfamiliar Words and Predicting and Clarifying Meanings

The Vocabulary Self-Collection Strategy (VSS) (Haggard [now Ruddell], 1982, 1986) is a cooperative structure that provides practice in identifying important terms and using context to predict meaning.* Although it takes place after students have read, its goal is to teach students to identify important key terms as they read and to access appropriate sources—from context, to dictionary, to other people—to obtain meaningful definitions.

Steps in Vocabulary Self-Collection

Step 1. *Preparation:* Use this method with concept-rich reading selections that contain several important vocabulary terms. Identify the terms you would expect students to have difficulty with. When using VSS for the first time with a group of students, prepare an example to use in introducing the method. After students have completed the reading assignment and some type of comprehension check, form small groups (nominating teams) of two to five students.

Step 2. *Small Group Work:* Each group's task is to identify and nominate one vocabulary word from the reading assignment for further emphasis. When the team has agreed on a word, it prepares the following information for the team spokesperson to present to the rest of the class. (When this activity is new to a group, the teacher gives a pre-prepared example.)

Step 3. Read the word in context.

*Adapted from: Ruddell [formerly Haggard]. Martha Rapp. (1982, December). The vocabulary self-collection strategy: An active approach to word learning. *Journal of Reading,* 26(3), 203–207. Copyright (c) 1982 by the International Reading Association.

Step 4. Tell what the group thinks the word means (it may use context and/or any other resources available in the classroom).

Step 5. Explain why the group thinks the word should be emphasized.

Step 6. *Whole Class Reporting:* Each group's spokesperson provides the information his or her group has prepared. The teacher facilitates by writing the words and meanings on the board, along with any additional information and clarifications provided by the class.

Step 7. *Recording:* Students record the information from the board in their vocabulary notebooks or journals.

Research has provided support for VSS as an effective means for increasing student vocabulary and for developing student abilities to be strategic, independent word learners, including with at-risk readers (Ruddell & Shearer, 2002). This method provides a natural link to the next level of Postreading vocabulary/concept development.

▶ METHODS FOR POSTREADING AND GENERAL VOCABULARY/DEVELOPMENT

Once a new word has been noticed and its meaning has been either predicted or determined, it can be thought of as clinging lightly to the appropriate schema location. To learn the word, it needs to be more tightly affixed. This is achieved through cross-referencing it with numerous other bits of information and experience and through repeated exposure. Word knowledge is transformed into concept understanding by means of inclusion, exclusion, subordination, and superordination.

1. *Inclusion.* Which other words belong in the same category with this word? What are its relevant characteristics or properties? What are some specific examples/applications of the word?
2. *Exclusion.* Which similar words do not belong in the same category with this word? What are some related but inappropriate examples/applications? What are some nonrelevant characteristics?
3. *Subordination.* What are some words that would fall into subcategories of this word?
4. *Superordination.* Which broader category does this word fall under?

This section deals with the deepening of understanding that converts word meanings to concept knowledge. The following section provides activities for repetition and practice.

Typical to Technical Meaning Approach

Common words often have special, technical applications in a particular content area. For example, the word *true* is used in mechanics to indicate that gears are well synchronized; hence, *not-true* means "poorly synchronized." Today this phenomenon often occurs with tech terms such as *cookies* and *spam.* In the Typical to Technical Meaning Approach (Welker, 1987), the teacher prepares a worksheet exercise that provides practice in using a term in both its typical and its technical meanings. Although these practice sheets require considerable preparation time, once students have become familiar with the format, the teacher simply can ask, "Do we have any terms in today's material for which there is a common as well as a technical meaning?" and the rest of the lesson will unfold from previous practice.*

Steps in the Typical to Technical Meaning Approach

Step 1. Discuss a term's common meanings and then introduce its technical meaning.

Step 2. Have students complete a word-to-meaning exercise, matching each term with both its common and its technical meanings (see Part 1 in Figure 7.6). Then have students complete a cloze-type exercise, filling in the blanks where the terms are used in either the typical or technical sense (see Part 2 in Figure 7.6).

Step 3. Briefly discuss students' responses prior to presenting information based on technical uses of the terms.

Subject Area Vocabulary Reinforcement

Learning is a process of placing new information into existing categories until a special feature that does not fit is encountered. Then a new category must be created to expand the schema. Semantic Feature Analysis (Johnson & Pearson, 1984) is a method designed to permit students to engage in this process in a conscious and focused way. A variation on this method, called SAVOR, or Subject Area Vocabulary Reinforcement (Stieglitz & Stieglitz, 1981), is designed specifically for content area use.

Steps in SAVOR

Step 1. Identify a category of words. Then, have students brainstorm words that fit in this category, and list these examples in a column on their own paper.

Step 2. Then, have students brainstorm specific features of the words they have listed. These features are listed as column headings across the top of their paper (see Figure 7.7 for an example of how the chart is constructed).

Step 3. Next, have students fill in the charts individually, using plus (+) or minus (−) signs to indicate whether each word has a particular feature.

Step 4. After students have completed their charts, the teacher encourages discussion about the patterns of pluses and minuses to discover the uniqueness of each word.

*Welker, W. A. (December, 1987). Open to Suggestion: Going from typical to technical meaning. *Journal of Reading 31*(3), 275–276.

Part 1

Directions: For each term below, write the letter of its common meaning and its technical meaning under the headings given.

Terms	***Common Meaning***	***Technical Meaning***
acute		
supplementary		
complementary		
angle		

Meanings

A. A person's point of view

B. Making whole, or completing something

C. Something additional to the basic requirements

D. Space between two lines or surfaces that meet

E. Having a sharp point

F. Either of two angles that combine to equal 90 degrees

G. An angle [that] is less than 90 degrees in value

H. Either of two angles that together form exactly 180 degrees

Part 2

Directions: Select the best word from the word bank to complete each sentence below. Each word will be used twice.

Sentences

1. The sword had a very ____________ cutting edge.
2. The ____________ angle for a 50-degree angle is a 40-degree angle.
3. Our reading textbook comes with ____________ materials such as workbooks and ditto sheets.
4. If an angle is 53 degrees, it is called an ____________ angle.
5. A black tie with a white shirt would be considered a ____________ match.
6. Now that I have gotten my thoughts on the subject, what is your ____________ (or opinion) on the matter?
7. A pie can be sliced into pieces with many different ____________.
8. Two angles that together equal 180 degrees are ____________ angles.

Word Bank

complementary *acute* *angle* *supplementary*

Figure 7.6 Typical to Technical Meaning Exercises

Source: Welker, W. A. (December, 1987). Open to Suggestion: Going from typical to technical meaning. *Journal of Reading 31*(3), 275–276.

Shapes	Four Sided	Curved or Rounded Lines	Line Segment	All Sides Equal in Length	Right Angles
Triangle	–	–	+	–	–
Rectangle	+	–	+	–	+
Parallelogram	+	–	+	–	–
Circle	–	+	–	–	–
Trapezoid	+	–	+	–	–
Semicircle	–	+	+	–	–
Square	+	–	+	+	+

Figure 7.7 SAVOR Example in Mathematics
Source: Stieglitz, E. & Stieglitz, V. (1981, October). SAVOR the word to reinforce vocabulary in the content areas. *Journal of Reading,* 25(1), 46–51. Copyright 1981 by the International Reading Association.

As students gain experience with the Semantic Feature Analysis format, the teacher may wish to switch from a plus/minus system to a numerical system (0 = none, 1 = some, 2 = much, 3 = all). The method is viewed as a culminating activity for reinforcing and expanding concepts introduced in the conventional content area lesson or following reading.

Notes on SAVOR

Semantic Feature Analysis has been found to be significantly more effective than traditional methods for clarifying frequently confused terms (Johnson, Toms-Bronowski, & Pittelman, 1982). It also has been shown to improve Content Area Reading vocabulary and comprehension in learning disabled adolescents (Anders, Bos, & Filip, 1984).

▶ CULTURAL-ACADEMIC TRIVIA

The Cultural-Academic Trivia, or CAT, game (Manzo, 1970b, 1985) is conducted similarly to an old-fashioned spelling bee, with three important differences: Students are asked to define rather than spell the words, extra points are given for a definition that includes a good example of or elaboration on the basic word meaning, and the words used are located and brought in by students themselves. This latter aspect of the games builds word consciousness by sending students out to look and listen for words of whatever sort the teacher has directed.

Steps in Cultural-Academic Trivia

Step 1. The class is divided into two groups. A chairperson is assigned to each group and given a set of index cards initially prepared by the teacher. On the front of each card is a word or phrase with a number from one to three designating its relative difficulty. On the reverse side is an explanation or definition of the word or phrase.

Step 2. The chairperson of one group chooses and writes a word or phrase on the board and then asks students in the other group if they know that word or phrase. All the information gained from the members of a group constitutes that group's total response. If that information amounts to merely an identification or recognition of the word or phrase, only the number describing the level of difficulty (from one to three) is awarded to the group. If any worthwhile elaboration, as determined by the teacher, also is contributed, the score is doubled. Conversely, if the students on one team cannot respond successfully, the opposing team is given the opportunity to win points.

Example

In a high school class, the word *utopia* might be assigned a difficulty level of two. If one team volunteers that the word means "a perfect political and social system," it gains the two basic points. If team members add that *utopia* is also the title of a book by Sir Thomas More, or that it came from Greek, they receive two additional points. After the first round of the game, students are asked to submit terms they have selected from their reading, viewing, and living environments.

Notes on Cultural-Academic Trivia

Students' contributions are essential if students are to be resensitized to the language they encounter around them. In the particular setting in which this game was first played, the cards were treated as "admission tickets" to class. Students who arrived without cards were sent scurrying to the library to find an appropriate term. Today, we would urge students to browse the internet for new terms. See Figure 7.8 for some ideas.

Of course, not all words are created equal. The success of this game hinges on the terms used. Well-selected words and phrases should key students to central, or schema-enhancing, academic ideas and allusions (e.g., hieroglyphics, Communist Manifesto, citizen's arrest, Chaucer). If the teacher intends to develop students' sophistication in just one area, the name of the game can be altered accordingly—for example, BAT (Biological-Academic Trivia) or HAT (Historical-Academic Trivia).

Themed Vocabulary, Webbing, and Semantic Clustering

One of the most logical approaches to vocabulary enrichment is based on grouping words by themes. Themed Vocabulary Study, also called Webbing and Semantic Clustering (Marzano & Marzano, 1988), permits students to take well-known, partially known, and barely recognized words and link them together into a semantic web that will catch and hold yet newer words as well as nuances of meaning and connotation for familiar words. Paradoxically, it helps students understand that words do not always have precise, distinct, and unchanging meanings (Anderson & Nagy, 1989). Most important, themed vocabulary study imparts an effective strategy for

Technology is the language *du jour*. It permeates our style of speaking/writing and is an analogical, or metaphorical, means of thinking and hence communicating. Vocabulary knowledge itself could be likened to a computer's random access memory (RAM). The human equivalent of RAM pretty much defines the type and sophistication level of the learning software, or content and concepts, that a mind will be easily able to recognize and run. Of course, this need not be the case. RAM is mechanical, fixed, unreflective, and indeed bogs down with demand. Minds are organic, have no apparent limitations, and can reflect on and, with proper stimulation, restructure themselves in ways that actually permit them to grow greater, wiser, and more efficient with each additional word and concept that is strategically added. If there is a limit to the mind's capacity to learn, we have yet to discover it; thus far it seems to expand further with each breakthrough means of teaching it.

In any case, once it was trains that captured human imagination with images like "building up a head of steam"; now we speak of someone's "bandwidth" to describe his or her capacity, or ask ourselves if we have enough "cycles" to get something done. New dictionaries are listing between 300 and 400 new and new-meaning words.

By the way (or BTW, in e-mail lingo), if you need a dictionary before one is available for terms such as *digerati* or *cookie* or *Netiquette,* try www.whatis.com.

Figure 7.8 Tech Talk—new members of our community of language and allusions

lifelong word learning. The act of categorizing terms also is one of the most fundamental forms of human thinking and, therefore, no doubt contributes to improved cognitive processing.

Steps in Themed Vocabulary Study

Step 1. Identify a theme. For example, the theme "talk" is used in Figure 7.9. In this example, the easier synonyms for "talk," that most elementary students might know, are extended outward to increasingly more difficult synonyms that might not be acquired until middle or high school.

Step 2. Ask students to suggest words they think are related to the theme.

Step 3. If necessary, use dictionaries to check word meanings and to find additional synonyms, antonyms, and subtly different meanings.

Step 4. Link the relevant words to one another (with brief definitions) in the form of a semantic map or web as shown.

Step 5. Reinforce and evaluate by testing students' recall of word meanings and distinctions by having them write sentences or descriptive pieces designed to elicit the new words.

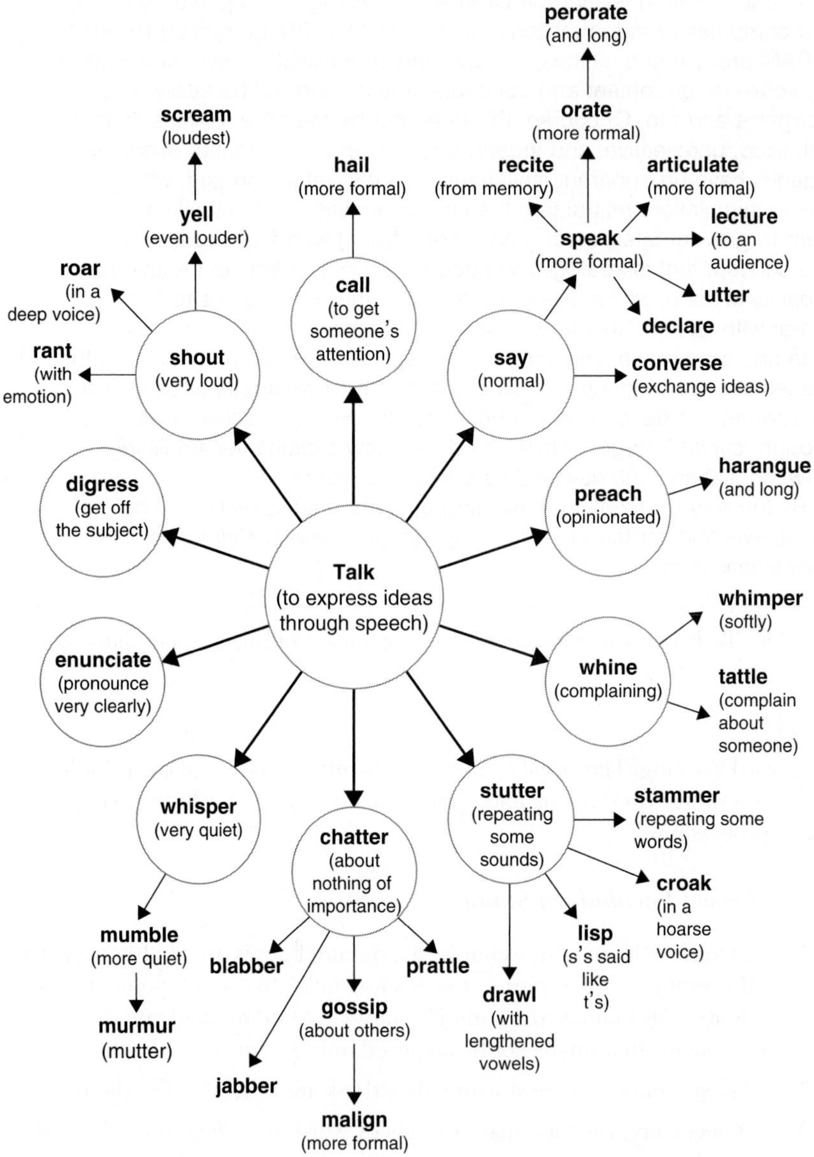

Figure 7.9 Themed Vocabulary Study—semantic cluster web for *talk*

Source: From MANZO. *Teaching Children to Be Literate,* 1E. ©1996 Wadsworth, a part of Cengage Learning, Inc. Reproduced by permission. www.cengage.com/permissions.

Notes on Themed Vocabulary Study

Themes for vocabulary study can be selected based on the guiding concept of instructional units. The possibilities are as broad as one's imagination. Here are some themes to consider for general word study that we have found to be of particular interest to middle and senior high school students:

- Noncomplimentary but nonvulgar terms (pesky, brusque, prissy, scattered, antsy, bawdy, addlebrained.)
- Behavior-related terms (manners, antsy, comportment, deportment, inappropriate, maladaptive, poised, irascible.)
- Character traits (endurance, restraint, perseverance, reflection, tolerance.)
- Thinking terms (abstract, concrete, rational, irrational, creative, critical, cognitive, diffusive, constructive, coherent.)
- Temperament labels (sanguine, industrious, hyper, choleric, mercurial, pensive.)
- Attitudes (positive, negative, hostile, aggressive, assertive, constructive.)

The impact of Themed Vocabulary Study can be amplified by combining it with other vocabulary methods previously described. It also can be linked to the next method as an incidental means of building word power.

Multimedia Vocabulary Review

Two formats are suggested by Baines (1998) for transforming vocabulary worksheets into a multimedia experience.* The first has students working in pairs to create word posters.

1. Place students in pairs.
2. Give each pair of students the responsibility for one vocabulary word.
3. Give students 10 minutes to illustrate their word. Students may draw pictures, cut out pictures in magazines, use computer clip art, or use images from the internet. After the images have been selected (printed and cut out), students should paste them on a large piece of posterboard and beside them write their own brief definition in large letters. Encourage students to use mnemonic devices.
4. Have the students explain their posters and then perform a live 30-second skit that illustrates the meaning of their word.
5. Give an extra point on the next vocabulary test to the first student each day to use one of the vocabulary words in class in "everyday conversation."
6. If more than one class has the same vocabulary words, place all the posterboards with the same words in the same area. Hang the posterboards conspicuously around the room until the exam is given.

*Baines, L. (1998). The future of the written word. In J. Simmons & L. Baines (Eds.), *Language study in the middle school, high school, and beyond* (pp. 207–209). Copyright 1998 by the International Reading Association.

The second format is the Vocabulary Chain E-Mail (Baines, 1998, pp. 208–209).*

1. Create a flowchart with PowerPoint, Persuasion, or another presentation software package, or by hand. Draw a flowchart in which one green box is at the top, five red boxes are under the top green box, and five more blue boxes are under each of the red boxes. This is a flowchart for 31 students that is easily modifiable for more or fewer students.
2. Give the student whose name is in the top green box the vocabulary list a day before you hand it out to the rest of the class. The student should write definitions of the words, be able to pronounce them correctly, and use them in a sentence.
3. The next day, speak individually with the student whose name is in the top green box. Answer any questions he or she might have about the vocabulary. Then hand out the list of vocabulary words to the rest of the class.
4. A day or two before the vocabulary test, the student whose name is in the top green box e-mails or calls the students whose names appear in the five red boxes and helps them review for the vocabulary test. Then, each of the students whose names appear in the five red boxes e-mails or calls each of the students whose names appear in the five blue boxes. By the day of the exam, everyone in class has received an e-mail message or a telephone call and has reviewed for the exam.
5. Shift responsibilities weekly. At the end of the term, give a prize to the individual whose name was in the top green box when the class scored the highest on the exam.

▶ CONCEPT SUMMARY

Most of the words known by the average adult, 80% in fact, are acquired incidentally, rather than through direct instruction and/or independent study. This suggests that equipping students with strategies for learning words is more important than teaching the meanings of any given sets of words. That said, key content/concept vocabulary can be selected and taught in ways that concurrently teach vocabulary learning strategies. Perhaps the most important of these strategies is *word consciousness*—simply noticing an unfamiliar word on the page or in the environment.

*Baines, L. (1998). The future of the written word. In J. Simmons & L. Baines (Eds.), *Language study in the middle school, high school, and beyond* (pp. 207–209). Copyright 1998 by the International Reading Association.

CHAPTER 8

TEACHING FOR CRITICAL AND CREATIVE RESPONSES TO READING

Educators are the primary trustees of the future.
—the authors

This chapter is more akin to reading (way) *Beyond* the lines. The ideas presented in this chapter are aimed at the heroic and evolving twenty-first-century goals of improving critical-constructive thinking and problem solving at all levels of reading proficiency. This type of teaching has been given lip service in the past but little real support in school or society at large. Achieving this aim implies the need for instructional approaches designed to *transform* rather than merely inform thinking. The chapter focuses on three interlocking approaches to transformation. One is aimed at converting inert knowledge to dynamic knowledge, an objective that has been described as moving the simple thinking of "ungeared minds" to the more complex thinking of connected minds (Chase, 1926). This is accomplished largely through brief, multiperspective writing and exchanges with other reader-writers. The second approach is to stress knowledge *making*, or original thought, as well as the more traditional goal of knowledge *taking*. Ironically, this is accomplished by reeducating minds to patterns of thought that could make creative thinking part of school tradition (Manzo & Manzo, 1997b). The third approach is to connect students globally to virtual communities of learners whose knowledge quests and idea exchanges match the most idealized campus environments of the past.

▶ WELCOME TO THE 21ST CENTURY—AIMING HIGHER TO CONSTRUCTIVE THINKING

Chances are that you already know something about *critical* reading–thinking. However, your own schooling and teacher education probably have not tended to address issues in *constructive-creative* thinking: It is a fairly new development in school programming. Much of the fundamental concept is captured in a helpful book by Rebecca Luce-Kapler (2004) called *Writing With, Through, and Beyond the Text: An Ecology of Language.* Despite its newness, teaching for constructive-creative outcomes does have some history associated with it. Knowing some of this will help you be ready to learn more. So here is a quick summary of some of the key ideas that should make your reading of the Content Area Literacy contributions to constructive thinking more profitable. First, we briefly address the role of text in constructive reading, then the relationship of constructive reading to constructivism and conventional critical thinking, we then move on to the affective side of this process, and, finally, to some general guidelines for promoting constructive-creative thinking outcomes in every content area classroom. Think of this initial information as *frontloading* for reading the remainder of this chapter, which in turn is front material for personally joining this exciting twenty-first-century development in professional education and hope for the future. See Figure 8.1 for a cognitive map of some similarities and differences between creative-constructive and critical thinking. The key differences as noted in Figure 8.1 are that critical reading–thinking is about finding flaws; constructive reading–thinking is about finding the best solution for a given time despite imperfections. Both require awareness and management of our sometimes blind inclination toward self-interest. In general, critical thinking alone can become a matter of finding peace of mind by selecting between dueling dogmas, whereas constructive thinking can be a bit unsettling since it most often involves stepping outside of dueling dogmas to provisional solutions that may need careful monitoring and testing.

The Role of Text

An English teacher in Brookline, Massachusetts, wrote an article on her remarkable three-month effort to teach to students *To Read Beyond the Plot* (Metzger, 1998). She used her own variations on Socratic Seminars and other elaborate techniques to foster such in-depth thinking. Along the way, in reading *Romeo and Juliet, The Great Gatsby*, and the poem *Ozymandias*, the class she led and tutored in discussion

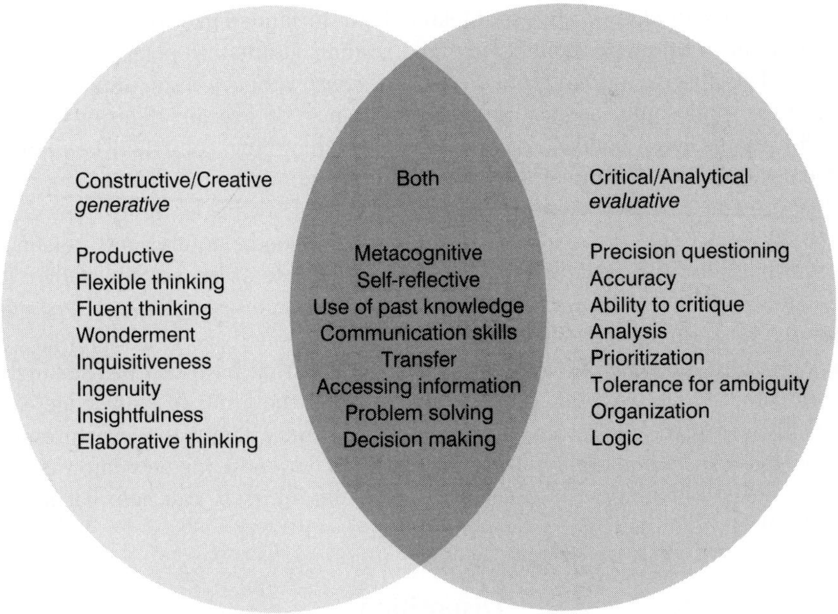

Figure 8.1 Cognitive map of major similarities and differences between creative-constructive and critical thinking

Source: From Fogarty, R., & McTighe, J. (1993). Educating Teachers for Higher-Order Thinking: The Three-Story Intellect. *Theory Into Practice*, 32(3), 161–169. Copyright by the College of Education, The Ohio State University. All rights reserved.

techniques did something else that can be easily forgotten when reaching "Beyond the lines": They read "the lines" again, and again.

> At the beginning of each discussion, we read the passage two or three times, each time more slowly. Therefore during a single class period, the same page was read four to six times. . . . The act of re-reading helped students focus and notice details . . . [and] words. . . . It was no longer enough to skim over an assignment and consider it finished.
>
> (From "Teaching Reading: Beyond the Plot," by Margaret Metzger, PHI DELTA KAPPAN, November, 1998, p. 246. © 1998 Phi Delta Kappa International.)

This teacher's experience tells how important the words are in teaching thinking beyond the text. Literal understanding is essential, although it need not be completely achieved before there is any discussion; which is to say that all the factors stated are necessary but not sufficient for promoting higher-order literacy. Also on the matter of words, it is important to talk about how certain words can be overly influential or underinfluential on thinking. Words and phrases can start wars, win or lose elections, or settle hostilities. This is a particular concern with textual/printed material from the past that cannot always be edited for each passing era.

Constructive-Creative Thinking and Constructivism

By *constructive thinking*, we mean thinking that is grounded in *critique more than criticism*, and critique is pointed toward building alternative perspectives and options. This approach is not quite the same as *constructivism*, a sometimes overly subjectivist philosophy advocating the importance of learners figuring things out for themselves. Unlike constructivism, teaching for constructive-creative outcomes does not contradict the value of old-fashioned lecture, recitation, and factual learning—three potentially powerful forms of "verbal learning" (Ausubel, 1960). What it does do is emphasize the greater good, inquiry, and personal responsibility for one's own knowledge and for the state of human knowledge. It raises this seemingly abstract responsibility to a conscious goal for teachers and students. In so doing, it should help increase internal motivation, grasp of larger concepts, and appreciation for existing "knowledge" that has been painstakingly accumulated. Done properly, efforts to teach about the limits of knowledge can implicitly impart ways to respond to the irritation of uncertainty, that ever-present feeling that can either immobilize the will or stir its quest for new knowledge. This is almost a definition of a higher purpose and, of itself, can help balance a worldview based on self-interest.

Disposition

The way in which a person typically deals with life problems foretells whether and how he or she will address problems in reading, writing, thinking, and knowledge acquisition. There are five characteristic dispositions for responding to a barrier, conflict, or paradox:

1. Ignoring it.
2. Saying it is unsolvable.
3. Working harder at the same solution hoping for a different result.
4. Trying for more inventive solutions.
5. Considering the possibility that the wrong questions are being asked.

The first three tend to be counterproductive. The latter two—looking for inventive solutions and reconsidering the question—are the prime movers of human progress and lives well lived. These are chief aims of this chapter, and well within the scope of most any classroom. Teaching for creative outcomes is not a tedious new challenge; it is a pragmatic solution for schools that in some cases have been reduced to teaching the "basics," when these elements are, in fact, a significant part of the basics.

Guidelines for Teaching Creative Outcomes

Successful teaching for creative outcomes tends to require creative teaching. Guidelines for inviting creativity include the following:

- Believing students are capable of creative production.
- Simply asking for creative responses.
- Providing critical-constructive feedback.
- Inviting and welcoming expressions of curiosity.
- Illustrating and underscoring new twists on old patterns.
- Teaching students how to give as well as receive critical-creative critiques.
- Readying students for a much greater level of error or mistakes than most of us are used to experiencing.
- Inviting contrary or opposing views.
- Finding ways to grapple with authentic as well as academic issues (Manzo, 1998).

In addition to these classroom-based considerations, there is a need to build systemic support in the society at large for inventive thinking, especially for procedural and social solutions, for which society provides few incentives such as patents or royalties.

Much of what you will be reading and thinking about from this point forward is one of the chief quests or pioneering realms of Content Area Literacy and professional education in the twenty-first century. Read ahead with the mindset of thinking both critically and constructively about how this might be done better in schools and, by extension, in society.

Unattended Needs of Even the Most Proficient Readers

Educators carefully note that there are subgroups of readers who are *dyslexic, remedial,* and *corrective.* However, when discussing *developmental readers,* or those on grade level and above, the implicit belief is that these students are a homogeneous group who are progressing as expected and need no further examination or assistance. Lack of attention to this issue masks several reading–thinking problems that need to be acknowledged before they can be addressed. Recent research is lending new insight into the needs of developmental readers.

Four subtypes of otherwise proficient readers seem to be emerging. Each subgroup has strengths and weakness that Content Area Literacy, and specifically the critical-creative thrust of this chapter, could be addressing. A recent study found that only one of the four subgroups seemed to be making real progress toward reading maturity, and even this group had a weakness in what could be called "entrepreneurial literacy"—again, the making as much as taking of jobs and commitment to knowledge creation—arguably one of the strongest needs in contemporary life. (See Figure 8.2 for descriptions of the four subgroups identified.) Two other subgroups of proficient readers had a decided gender-dominated bent, and the fourth appeared to have mastered the mechanics of language but not much of its subtleties' complex implications (Manzo, Manzo, Barnhill, & Thomas, 2000; Thomas, 2001). These subtypes, or *Reading Personality Profiles,* were deduced from a 148-item self-report inventory given to college-level students.

A Culture of Creativity

We do not yet know for certain when the characteristics identified had their developmental onset. However, one point seems logically supportable: Students are more likely to be "transformable," or guided toward a critical-constructive disposition, when they are younger rather than older. Therefore, efforts to promote higher-order reading, writing, and thinking probably should be cultivated as part of a culture of creativity for all students, from the earliest grade levels, no matter how proficient they might appear on conventional measures of reading comprehension.

The Need to Cultivate Multiple Literacies as Opposed to Merely More Reading

Jane Fell Greene, in a conference title for a presentation that frankly we did not get to hear, unpacks much of what concerns us in this tag line: "We Confused Literature with Literacy. . . So What Do We Do Now?" Higher-order literacy is not likely to be achieved merely by *more* story reading, nor by reading that is totally limited to one's narrow field of interest. Becoming more informed in a variety of fields and topics, or achieving multiple literacy, as in computer literacy and financial literacy and historical literacy, is the most basic and traditional way to enrich schema and broaden orientation. These *multiple literacies* amount to ingraining implicit questions, or quests, that engender the interests, motivation, and ability to

SUBTYPE I: DEVELOPMENTALLY MATURE ANDROGYNOUS READERS

These most highly optimized subtype readers report that their reading is characterized by concentration, critical analysis, concept formation, inference, and interpretation. They think creatively with minimum prompts, and write fairly well. They have eclectic reading interests and seem confident and comfortable with traditional schooling. Since they did not have the strong, conventionalized male or female schema orientations noted in other subtypes, they are characterized as androgynous, or in touch with both their male and female sides. The only hypothesized characteristic of mature readers that these individuals lack is the entrepreneurial spirit that has become so necessary in contemporary life.

SUBTYPE II: CONVENTIONALIZED NONFICTION MALE ORIENTATION

This subtype tends to have a conventionalized orientation that is most often associated with males in Western cultures. They have an action stance and a fair transfer-of-training (the application level of thinking), and are disinclined to self-examination. They have conventional male interests in sports, outdoor life, business, gambling, social studies, and the mechanics of how things work. However, they indicated that they do not enjoy reading for pleasure, and even report some physical discomfort in doing so. They further indicate that they have trouble paying attention while reading and suspect that they may be "learning disabled," to the point of being unable to stay attentive without active, pencil-in-hand, reading. They indicate that they are only moderately creative, and prefer repetitive tasks. Yet, they are critical and reflective: they engage in a great deal of active questioning while reading, attempting to convert what is read into action plans. Overall, they prefer to read in short spurts, and for pragmatic purposes.

SUBTYPE III: CONVENTIONALIZED STORY-READING FEMALE ORIENTATION

This subtype tends to have characteristics traditionally associated with females in literate cultures. They enjoy reading fiction, and report little interest in thinking deeply about what they read, and *no* interest in self-examination. They have virtually no interest in things mechanical, political, functional, or pragmatic. They have narrow, traditionalized female interests in fashion and children. They read for pleasure and escape with a self-declared tendency to be too literal, and to lack confidence in their understanding of what they read. Contrary to the image of the female diary keeper, they do not feel as if they learn from writing, and they find it very

Figure 8.2 Proficient-reader subtypes

taxing. Overall, they are story-readers with solid literal comprehension and strongly expressed enjoyment of reading, but who see little connection between what they read and their own lives. Since it is the nature of fiction to unveil the complexities in understanding "relationships," it is possible that this is a desired, pragmatic goal.

SUBTYPE IV: DETAIL-DEPENDENT RULE FOLLOWERS

This subtype tends to be passive reader-learners with apparently good mastery of the mechanics of language, such as grammar and spelling, but who feel that they tend to get lost in details when they read or write. They have an expressed interest in magic, which suggests less emotional maturity and relatively unsophisticated patterns of thought for otherwise capable minds.

Figure 8.2 *(continued)*

use metaphors, and analogical thinking ("Oh, this is like that . . . ") to comprehend and reason beyond the lines. Real experts in any field are those who leverage their primary interest area to find more universal meanings and levels of meaning in various other knowledge areas. Further, they return from forays into other knowledge areas with new metaphors and analogies that excite clearer thinking in their areas of expertise.

Complex Thinking Is Not Synonymous with More Information

The transfer from information to knowledge to complex thinking does not seem to occur naturally (Kirshner & Whitson, 1997). A study of mathematics majors had results similar to one found in the proficient reader study referenced previously. It showed that among those college students who had considerable experience with mathematics, there was not a commensurate improvement in thinking that even vaguely resembled that of mathematicians (Stenger, 1999). The primary reason to study in any field is often said to be to learn how to "think in that subject" (hence, the section at the end of this chapter on "Thinking-Like-a-Teacher"). Current schooling does not seem to be accomplishing this objective to the extent that modern teaching and ancillary technologies suggest we could and should. The next section suggests some possible reasons for the difficulty of teaching toward this transfer of disposition or social-emotional intelligence and learning, and some viable classroom solutions that would be within the reach of content area teachers in middle and secondary schools.

Problem: Inert Knowledge
Solution: Theme Study and Reflective Writing

Traditionally, two of the highest objectives of literacy education have been to keep learning continuous or ongoing (Bruner, 1966) and to help students transfer learning from one situation or context to another—sometimes called the *evaluation/application level of thinking* (Bloom, 1976; McKeough, Lupart, & Marini, 1995). Fundamental to these interrelated objectives is the need to have knowledge rise above the level of the *inert.* One of the main ways that this is done can be represented in a single word: *connections.* New experiences, ideas, and facts become usable, or transferable, only when they are connected with prior experience and knowledge or the intrinsic interconnectedness of themed study. We have discussed several ways to do this in previous chapters under the labels of *schema activation, frontloading,* and *reading between the lines.* Addressed now are several other reasons and ways to *excite* acquired knowledge, making it more active and potentially attachable to other sources of incoming information.

It is now commonly held that the conversion of *inert* to *dynamic* knowledge is not best done merely through conventional *transmission* education—with which information and knowledge are transferred from those who are "in the know" to those who are ignorant. Nor is it done merely through *transactional* education—with which the object of teaching/learning is the individual's unique subjective, constructivist perceptions of experience and information. Achieving dynamic learning requires a certain level of *transformative* education—with which learning and thinking are intended to change the learner's attitudes and dispositions, providing a more solid preparation for the feature that cannot be predicted. This form of learning is based on the connective tissue of real thinking and therefore the extension of cognitive modeling or *cognitive apprenticeship* approaches that have been illustrated earlier in this text. These apprenticeships can be conducted in a variety of settings and from a variety of perspectives (Rogoff, 1990). Aiming these approaches toward transformative goals tends to require

- themes and problems that are stated in evocative ways.
- reciprocal interactions that shape the thinking of learners and the offerings of teachers.
- frequent, brief writing on varied aspects of an interconnected theme.
- the environmental impact of the internet on information sharing and our social images of literate people.

To overlook the wraparound effect of the internet is to miss a developing opportunity to capitalize on its benefit to influence learning and thinking around the clock, around the home, in the community, in classrooms, and around the globe.

Writing in response to reading is a traditional means of teaching comprehension and developing thinking strategies. The types of responses students are guided toward reflect the teacher's theory of teaching-learning. The next section summarizes the primary schools of thought in this area.

Reader-Response Theories: Toward Transformational Turnabouts, Tiny Rebirths, and Epiphanies

For some educators, the primary purpose of reading in school is to achieve cultural and historical *transmission* (Hirsch, 1987), or (again) the *orderly* transfer of knowledge from those who have it to those who would then be sufficiently informed to do likewise. For others, response to text largely should be a *transaction* (Harste, 1994; Rosenblatt, 1938), or a personal construction of meaning that is highly subjective and unforced by the teacher or some other higher authority. This can be somewhat disorderly, since it seems to imply that there are no limits to the number of different ways that text can be interpreted. For a growing number of educators, such as the English teacher who e-mailed us from Brookline, Massachusetts, response to text has many, but not an "infinite number of, possible interpretations." As such, responses to text should be, at least in school, based on certain grounded outcomes that are both informative and transformative. That is, students should become more willing to reformulate as well as formulate ideas through what have been called *reflective turnabouts* (Santa, Dailey, & Nelson, 1985) and *tiny rebirths* (Burke, 1950/1969), or changes in personal views. Such change may follow from receiving sound arguments and evidence contrary to their initial views (Manzo, Garber, Manzo, & Kahn, 1994; Manzo & Manzo, 1995) and from exchanges of different perspectives. In some cases, the change may come as a sweeping epiphany triggered by new experience, but it is more likely to be a gradual transformation, or tiny rebirth to more qualified thinking. These enlightenments seldom come about through argument. They tend to culminate from stories as much as from statistics. Literature can be a very effective teacher of social-emotional intelligence as well as of empathy. The challenge seems to be to impart a balance of intentional information that is "suasive," though not blatantly persuasive (more on this later), along with a continuing supply of stories and perspectives that encourage deeper sensitivity to the incongruities in language and common conceptions. Salibrici (1999) refers to these as "Burkean moments," a reference to the writings of Kenneth Burke on what we would characterize as the "implosive" or mind-altering effect on learning and thinking that can come from attempting to reconcile incongruities and paradoxes or seemingly conflicting stories and statistics.

Comparative Studies Support Transformative Teaching

A comparison study of the effects of each of these three approaches on measures of complexity of thinking and socioemotional adjustment showed that *transmission-type* teaching was the least effective, *transactive* (constructivist) was next best, and *transformative* teaching was by far the most effective (Garber, 1995). This finding has been richly supported in a second study with college students (Jackson-Albee, 2000). For a rhetorical picture of the distinctions among these three perspectives in terms of the role of the text, the reader, and the teacher, see Figure 8.3. For a more personal account, consider Mary Salibrici's (1999) anecdotal report. She describes how her students reacted to a unit of reading, writing, and discussion of the Rosenberg trial of the early 1950s. Julius and Ethel Rosenberg were the only Americans ever executed for treason during peacetime. They were instrumental in helping the then Soviet Union gain access to secrets on how to build an atomic bomb. What started as a topical unit in literature soon became almost indistinguishable from a unit in social studies on the mass psychology of fear. In this case, what would have been a mildly interesting story of an earlier era is converted to a potentially transformative reminder to

TRANSMISSION MODEL PERSPECTIVE

Role of the Text:	The text is a means of transmitting society's dominant historical, literary, and cultural canon. It has fixed meanings and values irrespective of the reader. The text remains virtually static over time.
Role of the Reader:	The reader is expected to acquire the precise facts and ideas being conveyed by the author and reproduce these in the same formats in which they were presented. Little attention is given to the reader's personal or critical examination of the text. The reader is simply responsible for reconstructing the author's ideas.
Role of the Teacher:	The teacher focuses classroom discussion on the author's biography, the historical and political context of the author, and the traditional literary elements.

TRANSACTION MODEL PERSPECTIVE

Role of the Text:	The text means unique things to different readers regardless of what the author may have intended to communicate. There is no static or inherent meaning incorporated within the text itself. Instead, the text is viewed as dynamic and subjective.
Role of the Reader:	The reader brings a host of associations and inferences to every reading experience. These reader-based conceptions are a chief consideration as the reader attempts to build meaning from the written words. The reader makes fresh and unmediated interpretations, which may reflect the emotional and aesthetic needs of the reader.
Role of the Teacher:	The teacher focuses classroom discussion on the reader's feelings, associations, and personal interpretations of texts.

Figure 8.3 Theoretical perspectives on guiding students' responses to reading
Source: From *The Effects of Transmissional, Transactional, and Transformational Reader-Response Strategies on Middle School Students' Thinking Complexity and Social Development* by K.S. Garber, 1995, unpublished doctoral dissertation, University of Missouri, Kansas City. Adapted by permission.

think clearly about whatever time we are in just as you would try to rise above the preoccupations of a particular clique. (By the way, releases of previously secret Soviet files have confirmed that the Rosenbergs were communist spies who were ideologically motivated.)

In simplest terms, the key element in transformative theory is a commitment to providing students with some basic values, such as those associated with democratic

TRANSFORMATION MODEL PERSPECTIVE

Role of the Text:	The text is a tool for critical and constructive thought. It not only reflects the ideas and contexts of the author but also invites the thoughts and feelings of the reader. The text is a stimulus for critical-evaluative, or formative, thinking.
Role of the Reader:	The reader examines the text critically with the goal of becoming a constructive thinker and solution-creator/implementer in the context of the surrounding society. The reader approaches each text consciously, separating what the author says from the reader's own thoughts and feelings. The reader suspends final judgment until he or she has developed legitimate and rational positions through a process of rigorously examining multiple interpretations. The reader sometimes reformulates thinking and/or becomes a producer of new knowledge and new texts as a result of this examination.
Role of the Teacher:	The teacher focuses classroom discussion on generating and supporting varied interpretations with examples of multiple reader-response options. The teacher may ask students to make judgments about the author's intent, purpose, accuracy, logic, reliability, and literary form, or about others' responses to the same text.

Figure 8.3 *(continued)*

life, without pedantically serving up unnecessarily biased views of life's options. Needless to say, this isn't easy and we will all do it poorly sometimes. Therefore, we should judge ourselves by our long-term commitment more than our occasional lapses as all-too-human teachers. Writing and encouraging writing can be useful in clarifying one's thoughts and message.

▶ CRITICAL READING-WRITING-THINKING: A TRADITIONAL AND EVOLVING GOAL

With a background now in place on the general idea of *critical-constructive* reading, writing, and thinking, and the transformational approach to teaching toward these ends, we turn to a review of *critical* thinking, including some new concepts and challenges in this field. We then will recombine critical-constructive reading, writing, and thinking into one more or less unifying concept and speak to several concrete methods for promoting this highest level of literacy. By the end of the chapter, you will have recapitulated much of the evolution of knowledge and art on these topics, from critical to critical-constructive to the, perhaps, coming age of constructive-creative reading, writing and thinking. Ideally, this story should be orderly, unambiguous, and without redundancies. In fact, helping to finish construct this story may be part of each reader's contribution to the science and art of professional education.

Critical Thinking

Critical reading-writing-thinking clearly is one of the most written and talked about topics in modern history. Nonetheless, it remains one of the least well understood. Critical reading is merely the use of critical thinking in the act of reading (Ennis, 1962). Hence, most anything said about one is likely to be true of the other. David Russell, writing more than forty years ago, provides a most basic way for educators to understand critical reading and thinking. He says, essentially, that it is best defined as a three-factor ability, to which most contemporary educators would add a fourth, as shown here. Critical reading is

- an attitudinal, or dispositional, factor of effective questioning and suspension of judgment.
- a functional factor of logical inquiry and problem solving, sometimes known as *dialogical* or *dialectical thinking*.
- a judgmental factor based on some set of norms growing out of consensus, now called *cultural imperatives* (Russell, 1961).
- a matter of being able to imagine alternative perspectives often not represented (Lenski, Wham, & Johns, 1999; Paul, 1993), and which now we would now more generically call *constructive-creative thinking*.

There are several paradoxes to overcome in teaching for and even talking about critical reading-thinking. For one, it is a *process*, the merit of which people tend to acknowledge based on whether the *product*, or conclusion reached, pleases them. In general, the term *critical* is applied only when the facts are incomplete or in dispute and therefore when "right-thinking" people are likely to disagree. In other words, to teach critical thinking one must broach some controversial and even sensitive topics.

Critical Reading-Writing-Thinking Objectives

Certain functions sketch out the teacher's and students' thinking processes in achieving progress toward this higher level of literacy. Later in this chapter these ideas begin to lean toward a more holistic concept of critical-constructive thinking rather than some kind of step-by-step process.

- Growth past reductionist thinking, or the tendency to oversimplify complex matters to black and white, either/or choices.
- Overcoming the tendency to be deceptive and self-deceptive, as occurs when sound information is disallowed because it does not suit one's purpose.

- Learning to unpack one's own and a writer's intentions/motivations.
- Learning how to read-write-think in ways that are not immediately comfortable to us, since various domains of learning and influence have their own characteristic ways of conducting discourse (e.g., science talk, literature talk, business talk.)
- Achieving a certain measure of the goal of "critical pedagogy," which is to increase insight into the ways in which one's reading-writing-thinking are bound to our cultural perceptions of race, gender, representations of self-image, and hence personal power.
- Recognizing that language is "symbolic action" (Burke, 1950/1969), which implies a need to interrogate one's own and a writer's choice of words and positions in terms of their consequences to others.
- Belief that one is responsible in some ways for the production or creation of knowledge and insight as well as for its consumption.
- Realizing that in some situations there is not so much one "truth," but that often truth is a multilayered and multiperspective decision.

There probably is no better, though no more disquieting, way to become a better critical-constructive reader-writer-thinker than to start with a thorough examination of one's own assumptions. This is especially urgent for teachers, ministers, administrators, and lawyers since assumptions guide the way they implicitly teach others to think critically.

Watch Your Assumptions

Most faulty conclusions can be traced back to faulty or unexamined assumptions. Of course, these seldom seem unexamined at the time. Some assumptions go unexamined because they are traditionally accepted givens. For example, the conclusion that one needs to have a college education to be successful in life is based on employment practices and cultural expectations that are changing rapidly. Other assumptions go unexamined because they too ride into town as innovations or movements that reveal the error or outdatedness of the old or traditional ways of thinking and/or acting. The other side of the example is the conclusion that the cost of a college education may now have exceeded its value. This conclusion, being reached by many young people who in prior times would never have raised the question, can be justified by numerous facts. However, it is based on the assumption that the primary benefits of a college education are financial in nature.

Examining assumptions involves a set of thinking strategies that form the core of insightful critical-constructive analysis. These include:

- Asking a lot of relevant questions, even when the answers may seem self-evident.
- Acquiring and objectively dealing with available information, whether or not it is personally "pleasing".
- Avoiding overly simplistic good/bad dichotomies.
- Recognizing the persuasive effects of emotionally laden language.

- Examining the author's motivation (reformers' identities can get so tied up in the struggle that perpetuation of the cause becomes more important than its achievement).
- Examining one's own motivation (this may involve coming to grips with that egoistic voice inside each of us and recognizing self-serving myths and convenient distortions of the truth; in other words, internalizing the spirit of the old saying, "If the truth is getting in your way, chances are that you're going the wrong direction.").

These habits of thought are fairly self-evident. Teaching them, however, requires some powerful instructional actions to stir minds out of comfort and complacency. The next subsection provides a set of questions for modeling critical thinking strategies on any issue.

"Pentimento" Questions Help Adolescents Think More Critically

- Is there more here than first meets the eye? A useful metaphor for critical reading/thinking is *pentimento*, a term used in art restoration for finding a (sometimes more valuable) oil painting underneath another one (because canvases were expensive and artists often painted over their own works)
- Has this been proposed before, and under what label or name?
- What are the credentials, background, and interests of the major advocates and adversaries?
- What assumptions are nested in the competing proposals?
- What factual evidence and logic support and refute this proposal?
- What other issues or matters are affected by accepting or rejecting this proposal?
- How might critics label or name this proposal?
- How do the choices affect me, and can I think clearly about this?
- Chances are that there is something of value and something needing correction in the competing proposals. Can these be reconciled?

We'd now invite you to exercise *your* critical-constructive powers of analysis on some issues that are current in literacy and general education (see Figure 8.4, "Examples of Evocative and Critical Issues in Literacy Education").

Guidelines for Critically Reading a Writer's Intent

In most print materials intended to inform, the writer has attempted to build an orderly progression of thought and information toward an unambiguous conclusion. Relevant examples and details are interwoven to add clarity and support. Depending on the author's intended or unintended purpose, however, the "facts" may be more or less complete and verifiable, and there may be more or less acknowledgment of alternative perspectives. Some theorists would argue that virtually everything written, from the Declaration of Independence to a

Would you agree? Disagree? What are some of the issues to consider?

- Never teach or drill anything in isolation.
- Graded books (written to be at a given difficulty level) are inauthentic and hinder learning at every level.
- The only way to improve reading is to read, read, read.
- Students need to be taught to love reading.
- Education should be conducted so that it is a liberating force, rather than an indoctrination.
- Literature is literacy.
- Lecturing is bad teaching.
- Any subject can be taught through literature.
- Diversity is good; core culture is bad.
- Teaching declarative facts and consensual interpretations is bad.
- Teacher talk is bad; student talk is good.
- Constructivist philosophy is good for learning; traditionalist philosophy is bad for learning.
- Teaching phonics rules is bad.
- Teaching context clues is good.

Figure 8.4 Examples of evocative and critical issues in literacy education

cereal box, is intended to convince the reader of something, thereby shaping the reader's views and behavior. In the end, it is up to the reader to determine what to believe. Several sets of lenses can heighten critical analysis of a writer's intent and credibility.

The first aid in critical reading is to determine whether the author is attempting knowledge telling or knowledge making (Flower & Hayes, 1981). Knowledge telling typically is the attempt to articulate something one knows, or presumes to know, in the clearest and least ambiguous way possible. Knowledge making is that plunge into the murky unknown in an attempt to discover what the author is thinking or how he or she really feels about something. This also is the most transformative mode of writing. It tends to induce deeper thinking and to result in more conclusions that influence, if not radically change, a great deal of subsequent reading, thinking, attitudes, and human behavior.

Another set of critical-reading lenses involves recognizing and analyzing the nature of the claims used by the author to support a conclusion. A claim is a statement presented as truth when in fact it is open to question. Unrau (1997) details six types of claims that should alert critical readers to consider alternative propositions:

- What the writer believes to be true (*knowledge claims*).
- What or how something causes something else (*causal claims*).
- What is likely to result from current conditions (*predictive claims*).

- What is good and noble (*evaluative claims*).
- What is right and wrong (*moral claims*).
- What should be done (*policy claims*).

A final set of lenses for critical reading is awareness of the classical propaganda techniques that have evolved from marketing and politics. These techniques, detailed in Figure 8.5, provide a useful language for talking about critical reading as well as persuasive writing, debate techniques, and oral presentation.

Impediments to Critical-Constructive Thinking

A final consideration in melding a new focus on constructive reading–thinking with traditional and emerging concepts of critical analysis is to articulate why this is not already being done more systematically. Careful articulation of a problem is one way to overcome the human instinct to deny problems, avoid problems, or simply say that a problem is unsolvable. Furthermore, stating the question or problem often translates into 50% of the solution.

The human instinct to avoid problems is so deeply rooted that at one point in the late 1980s, it reached national concern. This led to an announcement by the Education Commission of the States of a large "Higher Literacies" project to look into state policies that either "constrain or promote" schools' efforts to teach "writing, problem-solving, critical thinking, argument, analysis, synthesis, interpretation and evaluation" (Tchudi, 1988). Here is a partial list of likely impediments to acknowledging and hence addressing problems:

- Textbooks tend to be inane and therefore fail to evoke critical thought.
- The printed word generates a "halo" effect: Because it is in print, it is true and therefore not worth questioning.
- Many school administrators and teachers are afraid to broach controversial subjects with students.
- There is a general emphasis on conformity in almost all aspects of life.
- Personal emotions and prejudices often tend to disrupt clear thinking.
- Critical reading–thinking is not routinely assessed and therefore is assumed to be less important than basic objectives.
- There is a lack of models (persons and programs) that epitomize or focus on constructive and critical thinking.
- Curriculum requirements generally do not include addressing or teaching specific critical reading–thinking strategies.
- There is a pervasive fear among students and teachers that criticism of *anything*, including introspective self-appraisals, ultimately unleashes criticism of *everything*, including schools, teachers, society, and self.
- It is a paradoxical fact that classroom questioning is used on the one hand to stimulate curiosity, reinforce knowledge, and ignite discussion and on the other to scold, embarrass, and test.

Critical reading often involves recognizing an author's use of propaganda, or selling techniques. These techniques are designed to convince, persuade, or move the reader/listener to action.

Bandwagon:	Everyone is doing a certain thing, so jump on the bandwagon and go along with the crowd. ("More kids want _______ than any other toothpaste.")
Testimonial:	A well-known person endorses a certain product or course of action even though he or she is not an authority on the subject. ("Take it from me, _______, this is the niftiest video game you can buy for the money.")
Plain folks:	People who appear to be "just plain folks," or "just like you and me," suggest that we think or act in a certain way. ("My family has been in farming for fifty years; you know I won't forget you when I get to Washington.")
Snob appeal:	The opposite of plain folks. ("These beautiful designer jeans were created for the with-it girl.")
Name calling:	Applying a currently unpopular put-down to a person or movement without seeing if it really applies. ("That teacher is a geek—look at those ancient-looking clothes.")
Glittering generalities:	Words or phrases with favorable suggestions that lead us to support a person or movement without examining the evidence (can also be used with unfavorable words). Such abstract words or phrases (e.g., "public spirit," "time for change," "patriotic duty," "fiscal responsibility") are used to make us support some person or idea with little further analysis. ("We need a leader who will guide us to greater fiscal responsibility, an improved standard of living, and a fairer system of taxation. It's time for a change.")
Transfer:	A commercial symbol that trades off our respect for something to which it really is not connected. ("Buy Red Cross shoes.")
Scientific slant:	Use of scientific terms and phrases to persuade us to accept something as being more than what it really is. ("The titanium light bulb burns for 7,000 hours"; "Four out of five dentists surveyed . . .")
False analogies:	Use of an analogy or comparison situation that is not really parallel or simply is divergent on a critical point. ("Learning to read is a language process; it is no different from learning to speak.")
Confusing correlation with cause:	This deception amounts to attributing causation to things that may be related, but are not necessarily related in a cause-and-effect way. ("In the two years that I have been president, we have had nothing but prosperity").

Figure 8.5 Propaganda techniques

- Great ideas often are conceived and forged in passion, and we haven't quite figured out how to endure, let alone allow, passion in our schools and policy-making arenas.

The methods described next were designed to expose, circumvent, or even build on these innate human dispositions. *Intra-Act,* for example, capitalizes on adolescents' natural interest in predicting the opinions of their peers and in informal small group interaction.

Multiple Literacies and Pop and Hybrid Culture

Multiple Literacies involve modern age changes to communication, such as the integration of various *designs,* for example, visual, linguistic, and audio within one text (Kress, 2003; Luce-Kapler, 2007; *New London Group,* 1996). The act of reading is no longer limited to the printed page, nor are texts perceived in the narrow sense of traditional print media. Virtually all systems of signing, from that employed by musicians and artists to that used by choreographers and television dramatists and comedians, are sending signals about what one might feel, believe in, or live by. This has led to two relatively new fields of study: *semiotics,* or the study of the history and impact of different signing systems, and *multiple literacies.* There also is a more didactic form, called *critical media literacy,* that makes use of popular culture texts and symbols in teaching, such as in advertising and story-based persuasive techniques, in which the story, such as Pearl Buck's *The Good Earth,* sends a penetrating message.

"Everything Bad Is Good for You:"

This heading is borrowed from Johnson (2005). The best part of the message follows the colon: "Today's popular culture is actually making us smarter." One of the newest additions to *multiple literacies* is *fanfictions.* Kelly Chandler-Olcott and Donna Mahar report on the intriguing electronic exchanges of two teenage girls built around an art form called *Anime*—a Japanese animation, also available as video, comics, and with memorabilia, and in this case entitled "The Shrine of Vegeta" (Chandler-Olcott & Mahar, 2003, p. 557). The researchers point out that although they do not consider that "cartoons in-and-of themselves are imperative for literacy educators to consider" (p. 558), they are, nonetheless, a primary influence on the writing that adolescents produce. There is a hub for such interactions and intertwined storylines. It can be found at the Anime Web Turnpike (*http://www.anipike.com*). This hub is part of a process that links and creates new meanings and new genres that is being called *hybridity.*

Pre-Adolescent and Adolescent Scene

We find ourselves more fascinated by a slightly different meaning for this root term, *hybrid cultures* (Manzo, Manzo, & Albee, 2004). Our sense is that much of this play and interplay has even more significance than in the recent past. This is because it is not merely something to chat about and claim as a *teen scene,* but that it actually is creating a hybrid culture that seems just as inviting to the youngest of children (think *Pokemon* and *Harry Potter*). It offers a common frame of experience shared by children from otherwise diverse linguistic and cultural backgrounds and an almost immediate foreground for social connecting. As such, a valuable goal is to find ways to harness this trend toward hybrid cultures to enhance content learning and student growth. Let's continue to speak of the values and possible traps of exploiting this trend with adolescents.

Reality TV shows, such as *Survivor*, are a poignant frame of reference for discussion before and in school. But even though a sensible and resourceful teacher will use and accept such references, doing so is not without some risks. Lewis (1999) writes about *popular cultural studies* in a forward to a book on the topic by Alvermann, Moon, and Hagwood (1999). She lists several interesting advantages, and at least one possible problem, to consider as one ventures out in the direction of popular cultural studies and references in English and social studies. She states that:

- Popular cultural studies are inherently interdisciplinary.
- Popular cultural studies allow youth to self-examine the pop culture that may be strongly influencing their lives.
- Popular cultural studies tend to create a more student-centered classroom.

However, she notes—and we concur—that there is a certain degree of contradiction in teaching kids more about what they are expert in and about which we are relatively naïve. Pop culture, by its very name, is trendy and, as such, often quickly passing and hard to keep track of. There also is a strong likelihood that kids don't really want us in this, their nonadult world. This may be one of the reasons that they often carefully craft it to look, feel, and be different from whatever it is that their parents and their schools are embracing. During this, the greatest period of divorce and youth disorientation in modern history, kids also are still fully tuned into the sedate, traditional, and innocent, watching reruns of such as shows *The Brady Bunch* and the *Cosby Show* in record numbers. This all needs more careful examination and deeper consideration before we launch too many units and courses on pop culture and its transient icons. For the moment, we suggest that educators continue to monitor pop culture but use it sparingly. For all the difficulty associated with reading Shakespeare and Chaucer, these are still the coin of the realm and the source code for many referents and standardized test terms; although they do not, and should not, remain unchallenged. They, too, were once "pop culture."

▶ WRITING-BASED METHODS FOR GUIDING CRITICAL-CONSTRUCTIVE READING

One of the most effective ways to teach students to respond critically and constructively to what they read is through various types of written response. This is traditionally done in the form of the research paper, a lengthy process in which students collect information from various sources and then synthesize it in their own words and toward their own points and conclusions. This process of "transforming text," according to Moffett (1989), is the highest level of writing. When students translate information from the words of various authors to their own choices of words and phrases, the ideas and information become integrated into the students' personal knowledge bases. In this more personal form, it is less likely to be forgotten and more likely to grow into more sophisticated language and thought.

The challenge always has been in just how to teach the multiple perspectives and attitudes necessary to enable such transformation of text and *turnabouts* of student thinking. The methods in this section provide various ways to do this with reading materials of any type, any length, and in any discipline. The first method is something of a template for eliciting students' thoughts and reflections on a variety of possible topics, whether they be in pop culture, traditional literature, or wide-ranging ideas. It involves prompting students to make evaluative responses, predict the responses of their peers, and discuss the reasons for their judgments.

Intra-Act: Values-Guided versus Values-Driven Reading and Evaluative Thinking

The challenge to educators, and virtually all thinking people, is how to be reasonably guided by a set of values but not so driven by these as to lose clarity and objectivity. One way that has been suggested by reflective educators is to provide more experience in school with the examination of authentic critical issues, and hence more experience with *evaluative thinking*, the cognitive psychology name for value-based reasoning. Intra-Act (Hoffman, 1977) is a teaching method that is representative of this class of methods and one that is especially compatible with Content Area Literacy.

Intra-Act was designed to develop readers' ability to draw on their personal values base, which permeates and colors their sense of what they read and what they do with what is read. Intra-Act was influenced by the earlier work of Raths, Harmon, and Simon (1978) on "valuing process" and of Manzo and Sherk (1978) on "languaging," the process of using language to more deeply process complex issues. It involves group problem solving and cooperative learning. A study of the efficacy of the Intra-Act activity conducted by Hoffman (1977) concluded that the method was an effective means of teaching basic comprehension, that students were willing and able to "go beyond the material in projecting and perceiving personal values related to the content of the selections," and that "given an appropriately structured learning environment . . . students can and do learn from one another" (p. 63).

Steps in the Intra-Act Procedure

Preparation. Create two worksheets based on the reading selection. One is a set of non-fact-type questions, which could be answered, and argued, from several perspectives. The second is a set of related values-based (agree-disagree) statements (see example of the second kind of worksheet in Figure 8.6).

Step 1. Students read the assigned selection and individually answer the comprehension questions on the first worksheet.

Step 2. Form cooperative groups of four students each. A chairperson is appointed. (The chairperson's role is rotated each time the activity is

Your Name: ____________________ Date: ______________
Group Chairperson: ______________ Hour: ______________

Directions: Circle A for "agree" or D for "disagree" to indicate your own responses to each statement. Then circle A or D to indicate how you think each other member of your group responded to each statement

		Group Members			
		Me	*Mary*	*Jack*	*Helen*
1.	Men are usually better bosses than women.	A/D	A/D	A/D	A/D
2.	Once elected, a legislator should vote according to the wishes of the people he or she represents, not according to personal feelings.	A/D	A/D	A/D	A/D
3.	I would have voted the way the main character did in this story.	A/D	A/D	A/D	A/D
4.	I probably would have reacted as negatively to the main character as her "constituents."	A/D	A/D	A/D	A/D

Figure 8.6 Sample valuing statement exercise sheet for Intra-Act

performed.) Students compare their answers to the questions within their groups and *discuss the reasons* for their answers.

Step 3. The second worksheet is distributed, and students individually record their own responses to the values-based statements and predict the responses of the other members of their group (see Figure 8.6).

Step 4. The chairperson reads the first statement, tells his or her response, and asks each group member to share his or her response. Students "check" their own predictions of their classmates' responses as the chairperson guides them through each item.

Step 5. The teacher leads a whole-class discussion of students' personal judgments about the valuing statements and the accuracy of their predictions of the other students' judgments.

Related to the valuing process, the next method is applicable from kindergarten to graduate school. It promotes reading, cognitive development, and even civics.

Polar Opposites Spur Higher-Order (Critical) Literacy

A new third grader once managed the complex wording that essentially said to us "Are we going to do more on what we think and feel about things, or do you have to explain *why* now that we're in third grade?" Evaluation and critique questions, presumably the highest order of thinking, are little more than gut-level sentiments without careful reflection and reasoned thought. Thomas Bean (1981) developed a sensible method for urging such thinking; it included stages of both scaffolding and fading to assist students with making evaluation-explanation responses, the implicit intent of higher-order questioning. Later the method was refined and further examples were added (Bean & Bishop, 1992). Bishop had great enthusiasm for the method from the beginning and has provided some touchstone examples of its worth down to the second-grade level (A. L. Bishop, personal communication, 2003). Here now is an abridged and edited version of Polar Opposites, largely from Bishop's Course Supplement (2003).

Polar Opposites: Rationale, Steps, and Examples

This method was designed to *spur students to higher levels of critical analysis.* The core idea is an adaptation of a means, called Semantic Differential, that originally was developed in the mid-1960s and often attributed to Murray Myron to assess possible shifts in attitudes pre - and post certain interventions. Polar Opposites consists of establishing some gritty adjectives at either end of a five- to seven-point scale and having students indicate where on the scale they find their personal feelings and thinking.

Step 1. Select a book or article that is reasonably familiar to the majority of students. (*Example:* the book *The Day Jimmy's Boa Ate the Wash* [Trinka Hakes Noble/Puffin, Reprint Edition, 1992.])

Step 2. Develop four to five polar opposites that address key characters, concepts, and/or events in the story. The following are illustrations from *The Day Jimmy's Boa Ate the Wash*:

A boa constrictor is a very ________snake.

Small				*Large*
1.	*2.*	*3.*	*4.*	*5.*

The fight at the farm was started...

On Purpose				*Accidentally*
1.	*2.*	*3.*	*4.*	*5.*

It probably was a ________idea that Jimmy brought his snake to the farm.

Bad				*Good*
1.	*2.*	*3.*	*4.*	*5.*

The girl telling the story found the field trip to the farm...

Unexciting				*Exciting*
1.	*2.*	*3.*	*4.*	*5.*

Step 3. Either orally read the book or selection to the class or have students read it silently. (It is best to read it to them in early trials. At the least, read an initial page or two before they continue silently.)

Step 4. Show and model how you would circle a choice for the first opposite. Defend your rating as a simple logical extension of saying anything evaluative. Explicitly state the importance of supporting one's position.

Step 5. Complete the second and possibly a third polar opposite as a group. Allow differences to be voiced, and encourage supporting evidence and logic. (Kids will quickly learn to challenge one another and therefore to think before they speak and while they are speaking. *Self-editing is itself a higher level of metacognition and self-regulation.*)

Step 6. As students become more comfortable with this elementary process, it should be incorporated into most all class discussion as a seamless part of "saying what (and why) you think and feel as you do."

To further fade and pass along independent functioning, have students create one or two polar opposites for Postreading discussion. To aid the deeper intent of this strategy as a *habit of mind* and way to do school and life, you might consider explicitly discussing why it is important to add the "whys" as well as the "whats" of evaluative thinking. This simple hook-up is one of the most fundamental requirements of sound critical analysis, antiprejudicial thinking, and civic responsibility. Writing in an analogous context, John McEneaney (2002) reminds us of how elementary this concern is to all social interactions with a reference to one of modern education's thought leaders: "It is not enough simply to assert, assertion must be *warranted*" [Dewey, 1938, p. 9 (as cited in McEneaney, 2002, p.330)].

Critical Discourse Analysis

More recently, Bean and Moni (2003) have stepped up and outside Polar Opposites by adding greater concern for Critical Discourse Analysis (CDA) (Fairclough, 1989). The point of such "critical literacy" is to further spur critical examination of the behind-the-scenes dimensions of text.

CDA, by the Bean and Moni (2003) account, "assumes that social conditions, particularly conditions of unequal power relationships, determine the properties of discourse" (p. 643). This suggests the need, at the very least, to add some Polar Opposites that might tap into this reservoir of hidden conditions, influences, and matters of judgment. In fact, in the story alluded to previously, Polar Opposites does just this when it asks:

It probably was a __________ idea that Jimmy brought his snake to the farm.

Bad				*Good*
1.	*2.*	*3.*	*4.*	*5.*

To open this door to the behind-the-scenes conditions, the teacher might raise questions such as, *What could have led Jimmy to bring his boa to the farm?* And, with older students, this could be followed with some more poignant questions: *Was Jimmy being controlling, reckless, or just naïve in bringing the snake? How do you suppose others felt? Is this just another form of bully behavior? What may have happened before and after?* In other words, discuss unseen motives and possible circumstances. Most often, poor judgment can be traced back to displays of power, efforts to acquire it, or lack of thought. Such misdeeds become vicarious learning experiences with more careful reading and analysis.

Extended Anticipation-Reaction Guide

An extension of the Anticipation-Reaction Guide described in Chapter 4 is an effective way to encourage critical-constructive reading and responding. After students have recorded their responses to the A-R Guide statements before and after reading, they are directed to write an essay elaborating on their response to any one of the statements on the worksheet. Figure 8.7 presents an example of an A-R Guide and a related student essay from a class in economics.

Active interaction of the type generated by Anticipation-Reaction Guides promotes several key ingredients of critical reading–thinking:

- Conflict identification and resolution (Frager & Thompson, 1985).
- Metacognitive awareness of the strategies one is employing while reading (Brown, 1980).
- Connections between one's knowledge of the world and comprehension of text (Waern, 1977a, 1977b).

Directions: Before reading, check Agree or Disagree for each statement. After reading, write a brief essay on one statement of your choice.

Agree	*Disagree*	
______	______	1. Supply-side economics favors the wealthy.
______	______	2. You cannot be a Republican and be against supply-side economics.
______	______	3. You cannot be a Democrat and be for supply-side economics.

STUDENT ESSAY

I think that supply-side economics favors the wealthy because it says that when profits go up, the number of suppliers will increase. This also is supposed to increase competition, and therefore reduce prices, since there would be more supply than demand.

The government, under this approach, is dedicated to helping create greater profits for suppliers. This, however, would tend to make the rich richer and leave the poor and middle class to be the perpetual shoppers, looking for oversupplies. In fact, though, whenever supply begins to exceed demand, the rich simply move their assets elsewhere, quickly reducing supply and competition.

Of course, supply-side thinking is basic to free enterprise. Without a profit motive, investors would not take risks. The role of government, however, needs to be balanced carefully so as to avoid unnecessarily restricting profits, but also avoiding measures that virtually guarantee profits. These include big tax breaks for industry or freedom to exploit the environment. When large corporations are legally permitted not to pay tax and/or to leave behind their industrial wastes, this amounts to a hidden surcharge on all the products bought and one that the rest of us, including future generations, eventually must pay.

Figure 8.7 Anticipation-Reaction Guide: Supply-side economics

Regarding the last point, Ericson, Hubler, Bean, Smith, and McKenzie (1987) point out that in the California Academic Partnership Program, in which professors used A-R Guides in working with teachers and middle school students, students often would leave class at the end of the period still arguing the relative merits of their various points of view. This act of carrying the classroom out into the students world may be the most powerful influence of all on learning and thinking. It extends the school day by increasing student time on task and reducing the sharp line of demarcation that often separates school learning from home and life experiences.

Opinion-Proof*

The Opinion-Proof method (Santa, Dailey, & Nelson, 1985) requires students to engage in four important aspects of higher-order literacy:

1. Evaluative thinking—forming an opinion.
2. Verification—supporting an opinion.
3. Persuasive articulation—writing about the opinion convincingly.
4. Forming a consensus—cooperatively critiquing and reviewing an opinion.

Steps in the Opinion-Proof Method

Step 1. Provide the students with an Opinion-Proof guide, either written on the board (or overhead, white board, or SmartBoard) or as a handout (see the example in Step 2).

Step 2. Have students write an opinion and supporting evidence for it from the text. Following is a guide for the short story "Old Horse," a popular selection about an elderly algebra teacher by Oliver Andersen:

Example:

Opinion Statement: Old Horse was sensitive.

Evidence to Prove My Opinion:

- Old Horse was sensitive.
- He was patient with Rabbit.
- He wanted Rabbit to belong.
- Old Horse forced Rabbit to dislike him.
- He put himself down for the sake of Rabbit.

Step 3. Students write a connected essay using their opinion and evidence as topic sentence and supporting details, respectively.

*Adapted from (and examples from) Santa, Carol Minnick, Daily, Susan C. & Nelson, Marylin. (1985, January). Free-Response and Opinion-Proof: A Reading and Writing Strategy of Middle Grade and Secondary Teachers. *Journal of Reading*, 28(4), 346–352. Copyright © by the International Reading Association.

Example:*

Old Horse was a very sensitive teacher. One reason I feel this way was because of his ability to understand Rabbit. Rabbit was not liked by the other students in his class because he was a friend of Old Horse's. In addition, Old Horse understood Rabbit's need to become a part of a group of friends, and Old Horse knew that he was part of the problem. Finally, Old Horse forced Rabbit to dislike him so much that he could become accepted by the other students. Therefore, Old Horse was a very sensitive man. He even sacrificed himself for the sake of his student.

Step 4. The final step is peer editing. In this step, students (1) develop specific criteria for evaluating their writing, such as the questions "Does my paragraph contain a main idea statement?" and "Do I have evidence to support my main idea?"; (2) divide up into pairs or small groups and read and react to one another's paragraphs; and (3) edit and/or revise their own paragraphs before submitting a final draft for teacher evaluation.

In addition to its role in reading and thinking, the Opinion-Proof process provides a useful sequence for organizing persuasive speeches, another important language art. It accomplishes this by having students state opinions and write out supporting and nonsupporting points. This often leads to the reflective turnabout that makes Opinion-Proof a good framework for teaching in the transformative mode.

Read-Encode-Annotate-Ponder: Brief Writing for Deep Learning

"Add Your Comments" is now everywhere. Shouldn't there be some training in school that can draw value from this ubiquitous innovation? There is such a method. The Read-Encode-Annotate-Ponder (REAP) method (Eanet & Manzo, 1976; Manzo, 1973; Manzo, Manzo, & Albee, 2004) was shown to be an effective tool for transformational teaching in two experimental studies (Garber, 1995; Jackson-Albee, 2000). At its most basic level, REAP is a way to teach students to write (and think) from a variety of perspectives a healthy antidote for unhealthy dogmatism. It also was among the earliest strategies developed for students to use to improve study-type writing, thinking, and reading. The basic REAP formula is as follows:

R: *Read* to discern the writer's message.

E: *Encode* the message by mentally translating it into your own words.

A: *Annotate*, or make written note of, your brief responses from several perspectives.

*Adapted from (and examples from) Santa, Carol Minnick, Daily, Susan C. & Nelson, Marylin. (1985, January). Free-Response and Opinion-Proof: A Reading and Writing Strategy of Middle Grade and Secondary Teachers. *Journal of Reading*, 28(4), 346–352. Copyright © by the International Reading Association.

P: *Ponder*, or further reflect on what you have read, thought, and written, through discussion of your own and others' responses to the selection and/or your and their annotations.

REAP introduces students to a variety of brief and poignant ways to critique or *annotate* what they have read. Although the written requirement is brief, the result of the entire process is deep learning. Annotation types range from simple summaries to highly challenging critical-constructive responses. Research on writing suggests that efforts to improve this type of critiquing, when taught concurrently with analytical reading and discipline instruction, result in enriched factual knowledge, conceptual development, writing improvement, vocabulary growth, and personal-social adjustment (Applebee, 1981; Bromley, 1985; Cunningham & Cunningham, 1976; Doctorow, Wittrock, & Marks, 1978; Eanet & Manzo, 1976; Garber, 1995; Tierney, Sorter, O'Flahavan, & McGinley, 1989).

REAP-Share: A Distributed Cognitive Network

Today, critiquing, annotating, and discussing are part of several online services whereby readers can exchange views on a variety of subjects and books (Leu, 2001). This *community of learners* can occur asynchronously (online, but at different times) or through chat groups (online, in real time). In either case, the exchanges tend to be open ended and "hit and miss" in terms of pedagogic value. REAP-sharing is more disciplined, an "enabling constraint" (Luce-Kapler, 2007, p. 214). As indicated previously, it is a structured system designed over a generation ago to guide and teach reading and thoughtful reacting in a pedagogically sound way, easily applicable to online interactions (cf. Thomas & Hofmeister, 2003). Students are introduced to the concept and value of writing from different perspectives in class. They then are led to discuss the merits of posting their annotations where they would be accessible to others. Students easily spot one basic value, namely that they can read one another's critiques of certain works before they read the longer work and/or following reading. Through guided discussion, they come to appreciate other values in sharing annotations. Benefits include having multiple representations of different perspectives on a variety of materials to guide higher-level thinking; having model critiques to guide the craft side of writing; and having the option to reread or further read annotations during the time they are reading a difficult longer work such as *A Tale of Two Cities*, with which it is easy to lose the thread of the plot. See the link provided at *www.LiteracyLeaders.com* for more information about internet projects based on REAP-Share, also called REAP ANX, for REAP Annotation Exchange. In addition, as course-delivery software platforms such as BlackBoard and WebCT become more integrated into classroom practices at the K–12 levels, as they are currently in many higher-education settings, the availability of using asynchronous discussion boards will greatly increase opportunities (and illustrate the increased need) to apply the sort of disciplined reading-writing-thinking REAP-sharing techniques discussed here.

Stages in Using REAP as a Teaching Tool

The first stage in using REAP is to teach students how to write several of the annotation types described next and illustrated in Figure 8.8. Note that the

"Travelers and the Plane-Tree: A Fable"

Two travelers were walking along a bare and dusty road in the heat of a mid-summer's day. Coming upon a large shade tree, they happily stopped to shelter themselves from the burning sun in the shade of its spreading branches. While they rested, looking up into the tree, one of them said to his companion, "What a useless tree this is! It makes no flowers and bears no fruit. Of what use is it to anyone?" The tree itself replied indignantly, "You ungrateful people! You take shelter under me from the scorching sun, and then, in the very act of enjoying the cool shade of my leaves, you abuse me and call me good for nothing!"

Reconstructive Responses:

1. Summary response
   Travelers take shelter from the sun under a large tree. They criticize the tree for not making flowers or fruit. The tree speaks and tells them that they are ungrateful people for taking shelter under its leaves and then criticizing it.
2. Precise response
   Travelers stop for rest and shade under big tree. Travelers say tree is useless. Tree tells them off.
3. Attention-getting response
   In this story, a tree talks back to people. The tree says, "You ungrateful people! You come and take shelter under me . . . and then . . . abuse me and call me nothing!"
4. Question response
   What tales might be told if inanimate objects could talk?

Constructive Responses

5. Personal view responses
   (a) We use resources like coal without thinking. Then we criticize the resource for damaging our lungs and dirtying our air.
   (b) Kids sometimes use their parents the way the travelers used the tree and then criticize them for letting themselves be used.
6. Critical response
   Not every word spoken in criticism is meant that way. The travelers were just a little grumpy from the long hard trip. The tree is being too sensitive.
7. Contrary response
   The travelers could be right. There are other trees that could produce something, as well as just providing shade.
8. Intention response
   The author wants us to be more sensitive to the people and things we depend on, especially those we see and use most often.

Figure 8.8 Examples of REAP annotations

9. Motivation response
   It sounds like the author may have felt used, after having a bad experience with friends or family.
10. Discovery response
    I wonder how many of us know when we are being "users." It would be interesting to take an anonymous poll to see how many people secretly feel that they have been used, and how many honestly see themselves as users.
11. Moral-ethical response
    I think we should ask how some of history's enlightened moral thinkers would respond to this, say Jesus, Confucius, Augustine, Thomas Jefferson.
12. Humorous response
    I can just see that poor tree thinking "I hope they are about to stop here to seek shelter and not firewood."
13. Discipline-connective responses
    (a) A poet would easily write an ode to such a tree; are there any?
    (b) A scientist might ask, "How does this tree manage to thrive where others cannot even manage to survive?"
    (c) A mathematician likely would want to calculate the probability of this tree's having rooted and found water before it was consumed by heat and drought; can that be done?
14. Creative response
    [Teacher guidance: What are some analogous situations this fable reminds you of?]
    (a) This fable made me think that teachers are sometimes used unfairly. They give us so much, and then we put them down if they make little mistakes. They're only human!
    [Teacher guidance: Having gotten the point of this fable, what should we do?]
    (b) We should put this fable on the bulletin board where it will remind us not to be ungrateful "users."
    [Teacher guidance: How would you retitle this fable if you were writing it?]
    (c) I'd call this fable "Travelers in the Dark," to show that we go through life without appreciating the many small "gifts" that come to us, while we're busy grumbling about what we don't have.

Figure 8.8 *(continued)*

15. Reading awareness (metacognitive) response
   (a) I feel like I'm beginning to better understand what the word "indignant" means from reading this, but I don't think I could define it yet.
   (b) This fable is too short. My mind feels like it needs more words, or something to really get this.
   (c) I keep wondering how a fable is different from a parable.

Figure 8.8 *(continued)*

annotation types represent a hierarchy from basic to higher-order levels of thinking, with the first four categorized as *reconstructive* level, requiring literal-level responding, and the next 10 as *constructive* level, requiring reading and thinking between and beyond the lines. It is best to introduce students to three or four annotation types initially, provide practice with these, and then add additional annotation types gradually. Experience suggests that a good cluster to begin with is summary, attention-getting/heuristic, and critical. If you have a sharp writing class, you might try the humorous annotation.

Reconstructive Responses:

1. *Summary response.* States the basic message of the selection in brief form. In fiction, it is the basic story line; in nonfiction, it is a simple statement of the main ideas.
2. *Precise response.* Briefly states the author's basic idea or theme, with all unnecessary words removed. The result is a crisp, telegram-like message.
3. *Attention-getting or heuristic response.* Restates a snappy portion of the selection that makes the reader want to respond. It is best to use the author's own words.
4. *Question response.* Turns the main point of the story or information into an organizing question that the selection answers.

Constructive Responses:

5. *Personal view or transactional response.* Answers the question "How do your views and feelings compare with what you perceive the author to have said?"
6. *Critical response.* Supports, rejects, or questions the main idea, and tells why. The first sentence of this type of response should restate the author's position. The next sentence should state the writer's position. Additional sentences should explain how the two differ.

7. *Contrary response.* Attempts to state a logical alternative position, even if it is not one that the student necessarily supports. This is an especially important way to represent a minority view that can easily be overlooked.
8. *Intention response.* States and briefly explains what the responder thinks is the author's intention, plan, and purpose in writing the selection. This is a special version of the critical response that causes the reader/responder to try to think like the author or from the author's perspective.
9. *Motivation response.* States what may have caused the author to create or write the story or selection. This is another special version of critical responding. It is an attempt to discover the author's personal agenda and hence areas of writing or unwitting biases.
10. *Discovery response.* States one or more practical questions that need to be answered before the story or facts can be judged for accuracy or worth. This type of response to text is the mode of thinking that leads to more reading and research and occasionally to a reformulated position or view.
11. *Moral-ethical response.* Requires reference to values and beliefs that guide, or one believes should guide, attitudes and behavior; and hence, both reflects and influences character development and complexity of thinking.
12. *Humorous response.* Can vary from bringing a slight smile to using jest to bring enlightenment.
13. *Discipline-connective (or interdisciplinary) response.* This is a conscious search for relevant ideas, facts, and factors that may seldom appear related to a topic because schooling, as opposed to learning, tends to have subject boundaries whereas ideas do not.
14. *Creative response.* Suggests different and perhaps better solutions or views and/or connections and applications to prior learning and experiences. Students usually need some guidance and/or examples to produce this type of response. Once they begin thinking in this way, however, the results can be remarkably constructive.
15. *Reading awareness (metacognitive) response.* Identifies or comments on a problem one may have had in reading and understanding a specific piece.

After students have had some practice in writing various types of annotations, these can be used in a variety of ways; a few are listed here:

- When giving a reading assignment, assign three annotation types for students to write and turn in.
- As students become more skilled at annotation writing, the assignment can be given with the requirement that after they have read, students themselves decide which three annotation types to write in response.
- Assign each member of cooperative groups a different annotation type to write. When groups meet, encourage group members to offer constructive suggestions by offering extra credit points to the group with the best annotation of each type (judged by the teacher or the class as a whole).

- Introduce a new reading assignment by having students read annotations written by students in a previous year (or from a different section of the class).
- Provide incentive to read and write reflectively by posting exemplary annotations, signed by the author, on a bulletin board or internet system.
- Encourage students to write from different disciplinary perspectives—"Write an annotation on *The Rainman* the way Mr. Kezlan, your math teacher, might, or like Mr. Willson, your English teacher, might write one." Expect some of these to be humorous, because they will be. (See item 13, "Discipline-connective responses" in Figure 8.8 for some representations that reduced the probability of humorous responses, should you wish to avoid these.)

REAP Responses as an Assessment System

To monitor student progress toward higher-order literacy, the teacher can use the preceding annotations listing as a rubric for reviewing student writings. The rubric can serve as a means of appraising the characteristic way in which a student or group of students responds to text. To use the REAP annotation types in this way, simply compare a student's writing to the preceding descriptions, and decide which annotation type it most closely resembles, keeping in mind that the annotations, as listed and illustrated here, already are roughly in order of difficulty: Lower numbers indicate more concrete thinking, and higher numbers more personal and abstract patterns of responding.

Acknowledging the Visceral Nature of Higher-Order Responding

One of the simplest ways to teach students to write constructively is to elicit quick personal responses to a piece they have read. Then the teacher should work with the class to form these initial highly subjective responses into more thoughtful critical and constructive ones. One way to do this is simply to ask students to give support for their positions—that is, to reconcile, or attempt to balance, their initial responses with the ethical and values-based positions that are fundamental to their communities and to higher ideals, such as liberty, as well as more practical ones such as how would their idea(s) be paid for or made workable. Again, students should not be forced to conformity here but should be encouraged to reprocess the rationale for societal goals and expectations. When students' responses differ markedly from one another, divide them into groups that produce critiques of their varied viewpoints. See Figure 8.9 for an anecdotal example from an eighth-grade social studies class we observed.

Letters to the Editor

Another means of stimulating cogent writing in response to text is to refer students to good approximations of it in the form of model letters to the editor in newspapers and magazines. Notice how the sample letters to the editor in Figure 8.10 help one get a better grip on one's own thoughts and feelings about problems in China. This is a good place to invite interesting perspectives that may come from trying to write

Following Silent Reading of a selection on the exploits of Hernando de Soto, an eighth-grade teacher, rather than first seeking a summary of facts, asked the class, "What did you think of de Soto?" Reactions included "sick," "cruel," and "loser." When asked to explain why they felt this way, students recited a litany of facts and events that amounted to a summary. Then the teacher asked them to get together in groups and form their reactions and reasons into personal comments on the selection. The following critique was typical of the results:

> *Hernando de Soto was a loser. After bringing gold back from Peru, the Spanish king encouraged him to go back to the New World by making him governor of Florida in 1539. He and 550 men looked for more gold. Even though some of them were priests, they mutilated and killed Indians in their search. After three years of this, de Soto died with nothing, and his men returned to Spain empty-handed.*

In this case, students' visceral and somewhat "cranky" responses seemed to help them distinguish de Soto from other explorers of his time and recall important information. In this way, the purpose of writing following reading was well served: Information was carefully processed, personalized, and stored for long-term recall. Further, the concept of "de Soto" and the context of the times replaced a collection of random facts about a vague historical figure named de Soto.

Figure 8.9 Encouraging higher-order responding

a letter as if it comes from a famous person, say Benjamin Franklin, one of our first foreign ambassadors (see "Ben Franklin on Tiananmen," in Figure 8.10).

Less Can Be More

Brief response-type annotations, such as letters to the editor, offer a challenge to sift through information and feelings and to struggle to take a thoughtful position. To this extent, such critiques can be more valuable than formal term papers and conventional book reports because they align more closely with student experiences and the faster pace of modern life. Additionally, this type of writing, because it is brief, provides more frequent opportunities for students to read, react, and write. On a very pragmatic level, such annotations can more easily be read and shared with peers and occasionally reviewed by a secondary teacher with an average load of more than 135 students per day, per semester.

▶ A FORMULA FOR PROMOTING CRITICAL-CONSTRUCTIVE THINKING

When the formula for teaching constructive reading, writing, and thinking is finally written, there is a good chance that it will contain at least these three factors: (1) respect for the past, (2) problem-based teaching, and (3) a collection of ways to invite creative production. See if the thoughts in the sections that follow meet these criteria.

"How tragic it is that to cope with change, China's leaders felt they needed to kill their young."

"The people of China will triumph. Deng Xiaoping and followers have forgotten their own history. It is impossible to repress an idea whose time has come!"

"China had to crush the democratic resistance. The blood spilled in Tiananmen Square is a small price to pay to prevent a civil war that would consume thousands, if not millions."

Ben Franklin on Tiananmen:

"China is a sovereign state whose internal affairs we cannot intercede in under international law. However, if we trade with them, we will be their customers, and merchants always try to please their best customers."

Figure 8.10 Letters to the editor exemplify cogent response to text

Exploring Ideas—Past, Present, and Evolving

Once we heard a popular futurist speaker at an educational conference say that when you are traveling at the speed of light, as we are now in the modern age, you don't need a rear view mirror. We respectfully disagree. The past is always important. It is the way we are able to escape the limitations of personal experiences and connect to the continuum of efforts and solutions that have proven workable. The challenge of course is to recognize the difference between a road and a rut. A problem-solving orientation is one way to deal with this challenge.

Engagement with problem solving teaches respect for the past, or what has been learned. Tussling with problems also can be empowering because it helps us tackle the daunting task of trying to have original thoughts, which it turns out we are more capable of than we ever realized. Teachers need to help students discover that they are capable of being *ideators*, that is, idea makers, problem identifiers, and problem solvers. Our collective tendency as teachers to almost never ask for creative production becomes a repeating, confirming lesson that this is hardly possible, let alone doable. For this problem, we are discovering some remarkably simple remedies with powerful implications for how students will read, write, learn subjects, and otherwise think.

"Just Ask for It" Taps Our Seemingly Innate Capacity for Inventiveness

The door to creative thinking is opened by putting question marks where there are premature periods. Or, in other words, to *ask for* new twists, innovative approaches, fresh thinking, saying, and expressing. Ollman (1996) compared seven formats for promoting higher-level thinking. Reflecting on the results, she noted, "I could see clearly that if I wanted a particular kind of thinking, I needed to *ask students for it*"*

*emphasis is not present in the original quote.

(p. 581). "Asking for it" begins with the teacher displaying his or her own enthusiasm for reading, learning, expressing, and inquiry.

There are some convincing clinical accounts and field studies suggesting that there is a great dormant force of creative energy waiting to transform the way in which we read and write in school, if teachers would "just ask for it." The question seems to impel the thinking and actions that follow.

One account, for example, tells of a professor of engineering's action research with his students. Students were randomly assigned to two groups and given identical plans to critique. However, one group was told to "critically" critique the plans, and the other to "constructively" critique them. The results showed that the "constructive" critiquers produced better criticisms and several very plausible, even creative, alternative solutions. The "criticisms" group offered weaker and more picky criticisms and virtually no constructive alternatives (Baker & Schutz, 1972). Apparently, the capacities of the students in the "criticism" group to be constructive-creative simply remained dormant with no trigger mechanism to activate them.

If you are inclined to celebrate the wonders and unique capabilities of the human mind from such stories, you may need to consider deleting the words *unique* and *human* after reading this next account. Louis Herman, director of a marine mammal laboratory, had taught dolphins to respond to directions communicated through hand gestures. In some way, not explained in the news account, he taught them, or they learned, to comprehend a gesture meaning "creative." In any case, one day he signaled to two of them to perform in tandem and to do "something creative." With only that prompt, the dolphins submerged for a few moments, then swimming in tandem leaped into the air and simultaneously spit out jets of water before plunging back into the pool. On another occasion, given the same command, they performed a synchronized backward swim culminating in a simultaneous wave of their tails (*Time*, March 22, 1993, p. 54). Of course, almost as amazing as the creative nature of this feat is the wonder about how these sea mammals were able to comprehend the concept of creative and to communicate intentions to one another for a tandem effort.

Nonetheless, this anecdote and some related empirical findings (discussed ahead) seem to give considerable creditability to the proposition that just asking for critical-constructive (i.e., creative) production is a solid way to begin to stimulate it. The simple logical explanation for this is the fact that higher levels of thinking tend to be *as much a matter of orientation and disposition* (Bereiter & Scardamalia, 1985)—or attitude, inclination, and focus—*as of aptitude*—or innate capacity that we apparently have, or we could not so easily answer this call to innovation.

Inviting Creative Production: Expressive-Artistic

A group of inner-city, once-failed-English, tenth-grade students was asked, as part of a *death and dying* literature theme, to try and create their own "communal poem"(Manzo & Martin, 1974). What they produced was called very worthy by several professors of literature, including the poet Dan Jaffe, who led this particular session. See Figure 8.11 for the Communal Poetry process and the poem.

Communal Poetry Process

1. The teacher asks questions designed to elicit fresh language and personal sensory responses about a chosen subject (e.g., "If death walked through that door, what would it look like?" "Who knows death best?").
2. Responses are recorded on the board. Clichés and other prosaic or hackneyed phrases are edited out as they occur.
3. Once the board is filled with raw material, students are asked to choose a beginning line from the material on the board.
4. The teacher writes the line and then aids students in selecting other phrases, helping them establish rhythm and/or continuity of thought.
5. The teacher reads the recorded lines aloud again and asks students for additional choices from the board, allowing changes as the group indicates need.
6. When students are satisfied with the product, the leader reads the finished poem aloud.
7. A final copy is prepared with the names of the student participants, and copies are presented to the class.

Figure 8.11 Communal poetry process and poem

The Communal Poetry process is an excellent way to build group cohesiveness and collaboration. The topic and mood are easily set with just a few words. For example, on another occasion, we observed a teacher leading a session in which she had conveyed a more humorous, "in-your-face" mood, and the students came back with a brief, rollicking poem that ended with a satisfying "Hurrah" for their effort (Manzo & Manzo, 1990a). Although we have not tried it yet, it seems as if it could be convened and conducted online in real time or asynchronously. Please e-mail us to let us know if you pilot this possibility.

Rousing Minds to Life: In the Realm of Idea Making (QuestMagnets)

You might wish to experiment with QuestMagnets (QM), a more wrap-around, or surround-sound form of "Just Ask for It." QuestMagnets are a self-discovery mechanism that evokes fresh thinking and writing. They are served up as an inviting variety of questions, problems, factoids, ideas, and musings that interrupt mundane thinking. Essentially, QMs are open-ended questions and dialogues about a wide variety of things encountered in and out of school. They are one way to begin to *convert periods to question marks and question marks to wonder and original thinking.* The goal is to enrich students' inner speech—which continues outside class hours—with reminders of the mysteries and questions that anchor much of what is taught in school and of how much more needs to be discovered. For example, in science one might ask the question, "How does gravity really work?" If you have ever thought about this, and who hasn't, you will be interested to discover that the answer is, "We haven't but a clue." Ironically, discovering this seems to benefit

Communal Poem

Somebody's Missing

Take a look around.
Somebody's missing
the dogs are howling
somebody's going to sleep.

The grandfathers know
what's going on:
the air is polluted with grief.

Down on the corner, in the grocery store,
he's about to touch you on the arm
with a silver knife
a black guillotine
a .38 pointed at your head.

Even the tough people are scared.

There I was slipping in the dark,
smelling the dumpyard,
the wrinkled dirt,
feeling so low I felt like getting high.

It's time
to let life into this poem!
Time to take a bath,
to pay death back with babies,
to make even a policeman cry.

It's true
not only an undertaker knows bodies.
Let's touch one another
and send Death Nowhere.

Figure 8.11 *(continued)*

attention and learning better than a lecture on the byplay between centripetal and centrifugal forces, words that describe more than explain how it is that the oceans don't empty into space.

There is no single way to stir and support higher-level reading, writing, and thinking, and yet there seem to be many ways. Clearly doing so must involve turning the attention of both teachers and students to the things about them that are worth pondering before being ingested as givens. Kristin Weissinger, a Manzo granddaughter, e-mailed us after a conversation on this subject with the contents of a poster she told us was on the bulletin board of every classroom in her middle school:

—What if . . . ?

—How would it change if . . . ?

—Is there another way to solve, write, or say this?

—What's wrong here?

—Why can't we do that?

Her e-mail with these potentially stirring questions also contained a note that has us wondering, "What's wrong here?" Her note continued:

> ... but no one really pays attention to them. I think they're mostly there for the teachers. Love, Kristen

Although these questions contain the basis for imaginative thinking, creative writing, innovative problem solving, problem identification, and plausibility testing, they are only inert when merely left posted on classroom bulletin boards. QuestMagnets are designed to be more participatory and to occur in a variety of ways and places. They are intended to "rouse minds to life" (Tharp & Gallimore, 1989).

QuestMagnets: Permission to Interrupt Granted by Students and Parents

To optimize the positive effects of QuestMagnets, the first and most important thing to do is to explain to students and parents, in a note home, their value and purpose to learning, thinking, and discussion. In other words, ask for permission to interrupt, much as modern advertising is based on "permission marketing" (Godin, 1999), a means of not only gaining attention to a product but interest in hearing more about it because of the personal value that it brings. To extend the critical-constructive, reading-writing-thinking "ad campaign," QuestMagnets could be

- posted on classroom bulletin boards, but also where one might not expect to find them, such as in locker rooms and on cafeteria walls.
- made into printed notes for the home refrigerator, where families can enjoy engaging and discussing them.
- invited from students, faculty, and parents (to further encourage thoughtful contributions, create blank post cards addressed to the school's Quest Learning Manager, and post names of submitters).
- treated as brief critical/constructive writing assignments in classes when they might tie in with a curriculum topic.
- entered and dialogued on a class's or a school's website.
- possibly submitted to global websites, such as the Registry for Better Ideas, a site that hopes to raise funds to make awards to incisive new questions as well as solutions (see the link provided at *www.LiteracyLeaders.com*).

Consider now some examples of QuestMagnets that might be used to stir REAP-like response writing and to generate additional similar submissions. The following categories are not mutually exclusive.

QuestMagnets: Writing the Future

- Why are eyeglasses not engineered to more easily adjust to the facts that most people's ears are of unequal height and that long hours of pressure on any skin surface, such as the nose, is irritating?
- Why aren't we doing more to develop something like a web-based universal voting system to complement and balance the influence of lobbyists on our current political system?

QuestMagnets: Factoids

- Deduce this: On what day are more take-out pizzas purchased than any other? (The day before Thanksgiving.)
- Southern California has fewer flying and crawling bugs per cubic foot of ground and space than the rest of the United States. Could this be the reason it also has less topsoil? Is topsoil largely bug guana and dead bug bodies?
- Females tend to see and remember more about what is in a room than do males; what can this mean?
- Single males are living home with their parents many years longer than single females, 29 years old versus 22.
- We're probably not all alike, and that may be our collective, adaptive advantage.
- Each U.S. acre contains an average of 400 lb of insects, compared with only 14 lb of people.
- It is frequently reported that the number of teen drivers killed in auto accidents is significantly greater than of urban teens killed by guns.

QuestMagnets: From the Heart

There are certain essential humanistic feelings that are not covered by law but that help us keep our moral-ethical bearings. Sometimes these gurgle up within us as an urge or counterurge that says, "This doesn't feel right." On a purely cognitive level, observing, thinking, and puzzling over these "gnarlies" is a fundamental way to build higher-order thinking, interdisciplinary problem-solving, and a sense of moral rectitude. Here are some examples:

- Isn't there some more humane way to kill and cook lobsters than to slowly boil them alive?
- Shouldn't we think twice about adopting pets that require more care and attention than we are ready to provide?
- Should there be a website on which one can post and date the license plate numbers of reckless drivers?

QuestMagnets: By Subjects

(Math)	Why did it take such a long time for humankind to discover and create zero (0)?
(Math)	What's all this business about "magic 9's"?
(Science)	Does anyone know how gravity really works? (Again, no they do not. For a fascinating new theory, see *http://amoureternal.com/oti/gravity/phen.htm*).
(Science)	How do electronic waves pass through the air and then recollect themselves in a radio or television set in the same patterns as they were sent?
(Social Studies)	If everyone has some money and keeps getting more, where did it first come from, and how does it continue to grow?
(Social Studies)	Why do some countries (like the United States) have "states" (which means independent countries, within the country as a whole), and doesn't this result in different laws and punishments in places that are separated only by an imaginary line?

QuestMusings: Wit and Wonder

School can be too serious and therefore a bit too confining. It can be liberating of the mind and spirit to think unseriously, and, ideally, wittily and amusingly. Invite such thoughts, more so than reactions, by sharing the wit and musings of some of the masters. Avoid heavy moralizing here; it's all in fun.

How come abbreviated is such a long word? (comedian Steven Wright)

Why do scientists call it "re-search" when they are looking for something new? (comedian Steven Wright)

CRITICAL-CONSTRUCTIVE TECHNIQUES FOR A ROUSING DISCUSSION

Many teaching methods have a step called "discuss." Following are two classical methods and one newly developing method for promoting discussions that also "rouse minds to life."

Developmental Discussion

The Developmental Discussion (Maier, 1963) and a rediscovered version called Guided Conversation (Gauthier, 1996) are intended to teach students about the full process of problem solving by involving them in all of its parts: identification and partitioning of the problem, collection of relevant data or information, generation of solutions, and appraisal of solutions. Most important, it emphasizes going beyond existing knowledge. As such, it should be basic to any program to improve creative thinking and problem solving. Much of this process can be shifted to an "asynchronous" system such as a website with a discussion board and/or an e-mail listserv.

Steps in Developmental Discussion/Guided Conversation

1. The teacher instructs students to try to identify certain conflicting points (rather than views) or problems inherent in material presented in text and lecture.
2. The teacher initially provides examples that can serve as models of problem identification (this usually requires comparing textual information to prior knowledge and experiences).
3. The teacher assists students in narrowing and partitioning the problem into manageable segments.
4. Students are divided into cooperative learning groups to solve the smaller parts of the problem. Each group is asked to jot down notes on individual and group members' answers using questions such as the following to guide their analysis:
   a. What do we know about this problem part?
   b. Which parts of the information we have are relevant to the problem?
   c. What more do we need to know to construct a possible solution?
   d. What are some possible solutions given what we now know?
   e. What additional information can we collect (and how) to formulate better solutions?
5. A large-group discussion is held to illustrate the different ways the problem can be viewed and solutions sought. The teacher reminds students to add to their notes during this discussion.
6. The class decides on a solution (usually a synthesis) or—in a significant departure from conventional school practices—may choose to table the matter until the class can collect additional information (see Figure 8.12 for an anecdotal account).
7. Students individually write out the solution as they see it and in the most convincing way possible. Then students exchange papers and give one another feedback on their essays. The teacher invites students and reviewers to read aloud phrases or sections that they believe were particularly well stated.

Devil's Advocate

One simple and direct way to encourage students to consider an issue from alternate perspectives is to get students into a discussion that evokes this type of reasoning. *Devil's Advocate* is an issues-based discussion that has a rich heritage (Alvermann, Dillon, & O'Brien, 1987; Roby, 1983). It was used by Socrates and Plato and is a common convention at synods of several religions around the world.

One of three things may happen in a Devil's Advocate discussion: Positions may be strengthened, modified, or abandoned. In any case, students involved in such a discussion tend to have a great many experiences with reflective turnabout.

Mr. Freeble, a high school civics teacher, works with a group of average ability students for fifty minutes each morning. In a previous class session the students had read a five page textbook assignment and had completed the accompanying study guide. The assignment covered information about the Supreme Court—what it is, its purpose and charges, and its relationship to the entire governmental system.

Freeble began the developmental discussion by reviewing the previous textbook assignment for five minutes. From the review, students were reminded of the following key concepts: the Supreme Court is the highest court in the land, the individuals sitting on the Supreme Court are charged with interpreting the Constitution, and members of the Supreme Court may change a previous ruling by another branch of the government.

Next, Freeble asked the students to supply current information about events in the news concerning recent Supreme Court rulings. Elicited were facts about prayer in school and nativity scenes set up on public property. Freeble noted that the seasonal influence (it was close to Christmas) play [*sic*] a large role in students' interest in a local newspaper story about a controversial nativity scene. After ten minutes of discussing that story and its implications for local residents, the class decided on a problem that was text based but of immediate interest to them—should religious groups be allowed to erect nativity scenes on public property?

The teacher guided the students in breaking the larger problem (separation of church and state) into three smaller problems: (1) Does setting up a nativity scene on public property violate the rights of individuals who do not have the same religious beliefs? (2) What information could the class add that would help solve the problem? (3) What would be a reasonable way to share what was learned with the people involved in the controversy?

The students broke into smaller groups and began to work on the first part of the problem. Freeble supplied each group with a one page summary of the Pawtucket case involving a Supreme Court ruling on the display of nativity scenes on public property. Freeble circulated among the groups, observing and offering assistance when requested.

During the last fifteen minutes of the period, students participated in a large group discussion in which they reported on their reactions to the Pawtucket case and whether they believed the case had any implications for the local controversy.

Over the next two days, the students worked in small groups to tackle the remaining problem parts. Solutions to the overall problem included working with community leaders to foster improved communication among the dissident groups and writing letters to the editor of the local newspaper on the topic of how the Pawtucket case compared to the local one.

Figure 8.12 Anecdotal account of developmental discussion
Source: Alvermann, D. E., Dillon, D. R., & O'Brien, D. G. (1987). *Using Discussion to Promote Reading Comprehension* (pp. 38, 40–41). Copyright 1987 by the International Reading Association.

They learn about the enormous complexity of issues that initially appear clear-cut. They learn about the paradoxes involved in trying to solve a problem only to find that the best solution can sometimes be more disruptive than the existing problem. Finally, they learn to use language not merely to state what they believe but to discover what they *might* reasonably believe.

Steps in Devil's Advocate

1. The teacher poses an issue to the class.
2. Students are paired but asked to individually prepare written arguments using the text for essential information. Sometimes there are more than two positions.
3. Students are instructed to describe to their partners their best arguments for each position. They should discuss each argument to determine whether it contains faulty reasoning.
4. Still in pairs, students are asked to discuss with their partners whether the positions they originally supported have changed as a result of this activity and, if so, why and in what way. Then they revise their individual written statements accordingly.
5. A class discussion follows based on students' arguments for each side of the issue, any changes in attitude that occurred as a result of the activity, and sources of further information related to the issue.
6. Students are offered a final opportunity to revise and prepare a final form of their position statements.

See Figure 8.13 for an example of the Devil's Advocate method. Notice how this method emphasizes critical examination of the issue with the possibility of changing one's mind, or reformulating a position, rather than winning a debate.

Regression Equation Technique: Fostering Rational Conclusions

It seems fitting that a chapter on critical-constructive reading, writing, and thinking should conclude on an innovative note. The *Regression Equation Technique* (RET) is a method under development for increasing the likelihood that discussion will detect a truth signal through the haze of social and semantic static, thus enabling participants to move more firmly toward sensible solutions. The method is based on a principle used in a statistical procedure of a similar name, the *multiple regression equation analysis.* The technique draws on group process methods that encourage less egocentric evaluative thinking, such as Hoffman's (1977) Intra-Act, and newer methods such as Moller and Bohning's (1992) *participatory ranking,* that are designed to get the best decision out of a diverse group. These methods are built around some form of guided value voting, tallying, discussing, and revoting. Here is the useable core of RET as it now is conceived.

Steps in the Regression Equation Technique (RET)

1. Set up an equation that represents an item, or "independent variable," that you wish to explore or better understand. Start by simply writing the entity or factor to be examined on the left side of an equal sign.
2. Place all other factors, or "dependent variables," that seem to explain that factor on the right side of the equal sign. Be sure that one of these dependent variables is titled "unexplained portion." Invite the group to add or restate any factors, except the one to be examined. (Rewording the independent variable changes the exercise and should only be undertaken advisedly or as another comparative exercise.)

Mr. Tennyson, a ninth grade social science teacher, used the Devil's Advocate strategy to structure a class discussion on banning nuclear testing. His students had read a section of their text that dealt with the horrors of nuclear warfare. As the discussion opens, Tennyson has just finished assigning the students to pairs.

"All right now, you and your partner find a place where you can talk quietly. Each of you should jot down why you believe the United States should stop testing nuclear weapons. Be sure to support your beliefs with evidence from the text. Then take the opposite stance (why the United States should not stop testing nuclear weapons) and again support your beliefs with evidence from the text."

(The students, working individually in pairs, take about ten minutes to complete this task.)

"Okay, now we're ready for the next step. Choose your best arguments and present them to your partner. Be certain that you discuss your beliefs with your partner; for example, seek your partner's ideas and evaluations of the pros and cons that you took on the issue. Is there evidence of any faulty reasoning on either one's part?"

(After approximately fifteen minutes, the noise level in the room drops, an indication that students have finished presenting the arguments they had with themselves.)

"May I have your attention. . . . There are two more things I would like you to do: (1) Think about how your ideas have changed on banning nuclear testing. For example, has your position shifted from your original one? If so, why? (2) Decide whether you have strengthened your original position, abandoned it completely, or only modified it. Then tell your partner your decision and see if he or she agrees."

(After approximately ten minutes, Tennyson drew the students into a whole class discussion by asking them to share some of their ideas on both sides of the issue.)

Figure 8.13 Example of Devil's Advocate method
Source: Alvermann, D. E., Dillon, D. R., & O'Brien, D. G. (1987). *Using Discussion to Promote Reading Comprehension* (pp. 38, 40–41). Copyright 1987 by the International Reading Association.

3. Have everyone in the discussion group independently distribute percentage weightings for each dependent variable to the right of the equal sign, including the "unexplained portion" (to total 100%).
4. Tally and record the range and average percent score for each factor.
5. Attempt to explain findings with briefly written personal notes and to reconcile differences through discussion.

Each time the researchers have used this basic discussion design in a domain in which the participants had real-life experience, they seem to have uniformly found their way back to some clearer signal (truth) and away from whatever static interference had been building around it. For example, the independent variable, or factor being analyzed, could be "academic success for inner-city youth," and the dependent variables or explaining factors could be elements such as structured classrooms; direct instruction; reading of core literature; reading of nonfiction material; vocabulary study; academic aptitude; recitation; transactional (subjective) reacting; self-esteem; family reading habits; and multicultural curricula. In such cases, the results often come out sounding as they did in a radio ad for a new charter school that emerged in a district that was disaccredited for failing to meet every one of its state's 11 criteria. It had experimented for 30 years with almost all of the aforementioned dependent variables, although often by misassigning their respective weightings as explaining outcomes on conventional standardized tests (arguably one of the basic means of quality control of schools and learning). The charter school ad essentially said the following:

> What ensures school success? Is it diversity, attention to differences between boys and girls, campaigns to end violence, efforts to increase social responsiveness, attention to learning styles, cooperative grouping practices? Not really. Important as each of these may be to someone or even everyone, success in school is determined in greatest measure by a focus on reading, writing, and content area teaching and learning.

If you think you would like to join the effort to further develop this critical-constructive discussion technique, look at *www.LiteracyLeaders.com* for details as they develop. Ideally, try using the method in either a professional discussion or in a classroom situation to which the independent variable can range from traditional fare such as "Rise of Labor Unions" or "Elements of Tragedy in *Hamlet*" to more contemporary issues such as "The Likely Power of Telecomputing in Modern Life" or "Factors Influencing Violent Behavior in Young Adults."

As you can see, this evolving technique is rigorous yet open ended. It brings several subtle points into focus that need to be better understood and dealt with in order to promote effective critical and constructive reading, discussion, and learning in school and in society. Some of these points are not immediately evident. For example, the person or group who gets to state the agenda or problem for review also has the greatest control over the discourse and hence the conclusions; therefore, teaching students how to articulate problems may be as important as teaching them how to solve problems. At least half of the solution to any problem can be found in its identification and statement.

The critical-constructive value of RET is amplified by the internet. An equation can be electronically published as a standing quest to which value can be added by each class and individual who reads, thinks, and writes about it over time. The equations should attract relevant positive and negative experiences in life, literature, and varied content areas. This ongoing discourse should help teachers and students to make better sense of the overly compartmentalized structures of school curriculum and the near-chaotic flow of information on the internet.

▶ CONCEPT SUMMARY

This chapter addresses the issues involved in encouraging critical and creative response to reading, including some of the reasons why this goal is often espoused but seldom seriously implemented. Skillful critical and creative response begins with development of the disposition to ask questions such as, "How important is this?" "How good is this?" and "Do I agree with this?" and the ability to understand perspectives other than one's own. These dispositions and abilities are best taught through project-based instruction, which, historically, has been difficult to implement. The writing-based and discussion-based methods assembled in this chapter lend themselves to implementation within a traditional classroom and curriculum program. Some, such as the Read Encode Annotate Ponder (REAP) system, have the potential to be expanded to a department or even schoolwide higher-order thinking program.

CHAPTER 9

EMERGENT CONTENT AREA LITERACY

The man who does not read good books has no advantage over the man who can't read them.
—Mark Twain

This chapter addresses three complementary topic areas: Emergent Content Area Literacy, the use of literature and trade books to teach content at all grade levels, and the use of writing to enhance student learning across the disciplines. The section on Emergent Content Area Literacy discusses how we could better prepare our secondary students for the challenges of Content Area Literacies from the earliest of grade levels. This has become a national quest for which there are very accessible solutions. Connected to this is the use of adolescent literature and trade books to enhance content learning during subsequent stages of human development. The chapter concludes with some practical and creative ways to utilize reflective writing as a thinking tool to enhance learning in all content areas.

- EMERGENT CONTENT AREA LITERACY: HOW EARLY ELEMENTARY TEACHERS CAN BETTER PREPARE CHILDREN FOR READING TO LEARN
- EXTENDING EMERGENT LITERACY

EMERGENT CONTENT AREA LITERACY: HOW EARLY ELEMENTARY TEACHERS CAN BETTER PREPARE CHILDREN FOR READING TO LEARN

The goal of this section is to move wonder-driven learning down to the earliest stages of childhood. It appears that teaching children to learn how to read may actually interrupt the rather natural interest in and development of content and concept learning. This is no small point since it suggests that pressing for greater factual knowledge at an early age would not be another ramped-up incursion into early childhood education but more an attempt to utilize children's ways of knowing and being to foster rather natural states of knowledge and vocabulary growth, which are the lynchpins linking *learning to read* and *reading to learn.*

Secondary School Teachers Lament. Secondary school teachers often bemoan the lack of preparation of students for the rigors of intensive discipline instruction. Just as the field of Content Area Reading has developed largely in response to the concerns expressed by college professors about the underpreparation of students in high school, a similar movement now seems to be afoot to elicit the aid of elementary teachers in preparing students for intermediate and high school.

Elementary Teachers Lament. For about 50 years now, textbooks on reading have either implicitly or explicitly suggested that progress in reading from middle through high school would be better if only the content teachers know more about how to teach reading. There is some truth in this belief, which is one of the reasons for the creation of the subfield of Content Area Reading, and the requirement that teachers of adolescents be so instructed. There is, however, another perspective on this. It is that elementary teachers have resisted teaching content and hence Content Area Reading as well as they might have. Here we will peel back some of the layers of this dilemma and see that an accessible solution is in the offering. Basically it is to rely more heavily on teaching about content in ways that better suit concerns for early childhood development.

Knowledge Deprivation? The Jesuits are fond of saying, "Give me the child until age seven, and I'll give you the man." The wisdom in this educational plan should not be lost in public education, but it is not being heeded as fully as it might. Clearly, knowledge begets knowledge. But what if children are knowledge deprived? After all, elementary teachers are expected to be generalists who have a working knowledge of all disciplines from math to literature (El-Hindi, 2003) and very extensive knowledge of children's nonfiction trade books (Moss, 1991). This puts something of a cap on what can realistically be achieved by a single teacher, but it also cries out for further attention, because the need for early and continuing content and concept growth in the disciplines is clear.

An observational study revealed that on average, a mere 3.6 minutes per day were spent on reading and interacting on informational material in the early grades, and far less in lower socioeconomic status (SES) school districts (Duke, 2000). If this has increased by 100% since 2000, it still would be significant when compared with academic expectations. Nonetheless, the early grades have a rich and sensible tradition of focusing on near-future needs of students: Children are taught to be good students by an emphasis on personal-social adjustment, language development, and learning how to read. However, primary school is not just preparation for life as a first, second, and third grader; it also must be a preparation for fourth grade and beyond. It is rather like Double A Little League: A team can win a lot of games by just hitting the ball to underdeveloped defensive players, but with hitting as its only focus, it isn't long before the other teams catch up in offense and games come to be decided by defense.

Children's Ways of Knowing

In literacy terms, building both skill sets means having a plan for better using this period of development (between four and ten years old, and spanning five years of summers, after-school hours, and in-school time) to offer wonderfully enriching opportunities for gathering some of the rich factual and conceptual bases of human interests and knowledge. This can be done in ways that are compatible with children's developmental needs and experiential ways of knowing. To capture the value of this opportunity and to position it as a complement to the current early school curriculum and standards, we suggest that it should be called *Emergent Content Area Literacy (ECAL)* and be built on the foundation of Content Area Literacy and Emergent Literacy, a branch of reading that attempts to impart attitudes, experiences, and skills that are simultaneously developmentally appropriate and also accelerate immediate and subsequent learning.

Teaching Without Teaching

This is achieved essentially with what strikes us as *intentional-incidental* teaching-learning, as opposed to either a heavily didactic or a totally incidental teaching-learning approach. This sort of intentional-incidental teaching-learning requires vastly more planning than either of the other two approaches since it must be instructionally robust and yet have the character of teaching without appearing to teach. Of course, this approach does not exclude some direct teaching, but on balance the early grades need to remain child centered; not because it cannot be otherwise but because *our society values early childhood as a precious moment, especially in our affective as well as our cognitive development.* This creates the challenge of not doing one at the expense of the other, but it also offers the opportunity of doing one in support of the other.

▶ EXTENDING EMERGENT LITERACY

Learning How to Read

The term *Emergent Literacy* is used most often to refer to the events and surroundings that need to be present to create a conducive environment for learning to read. The conceptual basis for this is that children's language acquisition—and interest in extending language to include reading and writing—is determined in large measure by the nature of their interactions with their environments. This idea often is attributed to Jean Piaget, the pioneer developmental psychologist, who showed that certain innate aptitudes and abilities would be substantially advanced in an environment that intentionally urged, more so than merely permitted, their "construction." In concrete terms, emergent literacy is made up of

- books, paper, and pencils.
- people reading and talking about what they are reading.
- a teacher who reads to the children from "Big Books" that incidentally teach children about the concepts of print, left-to-right decoding of words across a page, and recognition of letters and whole words.
- living models, primarily teachers at this stage, who impart a sense of the fluency and regard for punctuation that a reader needs to derive meaning from the printed page.

This strategy, along with direct instruction in phonemics and phonics, rapid word identification, and a good deal of storybook reading by children at ascending levels of difficulty, helps most children learn how to read.

Deceleration Requires Acceleration

Somewhere around fourth grade, however, children often reach a period of consolidation but also *deceleration.* From narrative material, they typically have mastered rapid recognition of most high-frequency words. They also have acquired a fairly sound sense of character development, conflict resolution, the search for a moral, and other such aspects of story organization. However, children also appear to plateau as their rate of progress levels off, particularly in reading comprehension and fluency with informational text. There are many possible explanations for this deceleration, some of which are as healthy and explainable as the slight weight gain that seems to precede each spurt of growth in height. Such periods in normal physical development often are accompanied by a need for more sleep—which, by the way, is the only time that growth can take place—and by a parallel need for more nourishment (as opposed to just calories) and increased exercise to support a larger, more agile structure. It has been noted that "instruction is, after all, an effort to assist growth" (Bruner, 1966, p. 1). Although this may appear to occur rather naturally, it also requires an accelerated, but careful, preplanning and seizing of a few propitious moments in early childhood development.

▶ EMERGENT CONTENT AREA LITERACY: *LEARNING FOR BEGINNERS*

Reading to Learn

Just as Content Area Literacy developed essentially in response to the belief that intermediate and secondary teachers need to assist students in their continuing developmental process of learning to read, a new subfield of emergent content area literacy likely is developing essentially in response to the belief that primary and elementary teachers need to assist students in more securely launching and continuing their developmental process of *reading to learn.* ECAL, however, is not merely about beginning learning but about *learning for beginners.* Early learning is much more challenging than subsequent learning. It is more about promoting a particular mind-set, or habit of mind, that, in this case, values facts and information and their byproduct: an active interest in continuing the growth of knowledge. The philosopher Nietzsche is frequently attributed to have once noted that "a man [person] has no ears for that to which experience has given him no access." *ECAL is about creating early experiences with the nature of knowledge and building an acquired taste for it.* It's a way to alert the ear and eye to the sound and sense of *things worth knowing.* The need to support such early learning is furthered by Jerome Bruner's popular dictum that it is possible to introduce a child to most any complex adult concept in some "intellectually honest way." Bruner referred to this model as the basis for a "spiral curriculum"—that is, one that introduces ideas, content, concepts, and problem-solving challenges that are mapped into children's predominant modes of representation and then reintroduced with increasing complexity as the child matures (1966). It also has been noted that some questions and points of information should be raised even as some children may seem to ignore these points, because informational knowledge has a way of "surfacing to consciousness at a later time" (Lee, Bingham, & Woelfel, 1968, p. 31). But this raises the question of just what it is that children can understand and learn. *Pokemon,* Yu Gi Oh, and other aspects of popular culture and modern media are providing some surprising and desirable (that is, serendipitous) clues to this perplexing developmental and philosophical question.

Reading Development May Be a Weak Indication of Actual Cognitive Development

A sustained look at *Pokemon,* Yu Gi Oh, and their now multiple variations speaks loudly to their significant complexity. These games and cards and stories would never have won approval as being age appropriate from a curriculum committee.

Yet children, largely boys, read and grasp the complex story lines and arcane games and guidelines for intelligently collecting and trading these inventive cards. Researchers are finding that boys are becoming literate "in spite of school instruction" and may end up better prepared for vocational careers because these skills are more useful than being able to write a narrative or analyze a work of fiction (Smyth, 2003). The lesson here is simple: Kids are more capable of understanding things of greater complexity than we have given them credit for. It seems that in the process of teaching youngsters to read, we have gathered a misimpression that their capacities to think are somehow tied to, if not arrested by, their rate of learning to read fluently, a two- to four-year process, on average. Now that we know otherwise, different implications present themselves. The challenge becomes one of asking, "What can we teach children about content and concepts and inquiry *while* they are learning to read?" because this will prepare them not merely for a smooth transition to reading to learn, but it will increase recognition of the complex ideas and factual information that our highly media-penetrating environment provides. In short, we may be seriously underestimating children's capacities to acquire knowledge, to think connectively, and to learn on their own.

Identifying and Promoting ECAL Curriculum and Practices

Soon there will be a new subfield that addresses *doing* emergent Content Area Literacy. This is not going unnoticed by others, such as Barbara Moss (1991), who has written extensively about the value of nonfiction books in the elementary school, and Karen Wood (2002), who pointedly writes about the new dimensions of Content Area Literacy that are not just for secondary teachers.

Essential elements have been identified for readers in today's world: Such readers must be code breakers, meaning makers, text users, and text critics (Luke & Freebody, 1997). We would add that they also must be more constructive-creative in their thinking than ever before simply to keep pace with a rapidly changing world and to be empowered and responsible for identifying its direction and its methods. Achieving these goals suggests several overlapping curriculum goals and objectives, gathered from several sources that seem to be leaning in this direction, some more than 30 years old (Bean, 2000; Desmond, 1997; Lee, Bingham, & Woelfel, 1968; Moss, 1991; Wood, 2000, 2002):

- It must involve learning from more avenues than just reading.
- It must lay the experiential foundation for peer-based speaking, writing and discussion.
- It must teach youngsters to gain and cross-reference information from multiple sources—sometimes referred to as "multiple source literacy."
- It must require more higher-order thinking.
- It must teach empathy for others—that is, concern for the means as well as the end.
- It must teach and promote foundational understanding of key concepts.
- It must be reinforced and enriched by a suitably precise vocabulary—an often undervalued objective of early schooling.

- It must teach collaboration, but also the reality of competition.
- It must result in greater self-regulation and self-teaching from environmental options.
- It must teach youngsters to be question raisers, or inquirers, as well as question answerers, or information acquirers.
- It must be conducted so as to connect new experiences and learning to what, in some way, is already known (Luce-Kapler, 2007).

Again, this must all be served up in ways that are compatible with children's ways of knowing. Simply put, *these efforts can in no way negate or undermine the current social-emotional-developmental goals of early childhood education.*

Will Efforts to Stir Early Learning Really Work?

This question has not yet been fully tested, but there is a growing body of evidence suggesting that efforts to influence patterns of interests and learning result in different outcomes, almost immediately. One of the more telling of these is based on an observational study of identical twins, Alan and Gordon, who were four years old, together at home, and separated at nursery school. Alan's verbal expression is oriented mainly to purpose and planning, even as he talks about his favorite book, *Caps for Sale.* Gordon's verbal expression is more primitive but much richer in narration and imagination and very influenced by the then popular TV series *Batman* and a *Batman* deck of cards that he would play with at every opportunity (Lee, Bingham, & Woelfel, 1968). As you will see in the next section of this chapter in another broader study of verbal (i.e., questioning) behavior, children clearly are very sensitive to environmental cues, whether they be encouraging or discouraging of certain behaviors and underlying attitudes.

Here are our candidates for this emerging, emergent field of primary and early-intermediate-grades Content Area Literacy development: (1) three simple methods that can be done before children can decode print; (2) one charting activity to help them learn to extract information from reading and others sources; and (3) a cluster of means for tying content learning to children's literature, to the benefit of both.

▶ NONPRINT ECAL METHODS

Show and Question-Only (Gambit)

This instructional strategy probably qualifies as a *Cambrian method* since it has one of the essential features of this new type of teaching-learning: It prepares children to engage in public speech that ideally becomes inner speech and, hence, to engage in self-teaching, in and outside the classroom. At a practical level, it simply involves playing show-and-tell with an occasionally different flare that lays the foundations for:

- Inquiry training.
- Self-guided purpose-setting in listening—the means by which 90% of new learning occurs—and soon reading.

- Aural-oral (listening-speaking) skills.
- Collaborative learning.

It also tends to be great fun. This is best launched with a little *gambit* (i.e., something done to open or focus conversation). It begins by demonstrating *Show and Question-Only* and then asking children to bring some things to class for student-led versions.

Steps in Show and Question-Only

1. Something interesting is shown to the class.
2. The class has 20 questions in which to discover what it is and what the presenter might wish to say about it.
3. The presenter may give some help by saying when they are getting "hotter" or "cooler."
4. The presenter finally tells all—usually to a very alert audience.

When this was done for the first time, as part of a study in the questioning behavior of kindergarten children, some remarkable things happened, immediately and thereafter (Manzo & Legenza, 1975). In this study a boy brought an old-fashioned hand-cranked coffee grinder to Show and Question-Only. The students gathered around and leaned forward, displaying the body language of attention and curiosity. At first they seemed to ask random questions but soon began to encourage one another to sequence their questions into a more orderly *inquiry.* Within about nine questions, they deduced that they were looking at an old grinder, and probably of coffee beans (which they suspected quickly because small electric bean grinders were popular at the time of the study). They conceded after a few attempts that they could not guess what the presenter might want to say about it, but they did narrow it down to it being connected to his grandparents. (His story was that the coffee grinder was given to his mother by his grandparents, who had it in the family from when his mother's mother brought it west to Kansas City from Virginia many years ago.)

Show and Question-Only as Epistemological Inquiry

This slightly different form of show-and-tell tends to yield more knowledge-driven (epistemological) inquiry, as compared with the majority of questions that children raise, which are more along the lines of social banter. In this example, the discussion drew a bead on concepts such as the westward migration and the intelligence in carrying coffee in the form of beans rather than preground, which would absorb moisture and grow stale.

Ideally, a gambit—or trial effort to stir interest and questioning—such as this one could be followed up with a brief reading from an appropriate book, much as is done in a conventional lesson, in which the teacher would have introduced some artifact to raise curiosity and interest before reading. Show and Question-Only has intrinsic value in building curiosity and knowledge that are justifiable whether with or without pre- or follow-up reading. One of its chief values is that it is *experiential* and, therefore, likely to be remembered for a long time. To that extent, it is *schema* building, more so than would be just another piece of relatively isolated information. Schema, like Java Script in computer programming, is not merely a message but a vessel that prepares the mind to seek out and carry multiple packets of new information that may come its way. As such, artifacts are now being used widely to accompany storybooks; some books are sold with accompanying *realia*, another name for artifacts, which are more typically associated with archeological finds.

Realia

Such artifacts, or realia, may vary from a wand for a lead-in to *Harry Potter and the Sorcerer's Stone* to a bonnet to stir focused interest in a historical piece about the early pilgrims to America, or story reading, *Little House on the Prairie.* We also have seen some imaginative teachers use the disassembled parts of a wristwatch, a toaster, and a VCR to induce curiosity and examination of small machines. Attention often gets focused on the simple mechanical parts of these, since the electronic components can be rather mystifying even for adults to grasp. Nonetheless, the lessons are valuable in providing a certain content orientation, and especially so to girls, who tend to be less inquisitive about the mechanical world and, hence, less likely to pursue studies in engineering. Lack of knowledge and orientation to the mechanical world also can have more immediate and prolonged effects: Each new body of knowledge learned is a potential analog, or parallel structure, for yet other complex content and concepts. Absent such knowledge, grasp of parallel, but different, concepts and content is considerably weakened. This orientational issue alone may explain the lower proportion of females in applied mathematics, physics, chemistry, and, as mentioned previously, engineering.

▶ PRINT RECORDS IMPORTANT INFORMATION AND WONDER RELEASES IT

Teachers should wonder aloud about all manner of things that easily-available print can quickly answer. Gestures as simple as these build an orientation toward, and respect for, the sheer utility and friendliness of print as a source of information.

- "I wonder how many crayons are in a box? Let's just read the box and see." (This can be followed by a count to see if there is the correct number in the box.)
- "I wonder what this color is called? It's a little red and a little purple. Let's see what it says on the crayon. Oh, it's called magenta!"
- "I wonder what all this writing is on this bottle of aspirin? Let's see if we can figure it out." *(Read aloud and discuss.)*
- "I wonder if the child who fell in the well will be OK? Should I read the news story to you that tells about it?" *(Read aloud and discuss.)*

Of course, today more so than ever, there are engaging informational books, such as David Macaulay's 1988 bestseller, *The Way Things Work*. But more on informational trade books and online questing for knowledge ahead. At the moment, the key question remains a very pragmatic one: How can content be used to release wonder? Pictures and streaming media are part of the answer.

Reciprocal Questioning of Pictures Procedure

In a fascinating field study with sixth-grade students, Luce-Kapler (2007) taught them to write and represent complex ideas by creating web pages in minutes with a software package called Launchpad. In the process she notes that many of the best-organized activities for these students were built around picture books. As students carefully noted what was happening in the pictures, they made story connections to the text and their sensory-rich environment.

In the study of the questioning behaviors of kindergarten children reported earlier (Manzo & Legenza, 1975), the authors developed a measure of students' "manifest curiosity" as expressed through their questioning about pictures. This measure, called the *Reciprocal Questioning of Pictures Procedure (RQPP)*, also serves as a useful method for teaching and assessing youngsters engaged in a careful content analysis of a picture that nicely parallels the thinking processes necessary in Content Area Reading. It is applicable anywhere pictures can be found and simply goes like this:

Step 1. Select a book with lively, interesting pictures. Manzo and Legenza (1975) developed a method for determining the language-stimulation value of pictures that suggested three characteristics to be most stimulating to children's interests and exploration: (1) pictures of children of the same age, (2) action pictures, and (3) pictures containing complex and multiple activities.

Step 2. Say to the children that you and they will have one minute to study the picture and try to recall all that is in it, after which, they, then you, will ask each other questions to see how many things each of you can remember as being represented when the picture is turned face down. After two or three rounds of this "recalling-retelling," the game is changed.

Step 3. Now say, "Let's take one turn asking others some interesting questions about this picture." The children go first. Most times they are uncertain as to what to ask, and say little, if anything. Oddly, this leaves them very attentive to the teacher's questions, since they are curious what these might be.

Step 4. The teacher then begins to ask a variety of who, what, where, and why questions and some inferential and conjectural questions having much the same form as these questions might if they were about something read: "Who/what is the main thing in this picture?" "What is happening?" "Why do you suppose mother put that cookie jar up so high?" "What do you suppose has happened before?" "What do you suppose will happen next?"

With this simple *teaching-without-teaching* procedure, children are taught how to exercise their own power of will and attention to increase recall—a fundamental function of content reading—and how to anticipate, and hence ask themselves the kind of questions that typically are asked of print material. Following are two lists of books, one without print and one stressing informational trade books, that can be used in the next stage of reading to learn. Further ahead you will find means of utilizing informational trade books in thematic ways that support, and in some instances out-do, the informational impact of standard textbooks, which sometimes can appear to be a stodgy litany of facts.

Picture Books. Books with particularly engaging pictures that enhance the theme, mood, and story line; encourage children to identify with characters and events; and heighten interest in the print:

Alexander and the Terrible, Horrible, No Good, Very Bad Day, by Judith Viorst, illustrated by Ray Cruz (K and up, 34 pp.)

Amelia Bedelia, by Peggy Parish, illustrated by Fritz Seibel (K–4, 24 pp.)

The Carp in the Bathtub, by Barbara Cohen, illustrated by Joan Halpern (K–4, 48 pp.)

A Chair for My Mother, by Vera B. Williams (K–3, 30 pp.)

Curious George, by H. A. Rey (PP–1, 48 pp.)

The Cut-Ups Cut Loose, by James Marshall (K–2, 30 pp.)

The Day Jimmy's Boa Ate the Wash, by Trinka Hakes Noble (PP–2, 30 pp.)

An Evening at Alfie's, by Shirley Hughes (PP–2, 28 pp.)

Frog and Toad Are Friends, Arnold Lobel (PP–2, 64 pp.)

The Giving Tree, by Shel Silverstein (K–4, 52 pp.)

Goodnight Moon, by Margaret Wise Brown (P–K, 30 pp.)

Ira Sleeps Over, by Bernard Waber (K–6, 48 pp.)

Madeline, by Ludwig Bemelmans (P–2, 54 pp.)

Mike Mulligan and His Steam Shovel, by Virginia Lee Burton (K–4, 42 pp.)

The Napping House, by Audrey Wood, illustrated by Don Wood (P–K, 28 pp.)

Tintin in Tibet, by Herge (2–4, 62 pp.)

Where the Wild Things Are, by Maurice Sendak (K–3, 28 pp.)

*Informational Books.** Nonfiction print satisfies and builds curiosity and reinforces the information value of books.

Planes, by Byron Barton (P–2)

Animals in the Country, by Kenneth Lilly (K–2)

*Source: From MANZO. *Teaching Children to Be Literate,* 1E. © 1996 Wadsworth, a part of Cengage Learning, Inc. Reproduced by permission. www.cengage.com/permissions.

Do Animals Dream? by Joyce Pope (3–6)

Here a Chick, There a Chick, by Bruce McMillan (P–3)

How Much Is a Million? by David M. Schwartz, illustrated by Steven Kellogg (P–3)

How the Human Body Works, by Giovanni Caselli (5–9)

The Kids' Question and Answer Book, by the editors of *Owl* magazine (4–7)

Life through the Ages, by Giovanni Caselli (5–8)

The Milk Makers, by Gail Gibbons (P–3)

The Post Office Book: Mail and How It Moves, by Gail Gibbons (P–3)

Trucks, by Byron Barton (P–K)

Wonder Charts*: Creating a Culture of Inquiry

A Wonder Chart provides a space for students to tell about anything that "wonders" them. Their purpose is to build interests and curiosity about the material in information trade books and textbooks. "Wonders" are recorded by the teacher or the child and signed by the contributor. Space is provided for illustrating pictures or additional related information. Additional space is provided for "Answers"—or explanations, illustrations, pictures, or book titles that relate. In this way, children are taught to be question raisers as well as question answerers (Figure 9.1).

The keenest part of Wonder Chart activities is that they not only broaden the circle of student participants but tend to include other teachers, library resources, newspapers, magazines, and parents. Every conceivable source of information soon becomes part of this cooperative learning activity. This activity also offers another opportunity for teachers to help children bring wonder and learning home to enrich family life:

"Dad, you're a mechanic, right? Well, we were wondering in school today how a car engine operates. Could you tell me how it works?"

"Mom, you said that you once worked in a fish-canning factory in Seattle. We were wondering today how those little sardines get so neatly into every can."

▶ LITERATURE- AND THEME-BASED (INTERDISCIPLINARY) EXPLORATIONS INTO CONTENT, CONCEPTS, AND VOCABULARY

Moss (1991) offers several sound reasons for promoting and using informational texts (trade books) in a thematic way, even when textbooks are the dominant medium. For example, textbooks tend to be written at a student's Instructional Level whereas trade books are often available on the same topic at a student's

*Source: From MANZO. *Teaching Children to Be Literate*, 1E. © 1996 Wadsworth, a part of Cengage Learning, Inc. Reproduced by permission. www.cengage.com/permissions.

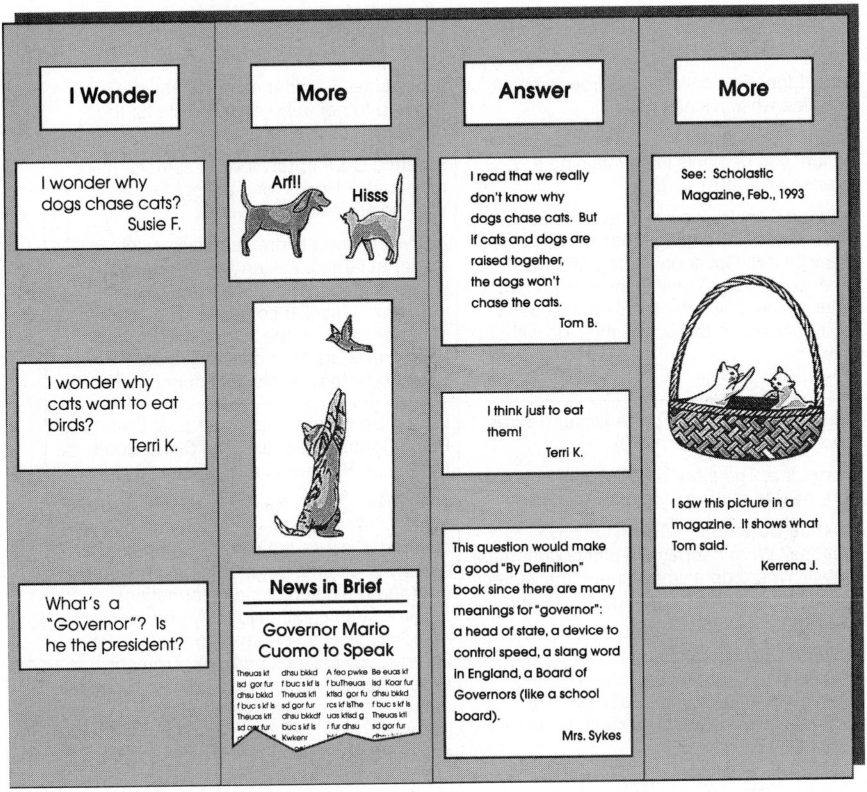

Figure 9.1 Wonder Chart

Source: From MANZO. *Teaching Children to Be Literate,* 1E. © 1996 Wadsworth, a part of Cengage Learning, Inc. Reproduced by permission. www.cengage.com/permissions

Independent Level. Further, trade books tend to be much more engaging, colorful, and detailed about a certain place and time—critical elements of children's ways of knowing. Beverly Kobrin introduced *Eyeopeners!* (1988) as a means of providing updates on available nonfiction children's books. Her first edition listed more than 500 entries. Today there are several other sources, such as *The Horn Book Magazine* and the *Reading Teacher's* section on *Children's Books.* Trade books tend to have children reading and learning before, during, and after the bell (Moss, 1991). Many of the themes discussed next are available with videos such as the audio-visual adaptations produced by Weston Woods (http://teacher.scholastic.com/products/westonwoods/).

No Lines Online

Today most any theme-based unit and lesson can be found instantly online. Topics and guidelines are in the thousands. The essential connections and functions of these wonderful online sites are part of a long legacy of theme-based study such

Literature Base: *Landslide* (Veronique Day, Coward McCann, 1963) **Story Line:** Five children are trapped by a landslide while hiking. **Science Concepts:** What is erosion? What is the function of plants in maintaining a balance in nature? **Activity:** Construct a box that has two parts with a board separating those parts. Fill each side with dirt. Cover one side with grass seed. Let it grow. Then tilt the box and run water evenly down the two sides. Observe what happens to the dirt on the side without grass.	**Literature Base:** *Charlotte's Web* (E. B. White, Harper & Row, 1952) **Story Line:** A spider named Charlotte uses her web to not only catch insects for food, but also to save a pig's life. **Science Concepts:** How do spiders make their webs? How strong are spider webs? Why do spiders make webs? **Activity:** Have children carefully catch a spider (a large black and yellow garden spider is ideal), and place it in a large terrarium or similar container. The children can then observe the spider spin its web. Live insects are then placed in the container to see how the insects are caught in the web.
Literature Base: *The Tough Winter* (Robert Lawson, Puffin Books, 1979) **Story Line:** The story is about how animals work hard to survive a tough winter. **Science Concepts:** Why do we have seasons? What happens to plants during the winter? Where do animals spend the winter? What is hibernation? What foods can animals find during the winter? **Activity:** Collect some cocoons from tall grass during February and March. Bring them into the classroom. Put them in a widemouth gallon jar. Cover with flyscreen. Observe.	**Literature Base:** *Little Cloud* (Eric Carle, Puffin Books, 1998) and *The Cloud Book* (Tomie de Paola, Holiday House, 1985) **Activities:** Over a several-week period, read either of these pieces to primary grade children. Discuss the different shapes and density of clouds. Begin to note, and ideally photograph, different cloud formations outside. Help children identify and properly name at least two of these formations. Read and discuss the second book. From this experience students would learn to be aware of the fact of and weather conditions associated with different cloud formations, and hence be open to the continuing growth of knowledge in this domain. Ideally, a few children may wish to build a relatively complete picture book of many formations.

Figure 9.2 Literature-based/themed science units
Source: Pond, M., & Hoch, L. (1992). Linking children's literature and science activities. *Ohio Reading Teacher, 25* (2), 13–15.

as is illustrated above. There is one major difference—the online world is ever growing and now in increasingly rich media forms.

Themed Science Units*

Pond and Hoch (1992, pp. 13–15) and Cerullo (1997) provide a number of examples to illustrate how literature can set the stage for activities that teach science concepts in meaningful ways. Four of these are detailed in Figure 9.2.

Children's literature is rich with books that can make science concepts more understandable. Maggart and Zintz (1992, pp. 400–402) offer these examples for developing units on animals and weather:

Books for a unit on animals

- *Born in a Barn* (by E. Gemming)—primary grades
- *Panda* (by C. Curtis)—primary grades
- *Animal Superstars: Biggest, Strongest, Fastest, Smartest* (by R. Freedman) —intermediate grades
- *Here Come the Dolphins* (by A. Goudey)—intermediate grades
- *Born Free* (by J. Adamson)—upper grades
- *Whale Watch* (by A. Graham & F. Graham)—upper grades

Books for a unit on weather

- *Blizzard at the Zoo* (by R. Bahr)—primary grades
- *The Snowy Day* (by E. J. Keats)—primary grades
- *Listen to the Rain* (by B. Martin Jr. & J. Archambault)—primary grades
- *The Cloud Book* (by T. dePaola)—intermediate grades

Literature-Based Mathematics Units*

For knowledge to be retained and transferred to other situations, it needs to be relevant and interesting to the student (Farris & Kaczmarski, 1988). Jamar and Morrow (1991) and Pauler and Bodevin (1990) have assembled integrated units for first and second graders. See Figure 9.3 for a practical example of how "the natural language in good children's literature provides a vehicle that allows teachers to present interrelated activities in reading, writing, and mathematics" (Jamar & Morrow, 1991, p. 29).

Wood (1992) offers some additional examples of Content Area Reading in mathematics that you might wish to examine. The methods she offers rely heavily on collaborative activities in reading, writing, and thinking aloud. One method, for example, uses a variation on "Big Books." Children produce enlarged versions of math word problems and then, using a pointer, show how they solved the problems (Figure 9.4).

Other Literature-Content Ties*

Wooten (1992) gives several examples of how the Martin books can be tied to subject area instruction. In one example, *Chicka Chicka Boom Boom* (Martin & Archambault, 1985), a colorful illustrated alphabet book typically used with kindergartners, was used with fourth graders to release these "layers of learning" (Figure 9.5).

Literature Base: *Cross-Country Cat* (Calhoun, 1979, NY: Morrow) **Story Line:** Henry, a sassy Siamese cat, takes matters into his own "paws" when his family accidentally leaves him behind at a ski lodge. Henry skis home, meeting a variety of animals along the way. **Mathematics Concepts:** Counting by twos; one-to-one correspondence; comparison; sequencing; map-making and map-reading. **Activity:** Use cut-out pairs of skis to practice counting by two's; use items of ski-clothing to reinforce the concept of one-to-one correspondence (2 shoes for 2 feet; 1 scarf for 1 neck; 2 mittens for 2 hands; 1 hat for 1 head, etc.); reinforce the concept of sequencing by having children list the animals that Henry met on his journey home; have children create maps of Henry's journey, illustrating where he met each of the other animals; have children use a cut-out ski to measure the length of Henry's trip, and to spark a discussion with questions such as, "How long do you think Henry's trip took? How long did it take Henry to get as far as he did before the family found him? How did you decide this? What clues did you find in the story or the pictures?" The map-making activity can be extended to creation of a neighborhood map, and estimation of distances.	**Literature Base:** *Millions of Cats* (Wanda Gag, 1928, NY: Coward, McCann, Geohegan) **Story Line:** Includes a refrain children can join in on when the story is read aloud, about hundreds, thousands, millions, billions, and trillions of cats! **Mathematics Concepts:** Place value, a mnemonic device for reading "big" numbers (a great motivator and confidence builder for young children) **Activity:** Note and list on the board the names of the number places: hundreds, thousands, millions, billions, and trillions. Explain how to read each hundreds and tens place ("three hundred seventy-eight *million* . . ."). Then show children how they can use the *Millions of Cats* refrain as a way to remember how to read numbers with as many as fifteen places.
Source: Jamar, D., & Morrow, J. (1991). A literature-based interdisciplinary approach to the teaching of reading, writing, and mathematics. *The Ohio Reading Teacher,* 25 (3), 28–35.	Source: Pauler, S., & Bodevin, D. (1990). Book-specific response activities: Satisfaction guaranteed. *Georgia Journal of Reading,* 16 (2), 30–35.

Figure 9.3 Literature-based math units

Indrisano and Paratore (1992) offer another literature-to-content connection. The book is a nonfiction piece by Barbara Bash (1989) called *Desert Giant—The World of the Saguaro Cactus.* Indrisano and Paratore's graphic organizer for *Desert Giant,* shown in Figure 9.6, illustrates its potential for teaching science and ecology in an altogether engaging manner.

Children's literature is also full of natural connections with social studies. Select children's literature that illuminates the values of the people about whom the social studies text is written: Books that teach something of the lives of the people, what daily living was like, what was fun, what games they played, what caused happiness and unhappiness, as well as fears and anxieties. Following are a few suggestions from Maggart and Zintz (1992, pp. 400–402):

- Biographies of historical figures, such as *Abe Lincoln Gets His Chance,* by Cavanah (1978).

Figure 9.4 Math word problems
Source: From MANZO. *Teaching Children to Be Literate,* 1E. © 1996 Wadsworth, a part of Cengage Learning, Inc. Reproduced by permission. www.cengage.com/permissions

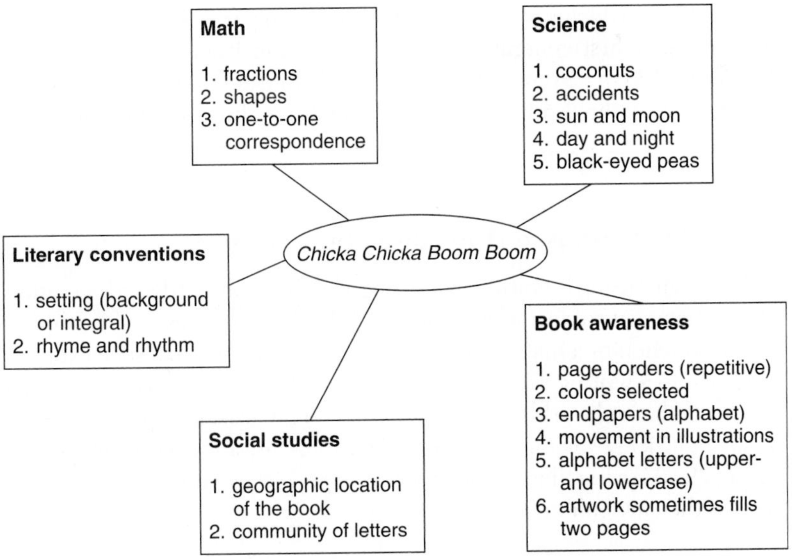

Figure 9.5 Interdisciplinary concepts through children's literature
Source: Wooten, D. A. (1992). The magic of Martin. In B. E. Cullinan (Ed.), *Invitation to Read: More Children's Literature in the Reading Program,* (pp. 72–79). Copyright 1992 by the International Reading Association.

How It Looks	*How It Grows*	*How It Is Used*
• Can grow as tall as 50 feet • Can weigh several tons • Has sharp spines • Has accordion-like pleats that expand when it rains to store water	• Begins under the canopy of a larger tree or "nurse plant" • After 50 years, it produces its first flowers • After 75 years, arms start to appear • At 150 years, it towers over the desert • Can live for 200 years	• Male woodpeckers make holes in the cactus for their mates' eggs • Elf owls and hawks live in them • Bats, doves, bees, and butterflies eat its flowers • Thrashers, lizards, and ants eat its fruit • Fruit is used for jams, candy, and wine • Hardened parts of dead cactus can be used for food containers • Termites feed on dead cactus • Snakes, geckos, and spiders use the dead stalks as a home

Figure 9.6 Graphic organizer for *Desert Giant: The World of the Saguaro Cactus*
Source: Indrisano, R, & Paratore, J.R. (1992). Using Literature with readers at risk. In B.E. Cullinan (Ed.), *Invitation to Read: More Children's Literature in the Reading Program*, (pp. 138–149). Copyright 1992 by the International Reading Association.

- Fictional accounts of historical periods, such as the Laura Ingalls Wilder series (c.f. Wilder & Williams, 1994).
- Books representing varied cultural worlds, such as *Fifth Chinese Daughter* (Wong, 1963), which reveals the conflict between parents and the children growing up as first-generation immigrants in San Francisco; and *Owl in the Cedar Tree* by Momaday (1975), which presents a conflict between the culture of the Native Americans and the culture of the European settlers.

Theme-Based (Interdisciplinary) Units*

Once a teacher begins using literature as a springboard for content-based activities, the boundaries between subject areas begin to fade. A science lesson leads naturally to the introduction of a math concept, for example, and on to a social studies activity, and back to a writing activity. This is the height of excellence in teaching because it reflects the real world, in which subjects do not exist as separate entities but as threads in a richly woven fabric. See Figure 9.7 for a lesson developed by Post (1992, pp. 29–35) as an illustration of how a single piece of literature can spark activities across the curriculum.

*Source: From MANZO. *Teaching Children to Be Literate*, 1E. © 1996 Wadsworth, a part of Cengage Learning, Inc. Reproduced by permission. www.cengage.com/permissions.

Literature Base: *The Camel Caper* (Kristin Casler, Grand Rapids Press—see Post, 1992, for reprint)

Story Line: In this humorous article, Casler chronicles the escape of the camel, Roxanne, from the John Ball Zoo; her travels through the neighborhood; the reactions of stunned observers; and, finally, her capture.

Language Arts Activities:

- Introduction—Show a picture of a camel on an overhead, and have students brainstorm what they know about camels. Distribute the article for students to read.
- Getting the Facts—Distribute note cards, and have students work in pairs to jot down the basic "who, what, when, where, why/how's" of the article.
- Application 1–Distribute a map of the area in which the camel wandered, and have students trace the camel's route from the zoo to where she was captured. Have students compare their maps with those of a partner—where differences occur, reread for clarification. Show the map on an overhead, and have one or more students or groups share their results with the whole class.
- Application 2–Ask several students to volunteer to give an extemporaneous radio broadcast, using their "who, what, . . ." card as notes. Tape record the speaking exercises. The teacher begins each "broadcast" by saying,

  "Good evening. This is station WGRX, Grand Rapids, Michigan, here to bring you the latest news."

  Students speak into a real or pretend microphone. Replay each "broadcast," giving the speaker positive comments and constructive criticism. Later, transcribe these "broadcasts." Instead of writing them as a paragraph, list and number the sentences, and use these as the basis for teaching aspects of grammar.

Figure 9.7 Example theme-based (interdisciplinary) unit
Source: Post, A. R. (1992). The camel caper: An integrated language arts lesson. *Michigan Reading Journal,* 25 (2), 29–35.

In the Upper Grades: Using Literature and Trade Books in the Secondary Content Area Classrooms

It is commonly expected that literature will be found in English class and that in the other content areas, a textbook will be the primary source of print instruction. However, increasing attention is being paid to the value of using a variety of adolescent literature, trade books, and even picture books to teach in and across the content areas. In some ways, the rationale is simple: Textbooks are broad, encyclopedic, and have a lot of information, but through the ages, it is clear that people often learn best through stories. Through stories, students learn not just the historical, mathematical, or scientific facts of a field but also are able to *experience* vicariously diverse affective and social issues—namely, a fresh variety of human thoughts, emotions, and actions. As students get the chance to learn in this way through literature and other forms of trade books, they are provided increased scaffolding on which to learn more of the content area materials that are expected to be covered in our classes. This way of learning also allows students to experience more of the true interdisciplinary nature of knowledge, as they see how interrelated much of their content learning is with other disciplines and with the human experience in general.

Because of this, there is now an increasing interest in the use of adolescent literature and trade books to supplement the textbook and other traditional instruction more commonly expected in our content areas. This extension of the *reiterative reading* concept, which we introduced in Chapter 4 (Crafton, 1983), is now burgeoning into entire courses and textbooks dedicated to the topic. Therefore, what we've included here is designed only to serve as a mention and introduction to this important literacy subfield. See Figure 9.8 for a collection of resources that might help you find out more regarding adolescent literature and trade books for use in your content area teaching.

▶ WRITING TO LEARN AND COMPOSING PAPERS

This section takes a closer look at two instructional uses of writing: writing to learn, and composing papers. Guidelines are given for increasing the use of writing

Textbooks	Textbook Chapters
Atwell, N. (1998). *In the middle: Writing, reading, and learning with adolescents* (2nd ed.). Portsmouth, NH: Boynton/Cook.	Chapter 9: "Literature-Based and Thematic Approaches to Content Area Teaching," in Roe, B. D., Stoodt, B. D., & Burns, P. C. (2001). *The content areas: Secondary school literacy instruction.* Boston, MA: Houghton-Mifflin.
Mueller, P. N. (2001). *Lifers: Learning from at-risk adolescent readers.* Portsmouth, NH: Heinemann.	Chapter 12: "Developing Lifetime Readers: Literature in Content Area Classes," in Alvermann, D. E., & Phelps, S. F. (2002). *Content reading and literacy: Succeeding in today's diverse classrooms* (3rd ed.). Boston, MA: Allyn & Bacon.
Hynds, S. (1997). *On the brink: Negotiating literature and life with adolescents.* New York: Teachers College Press.	Chapter 12: "Supporting the Textbook with Literature," in Richardson, J. S., & Morgan, R.F. (1997). *Reading to learn in the content areas* (3rd ed.). Belmont, CA: Wadsworth.
Nilsen, A. P., & Donelson, K. L. (2001). *Literature for today's young adults* (6th ed.). New York: Longman.	Chapter 2: "Learning with Textbooks, Trade Books, and Electronic Texts," in Vacca, R. T., & Vacca, J. A. (2002). *Content area reading: Literacy and learning across the curriculum* (7th ed.). Boston, MA: Allyn & Bacon.
Freeman, E. B., & Person, D. G. (1998). *Connecting informational children's books with content area learning.* Boston: Allyn & Bacon.	Chapter 7: "Literature," in Readence, J. E., Bean, T. W., & Baldwin, R. S. (2001). *Content area literacy: An integrated approach* (7th ed.). Dubuque, IA: Kendall/Hunt.
Science From the National Science Teachers Association: NSTA Outstanding Science Trade Books for Students K-12: http://www.nsta.org/ostbc	

Figure 9.8 Resources for learning more about using adolescent literature and other trade books in content area instruction

Web Sites	Journal Articles
From Reading Online, a review of 13 trade books for use in the content area of science: http://www.readingonline.org/reviews/literature/andersen/ Outstanding Science Trade books for Children: http://www.ucalgary.ca/~dkbrown/nsta98.html **Social Studies** From the National Council for the Social Studies---Notable Social Studies Trade books for Young People: http://www.socialstudies.org/resources/notable/ **Math** Mathematician Biographies Online: http://www-groups.dcs.st-and.ac.uk/~history/BiogIndex.html This site contains biographical and historical information on hundreds of mathematicians from antiquities through the present. Great resource for reiterative reading in the math classroom. Mr. Brandenburg's Books about Math: http://mathforum.com/t2t/faq/brandenburg.html This site contains an extensive collection of math-related trade books that can be used to supplement high school math instruction. **Language Arts and Other** Association for Library Service to Children: http://www.ala.org/ALSCTemplate.cfm?Section=ALSC This extensive site's "Literary and Related Awards" link provides information on collections of the mostly highly regarded children and adolescent literature and trade books. Making Multicultural Connections Through Trade Books: http://www.mcps.k12.md.us/curriculum/socialstd/MBD/Grade_index.html#top This site contains lists of trade books that can be used in making multicultural connections in teaching across the disciplines (grades K-6 emphasis).	**Multiple Content Areas** Moss, B. & Hendershot, J. (2002). Exploring sixth graders' selection of nonfiction trade books. *The Reading Teacher,* 56(1), 6-17. Daisey, P. (1997). Promoting literacy in secondary content area classrooms with biography projects. *Journal of Adolescent & Adult Literacy,* 40(4), 270-278. Palmer, R.G., & Stewart, R.A. (1997). Nonfiction trade books in content area instruction: Realities and potential. *Journal of Adolescent & Adult Literacy,* 40(8), 630-641. Moss, B., & Noden, H. (1995). Resources for choosing and using trade books in the classroom. *The Reading Teacher,* 48(8), 724-726. **Science** Shackleford, B. (2003). Teaching through trade books: Seeing the seasons. *Science and Children,* 40(6), 14-16. Outstanding science trade books for students K-12: Books published in 2002 (2003, March). *Science and Children,* 40(6), 31-38. **Social Studies** Albright, L.K. (2002). Bringing the ice maiden to life: Engaging adolescents in learning through picture book read-alouds in contents areas. *Journal of Adolescent & Adult Literacy* 45(5), 418-428. **Math** Hellwig, S.J., Monroe, E.E., & Jabobs, J.S. (2000). Making informed choices: Selecting children's trade books for mathematics instruction. *Teaching Children Mathematics,* 7(3), 138. **Picture Books for Content Area Instruction** Carr, K.S., Buchanan, D.L., Wentz, J.B., Weiss, M.L., & Brant, K.J. (2001). Not just for the primary grades: A bibliography of picture books for secondary content teachers. *Journal of Adolescent & Adult Literacy,* 45(2), 146-153.

Figure 9.8 *(continued)*

Web Sites	Journal Articles
Bilingual Books for Children: http://www.ala.org/Content/NavigationMenu/ALSC/Resources3/Book_Lists/Bilingual_Books_for_Children.htm This site contains a bibliography of books currently available with bilingual text. Great Websites for Kids: http://www.ala.org/gwstemplate.cfm?section=greatwebsites&template=/cfapps/gws/default.cfm&CFID=97761408&CFTOKEN=2017043 From the Association for Library Service to Children, this site has links to content area sites for Animals, Literature and Language Arts, Mathematics, Fine Art, Sciences, History, Social Science, and Reference.	Billman, L.W. (2002). Aren't these books for little kids? *Educational Leadership,* 60(3), 48-51.

Figure 9.8 (*continued*)

to learn—possibly the most underused teaching/learning tool at secondary teachers' disposal. The Writing Process is offered as a framework for guiding students' writing of various types of papers, from research papers to creative writing activities. The Writing Process is widely acknowledged as a means of teaching students how to write rather than simply grading the products of their writing.

Writing Process and One-Process Writing

There is a caution in following the Writing Process that deserves explanation. The Writing Process is a grammar for writing that can be as constraining as is grammar in language. It keeps management of classwork on a steady keel. However, it is not really the process by which we write. The process by which we write is less linear, more free-form, and when it is really cooking, much more passionate. Educators are thinking hard about how to better reconcile these two processes.

Writing: Encouraging the Process and the Products

The process of simply writing something down—a note while reading, an item on a to-do list, a message to a friend, or an answer to a study guide question—adds a slight but significant element of commitment to that thought that it previously did not have. It becomes more real, more concrete, more likely to be remembered. Any form of writing prior to reading or listening tends to activate prior knowledge and experience and heighten the reader's anticipation of the author's focus and key points. This could be called *engaged* reading and listening. It is a more active, interactive, and memorable mode of operating than is the passive, or disassociated, reading and listening that tends to occur in school. Additionally, each effort to write *after* reading also provides considerable benefits to learning. It requires active reconstruction of text and thereby increases sensitivity to the text's content, logic, and organization. Further, each effort to write in reaction to or evaluation of text constitutes that invigorating plunge into the unknown where language and thought trigger each other to discover and organize the "inchoate lump of meanings" (Henry, 1974) that we often are left with following typical passive reading.

Simply put, a routine requirement to write something—almost anything—before or after reading ignites more active thinking before, during, and following reading. In spite of these benefits, writing tends to be an underused tool in content classrooms. There are three primary reasons for this nonwriting orientation in school:

1. Most teachers have not themselves experienced a requirement for frequent writing as students, other than for an occasional book report or essay in English class and perhaps a research paper in social studies.
2. Relatedly, teachers are unaware of the many informal ways in which writing can be used as an aid to thinking.
3. Most teachers are reluctant to require frequent writing because of the time required to provide feedback.

Speaking to each of these three points now, let's see if we can become the generation of teachers that sets the example for others to follow. Our chances of accomplishing this goal are much improved over those who have preceded us. There is much that is new in the literature on writing, reading, and thinking to call on, in addition to the enabling possibilities inherent in use of the internet in increasingly wired classrooms.

Righting Writing across the Curriculum: Road under Construction

The most important point to be made about writing as a thinking tool is that teachers should help students distinguish between writing as a tool and writing as a product. When writing is used as a tool, *not everything students write has to be graded, or even read, by the teacher.* In the following suggestions, student writing may be followed by short cooperative group sharing of the writing, or added to a folder to be collected for "credit/no credit."

Before Reading

- *Timed prewriting:* Tell students the topic of a reading assignment, and give a short time (3 to 5 minutes) to write what they think it will be about.
- *Prompted prewriting:* Give a specific prompt related to the content of a reading assignment, and have students write brief responses before reading.

While Reading

- *Main idea notes:* Give the reading assignment with directions to write the author's main points (in students' own words), with supporting details noted.
- *Factoids:* Direct students to look, while reading, for brief, interesting facts as might appear on CNN, or set out in bold print to capture a reader's interest in a magazine or textbook.
- *Rewrite for different audiences:* Direct students to look, while reading, for a section to rewrite for a different audience (e.g., a younger person, a grandparent, corporate/government leader).
- *Write the author:* Direct students to think, while reading, about how the material might be presented more clearly or interestingly, and to write a note to the author informing him or her of their ideas.
- *Add to it:* Direct students to write a paragraph or two that could/should be added to make the information clearer.
- *Write an example:* Direct students to look for points that remind them of relevant examples or stories that help make the author's point.

After Reading

- *Press release:* A public relations press release on a worthy idea or finding.
- *More information:* A letter of request to an author or other authority for more information.
- *Connections:* Tell about a related television program, website, book, article, idea, or related moral/ethical conflict.

Notice that most of these suggestions can be done quickly and with little preparation. However, they add considerably to a student's anticipation and/or deeper processing of most any fundamental set of information and ideas. It's a good bet that you can see yourself doing any of these. With another few moments of thought, you surely can come up with many similar and manageable writing-learning activities for almost any discipline, from the more obvious content areas such as English and social studies to some that at first blush may seem less amenable to writing, such as physical education, music, and art.

Next, we turn to the nuts and bolts of guiding effective writing and thinking. Traditional efforts to teach writing have focused on the final *product.* More recently, an instructional framework for guiding student mastery of the *process of writing* has been evolving. This instructional framework was presumably designed to parallel the process one would reasonably go through in writing. In fact, it is merely an approximation that is quite mechanical, although as necessary to know as are the rules of grammatical speech. Therefore, it has come to be called simply the Writing Process. The Writing Process framework is analogous to the three-step framework for planning prereading, guided silent reading, and postreading instruction—or *into, through,* and *beyond* reading. It indicates what should be done at each stage in general terms but leaves considerable latitude in just how to do it.

The Writing Process: A Grammar and Framework for Guiding the Process of Paper Writing

It may be easy to request students to write, but writing is not easy to learn or to teach. It is a habit of mind, it is inherently chaotic, it involves a great deal of sifting and sorting, and it is always hard work. The prolific writer and economist John Kenneth Galbraith said it most sincerely: "There are days when the result is so bad that no fewer than five revisions are required. In contrast, when I'm greatly inspired, only four revisions are needed" (interview, CNBC, May 1996). For novice writers, the mere prospect of writing any type of paper is daunting. Traditionally, writing is a sink-or-swim proposition. A topic is assigned, and a due date is given. Sometimes a draft is critiqued by the teacher, but most of the real work of writing occurs before the initial draft is produced. The Writing Process framework is a way to provide guidance, from initial reflections through final editing stages.

Steps in the Writing Process

Step 1. *Prewriting: Getting It Together.* In the idea-building phase, the teacher prepares students for writing by:

- Raising motivation and interest.
- Calling up relevant prior knowledge and experiences.
- Encouraging exploration of the topic and suggesting resources.
- Reminding students to document sources of possible materials located in the library or on the internet.
- Eliciting additional details, reasons, or examples.
- Providing basic expectations for the final product, usually in the form of a rubric.

Step 2. *Drafting: Getting It Down.* In the drafting phase, students attempt to shape the unwieldy ideas, purposes, facts, personal feelings, and biases into the linearity of words and structure. This includes finding out what you really think and then how to say it best. During this phase, the teacher's role is to:

1. Help students express initial thoughts and ideas on paper.
2. Remind students to refer to prewriting notes and experiences. Word processors are a tremendous aid at this stage. Notes can be copied and pasted quickly and easily.
3. Help students keep in mind the audience who will be reading their work, as a guide to the form and character of the composition.
4. Encourage the free flow of ideas by emphasizing content rather than mechanics or structure.

Step 3. *Revising: Getting It Organized.* Revising is an evaluative and reconstructive phase. It requires a good deal of introspection and willingness to critique oneself, to be critiqued, and, in several strategies described later, to think like an editor and to critique the work of others. In this phase, the teacher provides guidance by:

1. Arranging for students to receive feedback from peers and/or various audiences. Draft copies can be e-mailed to a family member, an online tutor, or other willing helper.
2. Encouraging students to reorganize, rewrite, and revise as needed for fluency and coherence.
3. Guiding discussions that clarify and thereby point to specific areas of composition that require rewriting.
4. Encouraging redrafting as needed with an eye toward initial purpose and audience.
5. Helping students consider how well others have understood and interpreted their writing.

Step 4. *Editing: Getting It Right.* In the final editing phase, the composition is reviewed for correct mechanics such as spelling, grammatical usage, and punctuation. The teacher assists by

1. Encouraging students to fine-tune their work. Here again, word processors are quite useful in checking spelling and grammar.
2. Noting common mechanical problems and providing class instruction in these areas.

Step 5. *Publishing: Going Public.* In the publishing phase, the final copy is shared with an audience. This can be done in a variety of formal and informal ways. The point is that writing becomes more real and serious when it is to be read by someone other than the teacher. The teacher aids in this process by

1. Employing methods that ensure that there will be readers for students' efforts. The internet opens unlimited opportunities for creative ways of publishing student work.

2. Offering evaluative feedback based on a rubric for the assignment.
3. Offering opportunities for student papers to serve as a foundation for reading, discussion, or study.

▶ CONCEPT SUMMARY

This chapter is a reminder that Content Area Literacy is broader than subject area classroom curricula. The purposeful inquiry that drives content learning and strategy acquisition can be nourished and guided from early elementary grade levels. In real world applications and problem solving, literacy strategies are applied across disciplines, and incorporate listening, speaking, and writing as well as reading. This chapter focused on three aspects of this broader nature of CAL: Emergent Content Area Literacy; the use of literature and trade books to teach content at all grade levels, and some practical ways to use writing to enhance student learning across the disciplines.

CHAPTER 10

INTERACTIVE ASSESSMENT FOR ACTIVE SELF-MONITORING AND SELF-TEACHING

The examiner pipes and the teacher must dance—and the examiner sticks to the old tune.
—H. G. Wells, 1892

Interactive teaching is characterized by interactive assessment. To achieve this, it is essential that assessment techniques be selected that invite a reasonably high level of student involvement. This chapter details several such techniques that are both timely and have withstood the test of time. These include an informal textbook inventory designed to assess and teach students about the parts of their books, a rationale for portfolio evaluation of student progress, and a rubric system for easy evaluation of student writing. The chapter then addresses several simple ways to estimate the difficulty level, or readability, of textual material. Appropriate shortcuts and computer-based alternatives are noted along the way.

- ▶ INTRODUCTION TO STUDENT ASSESSMENT
- ▶ TOOLS FOR ASSESSMENT OF STUDENT READING
- ▶ EVALUATION OF STUDENT WRITING
- ▶ PORTFOLIOS: RATIONALE, FUNCTIONS, PROMISE, PROBLEMS
- ▶ ASSESSING TEXT DIFFICULTY
- ▶ AFFECTIVE ISSUES AND MEASURES
- ▶ CONCEPT SUMMARY

▶ INTRODUCTION TO STUDENT ASSESSMENT

The Power of the Examiner

The power of the examiner is a long-standing and deeply rooted issue in education. In fact, the influence of testing may be greater now than at any time in our history. In the past 10 years, most states have first instituted and then dropped or redirected assessment procedures with names such as *basic competencies, mastery learning, criterion-referenced* testing, and, more recently, *holistic, authentic, outcomes-based,* and *performance-based* assessment. One measure, however, remains a constant since federal law (NAEP: The National Assessment of Educational Progress) mandates it.

National Assessment of Educational Progress (NAEP)

NAEP is one of the major literacy benchmarks. It was mandated by the Congress in 1969 and carried out on a mixed-subject schedule every two or three years. Students in fourth, eighth, and twelfth grades receive 50 minutes to read graded passages and answer questions, both multiple choice and written. There are four possible levels of competency that one can achieve: *below basic, basic, proficient,* and *advanced.* Four sets of data are relevant: 1992, 1994, 1998 and 2002. The 1994 data were among the most shocking to the national conscience.

In that year, about 60% of adolescents, according to NAEP performance indicators, were able to read at a basic level. They could gather details, identify a main idea, and recognize connections among textually explicit ideas. Fewer than 5% of students surveyed, however, were able to perform at *advanced* levels, where they were required to examine, extend, and elaborate meanings from representative fiction and nonfiction materials (Campbell, Donahue, Reese, & Phillips, 1996). Results of an NAEP *writing* assessment (Applebee, Langer, Mullis, Lathan, & Gentile, 1994) revealed that *most all* students in grades 4, 8, and 12 had difficulty with writing tasks that required higher levels of coherent thinking and the important capacity to provide details to support points made. Some have called this a national crisis (Vacca & Alvermann, 1998). We tend to see it as a growing awareness of one of the challenges inherent in the field of Content Area Literacy: In addition to the need for systematic direct *instruction* in reading-thinking strategies across the disciplines, we need systematic ongoing *assessment* and feedback at the classroom level. Several basic formats for classroom assessment are described next.

Higher-Order and Performance-Based Assessment

Of the many recent efforts to reform educational assessment, the movement toward higher-order thinking and performance-based assessment, or the representation of real-life tasks in assessment, may be the most welcome (see Figure 10.1). The logic of mastery learning, which so strongly influenced teaching and testing in the past, now finally is being replaced with assessment more firmly grounded in interactive and integrated performance. Where mastery learning stressed the passive acquisition of facts and skills, newer interactive assessment models tend to emphasize the active role of readers and learners in using print to construct meaning and solve problems. Thus, there is a decreased emphasis on product outcomes of learning, such as information acquisition, and an increased emphasis on how well students are internalizing the thinking processes they will need to learn both in and out of school.

As more states move away from use of standardized test scores as the primary approach to evaluation of schools and school districts, it is expected that educators will feel less obliged to concentrate on simple fact acquisition and more committed to engaging students in authentic learning activities. Of course, this does not mean that standardized test scores are without value. See Figure 10.2 for an example of how such data can be used to suggest programmatic decisions.

For a more authentic and interactive means of assessing students' needs, consider the Informal Textbook Inventory. It is a means of introducing a textbook to

The goal of traditional assessment is to evaluate acquisition of information. The goal of performance-based assessment is to evaluate the processes for acquiring and using information. To do this, performance-based assessment is expected to have several of the following characteristics:

- Is problem centered
- Requires use of facts rather than recall of facts
- Requires higher-order thinking along inferential and evaluative lines
- Is more constructive than reconstructive in format
- Does not necessarily have a single correct answer
- Involves more hands-on doing than conventional knowledge testing
- Is more authentic, or real life
- Reflects more fairly the diversity of perspectives in American cultures

Figure 10.1 Performance-based, or authentic, assessment: The current trend.

The following standardized test score information was reported for a local high school in a major city. Of 34 high schools recently tested in the state, this high school was

first in mathematics.
first in social studies.
first in science.
second in narrative (story) reading.
sixth in expository (contentarea) reading.

These data suggest the following conclusion: If the youngsters in this school are first in the three traditional areas of knowledge acquisition but sixth in ability to comprehend (i.e., think) in these subjects, then a program to further maximize application and Content Area Reading in the disciplines is in order.

Figure 10.2 Local high school excels in knowledge but lags in reading.

a class, having students tell the teacher about their preparation for using it effectively, and seamlessly teaching them how to use it to full advantage. This technique sometimes is referred to as a Classroom Reading Inventory (CRI).

▶ TOOLS FOR ASSESSMENT OF STUDENT READING

The Informal Textbook Inventory

An Informal Textbook Inventory (ITI) essentially is a special type of open-book test designed to familiarize students with using one of education's most basic learning tools: the textbook. This "new idea" is more than 75 years old. We have seen an excellent 10-question version of the ITI in a 1924 edition of a fifth-year reader (Walker & Parkman). Since most texts on the market do not contain such a ready-made inventory, you probably will need to construct your own. There are several good reasons for creating and using an ITI at the beginning of the school year:

- It is easily administered in group, paper-and-pencil format.
- It tests and teaches simultaneously.
- It draws the teacher's and students' attention to the processing strategies involved in using text parts, text aids, and related resources.
- It provokes active awareness and discussion of text features.
- It lends itself well to computer (hypertext) presentation and scoring.
- It is purposeful and well structured but nonthreatening.
- It reflects the highest current standards of performance-based assessment.

When used early in the school year, while student attitudes and expectations are still being formed, the ITI provides an excellent means of establishing a disciplined, well-managed classroom tone. By simply tallying the results of the inventory, the teacher can obtain a record of each student's ability to deal with the textbook as well as indications of some of the potential benefits and shortcomings of the textbook itself.

Such assessment can take time to prepare, but it also stores well and improves with age and use. It is the type of activity that is the mark of a professional teacher. Students appreciate the help, and supervisors rarely fail to take note. The second and subsequent times you use the ITI, you will be even more pleased because you will have refined it and will know better what to expect and how to better orchestrate the full activity.

Constructing the Informal Textbook Inventory

The following outline illustrates the general form of the ITI:

I. Organization and Structure of the Text

- A. Understanding the Textbook Organization
  Develop three to five straightforward questions about how the text is structured and how to use the comprehension aids provided within the text.
- B. Using the Text Organization Effectively
  Develop three to five questions that students can answer by referring to the index, table of contents, glossary, appendices, or other text sections and/or aids.

II. Basic Comprehension
Select a short portion of the text that contains an important concept with supporting details and at least one graph, chart, or picture. (The same selection can be used in the following section on applied comprehension.)

- A. Comprehending the Main Idea
  Develop one or two fill-in or multiple-choice questions that direct students to state or select the main idea of the material read.
- B. Noting Supporting Details
  Develop three or more fill-in, multiple-choice, or matching questions about specific facts or ideas in the selection.
- C. Understanding Vocabulary in Context
  Develop three or more fill-in, multiple-choice, or matching questions that direct students to state or select a definition for key terms used in the selection.
- D. Understanding Information Presented in Graphic or Pictorial Form
  Develop one or more questions requiring students to state or select an interpretation of a graph, chart, or picture that adds information not explicitly stated in the selection.

III. Applied Comprehension

Questions in this section can be based on the same text selection used in Part II.

A. Drawing Conclusions and Critical Thinking

Develop one or more questions that require students to draw valid conclusions based on the information presented.

B. Evaluating and Judging

Develop one or more questions that require students to evaluate and apply information from the text in terms of their own experiences, values, and existing knowledge base.

IV. Specialized Options

A. Assess special requirements of the discipline. This could mean understanding geographical directions in social studies, a section on understanding style or mood in literature, or a section on applying symbols in mathematical formulas. Examples are found in Chapter 12 on content-specific applications.

B. Assess pupil abilities to deal with the linguistic features of the text with a Standard Cloze Passage test (described later in this chapter).

Administering and Evaluating the Informal Textbook Inventory

Before asking students to tackle the inventory, explain some of its features and purposes: It is not a test in the usual sense of the word; every text differs slightly from every other, and this is a way to find out how. Point out further that although answers will be discussed as a group, each student will need to complete the inventory independently as thoroughly and accurately as possible.

Once all students have completed the inventory, collect and score the results. For diagnostic purposes, any error is taken as a sign of need in that category.

Much of the diagnostic-teaching value of the inventory comes from the group discussion of the items when the tests are returned to the students. Compare and contrast student strengths and weaknesses among the various categories of questions. Review and discussion of the inventory with the class can take from one-half to two full class periods, depending on individual students' abilities, the difficulty of the text, and the objectives the teacher may wish to achieve.

The next assessment instrument, the Standard Cloze Passage test, also can be constructed from a class textbook. It is much easier to construct, but it yields a more general account of a pupil's ability to handle a given textbook at the linguistic, or language and syntactic, level.

Standard Cloze Passage Test

The term *cloze* refers to a written passage with certain words blanked out to be filled in by the reader. Early studies of this task revealed that it is closely related to reading comprehension across age and most grade levels (Bormuth, 1965). Other studies, however, indicated that cloze was not a direct measure of reading comprehension. Instead, it was a fairly accurate measure of one of the factors that contributes to comprehension, namely, familiarity with the language redundancy patterns, or repetitive sentence structures and phrases in prose (Culver, Godfrey, & Manzo, 1972; Weaver & Kingston, 1963). Technically speaking, this means that cloze and reading comprehension have relatively little in common, but both are strongly related to a third thing (probably verbal reasoning), and therefore either can be used to infer the other.

This and related work added several points to our understanding of the potential values and possible shortcomings of cloze passage testing. These points are summarized in the following list:

1. Cloze is a good, quick assessment strategy for sampling students' ability to handle the language patterns common to different types of content material—and therefore is a good complement to an ITI.
2. Cloze will tend to underestimate the comprehension abilities of students with weak standard English backgrounds, since comprehension is inferred from familiarity with English language patterns. However, when compared with conventional measures of comprehension, this also makes it a fair measure of the degree to which English language learners are experiencing difficulty as a result of lack of familiarity with the new language.
3. Cloze tends to penalize students who are divergent thinking, impulsive, or perfectionistic, since the task is rather tedious, with an error rate higher than what students are used to.
4. Independent practice on cloze tasks does not contribute to improvement in reading comprehension; however, guided discussion of which words work best in each blank, and why, does result in improved comprehension.

The general cloze task can have many forms and purposes. The specific form of the cloze task described next, the Standard Cloze Passage test, is a useful assessment tool for content teachers.

Purpose of the Standard Cloze Passage Test

When constructed, administered, and scored as described next, the cloze test provides a fair indication of how a particular group of students will be able to read and understand a particular piece of reading material. Students' individual scores can be categorized to indicate whether the reading material used is at their own Independent, Instructional, or Frustration level.

Preparation of the Standard Cloze Passage Test

To prepare a Standard Cloze test, select a passage of about 300 words from a textbook. The passage should be one that students have not yet read. Copy the first sentence with no deletions. Then select a word at random in the second sentence. Delete this word and every fifth word thereafter until 50 words have been deleted. Finish the sentence containing the fiftieth blank, and copy the next sentence with no deletions. The blanks should be typed as lines five spaces long and numbered from one to fifty. Students record their responses on numbered answer sheets.

Cautions for Administration of the Standard Cloze Passage Test

To administer the Standard Cloze test, first talk through a few sample cloze sentences. See Figure 10.3 for suggestions about how to do this. Tell students that the task is more difficult than what they may be used to, but that even if they miss half of the items they will have done very well (actually, 40% correct is still Instructional level). You may also wish to assure students that their scores will not be part of their course grades but are an important means for teachers to better understand and provide for their reading needs. This introduction should encourage most students to do their best while reducing the problem noted earlier with this type of task.

Scoring the Standard Cloze Passage Test

To score the Standard Cloze Passage test, simply count the number of words filled in correctly. Count only exact words; do not count synonyms as correct. Multiply this number by 2 (since there are 50 items) to get the percent correct. Scores below 40% mean the material is at the students' Frustration level: It is too difficult for them to read and learn from even with instructional support. Scores from 40% to 60% mean that the material is at these students' Instructional level: They can read and learn from the material with some assistance and guidance. Scores above 60% generally indicate ability to read and learn with no special assistance, or the Independent level.

Why Synonyms Won't Do

An understandable concern of teachers is the fact that only exact replacement words are counted correct in scoring the Standard Cloze test. Synonyms are not counted in such testing for three reasons. First, the assessment format was standardized according to exact-word scoring; therefore, the evaluation criterion cannot be used if synonyms are accepted. Second, the rank ordering of students does not change appreciably when synonyms are accepted; everyone simply has a higher score. Finally, if synonyms are allowed, scoring for the teacher becomes a much

Two elements must be considered for proper word replacement, *semantics*—or meaning—and *syntax*—or grammatical function. Demonstrate these by making choices available on the first two examples that make this point. Then increase the difficulty level of the examples to the actual testing task with two or three more deletions that offer no choices.

Example

> Germany today is reunited, but its people still feel the differences from the period of Soviet domination. West Germans are highly (industrious/frivolous), in the tradition of (ancient/old) Germany. The East (Germans) feel less industrious and (are) given to reliance on (government) for their support.

Figure 10.3 Pointers on demonstrating cloze testing.

longer and more tedious process. You may, nonetheless, wish to use a more interactive version if you believe that the standard form is inappropriate for your students.

Interactive—Non-Standard-Cloze

For a more interactive version of cloze testing, consider these guidelines for a nonstandard form: Have students score their own papers with an allowance for synonyms based on class discussion of reasonable alternatives to the exact word deleted. Increase the Independent reading level score to 70%.

To further encourage self-evaluation and strategic reading, ask pupils to write a sentence or two telling what they think their score indicates about their ability to read the material and what they think they should do to read better in the particular textbook from which the passage was taken.

Next, we turn to the topic of writing. Of all the things we attempt to evaluate in school, writing is one of the more difficult to assess satisfactorily. Nonetheless, it is an area of considerable interest in modern education.

▶ EVALUATION OF STUDENT WRITING

Teachers' enthusiasm for activities that involve student writing often is dampened by the prospect of piles of papers to be painstakingly graded. Fortunately, the recent renovation of an old idea called *rubric evaluation* of student writing cuts down on the paper load. As a result, it is making student writing a more attractive option for more teachers. Two types of rubrics are discussed next, one done essentially by teachers and one done by students.

Using Rubric Evaluation to Enhance Writing Activities

A writing rubric is a set of guidelines for holistic scoring of compositions. It is a teacher-constructed list of characteristics for ranking the quality of student papers, generally on a number scale or simply as *high*, *medium*, or *low*. The teacher uses a rubric to grade student compositions by simply determining which rubric level each composition best matches. Grading compositions thus becomes a speedy process of categorizing papers by level rather than a tedious chore of red-penciling each and every error and composing brief but time-consuming written comments on students' papers.

Ideally, the teacher gives the rubric for a writing assignment to students along with the topic. This encourages students to participate in self-evaluation, to internalize high standards and, hence, self-correct and self-teach. A partner-student reads a student's working drafts, using the rubric to make editorial suggestions. As teachers drop in on these peer-editing sessions, their suggestions become more meaningful to these works in progress than conventional written comments on a final product paper. Used in this way, rubrics are a valuable way of stimulating individual and peer revisions of school compositions.

Depending on the importance of the objective of the writing assignment, the rubric may be simple or quite complex. Figures 10.4 and 10.5 provide two sample rubrics, one addressing a specific writing objective and the other addressing content objectives of a particular writing assignment.

3	The topic sentence is clearly written and strongly supported by lucid and interesting examples. Transitions tie the paper together in a fluid manner. Mechanical errors are slight.
2	The topic sentence is present, but support from the examples needs to be stronger and better organized. Transitions are used but need polishing. There are some mechanical errors.
1	The paragraph lacks a clear topic sentence. Examples are few in number and inadequately explained. Transitions are lacking, and mechanical errors are frequent.

Figure 10.4 Sample rubric 1: Using examples and illustrations.
Source: Adapted from P. Behle (Ed.) (1982), *The Double Helix: Teaching the Writing Process*, Florissant, MO, Ferguson-Florissant Writers Project. Copyright 1982 by Ferguson-Florissant Writers Project. Ferguson-Florissant School District, 1005 Waterford Drive, Florissant, MO 63033.

PAPER TOPIC: 1960s APPROACHES TO CIVIL RIGHTS IN THE UNITED STATES

High-Quality Papers Contain:

- ✦ An overview of civil rights or their lack during the 1960s, with three specific examples
- ✦ A statement defining civil disobedience, with three examples of how it was used and Martin Luther King Jr.'s role
- ✦ At least one other approach to civil rights, with specific examples, and a comparison of this approach with King's civil disobedience that illustrates differences or similarities in at least two ways
- ✦ Good organization, well-developed arguments, few mechanical errors (sentence fragments, grammatical errors, spelling errors)

Medium-Quality Papers Contain:

- ✦ An overview of black civil rights during the 1960s with two specific examples
- ✦ A statement defining civil disobedience, with two examples of its use and Martin Luther King Jr.'s involvement
- ✦ One other approach to civil rights, with examples, and a comparison of it with King's civil disobedience by their differences
- ✦ Good organization, few mechanical errors, moderately developed arguments

Figure 10.5 Sample rubric 2: A specific content assignment.
Source: Pearce, D. L. (1983, December). Guidelines for the use and evaluation of writing in content classrooms. *Journal of Reading*, 27(3), 212–218.

Lower-Quality Papers Contain:

- ✦ A general statement defining civil disobedience with reference to Martin Luther King Jr.'s involvement and at least one example
- ✦ One other approach to civil rights and how it differed from civil disobedience
- ✦ Fair organization, some mechanical errors

Lowest-Quality Papers Contain:

- ✦ A general statement on who Martin Luther King Jr. was, or a general statement on civil disobedience
- ✦ A general statement that not all blacks agreed with civil disobedience
- ✦ A list of points, poor organization, many mechanical errors

Figure 10.5 *(continued)*

Evaluating Expression and Concepts

A persistent problem in evaluating student writing is that some compositions will be organizationally, structurally, and mechanically perfect but lack originality and richness of thought, while others may have distracting errors in form but contain striking expressions and/or fresh conceptual approaches. A popular solution to this problem has been a dual-grade system—one grade for ideas and one for mechanics. A rubric that combines mechanics and content, such as sample rubric 2 in Figure 10.5, provides guidelines for students to assist one another in working toward an effective combination of both aspects of a quality composition.

The initial planning time spent in preparing a rubric tends to enhance the quality of student products as well as to simplify grading. A rubric-guided writing assignment at the beginning of the school year can provide a valuable addition to the ITI.

Self-Analysis of Writing Checklist

Recently, rubrics have been evolving into means of urging students to pay adequate attention to a chosen set of objectives in writing. The *Self Analysis of Writing*, or SAW (Figure 10.6), is a checklist-type rubric that is further intended to guide students in reviewing and self-improving their own work prior to submission.

Next, we discuss another form assessment that is growing in popularity. It is a means of incorporating and organizing many possible forms of assessment and is called portfolio collection and analysis.

Conventions (mechanics)	___	My work has been edited and proofread; it is easy to read.
	___	I used capital letters and punctuation correctly.
	___	I checked my spelling.
	___	You'd have to look hard to find mistakes in my paper!
Word Choice (vocabulary)	___	My reader will enjoy the words I chose.
	___	My words paint a descriptive picture.
	___	I think this is the best way to say it.
Ideas (topic)	___	It all makes sense, from title, to topic, to details.
	___	My reader will learn a lot.
	___	This is what I wanted to say.
	___	Details are adequate, but not overwhelming
Organization (sequence)	___	I love my beginning.
	___	I know where I am going; the middle nicely connects to the start.
	___	You can follow me.
	___	My ending is interesting and pulls things together.
Sentences (fluency & variety)	___	My sentences make sense.
	___	My paper is easy to read out loud.
	___	Some sentences are long and some are short.
	___	My sentences begin in several different ways.
Voice (overall impression)	___	This is what I feel, or believe.
	___	It makes you laugh, or cry, or even be angry.
	___	If you read my paper and it did not have a name on it, you would know that it is mine!
Rich Thinking (critical/constructive)	___	This is why I believe what I do.
	___	The paper rises above my personal feelings and beliefs.
	___	The paper gives a fair representation of other points of view.
	___	The paper seems to connect with certain other things we have learned.
	___	The paper raises some interesting questions that I will think about and perhaps write more about sometime.
	___	I'll bet I can find or think of a better idea or way to look at this.
Overall rating:	1 2 3 4 5 6 7 8 9 10	

Figure 10.6 SAW (Self-Analysis of Writing) checklist.
Source: Modified from a workshop handout of the Northwest Regional Education Laboratory, Shawnee Mission, KS, School District, May, 1998.

PORTFOLIOS: RATIONALE, FUNCTIONS, PROMISE, PROBLEMS

A portfolio is a collection of works intended to illustrate a range of abilities and possible special talents over time. The idea of a portfolio is to show what one can do and how one has progressed through various stages and periods.

Portfolios for students, in effect, are based on the proposition that pupils should be involved in assessing their progress and actively selecting and keeping samples of their best work for periodic review. There are two popular types of student portfolios: show portfolios, which include only a few selected samples of work, and working portfolios, which include a wide array of works in progress (Farr, 1992). Periodically, students should be helped to select pieces from their working portfolios to place in their show portfolios. The show portfolio should include the pupil's best current works, as well as some works that are representative of earlier stages of learning. The teacher's role is largely to serve as a consultant who councils students on the works that seem to reflect their progress in reading, writing, thinking, and content learning. The process of collecting, reviewing, and maintaining student portfolios tends to create interactions between teachers and students that can lead to greater empathy and a sense of common purpose.

Contents of Portfolios

Depending on the teacher's purposes, student portfolios may include any or all of the following types of entries:

- Quarterly writing samples from a variety of perspectives across genres: journal writing, personal narrative, fiction, nonfiction, poetry
- Evidence of progress in aspects of communications from phrasing to grammar and spelling
- Evidence of progress in comprehension and content knowledge
- Results from informal inventories
- Taped oral readings and presentations
- Drawings and other expressive works
- Photographs of special projects too bulky to store
- Year-to-year photographs of self, the teacher, and other students
- Periodic anecdotal accounts and comments from teachers

Teacher and student comments give the portfolio depth and dimension. Here are some sample comments:

> Jack, your account of the religious basis for the civil war in Bosnia is enlightening. I read it to my wife at dinner the other night.
>
> Mr. Ahkim, 10/23/07

Tamica, this algebra homework assignment tells me that you can read and follow word problems quite well. However, I think you should recheck your calculations.

Ms. Toma, 11/10/07

Students can be asked to write short explanations of why they chose certain entries for their show portfolios. For example,

I included this report on "Russia Today" because I think it includes my best work so far on using citations and references.

Mark, 11/10/07

This is a tape recording of me in the spring play. I was the narrator, and I thought I was pretty good. I'd like to listen to it again next year, and see how much I have changed.

Nina, 5/12/07

The single most important value of portfolio assessment is that it shifts the emphasis away from the errors and the false starts kids make while acquiring knowledge and skill. Instead, the emphasis is placed on preserving, and periodically reviewing, completed pieces that youngsters value. Unlike grade books and permanent record files, which few have access to, the portfolio collection may be kept in an easily accessible part of the room for others to view, with proper permission. Maintaining portfolios is something students do for themselves as well as for others. As such, the portfolio system helps build and expand interests that lead to further reading (Ediger, 1992).

Disadvantages of Portfolios

The most serious disadvantage of portfolios is that they can quickly become complex and cumbersome. Portfolios were originally intended to provide a means of balancing other more standardized forms of assessment with a concrete record of a student's actual work. The student portfolio itself, however, is only the raw data on which this balancing is based. Evaluating these data should be a simple, subjective, and self-evident process. It can, however, be turned into a tedious, overly objectified, time-consuming one. According to one research report, some teachers view student portfolios as too demanding, and "yet another means of increasing and controlling teachers' work while appearing to empower them" (Gomez, Graue, & Bloch, 1991, p. 621). On the other hand, electronic technology is making portfolio collection and analysis somewhat easier. Computer programs are being written that guide collection, assessment, and interpretation, all with a click on an appropriate icon. See Figure 10.7 for an example (Duckworth & Taylor, 1995) of a computerized portfolio. On a further cautionary note, girls tend to enjoy this "scrapbooking" process much more than boys do.

Now that you know about several means of estimating students' abilities and progress in reading and writing about materials at different levels of difficulty, learn next how to estimate the difficulty level of the textual material they are asked to read. This, too, is a "new" technology that is about seventy-five years old.

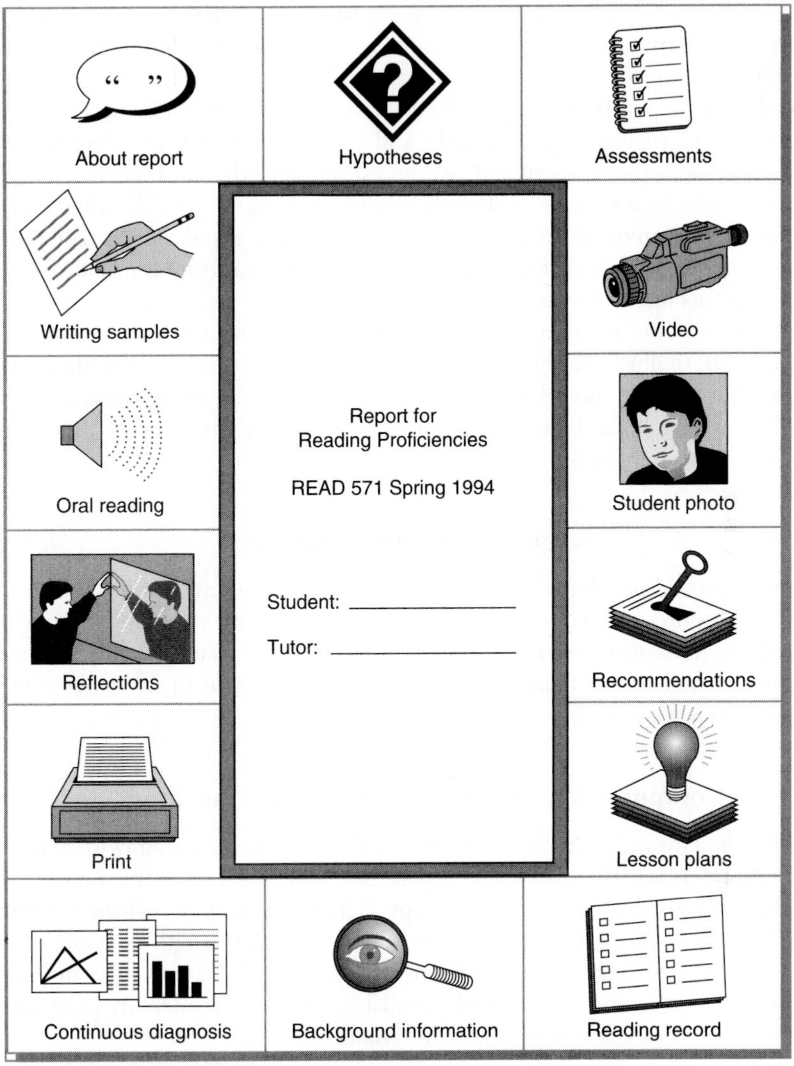

Figure 10.7 Assessing literacy through hypermedia portfolios.
Source: Duckworth, S. & Taylor R. (1995). Creating and assessing literacy in at-risk students through hypermedia portfolios. *Reading Improvement.* 32(1), 26–31. Reprinted by permission of Project Innovation, Inc., Mobile, Alabama.

▶ ASSESSING TEXT DIFFICULTY

Readability Formulas

The difficulty level of a text is referred to as the text's *readability.* Historically, middle and senior high school texts have been written with more concern for content than for difficulty level. A tenth-grade American history text, for example, might have a readability of grade 12. This has begun to change in recent years as members of school district text selection committees have started including readability as a major criterion by which to evaluate potential textbook purchases.

Readability depends on a number of factors, including the influence of print size, number and quality of graphic aids, and an individual's level of interest and prior knowledge in the topic area. The greatest influence by far, however, comes from two simple factors: average length of sentences and word difficulty, which largely are a function of the frequency of use of a word in popular print. The most commonly used procedures for estimating readability are formulas that employ these two factors in one way or another.

One of the more commonly used readability formulas is detailed next. It is presented here to illustrate the process of estimating readability level rather than to suggest that teachers should regularly undertake even these abbreviated analyses by hand. However, it can be enlightening to do a text analysis by hand, especially if no other means is available.

Raygor's Readability Graph

The Raygor procedure, illustrated in Figure 10.8, uses the number of words containing six or more letters and the average sentence length of three passages of 100 words each to estimate a text's difficulty. Baldwin and Kaufman (1979) found the Raygor formula faster than and as accurate as the original Fry formula (1968, 1977), on which it is based.

Computer Programs for Readability Checking

Even simplified formulas for estimating readability are time consuming to do manually. Fortunately, a wide variety of computer software now is available for obtaining readability estimates on textbook excerpts. This is much more realistic in terms of time and elimination of the human error inevitable with lengthy syllable/word counting and calculating. Microsoft Word has two readability formulas built in. For more information on commercially available computer readability programs, ask your local software dealer or school librarian.

There is another approach to evaluating readability that any veteran teacher can use effectively and that new teachers can use to increase their sensitivity to factors in a text that will influence the level of difficulty for students. It is called a readability checklist.

Readability Checklists

Checklists to guide readability estimates are totally subjective and do not necessarily yield a grade-level readability estimate. They do, however, indicate whether a given book is appropriate for a particular group of students. Checklists are most effective when several teachers rate the same material and then average (or otherwise compare) their judgments. A group of teachers from a given content area may wish to develop its own checklist that addresses specific content concerns.

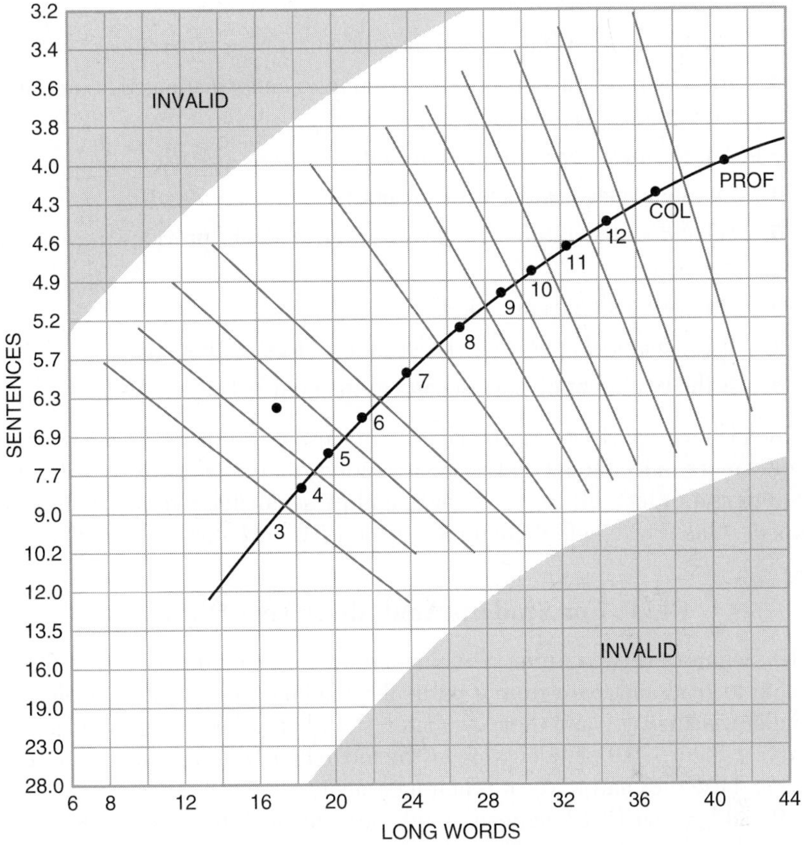

1. Count out three 100-word passages at the beginning, middle, and end of a selection or book. Count proper nouns but not numerals.
2. Count sentences in each passage, estimating to the nearest tenth.
3. Count words with six or more letters.

Average the sentence length and word length over three samples, and plot the average on the graph.

Figure 10.8 The Raygor procedure for estimating readability.

Source: From A. L. Raygor "The Raygor Readability Estimate: A Quick and Easy Way to Determine Difficulty" in *Reading: Theory, Research and Practice. Twenty-Sixth Yearbook of the National Reading Conference* (pp. 259–263), edited by P. D. Pearson, 1977, Clemson, SC: National Reading Conference.

One list includes the following items, to which the rater responds with a particular group of students in mind:

1. Are the concepts far beyond the students' direct experiences?
2. Are abstract concepts linked to examples and situations that are familiar to students?
3. Are technical terms defined in context as they appear?
4. Does one idea lead logically to another?
5. What does the author assume about the students' previous learning experiences?
6. Are textbooks aids provided?
7. Is the material appealing, or does it look too "textbookish"?
8. Is the writing brief, concise, and to the point? (Harker, 1977)*

Readability checklists can be adapted for use by students. To help students become more independent and strategic readers, they need a greater capacity for self-appraisal of text difficulty, text aids, and personal ability to negotiate a given textbook. One way to help them do this is the FLIP inventory, described next.

FLIP: For Student Analysis of Text Difficulty

FLIP (Schumm & Mangrum, 1991) invites students to judge how well they will be able to read and learn from a particular reading assignment by analyzing its *f*riendliness, *l*anguage, and their own *i*nterest and *p*rior knowledge, using a FLIP chart (see Figure 10.9). Students are instructed to FLIP through the reading assignment and use the chart to record their judgments.

By adding the FLIP elements rated, students are able to evaluate the general level of the assignment. They then proceed to interpret their assessment to determine an appropriate reading rate and to budget reading and study time (see Figure 10.10).

Following is a valuable closing thought on readability. It uses the idea of student input in a way that may have occurred to you when you first read about cloze testing.

Matching Student Abilities with Text Difficulty Through Cloze

The Standard Cloze Passage test described earlier is as much a readability strategy as it is a measure of students' reading ability. It does not yield a grade-level estimate of the difficulty of a given text, but it does predict how well a particular student or group of students will be able to read and learn from it. Hittleman (1978) pointed out that cloze measures readability, whereas other means predict text difficulty. He also noted that the cloze procedure is the only available procedure that can

*Source: Harker, W. J. (Ed.). (1977). *Classroom Strategies for Secondary Reading.* © International Reading Association. Used with permission.

Title of assignment ______________ # of pages ________

General directions: Rate each of the four FLIP categories on a 1 to 5 scale (5 = high). Then determine your purpose for reading and appropriate reading rate, and budget your reading/study time.

F = Friendliness: How friendly is my reading assignment?

Directions: Examine your assignment to see if it includes the friendly elements listed below.

Friendly text features

Table of contents	Index	Glossary
Chapter introductions	Headings	Subheadings
Margin notes	Study questions	Chapter summary
Key terms highlighted	Graphs	Charts
Pictures	Signal words	Lists of key facts

1————2————3————4————5

No friendly text features	Some friendly text features	Many friendly text features

Friendliness rating = ____

L = Language: How difficult is the language in my reading assignment?

Directions: Skim the chapter quickly to determine the number of new terms. Read three random paragraphs to get a feel for the vocabulary level and number of long, complicated sentences.

1————2————3————4————5

Many new words; complicated sentences	Some new words; somewhat complicated sentences	No new words; clear sentences

Language rating = ____

I = Interest: How interesting is my reading assignment?

Directions: Read the title, introduction, headings/subheadings, and summary. Examine the pictures and graphics included.

1————2————3————4————5

Boring	Somewhat interesting	Very interesting

Interest rating = ____

Figure 10.9 FLIP chart.

Source: Schumm, J. S., & Mangrum, C. T., II. (1991, October). FLIP: A framework for content area reading. *Journal of Reading, 35*(2), 120–124.

P = Prior knowledge: What do I already know about the material covered in my reading assignment?

Directions: Think about the title, introduction, headings/subheadings, and summary.

1————————2————————3————————4————————5

Mostly new information	Some new information	Mostly familiar information

Prior knowledge rating = ____

Overall, this reading assignment appears to be at

____ a comfortable reading level for me

____ a somewhat comfortable reading level for me

____ an uncomfortable reading level for me

Figure 10.9 (*continued*)

My purpose for reading is (circle one):

A. Personal pleasure
B. To prepare for class discussions
C. To answer written questions for class assignment or for homework
D. To prepare for a test
E. Other ______________________________

My reading rate should be (circle one):

A. Slow—allowing time for rereading if necessary
B. Medium—careful and analytical
C. Fast—steady, skipping sections that are about information I already know

Active reading time:

Chunk 1, pages ________–________, estimated time: ________ minutes
Chunk 2, pages ________–________, estimated time: ________ minutes
Chunk 3, pages ________–________, estimated time: ________ minutes
Chunk 4, pages ________–________, estimated time: ________ minutes
Total estimated time: ________ minutes

Figure 10.10 FLIP follow-up.
Source: Schumm, J. S., & Mangrum, C. T., II. (1991, October). FLIP: A framework for content area reading. *Journal of Reading, 35*(2), 120–124. Copyright 1991 by the International Reading Association.

take into account, in a natural setting, the constraints of the language system of the reading matter, the reading ability and other characteristics of the reader, and the background information needed by the reader. In other words, there are two ways to compare your students' reading levels with your textbook's readability level. One is to compare some form of student reading test score to a formula-based readability estimate in the text. Another is simply to give a Standard Cloze Passage test constructed from a representative portion of the text. Hence, the Standard Cloze Passage test permits a direct comparison using a single measure. To improve the quality of the match, you have only to construct more than one sample for the text.

▶ AFFECTIVE ISSUES AND MEASURES

It is an axiom of professional education that to know others, you must first know yourself. To reach this island of self-knowledge, however, one must navigate through the reefs of self-doubt and self-examination. This can be particularly formidable because, as the German writer Herman Hesse put it, "Nothing . . . is so distasteful to man as to go the way which leads him to himself."

When you are up to facing this process, you might wish to look into some of the personality and temperament inventories that are available for popular consumption in most bookstores. These may not always have the same level of accuracy as norm-referenced personality tests, but they tend to be sufficiently accurate for getting a look at yourself, since most of them essentially are made up of the more telling items of traditional measures such as the Minnesota Multiphasic Personality Inventory (MMPI).

▶ CONCEPT SUMMARY

This chapter offered a broad range of options for considering and conducting assessment in the context of the content area classroom. It described traditional and emerging options for assessing students' reading, text management, and writing. Finally, the chapter turned from student assessment to text assessment and provided a tour of available means for assessing the difficulty level of printed material.

CHAPTER 11

STUDY TECHNIQUES FOR READING, LEARNING, AND REMEMBERING

Study without reflection is a waste of time; reflection without study is dangerous.

—Confucius

The goal of *study skills instruction* is the *efficient* use of time spent in learning and remembering. As such, it includes an array of diverse topics such as time management, techniques for active reading and listening, note taking, and test taking. Study strategies may be taught in mini-courses or as units in a regular class and/or integrated with the content of various classes. Each approach has merit. The content class approach is gaining in popularity as more teachers learn about methods for imparting these strategies in teacher training and in-service programs. This chapter provides an overview of early efforts to provide learners with tools for more efficient study. A sampling of some of the time-tested and other more recently developed techniques address study reading, note taking, listening, and test taking.

- FROM STUDY SKILLS TO STRATEGIC STUDY
- METHODS FOR IMPROVING LECTURE NOTE TAKING AND LISTENING
- TEST-TAKING STRATEGIES
- CONCEPT SUMMARY

FROM STUDY SKILLS TO STRATEGIC STUDY

The development of approaches and methods for teaching study skills has tended to track the educational trends of the times. McMurry wrote the first study skills text for classroom teachers in 1909. It was a no-frills book simply called *How to Study and Teaching How to Study.* Its approach reflected the early-twentieth-century assumption that reading was a process of mastering and applying a series of discrete subskills.

This skills-based approach continued through the popularization of self-directed study techniques during World Wars I and II. Armed services inductees needed quick training in how to read and master the contents of the manuals that accompanied increasingly sophisticated weapons and machines. Later, returning veterans willingly enrolled in study skills courses to improve their reading efficiency and their grades in technical schools and colleges. By 1930, skills-based books with names such as *Outlining as a Study Procedure* (Barton, 1930) were available at the college level.

The open admissions policies initiated in many colleges in the 1960s created a further need to assist underprepared students in meeting college-level reading, writing, and study requirements. By this time, many educators were realizing that effective study, like reading, was not a skill to be mastered, but a collection of strategies to be personalized by the learner to meet the demands of varying situations. The emphasis on imparting study skills gradually evolved into an emphasis on the learner as an active doer and strategy user.

Some of the classic study techniques were based on sound intuition and align well with current understandings of reading and study processes. Others, such as the use of outlining as a study tool, were based on faulty assumptions and are no longer recommended. Let's continue our historical look at one of the first and still most widely known approaches to effective reading and study.

SQ3R: A Story unto Itself

The Survey-Question-Read-Recite-Review (SQ3R) technique is the acknowledged granddaddy of study formulas. It was developed by Francis Robinson (1946), who traced its roots back to 1923. Robinson developed it into its current form in response to a need expressed by the U.S. Department of Defense during World War II (Stahl & Henk, 1986). As noted earlier, U.S. troops had a great deal of technical information to learn and little time in which to learn it. They needed a rigorous, self-guided technique that they could use with minimal instruction in field-training situations. Note the alignment of the SQ3R steps with the three-phase study reading process of schema activation, comprehension monitoring and fix-up, and schema building.

Steps in SQ3R

1. *Survey.* Survey a chapter before reading it closely.
   a. Read the title, and think about what it says or implies.
   b. Read the headings and subheadings.
   c. Read the summary if there is one.
   d. Read the captions under the pictures, charts, graphs, or other features.
   e. See if there is a bibliography or a list of books related to the chapter.
2. *Question.* Ask yourself questions about what you are going to read.
   a. What does the title of the chapter mean?
   b. What do you already know about the subject?
   c. What did the instructor say about this chapter when it was assigned?
   d. Turn each heading and subheading into a question. Write these questions in the margin or on a separate piece of paper.
3. *Read.* Read actively.
   a. Read to write notes in answer to the questions you wrote in step 2.
   b. Read all the added attractions in the chapter (maps, graphs, tables, and other illustrations).
   c. Read all the underlined, italicized, or boldface words or phrases extra carefully.
4. *Recite.* Say what you read.
   a. Answer the questions you raised in step 2 without looking back at the text or your notes.
   b. Reread any sections that you don't recall.
5. *Review.* Periodically survey what you read and learned.
   a. Use your notes or markings to refresh your memory.
   b. Review immediately after reading.
   c. Review again periodically.
   d. Review again before taking an exam on the subject.

Efficacy of SQ3R for Independent and Content Class Use

The balance of opinion among specialists regarding the efficacy of SQ3R is positive but by no means unanimous. Several studies (Diggs, 1973; Donald, 1967; Gurrola, 1975; McNamara, 1977; Willmore, 1967; Wooster, 1958) found no significant differences between SQ3R and control treatments.

This conflicting evidence may result from the fact that as Robinson himself noted, SQ3R cannot be effective until it becomes "automatic" and "subordinate to the task of reading" (1946, p. 21). SQ3R has been modified in a variety of ways since its publication. The most recent modification is discussed next.

SQP2RS

SQP2RS, Vogt (2002) combines SQ3R and Russell Stauffer's (1969) Read-Predict-Read formula for teaching active study reading strategies. Like SQ3R, its intent is to teach students a study reading system that they will eventually be able to use independently.

Steps in SQP2RS

1. *Survey*—have students scan the text to be read for 1 to 2 minutes.
2. *Question*—have students generate likely questions to be answered by the text (teacher guidance should be greater at first, and faded thereafter to levels guided by class need and content density).
3. *Predict*—have students state 1 to 3 things that they think they will learn based on the questions generated.
4. *Read*—silently search for confirming and disconfirming answers to predicted questions, with an eye to answers to questions not raised.
5. *Respond*—orally answer questions raised, comment on questions that could/should have been raised, and formulate new ones for the next section of text that may be read in class or for homework.
6. *Summarize*—add a quick written summary, personal response, and/or notes for later to further supplement and help consolidate the impact of step 5.

The addition of the final summarizing step is of particular importance since it has been shown in another methodology, KWL-Plus (Carr & Ogle, 1987; Ogle, 1989, 1996), to have a positive effect on reading comprehension outcomes.

SQP2RS also meets most all of the criteria of *sheltered* instruction for English Language Learners. Four years of continuing research with SQP2RS largely with ELL students in grades 4 to 9 has been encouraging in terms of both learning outcomes and teacher response. Teachers and students have given it a nickname—often a sign of affection—*Squeepers* (Echevarria, Vogt, & Short, 2004).

Obstacles to Study Strategy Instruction— Habits Are Hard to Change

Teaching study strategies presents several unique challenges. At a basic management level, study strategy instruction is an additional layer of *content* to be taught and learned on top of existing demands.

The second challenge is the lofty goal of this type of instruction. The intent is to change reading and study habits—and habits are notoriously difficult to change. Teaching students to use study strategies such as SQ3R or SQP2RS is analogous to teaching teachers to use instructional methods such as the L-R-D. In each case, what is taught is a set of steps that students or teachers are expected to understand, remember, and then apply *on their own.* This requires preparation, guidance, and lots of practice. Even if students become convinced of the usefulness of a particular study strategy, they are likely to slip back into more accustomed patterns. To be effective, study strategies need to become new habits.

Another complicating factor is that people tend to resent being given advice, and most study strategies amount to advice. This problem persists even though the strategies and techniques are effective.

Finally, teachers tend to believe that what we do when we study is highly individual, and that no one strategy will work for everyone. Even though it is true that each of us tailors a particular strategy to our own personal style, fundamental principles of learning apply regardless of individual differences. In one of the early textbooks designed for college students with weak academic skills, Walter Pauk (1989) summarized much of what is known about effective learning and study in his "Eight Learning Principles." These research-based principles, shown in Figure 11.1, provide an excellent orientation to the field of developmental studies and a basis for evaluating any study strategies program.

Note in particular Principle 6: The Principle of Recitation. If plotted on a chart, there would be a sharp drop for the students who did not review immediately after learning. This has been called the "curve of forgetting." In contrast, the line representing students who *did* review remains steadily higher. Note how this principle is applied in the note-taking technique discussed next.

▶ METHODS FOR IMPROVING LECTURE NOTE TAKING AND LISTENING

Palmatier's Unified Note-Taking System*

Students need instruction in how to learn from lectures as well as from text. Palmatier's Unified Note-Taking System (PUNS) urges students to review lecture notes immediately after class and supplement them with memory cues and text information. The note-taking format provides a built-in study system by separating

**Source:* From Palmatier, R. A. (1973). A notetaking system for learning. *Journal of Reading, 17.* © International Reading Association. Used with permission.

1. **Principle of Motivated Interest.** We remember what interests us. Develop your natural interests, and try to create new interests by reading (e.g., magazine and newspaper articles) in diverse areas. If you find a subject boring, or irrelevant, try to find something in it of personal interest or use, and you will find it easier to learn.
2. **Principle of Selectivity.** Information must be grouped into units of a manageable size for efficient recall. In the nineteenth century, Hermann Ebbinghaus, one of the world's earliest experimental psychologists, found that it took 15 times as many trials to memorize 12 nonsense syllables as the number of trials needed to memorize 6 nonsense syllables. One would predict that it would take only twice as many trials.
3. **Principle of Intention to Remember.** Prerequisites to efficient learning include careful attending, getting the facts right the first time, and striving to understand. Recall that this is the basic principle underlying the guided reading procedure, a total reading and study lesson design covered in Chapter 6. Active reading the *first* time saves time in the long run.
4. **Principle of Basic Background.** What we perceive (see, hear, taste, smell, feel, and read) depends in large measure on what we already know. Whenever you are trying to learn something new, connect it to something you know.
5. **Principle of Meaningful Organization.** George Miller, the eminent Harvard psychologist, found that the immediate memory span of the general population seems fixed at approximately seven bits of information, plus or minus two. For effective recall, therefore, information should be categorized into meaningful groups of no more than seven bits. The telephone company heeded this research when developing the telephone numbering system. The U.S. Postal Service, on the other hand, has challenged it by implementing a nine-digit Zip Code system.
6. **Principle of Recitation.** Study reading must be an active process. Recitation is analogous to exercising a muscle: It builds and embeds information in long-term memory. Pauk reminds us of how H. F. Spitzer's classic study compared the amount of information recalled by students 7 and 63 days after learning. Students who reviewed immediately after learning remembered 83% after 7 days and 70% after 63 days. Those who did not review immediately after learning remembered 33% after 7 days and 14% after 63 days. Control groups of students who also did not review immediately after learning remembered approximately 55% after 1 day, 22% after 14 days, 18% after 21 days, and 1% after 28 days. Obviously, recitation-study works!

Figure 11.1 Pauk's eight learning principles.

Source: Pauk, Walter, *HOW TO STUDY IN COLLEGE* (Fourth ed), Copyright ©1989 by Houghton Mifflin Company. Adapted with permission.

7. **Principle of Consolidation.** Information must be harbored in the mind for a certain period before a temporary memory can be consolidated into a more permanent one. Numerous records of accident victims show that a period of unconsciousness can erase the memory of events that occurred from 15 to 5 minutes before the person lost consciousness. Spitzer's study, described in principle 6, further illustrates the effectiveness of an immediate review of new information.
8. **Principle of Distributed Practice.** A number of brief reviews are more effective than one long review session. Short sessions prevent physical and emotional fatigue and help sustain interest and motivation.

Figure 11.1 *(continued)*

key words from the body of the notes. PUNS is one of the few note-taking methods that has been validated through scientifically based replicated research (Palmatier, 1971, 1973; Palmatier & Bennett, 1974).

Steps in PUNS

1. *Record.* In a loose-leaf binder, use only one side of $8\frac{1}{2}$-by-11-inch notebook paper with a 3-inch margin on the left side. (Many college bookstores now stock this type of paper for this purpose.) Record lecture notes to the right of the margin. Use a modified outline form, simply indenting subtopics under main topics. Leave space where information seems to be missing that could be filled in from the textbook. Number each page as you record the notes.
2. *Organize.* As soon after the lecture as possible, add two sections to the notes. First, place labels inside the left margin. These should be questions about or a brief description of the information in the notes. Second, insert important text information directly into the recorded notes. If you need more space, you can use the back of the notebook paper.
3. *Study.* Remove the notes from the loose-leaf binder, and lay them out so that only the left margin of each page is visible. Use the labels as memory cues to recite as much of the information on the right as you can recall. Verify your recall immediately by lifting the page to read the information recorded to the right of the label. For objective tests, the labels can be approached at random, simulating the format of multiple-choice, true/false, and matching tests. For essay tests, group information into logical units, formulate predicted essay questions, and practice writing answers. Figure 11.2 presents a sample PUNS format.

The notes students take during lectures are influenced as much by listening habits as by note-taking strategy. The next sections suggest ways to improve attention and active listening to maximize learning outcomes for time spent in class.

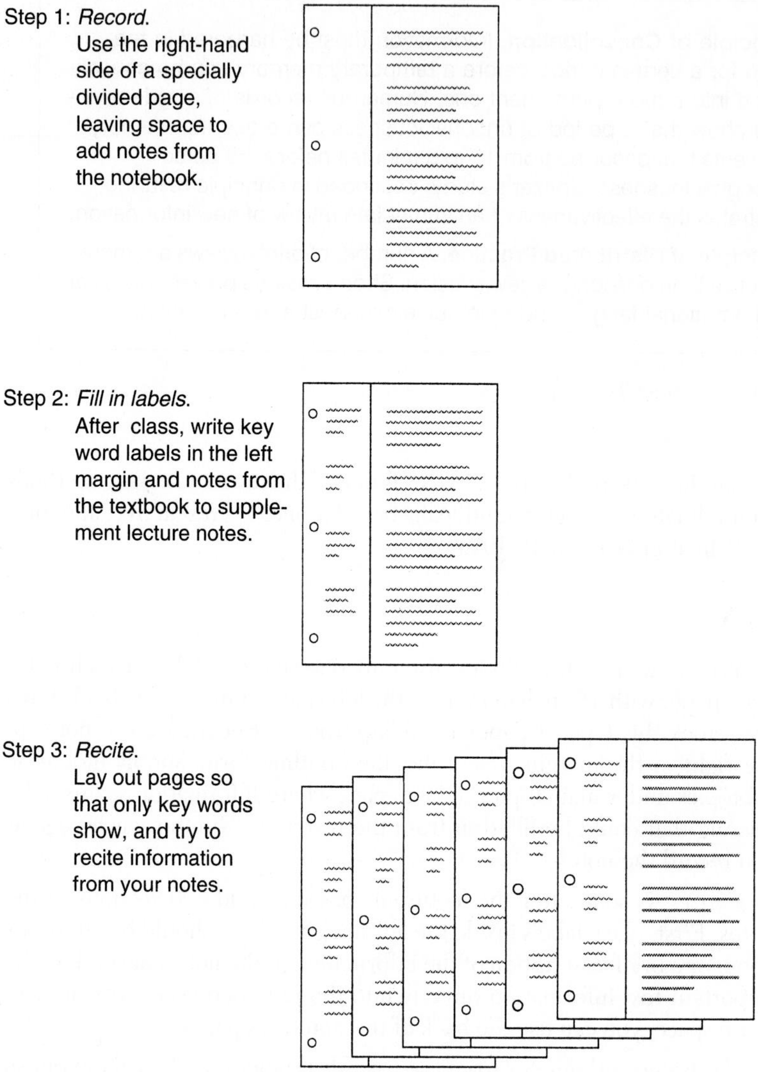

Step 1: Record.
Use the right-hand side of a specially divided page, leaving space to add notes from the notebook.
Step 2: Fill in labels.
After class, write key word labels in the left margin and notes from the textbook to supplement lecture notes.
Step 3: Recite.
Lay out pages so that only key words show, and try to recite information from your notes.

Figure 11.2 PUNS note taking.

Enabling Questions

The Enabling Questions procedure is a student-initiated strategy developed by the authors. It is a prepared set of questions that students can use to tune in and reduce distraction during lectures. Using Enabling Questions puts the listener into an active, evaluative thinking mode and invites the teacher or speaker to talk a little less and welcome more interaction. Students should be urged to translate these questions into their own words to further increase their sense of agency as learners.

Set 1: Questions That Help the Listener Organize and Clarify Information

1. What is/are the main *question(s)* you are answering by your lecture (or lesson) today?
2. Which key terms and concepts are most important for us to remember from what you have said (or will say) today?
3. What is most often misunderstood or confusing about the information or position you are presenting today?

Set 2: Questions That Help the Listener Get a Mental Breather

1. Could you please restate that last point in a different way?
2. Which points would you especially want us to note at this time?

Set 3: Questions That Invite Give-and-Take with the Speaker

1. How does what you have said compare with positions others have taken, and who might these others be? Are there other perspectives on this information?
2. What evidence that supports your position can you share with us?
3. What is the weakest part of your position?
4. How does this position (or information) affect previously held beliefs?
5. What would happen if you extended this point another step or two?
6. Would you mind pausing for a moment to see if there are other thoughts on this in the class/audience? This would help us better understand and follow your points.

Any one of the latter set of questions likely would put the listener into an active, evaluative thinking mode. It is important that the listener who wishes to use these types of questions does so with an eye toward using them to enrich comprehension, learning, and mature interaction, and not from an offensive stance. One way to help students learn the value of Enabling Questions is to *write these questions on index cards* and distribute a few to each class member. Then urge students to try to use the questions on their card(s) intelligently over a two- to three-day period. Schedule a day to discuss what happened and what students learned and what might need to be modified to make the Enabling Questions even more enabling.

Guided Lecture Procedure

The Guided Lecture Procedure (GLP) (Kelly & Holmes, 1979) is a teacher-directed method for improving listening.* It is the listening counterpart of the highly validated Guided Reading Procedure (Manzo, 1975).

**Source:* From Kelly, B. W., & Holmes, J. (1979). The Guided Lecture Procedure. *Journal of Reading, 22.* © International Reading Association. Used with permission.

Steps in the GLP

1. Students are directed to take no notes as they listen carefully to the lecture.
2. The teacher writes the objectives of the lecture on the board along with key technical terms.
3. The teacher lectures for about half the class period, then stops.
4. Students attempt to write down everything they can recall from the lecture.
5. Students form small cooperative learning groups to review and discuss their notes. This discussion, or language component, helps build related speaking, writing, and thinking strategies.

The GLP has been used effectively with classes from middle school to college levels (Kelly & Holmes, 1979). The small group activity that forms the latter part of the lesson is an excellent cooperative-learning and team-building activity.

▶ TEST-TAKING STRATEGIES

Taking Multiple-Choice Tests

It is difficult to overstate the effects of test taking on the body and the ego. If test taking were a pill, it probably would never pass the Food and Drug Administration guidelines for benefit-to-risk ratio. The growing emphasis on writing and performance-based assessment has begun to decrease the use of multiple-choice tests in the classroom. However, most schools still use standardized multiple-choice tests for program evaluation. Students' scores on multiple-choice tests can be more a reflection of their test-taking savvy than their knowledge acquisition. See Figure 11.3 for a brief list of helpful hints for taking multiple-choice tests.

PORPE: A Strategy for Taking *Essay* Tests

Predict-Organize-Rehearse-Practice-Evaluate (PORPE) was developed in response to students' anxiety about taking essay examinations (Simpson, 1986).* The method evolved from a review of the research literature to find practical ideas about how proficient readers prepare for essay-type tests. PORPE's five steps guide students to behave like "effective readers who have some awareness and control of their own cognitive activities while they read and study" (p. 408).

Steps in PORPE

1. *Predict:* Students are asked to predict essay questions that they might be asked. Teachers should make every effort to help students at this stage raise synthesizing, analyzing, and application questions as well as more

**Source:* From Simpson, M. (1986). PORPE: A writing strategy for studying and learning in the content areas. *Journal of Reading, 29*(5). © International Reading Association. Used with permission.

- ✦ Block out a rough time plan for timed tests. Note what time it will be when half the time is up, and how many items you should have completed by that time.
- ✦ Read slowly and answer quickly. Focus on the question instead of the answer choices. This prevents the frequent and irritating problem of misreading the question.
- ✦ Answer the easy questions first, and skip the hard ones. Spending time on difficult questions raises anxiety and may cause you to forget information you knew when the test began. As you go through the test, you may find information that will help you remember answers to earlier difficult items.
- ✦ Don't assume that the test is loaded with trick questions. This will cause you to read too much into the questions and spend too much time in needless internal debate. Read each question carefully, but concentrate on the main point rather than the details.
- ✦ Avoid anxiety reactions that break concentration: glancing frequently at the clock or the instructor, polishing eyeglasses, examining fingernails, gazing at the wall or ceiling, excessive yawning or stretching.
- ✦ Use all the time allotted. If you finish before the time is up, always check your work. Make sure you answered all the questions, but don't waste time reviewing the answers to easy questions. Change your answers if you have reason to. Research shows that contrary to common belief, three out of four times your changes will be correct. This may be because during a final check, the tension begins to lessen and thought processes are clearer.

Figure 11.3 Tips for taking multiple-choice tests.

literal *what-* and *when*-type questions. One way to do this is to introduce students to a glossary of the most common words used in essay questions, such as *explain, criticize, compare, contrast, react, support,* and *elaborate.* As follow-up, teachers should model the thought process they go through in preparing (predicting) and phrasing essay questions on a previously studied body of information. Students then should prepare and share their predicted questions with classmates.

2. *Organize:* Students are encouraged to organize the information needed to answer predicted questions. Students are encouraged to use semantic maps and outlines for this purpose. Again, teachers should model this strategy.
3. *Rehearse:* This is the conventional study or recall and recite step. Students should be encouraged to use appropriate memory devices.
4. *Practice:* In this step, students practice composing or answering essay-type questions. They should be reminded of the following in doing so:
   a. Work from an outline.
   b. Make sure your opening sentence rephrases the question and/or takes a clear position.

c. Make the structure of your answer clear by using transitional words and phrases such as *first, on the other hand, furthermore,* and *finally.*

d. Give examples of major points.

e. Reread what you wrote, and make appropriate editorial corrections.

5. *Evaluate:* This step continues logically from the latter portion of the last one but should occur after a brief pause. The idea simply is to consider how a teacher might evaluate your answer. It may be necessary to conduct several sessions during which students listen to, read, and discuss the relative merits of various essay answers before they acquire the ability to get outside of themselves and review their own work.

PORPE has been found to be significantly more effective than question-answer recitation in improving comprehension and essay writing (Simpson, Hayes, Stahl, Connor, & Weaver, 1988). PORPE also makes a great deal of sense at an intuitive level. It incorporates attention to metacognitive development, content mastery, effective predicting, organizing, and test writing. Structurally, it progresses in logical movements from teacher instruction, modeling, and guidance to total student independence and control—the purpose of all study strategies instruction.

Study Journals

Keeping a study journal can make students more aware of their present study habits and attitudes and more open to modifying these toward greater efficacy. A study journal is simply a written record of thoughts and feelings about studying and about school. Students should be encouraged to make four or five brief journal entries each week, without undue concern for form or style. Guiding questions should be, "What am I doing when I study?" and "How do I feel about it?" Some categories for consideration include the following:

- *Classes:* participation or lack of it, difficulty paying attention, confidence level
- *Homework:* difficulty concentrating or getting started, organization of materials, strategies for studying
- *Tests:* thoughts before, during, and after tests; controlling anxiety
- *Time management:* difficulty getting everything done; setting priorities
- *Symptoms of stress:* fatigue, headaches, worry, apathy, guilt, problems in interpersonal relationships, insomnia, excessive snacking, and so on

Following are some sample study journal entries:

9/10: Algebra class always begins in English, but it soon becomes Greek. There must be something I can do to keep from getting lost about midway?

9/14: When I get home from school, I can't stand to face homework. Soon it's dinnertime, then the good programs are on, and then I'm too tired. When are you supposed to do homework anyway?

9/25: I hate tests. I never seem to study the right things.

10/2: I've been having trouble falling asleep, and I wake up two hours early thinking about that darn paper due next week. I also find it impossible to stay awake after lunch.

After students have made several entries in their journals, they should be encouraged to look back over what they have written. Are there noticeable patterns? Are there certain kinds of situations that tend to precipitate stress? What coping strategies did they try? How effective were these? We have found that study journals are more likely to be kept when they are combined with the next strategy, which offers a place and time for their use and reinforcement.

Problem-Solving Approach to Study Skills

The *Problem-Solving Approach to Study Skills* (PASS) (Manzo & Casale, 1980) is an interactive method designed to communicate the attitude that school, learning, and living present typical problems that generally are quite solvable by critical, constructive analysis and personal resolve. PASS is a fundamental paradigm for teaching study skills that can be customized to each class's or student's particular needs.

Steps in PASS

1. *Count:* The teacher presents students with a list of common study problems and asks them to check those that apply to them (see Figure 11.4).
2. *Characterize:* The teacher guides students in defining selected problems, and themselves, in specific terms. The teacher may provide inventories of learning style, temperament, skills, abilities, and attitudes in an effort to reach a better sense of themselves as learners. Inventories of this type are increasingly available online.
3. *Consider:* Students consider how they typically have dealt with their learning and study needs and problems and the possible merit in these intuitive coping strategies.
4. *Collect:* The class discusses standard techniques for dealing with reading/study problems on the basis of their compatibility with each student's style and character. When these appear incompatible, the procedures are dismissed as inappropriate.
5. *Create:* Students seek inventive alternatives that match their personal styles. This step is best handled initially in small groups and then in larger group discussions.

PASS was evaluated in a case study approach and found to be a sound means of improving study habits and positive attitudes toward learning (Casale [now Manzo] & Kelly, 1980). The content teacher's efforts to teach students how to study will be time well spent. Learning is as much attitudinal as it is intellectual. Teaching students how to study tells them that they are as important as the content.

__1. Taking good notes in class
__2. Completing reading assignments
__3. Finding the main ideas when reading
__4. Remembering details when reading
__5. Figuring out what the author/teacher means
__6. Staying relaxed when studying
__7. Concentrating while reading
__8. Paying attention in class
—9. Asking questions in class
__10. Vocabulary meanings
__11. Writing answers to questions
__12. Writing personal opinions about class topics
__13. Writing research papers
__14. Planning and completing class projects
__15. Taking notes while reading/studying
__16. Finding reference materials in the library
__17. Participating in class discussions
Other: ______________________________

Figure 11.4 Checklist of common study problems.

▶ CONCEPT SUMMARY

Study skill is the effortless and habitual application of strategies that enable one to gain maximum learning in the amount of time spent studying. This efficiency can be achieved in study reading by using techniques such as SQ3R and SQP2RS that serve as reminders of key steps in reading actively. Greater efficiency in classroom learning can be achieved by using listening techniques such as Enabling Questions and note-taking techniques such as PUNS. The Guided Lecture Procedure builds students' confidence in their ability to listen actively and understand accurately. Guidelines for taking multiple-choice tests and PORPE for taking essay tests make time spent in test preparation more productive. The Problem-Solving Approach to Study Skills can be used to identify learning and study needs and to select and modify study techniques to meet those needs. The Principles of Learning outlined in Walter Pauk's classic textbook on studying are a useful guide to evaluating and adapting study techniques. One of the most important of these, the Principle of Recitation, is based on classic research showing that an immediate review after initial learning, and with no subsequent study of the material, results in about 83% retention after seven days, as compared to 33% retention without immediate review. Content area teachers can help students build study strategies, habits, and attitudes. Teachers who do so demonstrate their willingness to help students learn and succeed—a worthy outcome in itself.

SECTION

IV

CONTENT AREA APPLICATIONS: PROVISIONS FOR SPECIAL NEEDS AND THE SCHOOLWIDE LITERACY PROGRAM

An effective Content Area Literacy program needs planning and support at the school and district levels as well as from individual teachers in their own classrooms. Different literacy objectives might be emphasized in different content areas through such planning. Chapter 12 offers suggestions for content-specific planning of this type, and additional methods for specific disciplines. Collaborative planning can be extended to shared responsibility for addressing students' special needs, with approaches and techniques provided in Chapter 13. Chapter 14 describes the essential components that are needed to plan, drive, and guide the schoolwide Content Area Literacy program.

CHAPTER 12

DISCIPLINE-SPECIFIC APPLICATIONS

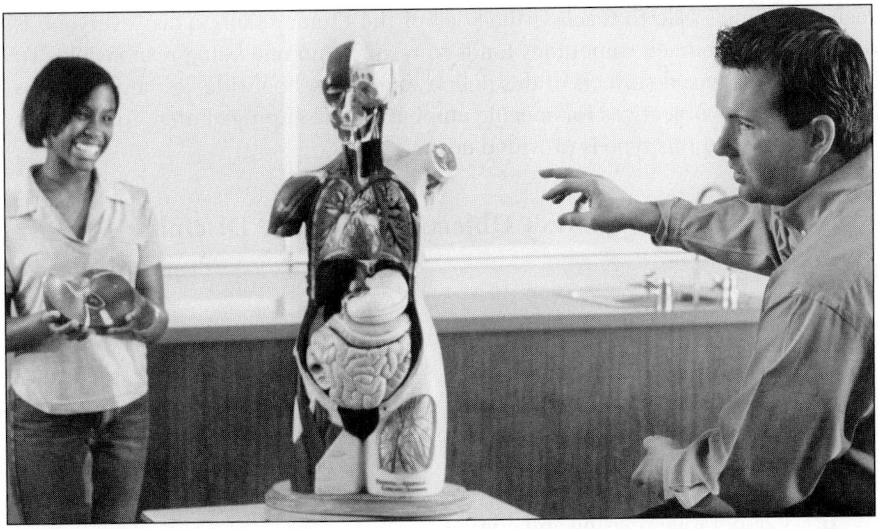

Too much new information can drive knowledge out of circulation. Knowledge is orderly and cumulative, an enduring treasure.

—Dan Boorstin

Many aspects of teaching and learning are common across the disciplines. Previous chapters have presented principles and methods for reading-based instruction in any subject. Each subject also has unique characteristics and potential for supporting the schoolwide literacy program. This chapter highlights a few of these distinct aspects of the core disciplines, with examples of reading-based instruction that are especially suited to each.

- DISTRIBUTED VERSUS UNIVERSAL RESPONSIBILITY
- ENGLISH/LANGUAGE ARTS
- FOREIGN LANGUAGES
- MATHEMATICS
- BIOLOGICAL–PHYSICAL SCIENCES
- SOCIAL STUDIES
- CONTENT AREA READING IN THE SUPPORT SUBJECT AREAS
- HEALTH AND PHYSICAL EDUCATION
- VOCATIONAL TECHNOLOGY

▶ DISTRIBUTED VERSUS UNIVERSAL RESPONSIBILITY

For some time, it has been the practice to educate teachers in the belief that it is each discipline's role to teach virtually all of the literacy skills. This "everyone is responsible" approach sometimes tends to result in no one being responsible. To counter the downside effects of this policy, effective schoolwide literacy programs identify literacy objectives for specific emphasis in each project area. An example of distribution of this type is provided next.

Distributed Literacy Objectives for Core Disciplines

English

1. Story comprehension
2. Poetry comprehension
3. Language patterns
4. Creative writing
5. Summary writing
6. Cooperative revising and editing
7. General vocabulary development
8. Research paper writing and referencing

Social Studies

1. Analytical discussion
2. Critical reading and writing
3. Debate
4. Cooperative study reading
5. Lecture note taking
6. Social studies vocabulary
7. Reading almanac, encyclopedia, and primary sources
8. Reading maps, charts, graphs, and cartoons

Science

1. Scientific training
2. Hypothesis formulation and testing
3. Evaluation of scientific evidence
4. Cooperative reading and writing based on laboratory experiments

5. Accurate recall
6. Science vocabulary
7. Abstract thinking

Mathematics

1. Recitation
2. Translation
3. Test taking
4. Mathematics vocabulary
5. Expository writing: What did this problem ask, and why did I solve it as I did?
6. Cooperative problem solving

This list could easily be extended to all other subject areas. For example, Health and Physical Education teaches students how to *follow complex directions* and to *image body movement* in games and sports and to plan and follow personal fitness routines. Music teaches reading and understanding an alternate means of coding sound. Art teaches visualization and sense awareness, a fundamental skill in story reading, and nonfiction accounts of actions and sensations. Each subject area has its own distinct and specialized ways of thinking that contribute to general language and literacy development and to the schoolwide Content Area Literacy program.

▶ ENGLISH/LANGUAGE ARTS

English is the only discipline that traditionally designates reading improvement as a key objective. It also has traditionally provided direct and systematic instruction in vocabulary, writing, critical literacy, and literary appreciation. Lately, it has taken on the responsibility for teaching mass media, and communications as well. As such, the English curriculum lays the classical and modern foundations for effective comprehension of text and for interpreting the contemporary experience. There are sound reasons for continuing explicit instruction in expressive and receptive language development up to and through graduate education. Listening, speaking, and writing, along with reading, are developmental processes that can be refined and enhanced throughout one's lifetime. They are the mechanisms through which learning, as well as the capacity to learn, can be developed.

One of the most difficult requirements of the English curriculum is reading anthologies of prose and poetry that often span hundreds of years in origin, context, and style. Finding value and meaning in "story" is the heart of the English curriculum. To this end, we provide next a basic set of questions to guide literature study. Notice that the questions raised reveal a good deal about author craft and therefore can serve as aids in teaching creative writing. They can also be used to "unpack" a video presentation or to compare several works. Keep in mind while reviewing this guide that it is just that, a *guide*. Literature is art, and art, like the life it imitates, does not lend itself to easy categorization and dissection.

Guide to Literature Study*

Character Study

Who is the protagonist, or main character, and why?

Who is the antagonist, and why?

Does the author use common stereotypes or some inventive ways to introduce and picture the main characters?

Are there any minor characters who seem to have special appeal or possibilities for future development?

Setting

Does the story take place in a real or totally imagined place?

How does the author create mood through setting?

How do the characters react to the setting?

Plot

How does the author tell the story—through a narrator, a character, or some other way?

How does the point of view help readers relate to the characters and buy into the plot?

What information is given and when?

What information is held back from the reader for dramatic effect?

Theme

What type of conflict is depicted (e.g., person against person, person against nature, person against self)?

Can you detect some idea or attitude being conveyed through the story?

Are there subplots, and do they convey the same or different themes?

How do characters grow or change?

How do they deal with problems?

Style and Tone

Does the story contain elements of the unbelievable, and how is it made believable?

How are facts, images, and words used to hook readers?

**Source:* Adapted from Patricia O. Richards, Debra H. Thatch, Michelle Shreeves, Peggy Timmons, and Sallie Barker (1999). "Don't Let a Good Scare Frighten You: Choosing and Using Quality Chillers to Promote Reading," *The Reading Teacher*, 52 (8), pp. 830-840. Copyright (c) 1999 by the International Reading Association.

How is tension/humor built?

How is tension relieved?

What sensory images are used, and toward what effect?

Universal Truths

What ideas and values underlie the story or piece?

In your judgment, are the ideas and values mature or immature?

Are the ideas and values central to the piece or simply a mechanism for telling an entertaining story or tale?

Genre Comparisons

How would you characterize the story by literary type (e.g., fantasy, mystery, survival, science fiction, biography)?

What are the genre features of a given story?

How would you compare stories of a similar genre for distinguishing characteristics?

Author Comparisons

What are some of the distinctive style features of authors working in a similar genre?

What are some of the distinctive style features of authors working in the same theme but in a different genre?

Can you describe different audiences that likely would be attracted to different author styles?

Which is/are your favorite authors/styles/genre and why?

Illustrations and Camera Work

Can you describe the style characteristics of the illustrations/camera work?

Are illustrations/camera work realistic or impressionistic?

What tends to be in focus, out of focus?

Beyond Literature Study to Academic Language

A newer view of the English/Language Arts curriculum says that a good job is being done with prose and poetry reading but that students need to be taught more about how to read specific academic or technical writing, something 19 other industrialized nations already do.

Much of the catch-up being called for, we believe, is occurring and will continue to occur at a lively pace largely because of the influence of the Content Area Literacy movement, which emphasizes it, and the internet, which is bringing terse, content-laden, high-tech language into schools and homes via electronic text.

Although almost all of the methods presented in previous chapters would serve the English/Language Arts curriculum, two are highlighted here: specifications for English textbooks that could be added to the Informal Textbook Inventory (see Figure 12.1) and Cloze-Plus (Blanc, 1977), a method designed to improve poetry comprehension—a special kind of academic language—more directly than most other approaches.

Cloze-Plus for Poetry

Cloze-Plus enhances comprehension of the meanings and techniques of poetry by dealing directly with the poem, using a cloze-type worksheet. Cloze techniques are most effective when they serve as the basis for an interactive discussion about language choices and forms. Used in this way, they also encourage peer teaching, urge students to generate their own guiding questions, and serve as a readiness step for poetry-writing activities.

Steps in Cloze-Plus

1. The teacher prepares a worksheet by writing the poem, deleting every fifth word beginning with the title (see Figure 12.2 for an example).
2. The teacher tells students that although they have not read the poem, they are to try to re-create it by filling in the deleted words as closely as possible to the exact words of the original. The teacher points out that the activity will be difficult, and students should rely on whatever clues they can find. Students then complete the poem individually.
3. Next, students work in small groups to discuss their word choices. The teacher stands back and lets it happen.
4. Once the groups have reconciled their choices, the teacher resumes a leader role, explaining terms such as *context, syntax,* and *rhyme* and asking students to express how they might have used these to fill in the blanks. (Further class discussion might include comments on poetic license, grammar, vocabulary, and style.)
5. The teacher reads the poem aloud, pausing at the previous blanks to give students time to correct their initial responses.

▶ FOREIGN LANGUAGES

No matter how the teaching of foreign languages is approached, its ultimate success depends on two rudimentary principles of learning that apply to all academic language learning: students must think *about* and *in* the language, and practice outside of scheduled lab and class times. For this reason, foreign language teachers have worked hard to network with English language teachers from around the world. In this way they have arranged for student pen pals and for students to visit one another's countries. This has been marginally successful. Now there is a new tool, the internet.

I. Use of Text Aids to Locate Information
Construct 10 to 15 questions that assess student's ability to use parts of the textbook, such as:

A. What is the title of the book?
B. When was it published?
C. Who wrote the book?
D. How are the chapters arranged or grouped?
E. On what page does Chapter 8 begin?
F. In which chapter can you find something about Langston Hughes?
G. In which chapter can you find "Types of Humor in Modern American Literature"?

II. Rate of Reading and Levels of Comprehension
Choose a passage from the textbook that has not been read by students. Have students read the passage and record the time when they finish it. Help them compute their rate of reading, or words per minute (number of words read divided by number of minutes spent = words per minute). Have students answer questions about the passage that require comprehension at literal, interpretive, and applied levels.

III. Vocabulary Development

A. *Contextual Analysis:* Choose sentences from the textbook that contain words that may be difficult for students. List these sentences, with the difficult words underlined. Have students predict the meaning of the underlined words, using clues from the context to make reasonable predictions (evaluate student responses in terms of "reasonableness" of prediction rather than accuracy of definition).
B. *Structural Analysis:* Select words from the textbook that are made up of affixes and recognizable English root words. Have students identify and explain the meaning or function of the root word, prefix, and/or suffix in each of these words.
C. *Dictionary Use:* Choose sentences from the textbook that contain a word or words that have multiple meanings. List these sentences, with the multiple-meaning word(s) underlined. Have students check a dictionary to select and write the appropriate meaning of each underlined word according to its use in the sentence. (From a term paper by Fengfang Lu, UMKC, 1986.)

IV. Use of Reference Resources

A. Using our textbook's Glossary of Literary Terms, define an "Epic Hero."
B. In an online dictionary (such as Merriam-Webster Online at www.m-w.com) find and then analyze and explain the history (etymology) of the word "sheriff."

Figure 12.1 Informal Textbook Inventory Questions for English

C. Using our textbook's "Reading Guidebook Appendix," list one thing you could do before reading, during reading, and after reading to help you better understand a literature assignment you may be given.
D. With Project Gutenberg (http://www.gutenberg.org) find the names of at least two stories available for free in full text written by Leo Tolstoy.
E. With the thesaurus feature in the word processing program of our class computers, list at least four words you could use instead of "nice."
F. Through Google Books (http://books.google.com) list two books written by Mortimer Adler and two books written by Jhumpa Lahiri.
G. Using the online quotation resource at www.bartleby.com, list the person to whom this quotation is attributed: "The present letter is a very long one, simply because I had no leisure to make it shorter."

V. *Determining Meaning and Interpreting Visual Aids*
A. Look at the picture and pull-out captions on p.____ of our text. What ideas does this give you for being a more active reader yourself?
B. The diagram on the bottom of p. ____ of our text illustrates the four main aspects of plot. Describe briefly how a story you have recently read aligns with these four items.
C. Look at the painting on p. ____ of our text. How would you guess the stark colors chosen by the artist for the sky and the wall of the house relate to the theme of the story in which it is placed?

Figure 12.1 (*continued*)

Richard Cory
Whenever Richard ____ 1 ____ went down town,
We ____ 2 ____ on the pavement looked ____ 3 ____ him;
He was a ____ 4 ____ from sole to crown,
____ 5 ____-favored and imperially slim.

____ 6 ____ he was always quietly ____ 7 ____.
And he was always ____ 8 ____ when he talked;
But ____ 9 ____ he fluttered pulses when ____ 10 ____ said,
"Good-morning," and ____ 11 ____ glittered when he walked.
____ 12 ____ he was rich,—yes, ____ 13 ____ than a king—
And ____ 14 ____ schooled in every grace;
____ 15 ____ fine, we thought that ____ 16 ____ was everything
To make ____ 17 ____ wish that we were ____ 18 ____ his place.

So on ____ 19 ____ worked, and waited for ____ 20 ____ light,
And went without ____ 21 ____ meat, and cursed the ____ 22 ____,
And Richard Cory, one ____ 23 ____ summer night,
Went home ____ 24 ____ put a bullet through ____ 25 ____ head.

—Edwin Arlington Robinson

1. Cory; 2. people; 3. at; 4. gentleman; 5. clean; 6. And; 7. arrayed; 8. human, 9. still; 10. he; 11. he; 12. And; 13. richer; 14. admirably; 15. In; 16. he; 17. us, 18. in; 19. we; 20. the; 21. the; 22. bread, 23. calm; 24. and; 25. his.

Figure 12.2 Example of Cloze-Plus

Newby, Stepich, Lehman, and Russel (1996) describe this new dimension through the story of a Spanish teacher whose students now regularly chat by e-mail with a classroom in Seville, Spain. The future of foreign language education will be in cultivating the many dimensions and values in this new, rapid, and easy-access means of writing, reading, and "speaking" in the vernacular(s) of other languages. Foreign language education need never seem tedious again. To further take advantage of this chat environment, foreign language teachers could develop some common pieces of material for students to read and react to, using the REAP system described in Chapter 8. Every part of REAP seems to meet some part of learning a foreign language: especially the requirements that it be used in authentic contexts with native speakers.

Other approaches and methods from earlier chapters that are well suited to foreign language instruction include:

- Frequent structured peer interactions to maximize opportunities for students to *use* the new language in purposeful ways.
- Reciprocal Questioning, using text in the second language, and asking the questions in English.
- Cloze passage–type worksheets, modified to delete only words students should have learned, rather than strictly every fifth word.
- The Subjective Approach to Vocabulary and Motor Imaging, to teach students strategies for connecting new words to existing schema.

▶ MATHEMATICS

Although some progress has been made over the past decade, reports of the National Assessment of Educational Progress and similar studies repeatedly reveal findings that are cause for concern about the state of mathematics proficiency in the United States (cf. NCES, 2001, 2003).

- More than 30% of eighth-graders are below the most basic level, indicating that they likely cannot handle elementary school arithmetic.
- Only 32% of fourth-graders perform at or above the proficient level.
- Only 29% of eighth-graders perform at or above the proficient level.
- Fifteen-year-olds in the United States score lower than their peers in 17 other countries in mathematics literacy.
- Scores for black and Hispanic students, despite modest gains, lag behind those of whites.

The difficulties students experience in dealing effectively with word problems and related mathematical concepts is unparalleled among current educational dilemmas. Clearly there are more math illiterates than there are people who cannot read. Until recently, however, this problem has been among the lowest-ranked national priorities. Weakness in dealing with math concepts, computation, and word problems—that is, academic language—is so pervasive that it tends to pass for a fact of life.

Mathematics as a Second Language

Mathematics is a system of coding reality that is, in effect, a language. In a book called *Mathsemantics: Making Numbers Talk*, MacNeal (1994) proposes that students can be taught to listen and speak the language of mathematics in settings and situations that closely parallel the ways in which people successfully learn language, and especially second languages. Using the principles of second-language instruction, the reason, purpose, and value of mathematical systems can be more easily imparted, reinforced, and internalized. One simple application of this idea is to *preteach* mathematics incidentally by using math terms in conversation. In the same way that the community of language approach builds word consciousness, repeated exposures to math terms increases students' inclination to be attentive when direct instruction is offered on one of these terms. Another approach is the use of "realia"—or real objects—to help make abstract concepts more concrete. In second-language instruction, realia typically are items associated with the culture of the language. Figure 12.3, a page from a mathematics textbook, illustrates how realia such as square tiles and graph paper are being used to ground abstract numerical operations. Notice also, in this figure, the repeated use of the words *area, perimeter,* and *plotting* in items 1a to 2c, and the conversational tone of these items.

Math Is a Trip: The Informal Textbook Inventory Is a Guide

Math is a trip, for some a good trip and for others a bad trip. Introducing students to their textbooks is a simple, sensible way to have them get to know this well-informed travel companion. The math teacher should plan on spending a minimum of three days on an Informal Textbook Inventory, such as the example provided in Figure 12.4, and giving 2 one-day refresher and extender sessions about two months apart. As students' skills and knowledge base in mathematics grow, so will their perceived need for, and therefore receptivity to, the helping features and value of the text.

The teacher should make an extra effort to conduct all sessions in a relaxed and supportive atmosphere. The Informal Textbook Inventory experience can be a nonthreatening, math-teacher–generated means of desensitizing and counter-conditioning math anxiety. Items 2, 5, 6, and 7 in Figure 12.4, offer useful ways to help students converse in conversational terms about mathematical systems. Note especially question 7 for its possibilities for making math something to be curious about and interested in.

The next method addresses the persistent problem of reading and comprehending word problems, which remain the most complex of academic languages. The one shown from the math book in the figure has five major parts and is difficult to translate into computational steps that most students know how to do.

The Dahmus Method for Word Problems

The Dahmus method for teaching word problems (Dahmus, 1970) emphasizes the translation of English statements into the academic language of mathematics.

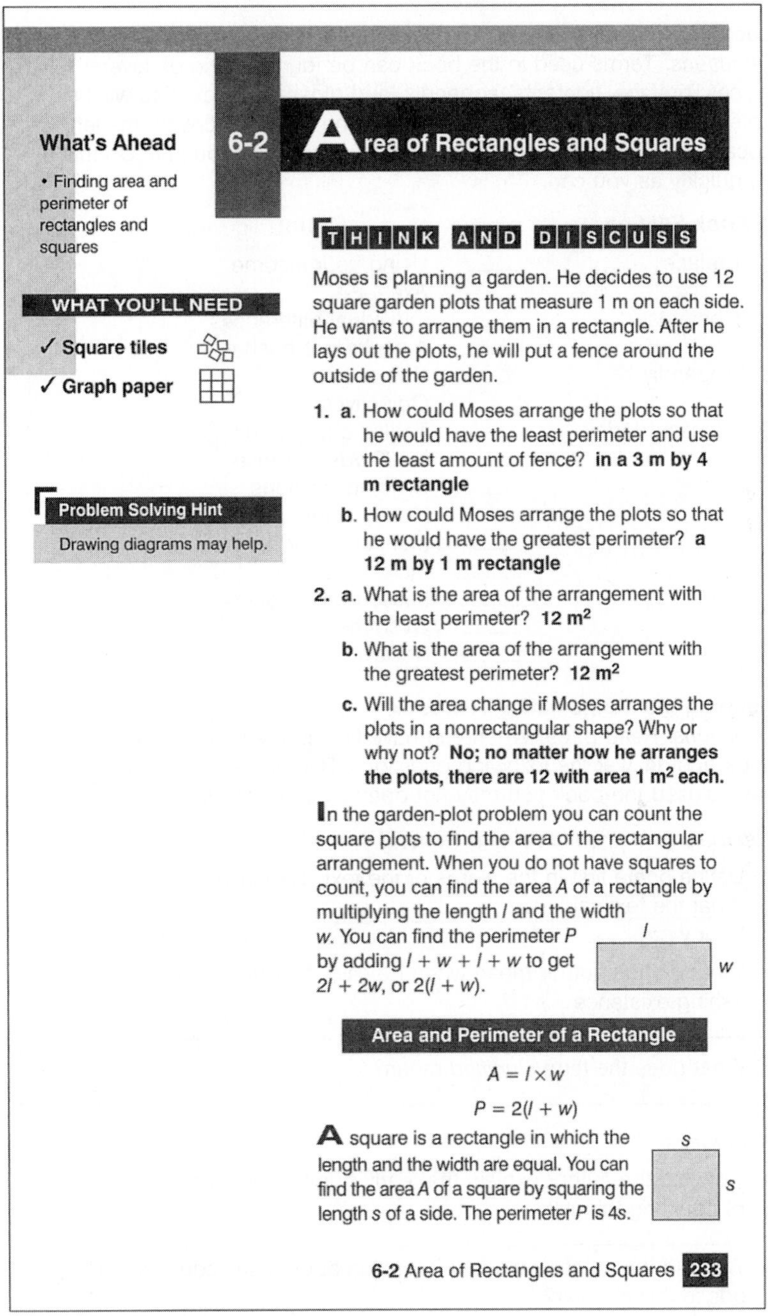

What's Ahead

• Finding area and perimeter of rectangles and squares

WHAT YOU'LL NEED

✓ Square tiles

✓ Graph paper

Problem Solving Hint

Drawing diagrams may help.

6-2 Area of Rectangles and Squares

THINK AND DISCUSS

Moses is planning a garden. He decides to use 12 square garden plots that measure 1 m on each side. He wants to arrange them in a rectangle. After he lays out the plots, he will put a fence around the outside of the garden.

1. a. How could Moses arrange the plots so that he would have the least perimeter and use the least amount of fence? **in a 3 m by 4 m rectangle**
   b. How could Moses arrange the plots so that he would have the greatest perimeter? **a 12 m by 1 m rectangle**
2. a. What is the area of the arrangement with the least perimeter? **12 m^2**
   b. What is the area of the arrangement with the greatest perimeter? **12 m^2**
   c. Will the area change if Moses arranges the plots in a nonrectangular shape? Why or why not? **No; no matter how he arranges the plots, there are 12 with area 1 m^2 each.**

In the garden-plot problem you can count the square plots to find the area of the rectangular arrangement. When you do not have squares to count, you can find the area A of a rectangle by multiplying the length l and the width w. You can find the perimeter P by adding $l + w + l + w$ to get $2l + 2w$, or $2(l + w)$.

Area and Perimeter of a Rectangle

$$A = l \times w$$

$$P = 2(l + w)$$

A square is a rectangle in which the length and the width are equal. You can find the area A of a square by squaring the length s of a side. The perimeter P is $4s$.

6-2 Area of Rectangles and Squares 233

Figure 12.3 Aids in modern mathematics textbooks

Source: From *Middle Grades Mathematics: An Interactive Approach* by S. Chapin, M. Illingworth, M. Landau, J. Masingila, and L. McCracken © 1995 by Pearson Education, Inc., or its affiliate(s). Used by permission. All rights reserved.

1. **Locating Information**
Directions: Terms used in the book can be found in one of several places: preface, contents, appendix, and glossary/index. You will be able to locate each term on the right in one of the places on the left. Locate the term and then mark the place where you found it. Do this as quickly as you can.

Book Section		***Term***
A. Preface	_____	Using your income
	_____	Axes
B. Contents	_____	Individual differences
	_____	4 pecks = 1 bushel
C. Appendix	_____	Cubic units
	_____	Objectives
D. Glossary/Index	_____	Tables and graphs
	_____	1,760 yds = 1 mile
	_____	Dividing fractions
	_____	Hourly wage
	_____	Measure your progress
	_____	Inch
	_____	Lesson organization
	_____	Overtime
	_____	Review

2. **Reading the Mathematics Textbook**
Directions: Read p. 69. When you have finished reading, close your book and answer the following questions. Remember, once you have closed the book you may not open it for any answers.

Vocabulary: Mathematical and General

a. Define *prime* first in the words of the text, then in your own words.
What the text said: ______________________________
Your words: ______________________________

b. What did the author mean when he said, "a simple hunting and fishing existence . . ."?
____

c. What does the term *signified* mean?
____

Main Ideas

d. How did the author explain that early humans needed a method of counting things?
____

e. Why did the author include information about early counting methods in this chapter?
____

Figure 12.4 Mathematics Informal Textbook Inventory

3. **Interpreting Graphs**
Directions: Turn to p. 259 and read the section entitled "Reading Bar Graphs." Study Figure 199 and answer the following questions:

a. How many students (total number) are represented on the bar graph? __________

b. Circle the two categories below in which the same number of students is found:

Poor   Fair   Good   Excellent   Superior

c. Use the graph to determine an approximate answer to each of the following questions:

How many students received "poor" grades? __________

How many students received "good" grades? __________

How many students received "excellent" grades? __________

How many students received "superior" grades? __________

d. Would you say that this test was a good test or a poor test? (Explain your answer.)

4. **Seeing and Using Text Markers**
Directions: Read pp. 119–121. When you finish, close your book and fill in the missing parts of the following outline. Do this in pen.

I. Units of Measurement
  A. Direct: measuring height with ruler
  B. ______________________________
    1. Measuring temperature — thermometer
    2. ______________—______________
    3. ______________—______________
    4. Measuring air pressure —barometer

II. Ancient Measurement Devices
  A. ______________________________
    1. thumb
    2. foot
    3. hand
    4. forearm
    5. ______________
  B. Difficulties of Ancient Measuring Devices
    1. ______________________________
    2. ______________________________

Directions: Now that you have written in your first set of responses in pen, open your book and try to complete the outline in pencil.

Figure 12.4 *(continued)*

5. **Summarizing**
Directions: You are going to read the section "The Metric System of Weights and Measures," p. 202. When you have finished this section about the consistency of the metric system, close your book. Write a summary of what you have read in four complete sentences.
____
____
____
____

6. **Where I Need Help!**
Directions: Think back to all that you just read and the answers you gave. Indicate in no fewer than two sentences where you think you need help in understanding the information presented.
____
____

7. **What More?**
Directions: Think again about what you have read. What are you most curious about? Write at least one sentence telling what you would like to learn more about.
____
____

Figure 12.4 *(continued)*

Recall from previous chapters that simple *translation* questions provide a bridge from literal to higher-order thinking skills.

Steps in the Dahmus Method

1. The statements and their parts in the translation must be in the same order as the verbal form.
2. No operations or substitutions should be performed until the translation is completed.
3. Students should read slowly and translate each idea and fact in the verbal form as it appears before reading. Dahmus recommends that students not read the entire problem beforehand.
4. All other facts suggested by the verbal form and required for the solution should be stated mathematically on students' papers. There should be no verbal forms of translation, only math notation.
5. Students should use deductive reasoning on the translated and implied facts to obtain a solution.

Figure 12.5 provides an example of the Dahmus method.

Mark is twice as old as John. In two years, the sum of their ages
M = 2× J. (M + 2) + (J + 2)
will be five times as much as John's age was four years ago.
= 5 × (J − 4)
How old is each now?
M = ? J = ?

Figure 12.5 Example: The Dahmus Method
Source: Dahmus, M. E. (1970), *How to Teach Verbal Problems.* School Science and Mathematics. © School Science and Mathematics Assn

▶ BIOLOGICAL–PHYSICAL SCIENCES

Bureaucratic reports are notorious for being dull and uninfluential. However, one written about 1945 by Vannevar Bush, director of the U.S. Office of Scientific Research and Development, has become one of the most important documents in modern times. Called *Science, the Endless Frontier: A Report to the President,* this document was the major impetus for getting the massive and sustaining investments by the U.S. Congress in basic scientific research and, indirectly, in America's willingness to support the advancement of knowledge and the education of its students in the scientific method. This priority competes successfully year in and year out with the many other concerns and critical needs of the nation and is largely responsible for our continued program for the exploration of space.

It was in this spirit that science education, for more than 50 years, has called for science to be taught as a narrative of inquiry with emphasis on self-discovery and hands-on learning. This view is now being reflected in science textbooks, state curricula, and teacher training institutions.

Contributions of Science to Reading and Reading to the Language of Science

The typical science curriculum, whether textbook or experiment based, already contributes naturally to growth in reading. Simply by teaching science well, the science teacher helps students better grasp the fundamentals of systematic observation, scientific thinking, problem solving, science vocabulary, science concepts, and the physical world. These elements promote progress in reading by enhancing student schemata, as well as important related linguistic and thinking processes. For these reasons, science and reading have been called a "harmonic convergence" (Johnson, 1995).

The characteristics of an expert reader, such as described in prior chapters, strongly resemble and therefore are greatly compatible with the characteristics of those who are "scientifically literate" as defined by the National Science Teachers Association (NSES, 1998):

> Scientific literacy is the knowledge and understanding of scientific concepts and processes required for personal decision making, participation in civic and cultural affairs,

and economic productivity. . . . Scientific literacy means that a person can ask, find, or determine answers to questions derived from curiosity about everyday experiences. It means that a person has the ability to describe, explain, and predict natural phenomena. Scientific literacy entails being able to read with understanding articles about science in the popular press and to engage in social conversation about the validity of the conclusions. Scientific literacy implies that a person can identify scientific issues underlying national and local decisions and express positions that are scientifically and technologically informed. A literate citizen should be able to evaluate the quality of scientific information on the basis of its source and the methods used to generate it. Scientific literacy also implies the capacity to pose and evaluate arguments based on evidence and to apply conclusions from such arguments appropriately (p. 22).

Problems in Reading Science

The problems students encounter in reading science material stem in large measure from five problem areas:

- Inadequate background of information.
- Misconceptions about the physical world.
- Inconsiderate—assumptive and inadequately explained—text.
- Difficulty in handling esoteric or technically overwhelming academic terms.
- Inadequate preparation and orientation of teachers, particularly at the elementary level, in the basic sciences.

Consider some solutions to these problems as they bear on effective reading and study in science.

Using New-Generation Science Texts

Science textbooks have been roundly criticized as being inadequate (Bradley, 1999). However, this criticism belies the fact that there is a new generation of science materials that offers great promise despite some rough spots that are not easily overcome because they are inherent to the discipline. The promise of the newer materials lies in their being better grounded in compellingly interesting issues; their attempt to stress scientific thinking; and the opportunities they offer for developing integrated reading, writing, and science skills. The inherent problem they pose is that issues-based materials tend to exceed the mental and social maturity levels of most students and can be controversial in some communities (e.g., the perceived conflict between theories and findings for evolution and beliefs nested in conservative religious views). Additionally, from a purely pedagogic perspective, *real issues cannot easily be disassembled and reassembled to meet a typical learning sequence.* These problems aside, the new materials do tend to do a better job of engaging students.

One of the reasons for higher levels of engagement in science texts may be traced to the casual use and reference to prose, poetry, and common experience as a known ground on which to build a sense of familiarity and a basis for new, less familiar knowledge (see Figure 12.6). Admittedly, these connections sometimes are

Guide for Reading

Focus on these questions as you read.

- *What is the function of the excretory system?*
- *What are the four major organs of the excretory system?*

5–2 The Excretory System

When the sixteenth-century English poet John Donne wrote that "No man is an island, entire of itself," he was actually talking about the human mind and spirit. However, this phrase can also be used to describe the human body: No human body can function without help from its surroundings. For example, your body must obtain food, water, and oxygen from its surroundings and get rid of wastes that may poison you. In order to do this, three body systems work together to provide a pathway for materials to enter and leave the body.

You have already learned about two of these systems: the digestive system and the respiratory system. The digestive system is the pathway for food and water to enter the body. The respiratory system enables oxygen to enter and carbon dioxide and water vapor to leave the body. The third system is the excretory (EHKS-kruh-tor-ee) system. **The excretory system provides a way for various wastes to be removed from the body.** These wastes include excess water and salts, carbon dioxide, and urea (a nitrogen waste). The process by which these wastes are removed from the body is called **excretion.**

You have just read about one of the organs of the excretory system: the lungs. Because the lungs get rid of the wastes carbon dioxide and water vapor, they are members of the excretory system as well as the respiratory system. The remaining organs of the excretory system are the kidneys, the liver, and the skin.

ACTIVITY READING

Reading Poetry

1 The first line of John Donne's poem entitled "Meditation XVII" was quoted in this chapter. Find a copy of this poem in the library and read it. Is there another line in this poem that is familiar to you?

The Kidneys

Have you ever made spaghetti? If so, you know that you have to use a strainer to separate the cooked spaghetti from the cooking water or else you will be eating soggy spaghetti! The strainer acts as a filter, separating one material (spaghetti) from the other (water). Like the spaghetti strainer, the **kidneys** act as the body's filter. In doing so, the kidneys filter wastes and poisons from the blood.

The kidneys, which are the main organs of the excretory system, are reddish brown in color and

118 ■ H

Figure 12.6 Poetry and the excretory system

Source: From *Prentice Hall Science Human Biology & Health* by A. Maton, J. Hopkins, S. Johnson, D. LaHart, M. Q. Warner, and J. D. Wright © 1994 by Pearson Education, Inc., or its affiliates(s). Used by permission. All rights reserved.

a bit strained, but our sense is that students would rather have them than not. It would be even more effective if teachers could use the language of science across disciplines to provide more instances of intentional-incidental teaching of scientific academic language and ways of thinking.

Use of Science Texts

One ready means of learning how effectively students are using their science text while helping them improve usage is to prepare an Informal Textbook Inventory on the basic text. See Figure 12.7 for examples of science-oriented items to add to an ITI.

Using Media, Magazines, and Computers to Build Familiarity with the Academic Language of Science

One effective way to build your own as well as students' background knowledge in science is to read popular-science magazines, watch public television, and access online. A new breed of lay-technical writers is turning out articles on such mind-boggling topics as quantum physics and string theory in crystal-clear language—which is not to say that these topics are easily comprehended even then. *Discover* and *Omni* are among the best-written of these publications. There are also a multitude of project activities in progress on the internet providing fun and collaborative activities. An example of this is the *Mars 2030 Project.* Originally created by the White House Millennium Council, the United States through NASA has created a project for students, all ages and grades, to design a community for Mars for the year 2030. Kits are available (www.Mars2030.net).

Adaptations of the Guided Reading Procedure for Science

Two adaptations of the Guided Reading Procedure (Manzo, 1975) are especially appropriate for *Into* and *Beyond*, or Pre- and Postreading, activities using science material (Spiegel, 1980). The GRP-based *Prereading procedure* has students identify clear purposes for study, become aware of specific gaps in their knowledge, and build the scaffolding necessary for forming new concepts. This is achieved by having students bring to mind what they already know about a topic and then organizing this information into an "advance outline" prior to reading. Then students read to test their preconceptions.

Steps in the Prereading GRP

1. The teacher identifies a unit or topic of study that is fairly narrow in scope, such as photosynthesis or spiders.
2. The teacher has students tell peer recorder(s) at the board (or overhead, whiteboard, or SmartBoard) everything they know about the topic prior to lecture or reading.

Using Supplemental Science Resources

Brian Greene has written some best-selling books, written for non-scientist readers, explaining black holes, quantum mechanics, and string theory. Using the Google Books Search (http://books.google.com), searching for "Brian Greene," please read the introduction and preface to his new edition of *The Elegant Universe*. Then, please summarize how this material relates to what we have studied in Chapter ___ of our class text.

Using the reading and multimedia resources that can be found at http://www.pbs.org/wgbh/nova/, search for "hydrogen cars" and explain how what you see there aligns with Chapter _____ of our class text.

Theories Applied to Everyday Life

The basis for the "Doppler Effect" is explained on pp. ___ of our text. How do you think this relates to what you hear when a siren or a car with loud music drives by you? What connection do you suppose there is between this and "Doppler Radar" that we often hear about on the evening news weather forecasts?

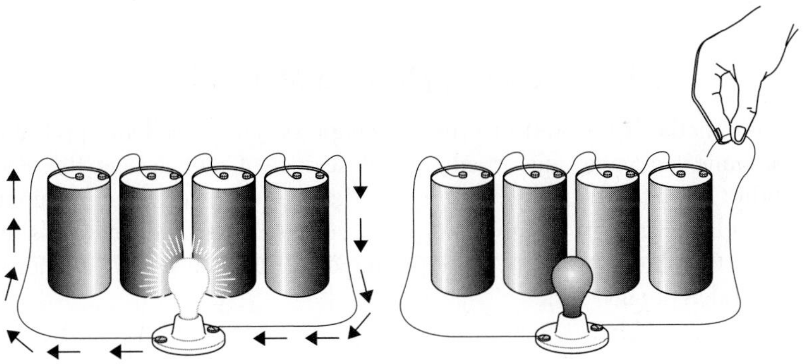

(Answer: Current flow requires a closed path)

Figure 12.7 Sample items for an Informal Textbook Inventory for a Science Text

3. The class identifies conflicting information and areas in which no information has been provided ("Hey, we don't know what spiders eat!"; "Are very large spiders insects or animals?").
4. Students construct an outline with conflicting information listed side by side ("Spiders have six legs/eight legs[?]"). Areas in which no information is known are listed by headings in the outline.

Spiders

I. How they look
  ?A. Have six legs/eight legs
  B. Have two body parts
  ?C. Antennae
II. How they live
  ?A. What they eat
  B. Spin webs
    1. Made of silk
    2. Lots of different kinds of webs
    3. Sticky
      ?a. What makes them sticky?
      ?b. Why doesn't the spider get stuck?

Figure 12.8 GRP Prereading Outline

5. The outline is displayed in the classroom throughout the unit of study.
6. The class is told to read to fill in or alter the outline (see Figure 12.8).

Other Science Application Methods

Several other methods covered in previous chapters have excellent application to the academic language and orientation of science. Chief among these are the Question-Only Strategy, which offers an effective means of inquiry training; the Oral Reading Strategy for giving direct assistance with science words and phrasing; and Graphic Organizers for imparting a "conceptual set" for numerous easily confounded details.

▶ SOCIAL STUDIES

Executive Training

The U.S. Constitution gives enormous executive power to every citizen. Social studies is the fundamental school-based source of the sense of *agency* that every citizen needs in order to read, interpret, and vote on the streams of raw and prepared information emanating from newspapers, magazines, broadcast media, and now the internet. The awesome responsibility facing all citizens with such executive power increases the responsibility of those of us who must agonize over what and how to teach them. Accordingly, today's social studies consists not merely of traditional fields such as history, government, and geography but fields such as psychology, sociology, and philosophy and several conceptual approaches that can be applied across these fields, such as social inquiry, moral education, and values clarification (Peters, 1982). Indeed, one of the more welcome changes in the teaching of social studies is that it is more about people. Look, for example, at the page from a contemporary text (Figure 12.9) to see how immigration has been reduced to human scale in the story of Sacco and Vanzetti; it's not *People* magazine, but it's also not the antiseptic and decontextualized social studies of just a generation ago. In fact, the effective way to teach history is to recognize that it is a *story*. Barbara Wertheim Tuchman (1912–1989), an American historian and author, made this point simply: She said that if you say that the king died and the queen died soon after, that is historical sequence. If, however, you say that the king died and then the queen, stricken with a sense of loss and grief, died soon after, then it becomes *story*. It calls up empathy and attention to the storyteller. It also ties the historical facts to the human capacity known as episodic memory. Our capacity to remember stories is extraordinary and near boundless. our ability to remember isolated facts is 7 plus or minus 2 (Tuchman, 1982).

Contribution of Social Studies to Reading

The principles, precepts, and actual content of social studies underlie almost everything written. This may explain why social studies as a discipline is so highly correlated with general reading comprehension (Adams, 1982; Artley, 1944). Also for this reason, the social studies teacher is especially well situated to enhance students' understanding of how best to read and think about nearly all things written. This is done naturally as the teacher and textbook report to students how others think and feel about a variety of issues such as economics, politics, and culture and the consequences of these beliefs on individual liberties. Most important from the standpoint of the reading process, social studies imparts a rich fund of general information, a specialized academic but also general-purpose vocabulary, refined critical thinking strategies, and the rudiments of cultural literacy, both about the "core" culture and the many diverse cultures within the American mainstream. It also is students' main source of information on our growing global awareness.

Obstacles to Reading and Studying in Social Studies

The major problems students encounter in reading in social studies stem in large measure from the very elements to which social studies ultimately contributes in general reading. Reading in social studies often requires conceptual and informational preparation. It also requires considerable assistance with objective reasoning and in connecting loose factual elements into a structure that subsequently can be used to read, grasp, and interpret still more.

Reasoning Guides

Reasoning Guides were developed and popularized in direct response to the aforementioned concerns. A Reasoning Guide is a specialized form of reading guide that strongly emphasizes interpretive and applied levels of reading and thinking (Herber, 1978). See Figure 12.10 for an example of the format and question types in a Reasoning Guide. Steps for using the Reasoning Guide are given next.

Sacco and Vanzetti *Millions of Americans mourned when Nicola Sacco and Bartolomeo Vanzetti were executed. They believed the immigrants were victims of prejudice. In this photo, the two men are shown handcuffed together as they await their fate.* **Citizenship** *How did the Sacco and Vanzetti case fuel anti-immigrant feeling?*

Middle-class Americans worried that communists and anarchists would invade the United States.

Congress responded by passing the Emergency Quota Act in 1921. The act set up a quota system that allowed only a certain number of people from each country to enter the United States. "America must be kept American," said Calvin Coolidge.

The quota system favored immigrants from Northern Europe, especially Britain. In 1924, Congress passed new laws that further cut immigration, especially from Eastern Europe. In addition, Japanese were added to the list of Asians denied entry to the United States.

Immigrants From Latin America

Latin Americans and Canadians were not included in the quota system. In 1917, the Jones Act made Puerto Ricans American citizens. Poverty on the island led to a great migration to the United States. In 1910, only 1,500 Puerto Ricans lived in the mainland United States. By 1930, there were 53,000.

Farms and factories in the Southwest depended on workers from Mexico. By 1930, a million or more Mexicans had crossed the border. Most came to work in the vegetable fields, orchards, and factories of the Southwest. The pay was low and the housing was poor. Still, the chance to earn more money was a very powerful lure. During the 1920s, more and more Mexicans began to settle in the large cities of the Midwest, too.

Solo in Chicago

UP CLOSE

Just before World War I, exciting news began filtering across the border into Mexico:

> "In the early days . . . one heard only of the states of Texas and California. The few Mexicans that left Mexico went there and wrote back from there. After a while we heard of New Mexico and Arizona, but beyond that there was no more United States to us. I remember distinctly with what great surprise we received a letter in our pueblo from a Mexican who had gone to Pennsylvania. 'Oh, where can that be! That must be very, very far away.'"

As news about jobs in the United States spread, young Mexican men made their way to El Paso or Laredo, Texas. There, they

700 • Chapter 24

Figure 12.9 Putting the story back in history

Source: From *The American Nation* by J. W. Davidson, M. B. Stoff © 1995 by Pearson Education, Inc. or its affiliate(s). Used by permission. All rights reserved.

Directions: Reread the sentences below taken from John F. Kennedy's inaugural address, which you just read in its entirety in your textbook. Then complete the exercises called for below.

A. The world is very different now.
B. For man holds in his mortal hands the power to abolish all forms of human poverty and all forms of human life.
C. . . . (T)he rights of man come not from the generosity of the state but from the hand of God.
D. United there is little we cannot do in a host of cooperative ventures.
E. To those people in huts . . . we pledge our best efforts . . . not because the communists are doing it, . . . but because it is right.
F. We dare not tempt them with weakness.
G. So let us begin anew, remembering on both sides that civility is not a sign of weakness . . .
H. Let both sides explore what problems unite us instead of belaboring those problems which divide us.
I. And so, my fellow Americans, ask not what your country can do for you, ask what you can do for your country.

Directions: Now consider each of the statements below, and decide based on the statements above whether JFK would have approved or disapproved of each. In column A, answer yes or no. In column B, write the letter indicating the quotation from JFK that influenced your decision. For number 10, write an original statement that you think JFK might have made. Quote some part of the address (in your text) other than the quotations listed above as evidence.

A	B	
____	____	1. The problems we are facing today are not much different from those that faced our forefathers.
____	____	2. The oriental world is immensely different from our own.
____	____	3. Our rights are given to us out of the goodness of humans' love for humankind.
____	____	4. If we are to win over the threat of world communism, we must give money, supplies, and help to underdeveloped nations of the world.
____	____	5. Let us demonstrate our goodwill to the world by disarming.
____	____	6. Only the federal government can solve the complex problems of our society.
____	____	7. We will never resort to violence.
____	____	8. The events of the past have helped us realize the truth of Washington's policy of isolationism. We should continue to heed the advice of our president.
____	____	9. The greatest threat to humankind is not famine and sickness but the threat of world communism.
____	____	10. ______________________________ ______________________________ ______________________________

Figure 12.10 Sample Reasoning Guide for social studies

Steps in Using a Reasoning Guide

1. The teacher constructs a guide that draws focused attention to the key portions of a longer section (see Figure 12.11).
2. Students read the longer selection first before using the guide.
3. Students complete the Reasoning Guide, rereading the key portions of the text as necessary.
4. A class discussion in which students compare their answers and their reasons follows.
5. Students further discuss what they learned about their own thinking and about thinking in general; for example,
   a. In what way(s) can we discover what attitudes we and others hold other than by what we/they say? (By our/their actions.)
   b. Is there really any value in trying to form generalizations without all the facts? (Life requires that we do, but any new piece of information may change all previous thoughts and conclusions.)

Building Good Judgment to Accompany Increased *Agency*

Increased power, or *agency,* carries increased privilege and responsibility for making weighty decisions requiring good judgment. No one is born with good judgment. It is painstakingly acquired. An interesting format for promoting good judgment, or critical-evaluative thinking, in social studies was borrowed from experimental tests (Manzo & Manzo, 1990a) and further developed by ninth-grade teachers Susan Tarwater and the late Phyllis McConnel. McConnel and Tarwater used these formats in a team-taught core curriculum program combining social studies and English. The team approach permitted team members to relieve one another from classroom teaching duties to enable them to develop the necessary materials.

In the Critical Judgments Exercise, students first decide and then discuss their judgments of the relative *values* of certain pieces of information. The format can be used with general or background information or with items selected from a section of text that students read in class. Figure 12.11 presents examples of both general-information and text-based items.

▶ CONTENT AREA READING IN THE SUPPORT SUBJECT AREAS

The contemporary forces that have led to the information explosion in the core areas of the curriculum have profoundly influenced the support subjects as well. The evidence for this is readily apparent in even a casual inspection of any support area syllabus. In music, students now study jazz, rock, and hip-hop as well as choral, orchestral, and symphonic works. Physical education now encompasses physiology and less popular sports such as badminton and soccer. In industrial arts, particularly automotive technology, there now is a strong emphasis on electronics.

PART 1: GENERAL INFORMATION ITEMS

Directions: Using your best judgment, decide what you think would be the value to society in knowing each of the statements listed below. Consider each statement to be true. We shall discuss these momentarily.

1 = of no use
2 = of little use
3 = of moderate use
4 = very useful
5 = extremely useful

____ 1. Mary Queen of Scots inherited the throne at the age of six days.
____ 2. Simplicity and elegance in writing are more desirable than length or vocabulary.
____ 3. The first European to sail into New York Harbor was Henry Hudson.
____ 4. The tomato is not a vegetable but a fruit.
____ 5. Left-handedness is a recessive genetic trait.
____ 6. Mary Goddard was the only woman to have her name on the Declaration of Independence.
____ 7. Diamond dust is black.
____ 8. Red meats are high in fat content.

PART 2: TEXT-BASED ITEMS

Directions: Indicate your judgment of the relative values of the statements below taken from your text. Use the five-point scale—1 = lowest, 5 = highest value—that we have used previously.

A. ____ 1. The Nobel Prize is given at least once every five years.
____ 2. The Nobel Prize is awarded for important discoveries or inventions in the five categories of knowledge.
____ 3. No Nobel Prizes were given in 1940–1942.
____ 4. The Nobel Prize was founded by Alfred Nobel, a Swedish chemist and philanthropist.
____ 5. Women as well as men have been awarded the Nobel Prize.

B. ____ 1. Oliver Cromwell was called "The Protector."
____ 2. Cromwell was born in 1599.
____ 3. Cromwell was a violent and persuasive speaker.
____ 4. Cromwell expanded England's territories and increased its commerce.
____ 5. Cromwell's court was frugal but dignified.

Figure 12.11 Critical Judgments Exercise

Family and consumer science (home economics) now addresses complex issues in nutrition, parenting, and diverse family relationships. Business education, which formerly meant typing and shorthand, now means word processing, inventory control, networking, purchasing, and self-initiated appraisal of what may need to be done. In short, the traditional separation between academic subjects and what once were known as "minor" area subjects has all but vanished. These support areas involve complex technologies and require considerable and ongoing reading, research, and critical analysis. In some very real sense, the support area subjects are our best hope for a curriculum that is both authentic, in the sense of real, and interdisciplinary. Nonetheless, these subject domains are in jeopardy because of underfunding, and they should be appreciated and mainstreamed into the new emphases on academics.

Today's teachers of these subjects rarely need to be convinced that their subjects contain a heavy academic component. Thus, the support area teacher now has a heavy investment in, and commitment to, nourishing reading, writing, studying, language, and thinking strategies.

Health Education

Health Education Today

Health education once was a collection of well-intended clichés. Today it is the centerpiece of critical information with lifelong implications. It addresses topics such as nutrition, weight control, exercise, sex education, and personal social behavior. The information provided is crucial and especially needed by those who are less privileged and by those English Language Learners who come from developing nations to more affluent ones that have their own set of new problems.

A typical textbook on most any aspect of modern health education is characterized by intrinsically relevant topics to pre- and adolescent students. They include the issues related to *coming of age* and many of the near irreversible implications for what can follow. The topics speak frankly and openly on sexual awakenings and of grim facts, such as the disproportionately high percentage of young deaths that occur due to motor vehicle crashes, pranks, homicides, and suicides. However, health education also tends to contain sophisticated vocabulary, content, and concepts. Access to the internet to follow up on topics and issues of personal interest now is common, but it can be difficult reading and students need help digesting such information. Methods such as Listen-Read-Discuss and Question-only are compatible with both the topics and content of health education texts. These methods perhaps more than others will prepare students to establish the "prior knowledge" and learning strategies necessary to investigate matters that they would shy away from in class. It also will assist them in safely engaging such topics when class routines require and in ways that are informative, but personally protective.

Health education is a good example of where education is working. Here are some examples as found in a text for teachers by Matza (2009–10):

- The prevalence of alcohol drinking and smoking continues to decline.
- Health literacy is climbing, and this is extremely significant long term since many of the newer threats to health are "social morbidities"—connected to social environment and specific behaviors.

- Evidence continues to mount that as far as costs for health education are concerned, we can *"either pay now or pay later."*

▶ PHYSICAL EDUCATION

"Reading is sport," wrote Gentile (1980). "It requires mastering the fundamental skills, sufficient practice, a well-balanced diet of literary experiences, and a lifetime of development" (p. 4). The artificial separation of physical and academic education that exists in most schools is unfortunate, unnecessary, and uncaring. Plato placed gymnastics at the highest level for training his philosophers.

The Physical Domain: Linking Physical and Academic Development

The relationship between physical and academic development is more than coincidental. As noted in earlier chapters, all learning enters through and takes place in the body as well as in the mind. The linking of motor involvement with language and academic learning can be a "natural" for the P.E. class, as illustrated in a recent news report, which went something like this:

> In the gymnasium at the Jackson Avenue Elementary School of Mineola, New York, 8-year-olds ran through the pathways of a human circulatory system drawn on the parquet floor.
>
> Pretending they were blood cells, they grabbed oxygen molecules (bean bags) from a bucket, raced through the heart chambers (red and blue Hula-Hoops) and completed the circuit by exchanging the oxygen for carbon dioxide (crumpled waste paper). Their warm-up finished, the panting pupils checked their pulse rates.
>
> Watching them, Kathleen Kern, the school's physical education teacher, said, "You can't teach kids about aerobic fitness until they understand the circulatory system."

In the same vein, Gentile (1980) suggests an interesting "metacognitive" activity involving reading, appreciation of the physical domain, and provocative discussion: In gym class, have students read and discuss statements, such as one from Michener's *Sports in America* (1976), which says, in effect,

> If I had a child determined to be a writer, I'd expect that child to take two courses: one in ceramics so that he or she could feel form emerging from inchoate clay and a second in eurhythmic dancing so that child could feel within his or her own body the capacity for movement, form, and dramatic shifts in perspective.

The highest goal of the reading curriculum, as noted several times previously, is not merely to teach students to read but to promote language, thinking, and social-emotional maturity. Here, in slightly paraphrased form, are a few methods recommended by Maring and Ritson (1980), professors of reading and physical education, respectively, for fostering Content Area Literacy in gym classes.

THE BASIC RULES OF BASKETBALL

Directions: Review the underlined information about the capitalized key terms below. Then answer the questions that follow.

Key Terms

1. Each team is composed of five MEMBERS who play the entire court area.
2. A team scores 2 points when the ball passes through the hoop during regular play (FIELD GOAL).
3. A team may score additional points by means of free throws when a member of the opposing team commits a PERSONAL FOUL (hacking, pushing, holding, etc.).

Questions

1. Where on the court do team members play?
2. Explain in your own words what a field goal is.
3. Name two kinds of personal fouls.

Figure 12.12 Reading to Reinforce Instruction
Source: Maring, G.H., & Ritson, R. (1980, October). Reading improvement in the gymnasium. *Journal of Reading, 24*(1), 27–31. Copyright 1980 by the International Reading Association.

Method 1: Reading to Reinforce Instruction

Make up one-page handouts that summarize and reinforce the physical education content and skills that have just been taught via lecture-explanation, demonstration, or charts and diagrams. Type key terms in all-capital letters, and underline portions of the text that explain their meanings. On the bottom or back of each handout, include a set of questions that relates to the main ideas in the lesson. After students have read the handout, have them form small groups to answer the questions (see Figure 12.12).

Method 2: Read and Do

Prepare "Read and Do" instruction sheets so that students will learn required content and at the same time improve their ability to follow written directions (see Figure 12.13).

Method 3: Book Checkout

In the locker room or near your office, place a revolving bookrack displaying high-interest paperbacks that relate to aspects of your physical education curriculum with checkout cards pasted inside the back covers. Consult the school librarian and reading specialist for assistance in book selection. Have the class or team elect a librarian to be responsible for the lending and returning of the books.

MOTOR DEVELOPMENT EXERCISE

Single-heel click: Jump into the air, click heels together once, and land with feet apart (any distance). This can be turned into an amusing exercise in which students try to write out totally unambiguous expository directions for their peers to follow. You might invite an English teacher to cooperate with you on this project.

Figure 12.13 Read and Do
Source: Maring, G.H., & Ritson, R. (1980, October). Reading improvement in the gymnasium. *Journal of Reading, 24*(1), 27-31. Copyright 1980 by the International Reading Association.

Method 4: "Testlets"

Evaluate students' performance skills and knowledge by giving short tests that require students to read and follow directions (see Figure 12.14). Each test can be presented on an individual card. Students should be familiar with this format before being tested.

Grapevine Test
Stand with heels together. Bend trunk forward, extend both arms down between legs and behind ankles, and hold fingers of hands together in front of ankles. Hold this position for five seconds. Failure: (a) to lose balance; (b) to not hold fingers of both hands together; (c) to not hold the position for five seconds.

Three-Dip Test
Take a front leaning-rest position. Bend arms, touching chest to the floor, and push body up again until forearms are in a straight line with upper arms. Execute three performances in succession. Do not touch the floor with legs or with abdomen. Failure: (a) to not push body up three times; (b) to not touch chest to floor; (c) to touch the floor with any part of the body other than hands, feet, and chest.

Full-Left-Turn Test
Stand with feel together. Jump upward, making a full turn to the left. Land at approximately the same place from where the test was started. (Feet may be separated when landing.) Do not lose your balance or move feet after they have touched the floor. Failure: (a) to not make a full turn to the left; (b) to move feet after they have returned to the floor; (c) to lose your balance.

Figure 12.14 Testlets
Source: Maring, G.H., & Ritson, R. (1980, October). Reading improvement in the gymnasium. Journal of Reading, 24(1), 27–31. Copyright 1980 by the International Reading Association

Method 5: Student Reports
Have students read and write a brief (half-page) report on any person making news in sports. Invite different students to give these reports in the opening five minutes of class. Tack up the best reports on a cork display board (Gentile, 1980).

▶ VOCATIONAL TECHNOLOGY

Problems and Goals

Federal Public Law 98–524, also known as the Carl D. Perkins Vocational Act of 1984, has as one of its main purposes the goal of improving the academic foundations of vocational technology students. Simply put, the objective was to create a workforce able to adjust to the "changing content of jobs." This act contains provisions to support schools willing to develop quality programming in reading, computing, and the vocational areas that now are again growing rapidly with new options and opportunities.

The justification for such programming is well supported by several studies that have shown that the average workday for nonprofessional workers requires between 24 minutes and 4 hours of reading per day (Rush, Moe, & Storlie, 1986). Related research indicates that workers themselves underestimated by an average of 45% the amount of time they spent reading (Mikulecky, 1982). Furthermore, job-related reading is by no means easy. The materials essential to job competency in 11 fields, ranging from account clerk to welder, have readability levels that rarely dip as low as ninth grade and typically reach as high as the sixteenth grade level. Secretarial reading is the most difficult, ranging from sixteenth to college graduate levels (Diehl & Mikulecky, 1980).

Not surprisingly, one of the nagging problems of vocational technology has been the difficulty level of school texts and the information and schematics that come up on computer screens. Although this situation is changing, there still are plentiful examples of "inconsiderate" text. Derby (1987) offers examples from one vocational technology textbook:

- *This chapter is devoted to a study of the various ways in which the basic engine theory and parts are utilized to produce multicylinder engines of several types.* This, Derby explains, is an awkward way of saying, *This chapter is about the different kinds of engines that are used in today's cars.*
- In a second example, the same textbook states, *Although a number of three-rotor and four-rotor experimental engines have been built, common usage at this time employs either a one-rotor or a two-rotor engine.* A more "considerate text" version would read, *Although a number of experimental engines have been built with three or even four rotors, most engines being built today have just one or two rotors.*

Here are some services and functions vocational technology teachers can offer to help promote literacy in this domain.

Six Services Vocational Teachers Can Provide

1. Work with students to use, and where necessary create, text aids such as Advance Organizers, pivotal questions, glossaries of terms, and concept maps.
2. Follow the simple steps of the Listen-Read-Discuss method so that students will be better empowered for reading dense and often inconsiderate text.
3. Using the Informal Textbook Inventory, give students practice and instruction in using basic texts and reference books. For students of electricity, teach the use of the National Electrical Code; for health assistants, demonstrate the Physician's Desk Reference on diseases; and for automotive students, develop familiarity with the Chilton Repair Manual and other motor company services manuals.
4. Use the Question-Only procedure as a Prereading and prelecture method: Instead of merely announcing a topic, show students a vital engine part and have them conduct a systematic inquiry into its nature, functions, and most frequent failure points.
5. Vocational technology subjects offer abundant opportunities to use the Typical to Technical Vocabulary Approach, as discussed earlier in Chapter 7 (Welker, 1987). This strategy also can be used to concurrently improve abstract thinking. Here are some examples of automotive terms, suggested by Piercy (1976), for which students might have culled meanings from everyday life:
   - *Differential*—a set of gears that permits rear wheels to revolve at different speeds
   - *Differential*—peculiarity; distinction; feature; earmark
   - *Governor*—a device for automatically controlling the speed of an engine by regulating the intake of fuel
   - *Governor*—the elected head of any state in the United States
   - *Distributor*— a mechanical device for distributing electric current to the spark plugs of a gas engine
   - *Distributor*—a business firm that distributes goods to customers
6. Guiding a Pre- and Postreading analysis of diagrams and illustrations is a powerful way to promote strategic reading. This can be done in a survey fashion prior to reading and in a careful way following Silent Reading. When this procedure is followed routinely, students will be keyed into the supportive graphic material as they begin to read and anticipate further analysis following reading. This combination should increase the probability that students will use the illustrations, like the one in Figure 12.15, to grasp and clarify meanings when they read silently. It also should help them become better strategic readers for the time when they must read independently in school and on the job.

Text and Picture*

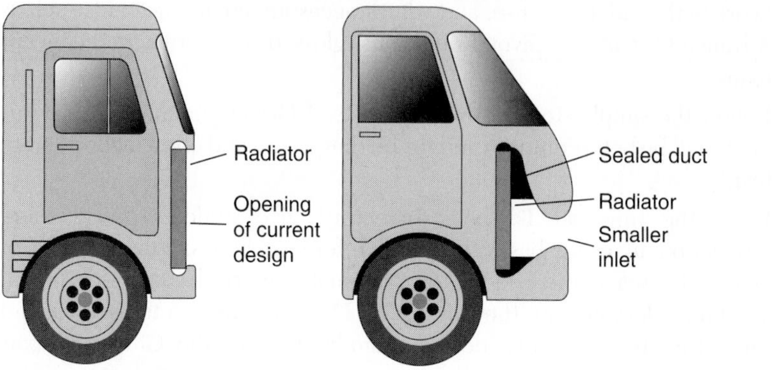

Current truck radiator installation design (left) requires flat front. Air resistance can be reduced by a streamlined design (right) where ducts bring sufficient cooling air to the radiator.

*Through design improvement, over-the-road trucks can function with radiator openings one-third as large as those used currently. Seating of ducts is necessary so that all cooling air is directed to the radiator. Applications of such truck designs have existed in the aircraft industry for many decades. Automotive engineers should examine aeronautical engineering practices in their quest for aerodynamic efficiency.

Figure 12.15 Using illustration to grasp and clarify meaning
Source: Rush, R. T., Moe, A. J., & Storlie, R. L. (1986). *Occupational literacy education.* Copyright 1986 by the International Reading Association.

Career-Oriented Literature

Apart from textbooks and manuals, the vocational technology teacher needs a ready and readable supply of career-oriented literature (COL). Career-oriented literature refers to articles and stories about jobs and career areas. It tends to reflect how real people feel about their jobs and vocations.

COL materials tend to touch on matters that textbooks and manuals rarely address, such as apprenticeship programs and various employee benefit options. For publishers who offer other special, hard-to-find, human elements, see Figure 12.16.

Language Experiences

Most activities undertaken in career and vocational education can be performed better with student input. Language Experience Activities (LEAs) provide such opportunities. Here are a few LEA-type activities that are especially suitable for the vocational technology class.

1. *"Celebrity" Interview:* Have students interview working people as though the latter were celebrities. Ask concerned questions such as might be asked of celebrities: "How did you first get into this business?" "Has this work been fulfilling for you?" "Have you ever wished that you could have

The Globe Book Company has two books (*All in a Day's Work* and *It Happened on the Job*) containing true, brief anecdotal accounts of work situations that are unusual and sometime humorous.

Pitman Learning offers *Pacemaker Vocation Readers,* a set of 10 high-interest, controlled-vocabulary books describing young trade-type people in challenging situations.

Scholastic Magazine has an Action Series that has a number of job-related storybooks such as the *Plumber's Line, Rosina Torres, L.P.N., Demolition Man,* and *Paramedic Emergency.*

Vocational Biographies, Inc. offers *Project Earth* and *Project Explore,* describing jobs and careers in the context of scientific principles and actual vocational biographies highlighting real individuals.

Career World (formerly *Real World*) is a color newspaper, written in the vein of *USA Today.* It addresses the work-a-day world and contains actual reading-skill exercises (Derby, 1987).

Figure 12.16 Career-oriented Literature

done something else?" "Can you tell me an interesting or amusing experience that you have had in this line of work?" Students could be instructed to watch television interview shows to get some ideas for "people questions." Discuss the questions they might ask before they ask them.

2. *Dialogue Journal:* As previously noted, have students keep a journal in which they write a sentence or two every other day regarding their career interests and experiences. Periodically, read and write a brief reaction to these: "Charlie, I didn't realize that your father is an electrician!" "Mary, if you will see me after class, I can tell you where to get more information on summer jobs with the city."

3. *Vocabulary from the Workplace:* To help build respect and support for the vocational program throughout the school, have students interview friends and family about words and expressions that they use on the job but laypeople would be unlikely to know. Ask English teachers, for example, to use the Vocabulary Self-Selection Strategy (Haggard, 1978) to include some of these words on English vocabulary lists. Vocabulary collections of this type can contribute to students' sense of accomplishment and make English teachers realize that many students who might not know what onomatopoeia means probably do know what a rocker-panel is (the name for the narrow shelf beneath all car doors). Terms such as these, which the English teacher probably doesn't know and which rarely can be found in most standard dictionaries, constitute a wider and richer language system than most academically oriented teachers have considered.

4. *Magazines:* Have students subscribe to a few quality news and trade magazines. These can be read in class or for homework. Assign groups to give well-organized reports on different articles.

5. *Computer Networks:* Browse the internet for home page sites that correspond to specific vocational technical interests.

▶ ART AND MUSIC

Art and music teachers are important advocates and shapers of a culture of literacy in the schools. Art and music offer a sheltering and enriching alternative to the sometimes harsh sounds and the challenges of life. They enhance emotional well-being and simple joy in living. Art and music also tend to reflect diverse perspectives, dialects, and historical periods and therefore contribute to a broader and more multicultural, global outlook. They provide pleasure and offer an outlet for more elevated expression. For these reasons, it is important to consider ways to gently weave together content area literacy and the art and music curricula, since each offers benefits to the other.

The Challenging Academic Language of the Arts

Writing in art and music almost by nature tends to be an academic language that is esoteric and difficult to read. Sentences often contain complex syntax, unusual phrasings, assumptive references, sophisticated ideas, and names and words of foreign origin. It has been said that "One does not really read a music theory book. One grapples with it. . . " (Tirro, 1969, p. 103, as cited in Duke, 1987, p. 154). A typical passage even from a popular library book on music reads like this:

> In all of art's best periods, creative people were brought together, and thus we had Pericles' Athens, the Medici's Florence, Elizabeth's London, Goethe's (and later Liszt's) Weimar, Beethoven's (and later Brahms') Vienna, Emerson's Concord, Lowell's Boston and Monet's Paris. These were by no means smooth waters, but they were lively (Bacon, 1963, p. 130).

One would need to be quite well informed in the areas of art, music, literature, and history and in the characteristics of several different cultures to take in the full significance of this almost casual observation by pianist and teacher Earnest Bacon.

Meeting the Challenge

Art and music teachers can help students meet and profit from the challenge of "inconsiderate text" in several ways. Some of these are specified next. Consider a suggestion to be applicable to both areas unless otherwise specified.

1. Use the Oral Reading Strategy to familiarize students with syntax, phrasing, proper breathing, enunciation, and pronunciations.
2. Ask frequent translation questions: "Can you say this in your own words?"
3. Add information as needed to enhance schema, or background knowledge: "Have you read or heard about the Medici family in world history class yet? They were a wealthy and influential Italian family in medieval

Florence—a thriving seaport city in Italy. They were great patrons of the arts."

4. Use the Listen-Read-Discuss method and Note Cue to guide reading and discussion.
5. Have students use the Subjective Approach to Vocabulary with illustrations: Divide a page into quarters, and have students write the new word in quadrant I, write its dictionary meaning in II, draw a pictorial representation in III, and write out the subjective association in IV. Then the students discuss these and store them in their notebooks.
6. Work with science, literature, and social studies teachers to have students produce various forms of artistic representations of significant ideas.
7. Work with the school principal to use music in appropriate settings. Music has been shown to facilitate creative writing, mathematics, spelling, and art (Greenhoe, 1972; Maor, 1979; Taylor, 1980). Although music sometimes can be distracting during reading, classical music has been found to be conducive to comprehension gains (Mullikin & Henk, 1985). The classical music played in the latter study was Pietro Mascagni's *Cavalleria Rusticana* "Intermeggio." A no-music condition produced better performance than did rock music, which is to say that rock is disruptive of thought. Apparently, something soft and slow and with methodical cadence is necessary to foster reading and thinking. The first author found this to be true while using taped music during "sustained Silent Reading" time with urban middle school reading classes. Music was played during the first 10 minutes of class, during which time students who were caught up with class work had the privilege of reading anything of their choosing. She began the year with a few classical and "easy-listening" instrumental selections that She used for free reading time. Not knowing about Mullikin and Henk's finding, She succumbed several times to students' pleas to use rock music instead. It never worked: With a rock music background, students were more distracted than they would have been otherwise. Even when She eliminated rock music, however, they appreciated the more traditional melodic pieces enough to hush one another rather than lose the privilege.
8. Outstanding television shows are dramatized with music. Work with the English teacher to have students think through and try to score selections of literature with appropriate musical pieces and/or poignant oral readings. This takes a good deal of thinking and analysis. If you feel daring, ask students to select or compose theme tunes for the school and/or individual teachers.

▶ ENCOURAGE CREATIVITY

A final suggestion is simply to invite students to be creative. Use Content Area Literacy to encourage creative-consructive, thinking and problem solving *and* to be encouraged to be creative in your own thinking and teaching. Again, the three main ingredients for encouraging creativity are to:

1. Connect your students and yourself to creative thinkers whenever and wherever you can. You might look up the web page of the Foundation for Better Ideas and the Global Idea Bank on the internet. This is one way to provide exposure to creative questions, creative answers, and even monetary and social incentives for creative production in a variety of disciplines and across disciplines.
2. Teach students to formulate good guiding questions, as purposes for reading and listening, and list these on your actual and/or virtual classroom bulletin boards. A good question is half-way to an inventive answer.
3. Request and expect creative production from your students, and they will not disappoint you.

▶ CONCEPT SUMMARY

The Prereading Guided Silent Reading, and Postreading methods in chapters 4, 5 and 6, the Vocabulary methods in chapter 7, and the critical and constructive response methods in chapter 8 were selected to be useful across content areas and grades. This chapter suggests that a schoolwide program might identify certain aspects of Content Area Literacy for particular emphasis in the different subject areas. Some previously presented methods are suggested and illustrated as especially appropriate for a given subject, and additional more subject-specific methods are introduced.

CHAPTER 13

PROVISIONS FOR SPECIAL LITERACY NEEDS OF ADOLESCENTS

A helping word to one in trouble is often like a switch on a railroad track—an inch between wreck and smooth-rolling prosperity.

—Henry Ward Beecher

As students progress through the grades beyond elementary school, in order to develop increasingly higher levels of reading ability—to achieve a year's growth in reading for each year of school—they must gain familiarity with increasingly difficult language patterns, vocabulary, and sets of knowledge; they must develop and apply strategies and "habits of mind" for constructing meaning from different types of text read for different purposes. Not all students "grow" their reading abilities equally, and many fall behind in one subject or another. This chapter outlines some of the special literacy needs of adolescents that can be addressed in the content area classroom and some that cannot, and it offers guidelines and approaches to meeting these needs.

SPECIAL LITERACY NEEDS DEFINED

The term *special literacy needs* is used here to refer conditions that cause learners to fall short of expected reading development. In any heterogeneously grouped classroom at middle and high school levels, students' reading abilities are likely to range from well above to well below grade level. Most classrooms will also include English Language Learners and students with specific learning disabilities. The literacy needs of all of these learners can be solidly addressed by regular use of the Framework for Text-Based Instruction that is the organizing principle of this textbook. Good prereading instruction *raises students' reading levels* for a given selection. Guidance of various types during reading reminds students to read actively and strategically. Postreading comprehension development reinforces, extends, corrects, and connects the understandings students bring away from the pages. Frequent opportunities to have prereading, during reading, and postreading interactions with peers in cooperative structures heighten self-efficacy and motivation as well as comprehension strategy acquisition.

Even with the best instruction, of course, there may be students whose reading level is so low that classroom instruction cannot effectively meet their needs. These students are easily identified by their inability to read grade-level material out loud with a *reasonable* degree of accuracy and fluency. These nonreaders will have had years of experience with school failure and will have little hope of any change for the better. They often are referred to in the literature as "struggling readers," but this may be optimistic. They may appear to "struggle" if forced to read aloud, but sadly, most such students have otherwise stopped struggling to read and devote their energies instead to a variety of successful means of diverting attention away from their inability to read, such as "hiding out," as Brozo (1990) aptly calls it. Brozo and colleagues observed an 11th-grade history classroom for a semester and subsequently identified and interviewed the three poorest readers in the class to determine the ways in which these students coped with their inability to read. The most frequently used coping strategy was to avoid eye contact with the teacher. The second most frequent strategy was to engage in disruptive behavior. Nonreaders need to be identified and provided with remedial-level reading instruction in settings that are, for the most part, outside the realm of Content Area Reading, although one simple technique for reinforcing basic decoding is described toward the end of this chapter.

The special literacy needs addressed in this chapter, more or less in order from least to most severe, are:

- Students reading at any level, needing encouragement and motivation simply to read *more.*
- Students reading below grade level, needing especially intensive applications of the inclusion methods used to implement the Framework for Text-Based Instruction.
- Students with personal-social adjustment needs that interfere with normal academic development.
- Students whose reading comprehension is hindered by lack of meaning vocabulary.
- Students whose learning is primarily hindered only by their limited English proficiency.
- Students whose reading and learning development is hindered by lack of familiarity with the social and language conventions of classroom discussion.
- Nonreaders who are "hiding out" in middle and high schools and need to be identified and provided with intensive remedial-level instruction in decoding and sight word acquisition.

▶ SPECIAL FOCUS ON MOTIVATION

The Three-Phase Framework for Text-Based Instruction is based on the teacher modeling strategies for Pre-, During, and Post- reading and providing ample opportunities for students to interact in cooperative groups to apply these strategies in verbal interactions with peers. As students begin to use these strategies on their own, simply spending more time reading will reinforce these habits. Content teachers can encourage wide reading in a variety of ways, as listed next.

1. *Establish a Sustained Silent Reading (SSR) program.* Once or twice a week, have students read anything they choose that is content related. Increase the time from 7 to 20 minutes over a few months. This lengthening period of SSR can become an effective management tool as well as a means of teaching students how to read in an increasingly sustained manner. To be sure that everyone has something to read and to allay students' sense that this is an idle-time activity, it is best to store SSR materials in class and periodically invite individual students to discuss what they are reading. This classroom-based activity can be broadened to include the entire school. It is most conducive if teachers, administrators, and all other personnel read for the sustained period as well. In our experience, doing this on a schoolwide basis provided a surprisingly settling effect in a school that frankly was rather chaotic. The sound of silence and an image of everyone reading produced a sense of peace, order, and purpose.

2. *Provide interesting materials.* Keep interesting newspaper and magazine articles, and make them available in the classroom for students to read before or after class or during downtime.
3. *Have students fill out a reading interest inventory, indicating the types of books they enjoy reading.* Invite the school librarian to help you select an appropriate inventory and to develop a list of suggested book titles related to areas of interest.
4. *Help organize book clubs.* Encourage students to join a book club and/or subscribe to magazines in areas of special interest. Concerned members of the business community often will pay for these, as will community members who contribute books and magazines.
5. *Become a reading motivator.* Almost everyone likes to be read to. Set aside a few minutes of classroom time to read a poem, newspaper or magazine article, or portion of a cherished book to the class. This simple gesture has been a staple of veteran teachers for generations.
6. *Encourage collaborations.* Allow two or more students read the same book for a book report to the class. Encourage them to discuss the book with each other.
7. *Use technology to encourage reading.* The school can buy multimedia CD-ROM disks or borrow them from libraries and/or hook up to the internet to encourage reading for pleasure and expanded knowledge. There are many sites that contain wonderful books and excerpts that are no longer under copyright protection.
8. *Use bulletin boards.* Cut out and display the weekly book review section of the newspaper. Add color pictures and captions from ads and reviews. Invite students to manage this in-class site.
9. *Combine with media.* Ask students to see a movie or television program either before or after reading a book on which one or the other is based.
10. *Have student groups create a book or article of the week poster.* Display books and articles with the caption "Read All About It." Invite students to share their books or articles with the class, noting the titles, authors, and sources of critiques.
11. *Invite local writers.* Invite local authors or poets to class to discuss and read their works. Perhaps call it the *Living (as opposed to Dead) Poets Society.*
12. *Give students incentives to read.* Students who read three or more books during a quarter or a semester can be rewarded with a donated gift certificate from a bookstore, record store, clothing store, or food store.
13. *Conduct reading conferences with students.* Personalized discussion and interest in a student's reading can be deeply motivating.

14. *Teach students to use the closed caption option on television to work incidentally on their own reading effectiveness* (Koskinen, Wilson, Gambrell, & Jensema, 1987). Similarly encourage weak readers to listen to books on tape while they follow along; however, this may have a slightly negative effect with above-average readers (Cloer & Denton, 1995).

▶ SPECIAL FOCUS ON INCLUSION

Federal Public Law 94–142 mandates that students with learning disabilities, developmental disabilities, and other physically handicapping conditions attend school in a least restrictive environment. This has been taken to mean that wherever possible, such students will be mainstreamed or expected to attend and be accommodated in regular classes.

Most of the methodology of the Content Area Reading movement is suitable for meeting this requirement. Maring and Furman (1985) have made an especially strong case for several whole-class, inclusion strategies for helping students read and listen better in heterogeneous, content area classes.

1. Use the Oral Reading Method (described in Chapter 2) at least once a week to increase familiarity and comfort with the language of the text.
2. Use the whole-class graphic organizer called *pyramiding* (Clewell & Haidemos, 1983). This activity offers group assistance to students with learning disabilities in identifying, classifying, and properly subordinating terms and ideas found in text.
    a. Each student reads silently to identify and write down key facts and ideas.
    b. The teacher leads a discussion, using the board to pyramid, or group, facts and phrases into logical categories.
    c. The class decides on a sentence that answers the question, "What is the author saying about these ideas?" This sentence forms the base of the triangle (see Figure 13.1).
3. Enhance and review the informal textbook inventory described in Chapters 10 and 12, and add some easier questions to help make the course textbook more instructive and user friendly. For example:
    a. How many pages are in the glossary?
    b. Where could you find more information about a term defined in the glossary? (Answer: the index.)
    c. What are the first and last page numbers of the index?
4. Use the Contextual Redefinition method, described in Chapter 7, to improve vocabulary while reading (Moore, Readence, & Rickelman, 1982).

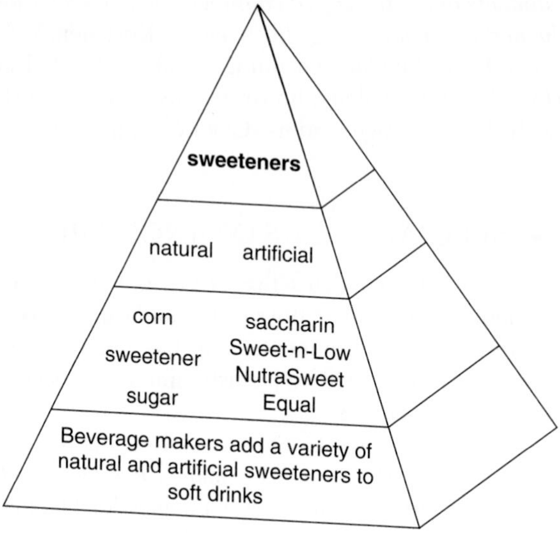

Figure 13.1 Pyramiding: A Graphic Organizer Method for Special-Needs Students.
Source: Maring, G.H., & Furman, G. C. (1985, May). Seven "whole class" strategies to help mainstreamed young people read and listen better in content area classes. *Journal of Reading,* 28(8), 694–700. Copyright 1985 by the International Reading Association.

5. Use Words on the Wall (Cunningham, Cunningham, & Arthur, 1981) as an uncomplicated means of providing students with learning disabilities and other students with an easily available set of key words from the text to which they can refer for meaning, significance, spelling, and increased familiarity. Simply write key words with a felt-tip marker on half-sheets of paper, and tape them on the walls during a given unit of study. (This can also be done with morphemes, as suggested in Chapter 7.)

6. Conduct the Guided Reading Procedure (see Chapter 6 for details) with the following specifications:

a. Use the procedure every two weeks, and administer a delayed retention test in the intervening week.

b. Try to get mainstreamed readers to contribute free recalls early in the lesson before the more able students contribute all of the easiest information.

c. Reread the information on the board as students try to decide which items are main ideas, which are related details, and how to sequence the information.

7. Build further crutches, or scaffolding, into reading guides:

a. Mark with asterisks those questions you think are most necessary and appropriate for mainstreamed students to answer. Tell them to answer these questions first.

b. Put page, column, and paragraph numbers after certain questions to better guide those students who might have difficulty finding these

(Wilkins & Miller, 1983); for example, "92, 2, 2" means page 92, second column, second paragraph.

▶ SPECIAL FOCUS ON PERSONAL-SOCIAL ADJUSTMENT NEEDS

The role of literacy in adolescent development is twofold: (1) It provides access to world literature with its many serious and humorous stories of coming of age and (2) it provides diversion from self-absorption in related literature of adult trials and tribulations and moral dilemmas. It also connects developing adults with an array of human quests in the form of baseline knowledge of many areas of human study. Simply put, the content areas offer possible engagement not merely in what is known, but in the acquisition of new knowledge. Since all knowledge is connected in some way to all other aspects of knowledge and human experience, acquiring a taste for a certain subject or discipline adds a higher purpose to one's life and a lasting interest in reading and thinking about things of fundamental value to a host of others sharing and appreciating those same interests. It is like joining a club. This is no small benefit; in modern life it grants one membership in a tribe—an area of comfort and affiliation that seems fundamental to us, and especially to those who have begun to grow past the strictures, but also the comfort of guiding parents, with whom, by the quirks of genetics, we may share much or relatively little. Interest and inquiry in a subject can be life enriching both socially and in terms of cognitive development. It can, in fact, be as meaningful as shared interest in a sport, hobby, or church.

At a practical level, these fundamental cognitive and social-emotional needs provide the opening for the teacher to invite each student into his or her subject area club, with perks such as signature occupations, language, and rituals. In adolescent development terms, engaging a new interest and area of continued reading and learning is equal to helping youngsters feel more capable, significant, powerful, and worthy, and to having a certain sense of group identity and purpose. This all equals higher levels of grounded self-esteem; that is, esteem based on real knowledge and a connection to, and affiliation with, some valued skills and, again, a larger sense of purpose. Good subject teaching and, implicitly, the selling of a life interest in certain disciplines and ideas can be therapeutic and life enriching. But let's turn now to the problem referred to as the *achievement gap*.

Story

Stories are one of the world's oldest tools for imparting values, guideposts, and enrichment of analogical thinking, the means by which minds establish parallel structures and understand the new from the previously learned. The archetypes of hero stories are not stereotypes but animated representations of good and bad in concrete, digestible form. Archetypes exist in relation to one another, serving as a map or record of the inner life of a single human and a society (Gurian, 1998). We are all a bit more complex and vulnerable than we are inclined to reveal. Good books can be good counsel.

Bibliotherapy

For students who are inclined to read, biblio-support (Manzo, Manzo, & Albee, 2004) can be an effective means of aiding with personal-social adjustment. Biblio-support is based on bibliotherapy, which essentially means healing through reading (Edwards & Simpson, 1986). Generally, it entails redirecting students' perceptions and attitudes in a healthy direction by getting the right reading material to the right student at the right time.

The sources of problems students encounter as they grow and mature are varied: cultural differences, family relationships, moving, divorce, peer pressure, physical handicaps, racial prejudice, death of loved ones, gender identification confusion, and many others. Biblio-support is merely a means of becoming more broadly informed on and dealing with these personal-social and identity formation dilemmas so that schooling does not suffer irreversibly. Several authorities are contributing to this rapidly growing aspect of using literature and content texts to meet some of the complex challenges of adolescent development (cf. Allen & Ingulsrud, 2003; Bean & Moni, 2003; DeBlase, 2003; Maloney, 2003; Simmons, 2003).

Whenever possible, the teacher or counselor who recommends a book to a student should invite the student to retell the story, highlighting incidents and feelings that are relevant to the central situation. Changes in behavior, feelings, and relationships should be looked at closely to permit reasonable identification and empathy with the textual characters (Heaton & Lewis, 1955). Most important, the reader should have an opportunity to form a conclusion about the consequences of certain behaviors or feelings to determine whether these behaviors or feelings improve the human condition, as well as one's self-centered concerns or personal situation.

Reading and discussion are most fruitful when they are built around two questions, one that most everyone can answer easily, "What have you read that reminds you of someone you know?" and another that few of us can answer easily, "What reminds you of yourself?"

Dialogue Journals and E-mail

Biblio-support can be greatly enhanced by the addition of a writing component. The easiest way to do this is to have students keep personal journals in which they write brief reactions—at least one sentence—to whatever they read. Be careful not to overdo this however; the majority of students really do not like to write, and certainly not continuously in pensive, reflective terms (Manzo, Manzo, Barnhill, & Thomas, 2000). Written materials can be stored in a box in the classroom or in a word processor, on which with students' prior approval, the teacher may read through them and write back personal notes and thoughts. Of course, notes and dialogue need not be limited to textual material; they can be extended to anything a student wishes to write or to anything a teacher may be interested in communicating. The idea of dialogue journals (Staton, 1980) is as old as conversation between caring friends. Teachers who use this approach regularly report touching insights revealed and warm relationships formed with students who at first appeared apathetic, hostile, or otherwise reluctant to learn (Kirby & Liner, 1981). In time, a teacher who uses this interactive means of teaching will learn a great deal about how to respond to many common complaints and potentially seething concerns of pre- and early adolescents. One teacher we know, for example, reminds teens, who frequently complain about the material things that they do not have, that even the poor today live better than the rich did 100 years ago, and infinitely better than did many kings and emperors 1,000 years ago. To dramatize the point, he has them list 10 things that most of them have that the czar of Russia did not have in 1900. Again, we all need a little reminder of our blessings to offset some of that existential (and real) angst of daily life. Adolescents especially appreciate these modest, little homilies; and, yes, they can be life saving to those who occasionally lapse into states of despair.

▶ SPECIAL FOCUS ON VOCABULARY

Cooperative Glossaries to Assist with Unfamiliar Word Meanings

A glossary is a handy mini-dictionary of terms used in a given book or field. Definitions are context specific and therefore concrete. Even proficient readers appreciate these when wading into a new field. Students spend each day wading through new fields. If there is no glossary in the class text, or the particular book or novel being read, there is a relatively easy and instructive way to create one cooperatively.

Steps in Constructing a Cooperative Glossary

1. The teacher constructs a simple glossary to a few pages of a longer selection or book.
2. Students are urged to use the cooperative glossary as they read.
3. Students are urged to read a few pages beyond those covered by the guide.
4. Discussion develops about how the guide helped and which additional words and/or phrases might need definition.
5. Each student is assigned to prepare a glossary for a few pages of the remainder of the text. Students should be told to note the page number for each word they select and to record *only* the dictionary definition that applies to the way the word is used in the selection.
6. Glossaries are compiled and reproduced for the entire class.
7. (Optional) The teacher adds a pronunciation guide. This step is optional because it is difficult to do; however, most students like—and need—one.

Figure 13.2 presents an example of a cooperative glossary.

Page	Chapter	Word	Definition	Pronunciation
67	3	inscrutable	cannot be understood	in-screw-ta-ble
68		lamentation	cry out	la-men-ta-shun
70		opiate	a drug to help a person sleep	o-pee-ut
71		perpetuation	continuting	per-pet-chu-a-shun
72		specter	ghost	speck-tur
81	4	consignment	delivery	cun-sine-ment
83		disconcerted	confused	dis-cun-sir-ted
84		oblivion	complete forgetfulness	o-bli-vee-un
85		sonorous	loud praise	sah-nore-us
87		supplicatory	begging	suh-pli-cu-tory

Figure 13.2 Cooperative Glossary for *A Tale of Two Cities.*

▶ SPECIAL FOCUS ON CLASSROOM DISCUSSION

Classroom listening and discussion remain the most fundamental means by which education is conducted. Nonetheless, students rarely are taught how to listen actively and participate in class discussion, that is, how to *ask*, *answer*, and make relevant and appropriate *comments*. English Language Learners, dialect speakers, and students from culturally different backgrounds have traditionally found these social-academic strategies especially difficult to acquire. These, as well as some students from lower SES (socioeconomic status) backgrounds, sometimes are unfamiliar with the more subtle aspects of the English language, such as tempo and volume, and social protocols, such as waiting one's turn to speak, and speaking cogently.

Note Cue (Manzo & Manzo, 1987) is a form of highly scaffolded, or sheltered, practice designed to show students how a well-orchestrated literacy lesson might occur. In some ways it resembles training wheels on a two-wheel bike and quickly thereafter, *spotting*, an independence-building technique used in physical education to guide initial attempts at tumbling (see Figure 13.3). Note Cue is a form of sensorimotor involvement in which the mind and the body learn complex new language, thinking, and social routines. The goal is to help students become more proficient in text-grounded instructional conversation about books and ideas. It resembles a cue card system described by Brown and Cambourne (1987) as a linguist activity to aid recall, paraphrasing, and content area instruction.

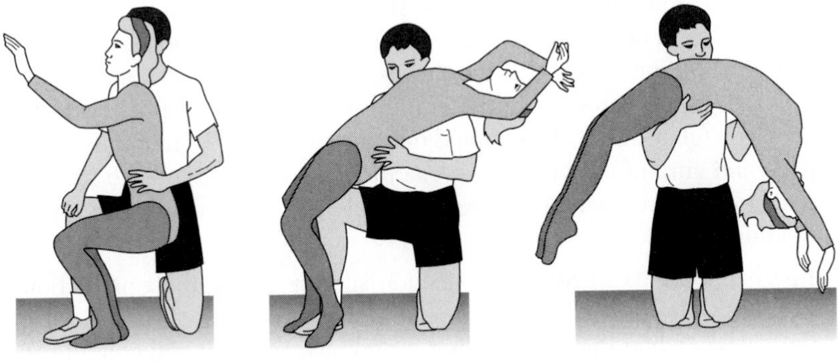

Figure 13.3 Note Cue is like acrobatic spotting.

Steps in Preparing for and Conducting the Note Cue Method

Teacher Preparation. Prepare two sets of cards, one for prereading and one for postreading. On the prereading cards, write prereading questions (one per card), answers (one per card), and comments (one per card). Write the label "Question," "Answer," or "Comment" at the top of each card. Leave a few blank cards, initially just one, then one more blank each time you use the method until only 20% of the cards contain statements. Questions, answers, and comments should focus on predicting main topics, important events, and outcomes. Write in pencil, and remember to reread and edit your cards. Prepare the postreading cards the same way but shift the focus from prediction to verification—what the passage actually states—and related evaluative questions and comments.

In preparing both sets of cards, be sure the answer card is phrased clearly enough to be easily matched to the question card (e.g., Q: Who followed Abraham Lincoln into the presidency? A: Andrew Johnson followed Abraham Lincoln into the presidency [not simply A: Andrew Johnson]).

Prereading Activity

1. Instruct students to survey the reading material to try to predict what it will be about. Inform them that a brief written test will follow reading and discussion of the selection.
2. While students are surveying, place one or more random or selected prereading cards on each student's desk.
3. Instruct students to read their card(s) silently and think about when they should read it (them) aloud, and about whether they wish to add anything else.
4. Instruct students with blank cards to think of a question, answer, or comment and, if time permits, write it on their cards.

5. Begin the prereading, or prediction, stage of the discussion by asking who has a question or comment that seems to provide a good idea of what the selection will be about. If a question is read, ask who has an answer that seems to fit. This process continues until students have a sense of what the passage will be about. This should take no more than 10 minutes; a brisk pace and aura of evolving a purpose for reading will convey to students that not all cards need to be read to establish a reasonable purpose for reading.
6. Instruct students to read the selection silently to test their predictions. Remind them to read their postreading cards, which will be placed on their desks while they are reading. Announce that you will come to the desk of any student who raises a hand for assistance.

Postreading Discussion

7. Ask, "Who has a good question to check comprehension of this selection?" then, "Who has a good answer to that question?" then, "Who has a comment that seems right to state?" and finally, "Who has reaction(s) or personal comment(s)?" The last question is intended to encourage extemporaneous statements as well as statements read from cards.

Follow-Up

8. Within the same class period, or later if preferred, give a test of five to ten questions that require brief written responses. Most questions should be taken directly from the cards to build an appreciation of the cooperative value in reading a cue card for all to hear and profit from.

Notes on Note Cue

If initial participation is slow to develop, try these options:

- Get things going by reading a question or comment card yourself.
- Simply call on students by name to read their card.
- Stimulate interest by inverting the process slightly: Request that an answer card be read; then ask, "What is the question?"
- Call on at least two students with question cards to read their cards aloud. Then, rather than immediately requesting an answer, ask, "Which question do you think should come first?"
- Have students write their names in pencil on the back of each card. Middle school teacher Betty Bennett says this heightens students' sense of ownership and accountability for the cards' contents and offers a good way to check afterward which students did not volunteer to read their cards.

To accelerate independence and transfer of learning, try these options:

- Reinforce high-quality extemporaneous responses by handing the student a blank card and saying, "That was very good. Would you please write it on this card for further use?"
- Divide the class into groups, and have them prepare the Note Cue cards for the next selections to be read.
- Once students are familiar with the activity, prepare some cards with prompts ("Try to ask a question to show that one should doubt what is being said") or an incomplete statement to be completed by students ("Make a comment by completing this statement: 'I enjoyed reading this story because. . . ' or 'The reaction would have been different in my family or culture. We would have. . . '"). Other types of prompter cards can be personalized ("Come on, Fred, don't you have something you can say about this selection?").

To foster higher-level thinking, develop evocative comment cards, preferably ones related to students' experiences. One vivid example of this kind of bridging comes to mind from a lesson observed in an English class. The selection read had been excerpted from a popular book. It described how a 15-year-old boy set out on a solitary voyage across the Pacific in a small craft. The questions and answers the teacher had put on the cue cards were primarily from the teacher's manual for the text. One of the comments that she added, however, raised the class's interest and even indignation: "How in the world did this young man raise the money and supplies to do this, and why did his parents permit him to risk his life in such a silly venture?" A student might not have worded the comment quite like that, but such real reactions tend to invite equally real responses and lively discussion.

Finally, Note Cue, unlike many conventional lesson designs, is cumulative. The cards a teacher composes for today's lesson can be stored for future use. Through cooperative work and sharing, teachers can develop starter sets of Note Cues for most key selections of a text. More important, with each use, previously written cards can be modified following use, and new cards generated by students can be added. In this way, lessons can be kept fresh and current.

SPECIAL FOCUS ON DECODING

The most essential facets of effective reading are decoding, or phonics, and comprehension. Poor readers, by definition, have difficulty with either or both. In fact, improving decoding is a fundamental way of improving comprehension. Here is a way for nonexperts to help with phonetic analysis, or phonics, and word learning.

Glass-Analysis Approach: Phonics Training, without Phonics Rules

There is an amusing scene in a Jack Nicholson movie (*Five Easy Pieces*) in which his character gets a waitress to make him a BLT sandwich, which she says they do not have, by starting with something else and removing this and that. Gerald Glass has done a similar thing to the teaching of decoding. In a stroke of ingenuity, he has taken the phonics out of decoding instruction, and somehow what remains is phonetic analysis without phonics instruction.

Glass-Analysis (Glass, 1973) is a simple procedure that enables virtually anyone who knows how to read to teach others how to do so. It can be used at opportune times as a whole-class method when introducing or reinforcing difficult content terms. Moreover, it takes some of the mystery out of dealing with the least able readers. Teachers need *not* know about diphthongs, digraphs, and other phonic elements and rules. Teachers simply provide occasional assistance, based on their own ability to decode, as time and circumstances permit. This approach is developmentally appropriate for postelementary and English Language Learners since it takes up the challenge of hearing, seeing, and decoding complex words beyond the level of simple "onsets" (initial sounds) and "rimes" (final sounds). Struggling, postelementary students tend to have the greatest difficulty with "medial" sounds, and particularly so in multisyllabic words (e.g., *photosynthesis, bureaucracy*).

Glass-Analysis is a fairly directive method based on two verbal scripts. The scripts are designed to teach students to focus attention on the unrecognized word and increase their familiarity with the sounds of the most common letter clusters in the English language. Ideally students internalize this cadence and exercise it as an internal mediational system, or self-spoken and, therefore, self-teaching strategy for unlocking unfamiliar words. The sound for *ing*, for example, has a high frequency of occurrence and is more easily learned as a cluster than as three separate letter sounds that then must be synthesized. Following are some general guidelines and steps for teaching with Glass-Analysis.

Guidelines for Teaching Glass-Analysis

Students should continuously look at the word. Never cover part of the word or point to letters when presenting the word. Generally, the Glass approach discourages including definitions of words in the instruction unless a student asks. The idea is to keep students focused on word analysis and recognition. However, when Glass is used in a content class, word meanings should be discussed following the word identification, especially if they are central to the content. In either case, reinforce students for correct responses. If a student cannot answer a word attack question, state the answer and return to the same question before finishing with the word.

Steps in Glass-Analysis

1. Write the word to be taught on the board or a large card.
2. Pronounce the word. Then teach it using as many combinations of letter clusters as are sensible.
3. Use the following questions or verbal scripts:
   "What letters make the <ch> sound?"
   After you have used this question with the possible combinations, ask *"What sound do the letters <c/h> make?"*

The teacher writes the word *forgetfulness* in large letters on the board. Then the teacher uses the Glass-Analysis script as follows:

In the word *forgetfulness,* what letters make the *for* sound?

The *or* sound?

What letters make the *et* sound?

The *get* sound?

What letters make the *forget* sound?
In the word *forgetfulness,* what letters make the *ful* sound?

The *forgetful* sound?

What letters make the *fulness* sound?

What letters make the *getfulness* sound?

(Notice how many structures can be learned in just one word—all transferable to other words.)

In the word *forgetfulness,* what sound do the letters f/o/r make?

What sound do the letters e/t make?

The g/e/t?

The f/o/r/g/e/t?

What sound do the letters f/u/l? make?

What sound does g/e/t/f/u/l make?

What sound does e/s/s make?
n/e/s/s?

In the word *forgetfulness,* what sound do the letters f/u/l/n/e/s/s make?

If I took off the letters f/o/r, what sound would be left?

If I took off the *ness* sound, what sound would be left?

What is the whole word?

Figure 13.4 Example of Glass-Analysis

Figure 13.4 illustrates how Glass would use this approach with a new word before silent reading. See Figure 13.5 for a listing of common letter clusters, grouped according to difficulty level.

Uses of Glass-Analysis

Glass-Analysis can be used in three ways to create an effective schoolwide remedial/corrective decoding program:

- Content teachers can incidentally use this simple letter-clustering approach each time a new technical or content word is introduced: "This word (showing it) is *photosynthesis.* What letters make the *photo* sound?

STARTERS KIT
(Nonreader 1st-grade decoding level, weak 2nd-grade decoding level)

1. at	11. am	21. ash
2. ing	12. un	22. ish
3. et	13. in	23. ed
4. it	14. ap	24. ig
5. ot	15. and	25. ip
6. im	16. ack	26. ud
7. op	17. um	27. id
8. an	18. ab	28. en
9. ay	19. ag	29. ug
10. ad	20. old	30. ut

MEDIUMS KIT
(2nd-grade decoding level and/or weak 3rd-grade decoding level)

31. ar	41. ame	51. ice
32. em	42. ape	52. ick
33. up	43. ace	53. if(f)
34. ate	44. ang	54. ink
35. ent	45. ank	55. ob
36. est	46. ong	56. od
37. ake	47. all	57. og
38. ide	48. aw	58. ub
39. ock	49. el(l)	59. uf(f)
40. ade	50. eck	60. ush

HARDERS KIT
(3rd-grade decoding level and above)

61. able	71. us	81. eat
62. ight	72. il(l)	82. as(s)
63. is(s)	73. ite	83. ev
64. on	74. es(s)	84. ind
65. or	75. om	85. oss
66. ul(l)	76. oke	86. earn
67. ac	77. ore	87. ost
68. af(f)	78. tow	88. rol(l)
69. ook	79. ast	89. one
70. fowl	80. ane	90. ale

COMPLETERS KIT
(Use after Harders)

91. ave	101. eal	111. ure
92. ove	102. tea	112. ur
93. folly	103. ee	113. ir
94. age	104. care	114. ai
95. er	105. deaf	115. au
96. air	106. oat	116. oi
97. ied	107. ue	117. tion
98. ew	108. soon	118. ture
99. ire	109. ou	119. al
100. ear	110. ound	

Figure 13.5 Letter Clusters (by difficulty level).
Source: Glass-Analysis for Decoding Only. ETL, Box 329, Garden City, New York, 11530. Used with permission.

What letters make the *syn* sound? The *thesis* sound? What is the whole word again?" This can also be followed by letters-to-sounds questions if needed.

- Content teachers also can occasionally preview textual material assigned for reading and use Glass-Analysis to teach other challenging words, especially foreign-language terms, that occur in text. "This is the Italian word *ciao.* Which letters make the *ch* sound in Italian? Which make the *ow* sound? How is the whole word pronounced again?" All students especially appreciate this kind of assistance with words that may be cause for embarrassment, such as saying *chick* for *chic*, which is a French word that is pronounced *sheek.*
- Students with serious decoding deficiencies can be scheduled for one to five 15-minute sessions per week in which Glass-Analysis tutoring is provided. *Decoding Stations* can be set up in convenient, unobtrusive places throughout the school. These can be staffed by teachers serving a duty period and/or by volunteer paraprofessionals.

▶ SPECIAL FOCUS ON ENGLISH LANGUAGE PROFICIENCY

Terminology

Generally speaking, the term *limited English proficiency* (LEP) is the larger category describing English dialect speakers and students for whom English is a second language (ESL). In recent times the ESL groups have come to be called English Language Learners (ELLs). This choice of terms remains fluid and not consistent across journals and scholars. However, ELL is the currently preferred term and the one that we have used in this text.

Learning Needs of ELL Students

If learning a new language while having to learn *in* a new language were not so common, it probably would be considered a serious form of learning disability since its impact on schooling can be considerable (Manzo, Manzo, & Albee, 2004). However, learning a new language while learning in a new language is not a learning disability, but a serious learning obstacle; students generally learn the informal conversational aspects of language in about two years, but it can take five to seven years to acquire skill in formal and academic language. Understanding this distinction becomes a necessary step in reducing the likelihood of mislabeling students as "learning disabled" and therefore misdirecting their instructional needs. In fact, this happens too frequently. Many teachers have difficulty differentiating the normal phases of learning a new language from "learning defects." This mimicking effect has teachers overidentifying English Language Learners for special education (Cummins, 2001; Ordonz-Jasis, 2002). Accordingly, this is a solid reason to also be very cautious in judging how many ELL students are low functioning and very generous in saying how many probably are average and above.

The increasing numbers of students pouring into our schools from foreign and diverse cultural backgrounds are once again hastening the need for all educators to be conversant with the precepts of teaching to those with limited English proficiency and/or are in transition as English Language Learners. Past efforts to accommodate non-English-speaking American youngsters have consistently resulted in a richer, more diverse, and stronger nation. To appreciate the nature of the challenge to ELL students is to begin to understand what needs to be done to accommodate them. Consider the following challenges. L1 refers to the students' first, or heritage, language, and L2 to the language (in this case, English) being learned.

Challenges of Learning a New Language While Having to Learn in a New Language

1. There is no word form in L1 for one in L2.
2. Lack of familiarity with the grammatical and syntactical structures (or linguistic patterns that we use to fluidly predict the next word in a sentence) in L2.

3. Inadequate vocabulary and concept development in L1.
4. Confusions arising from seeming parallels in L1 and L2 from similarities in letter clusters and idioms that are, in fact, not parallel and, therefore, are misleading.
5. Lack of, and/or incongruous, background schemata, values, customs, and attitudes.
6. Lack of skills and knowledge in interpreting the communicative intent of a speaker/writer.
7. Inadequate and incongruous experience and knowledge of the acceptability of various forms of oral and written discourse.

The CAL Tool Box

As previously noted, many of the *tools*— methods and means—devised and developed for Content Area Literacy have proven especially appropriate for use with linguistically and culturally different students. In many instances, these methods need not be modified but merely used as described. This certainly applies to methods that create a rich instructional conversation such as ReQuest, reported to be highly effective in English as a second language classes (McKenzie, Ericson, & Hunter, 1988), as well as other interactive methods such as Question-Only, the Cultural-Academic Trivia (knowledge) game, the Subjective Approach to Vocabulary, Vocabulary Development through Cooperative Learning, most variations on the cloze procedure, and the various response-to-text and discussion methods (such as REAP) presented in earlier chapters.

The most appealing feature of the general approaches presented next is that in addressing second-language and limited English needs, they simultaneously account for certain universal needs shared by all students. Among the most prominent of these are the need for a multicultural outlook; the need to reconnect ourselves to certain traditional human values and wisdom; the need to think abstractly as a requisite to thinking adaptively; and the need to actively participate in class, that is, conduct ourselves in harmony with others while pursuing individual goals (a specific method for which is detailed ahead).

ELL and Culturally Diverse Methods

The methods described next can be used to aid language development and support cultural diversity in almost any reading/language arts program and in almost any content class:

- Encourage students to watch captioned TV. This is a solid means of hearing and seeing new terms and customs of speech.
- Encourage students to comment on materials to be read by trying to predict what the selections in each unit of study might be about. Record students' predictions on a chart. At the end of a unit, encourage students to discuss whether their predictions were correct and why.

- Have as many books as possible available for students. Read the descriptions of books to them, encouraging them to select books from this list. In addition, select one book from each unit and orally read it to students to build familiarity with a content area's most frequent words and cadence.
- Have a variety of multiethnic literature available, including materials from the students' cultures and some in their native languages. Help them build on their strengths, from a strong base of confidence and self-esteem.
- Exercise materials in any lesson should be read to students and discussed, not merely assigned.
- Read poetry aloud to students and discuss. If possible, record the poetry on a tape so students can hear the poet's language again and again.
- Read plays to students before they are asked to take character parts. If possible, provide audio or video recorders so students can practice their parts and hear (and see) themselves before they are asked to read aloud.
- Read postreading questions to students and discuss answers with them before having them write out their own answers.
- Have quasi-bilingual, or *transitional*, students read and write with aides, parents, and former ELL students who speak a student's first language.
- English Language Learners are likely to have a developmental gap between their ability to read and their ability to write in the second language. These students will benefit by working through stages of the Writing Process as a group activity. After a suitable prewriting activity and/or discussion, students should be asked to talk through the drafting stage, while someone records what they say on chart paper. Students then should be asked to reread the composition and make any needed revisions. The recorder should make these revisions while students observe and suggest any editing corrections that need to be made (spelling, usage, punctuation, and so on). Each student should then copy the finished work from the board so that he or she has a sense of ownership. As students gain a sense of confidence in their ability to write, pair students and have them write their compositions together. Move from this to having students write independently.

▶ CONCEPT SUMMARY

This chapter offers approaches, methods, and techniques for supporting a range of special literacy needs of adolescent learners in the content area classroom. Teachers need to pay special attention to early identification of nonreaders who might be "hiding out" in their classrooms and refer these students for special remedial-level assistance. Other students' reading development can be supported by attention to possible special needs. Some classes may need ongoing special focus on one area of need or another; others may need a special focus for a short time only. Students reading below, at, and above grade level can benefit from the approaches to focusing on motivation, inclusion, personal-social adjustment, vocabulary, classroom discussion protocols, decoding, and English language proficiency.

CHAPTER 14

LITERACY LEADERSHIP IN THE CONTENT AREAS

We know what we will have if we operate as we have in the past—and the prospects are not promising.
—Carl D. Glickman

This chapter is structured to answer several organizing questions that a principal, classroom teacher, or literacy specialist would need to understand to be an effective participant in a school's Content Area Literacy program.

1. What is meant by "literacy leadership," and what shape does it take in today's schools?
2. What do schoolwide Content Area Literacy programs typically look like?
3. What are some newer directions for Content Area Literacy programming and curriculum?

- VISION
- ROLES AND RESPONSIBILITIES
- PROGRAM DESIGN
- STAFF DEVELOPMENT
- PROGRAM EVALUATION
- CONCEPT SUMMARY

LITERACY LEADERSHIP: PREPARE NOW TO LEAD LATER

The baby-boomer generation that is moving rapidly toward retirement is much larger than the generation behind it. This is creating a considerable leadership vacuum at every level of American life, and no less so in the nation's schools. For this reason, it is useful to be informed about the latest thinking on leadership. Leadership in today's schools does not begin or end with appointment to a position. It starts with inspiring a sense of shared responsibility for a school's mission and goals. Organizations of all types, schools included, now are being assessed in terms of "bottom-line" effectiveness. For schools this means increased demand for documentation of higher test scores, lower drop-out rates, improved school attendance, increased ratings on parent satisfaction surveys, and other indicators of effectiveness. Older models of school leadership, which tended to be based on charisma and connections, have not stood up to the new level of demand for accountability. Today, professional knowledge and skill are gaining new currency. Lambert (2005) offers key characteristics of effective leadership:

1. Leadership is about learning together. It is about conversations that generate ideas.
2. Leaders build leaders. They know when to follow someone else's lead. They avoid relationships that are based on "co-dependency," in which the leader is a benevolent authority figure and all others are the "led" and, therefore, more likely to be "mis-led."
3. Leaders pose questions that lead to reexamination of assumptions and beliefs.
4. Leaders raise a range of possibilities in order to avoid simplistic answers.
5. Leaders turn concerns into questions.
6. Leaders recognize that they sometimes will be wrong and acknowledge this with candor, grace, and humility.

A strong Content Area Literacy program relies on leadership at several levels. Ideally, the administration and all faculty are well informed about the study-reading process and effective practices in literacy assessment and instruction and maintain a regular staff development agenda to collaborate and keep abreast of new findings and techniques. The principal is a literacy leader and a core group of teachers on a Literacy Leadership Committee focuses and maintains participation of all content area teachers. Every teacher of every subject is a literacy leader in his or her classroom, theater, studio, or gymnasium.

In reality, there are few "ideal" Content Area Literacy programs. Principals may hold to outdated theories of reading and learning processes, as may groups of "set in their ways" teachers. Healthy change, or "developmental directionality," as Glickman (1985) referred to it, is an evolutionary more than a revolutionary process. Old ways die hard, and change does not occur in the same way or at the same pace across places and circumstances. Effective leaders are able to adjust their leadership style to effect a good match with a given group.

The probability of achieving durable change can be predicted from situational factors, especially those that characterize the performance readiness of the group as well as the designated leader. According to the Hersey-Blanchard Situational Leadership® Model (Hersey & Blanchard, 1977), the group's readiness to perform at a sustained and acceptable level can be characterized as high, medium, or low on three critical factors: (1) the achievement level, or self-motivation and confidence of the group; (2) the sense of responsibility or commitment of group members to assume the various leadership roles necessary to keep an organizational goal on target despite competing and distracting events; and (3) the background—education, experience and skills currently being demonstrated—of the group members to accomplish the subtasks comprising the larger goal.

To be effective change agents, leaders may need to adopt a leadership style that at least initially matches the culture or characteristic ways of functioning of the group rather than the one (based on performance readiness) the Situational Leadership® Model indicates as having the highest probability of successfully influencing the behaviors of the group members. Even great leadership can be dissonance producing and invite resistance (see Figure 14.1, Matching on the Hersey-Blanchard Situational Leadership® Model).

Glickman (1985) observed that what we have in education are *predicaments*, or recurring issues and needs, more so than one-time *problems* with final solutions. Thus, effective literacy leaders are familiar with many likely predicaments and continuously seek the specific knowledge and approaches to address these as they are encountered.

Needed: Informed Advocates

As far as Content Area Literacy is concerned, leadership is urgently needed. Most postelementary teachers are trained to give optimal focus to subject learning or product-over-process learning. Similarly, most elementary teachers have little training or orientation in fusing reading, writing, and thinking to subject mastery. Both as a cause and a reflection of this situation, few school districts and state departments of education emphasize Content Area Literacy objectives at elementary levels and almost none at the postelementary levels. Hence, Content Area Literacy often finds itself without informed advocates. A broadly sampled research report says that more than 50% of teachers do not know about current research-based Content Area Literacy methods, and of those who have been taught these in undergraduate or graduate school, few are using them (Spor & Schneider, 1999). Even the term *Content Area Literacy* is unfamiliar to many

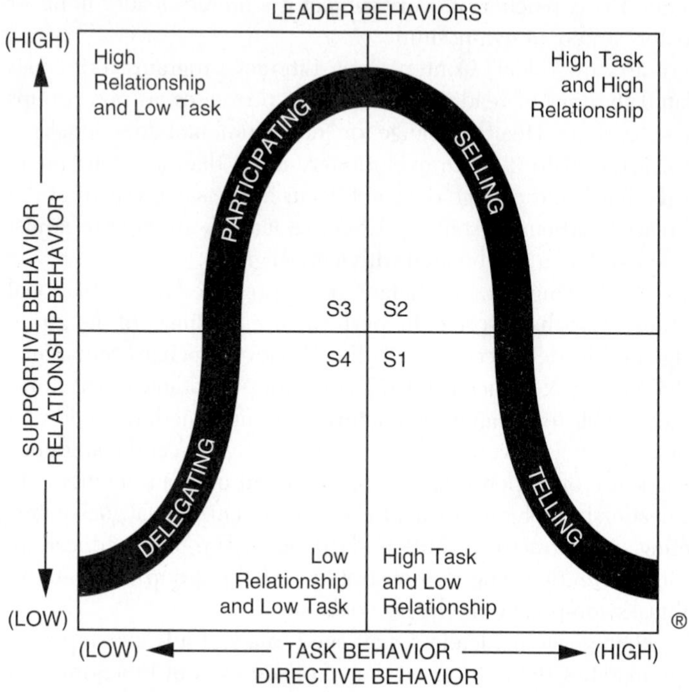

(HIGH) ◄— FOLLOWER READINESS —► (LOW)

Able and Willing and Conifident	Able but Unwilling or Insecure	Unable but Willing or Conifident	Unable and Unwilling or Insecure
R4	R3	R2	R1

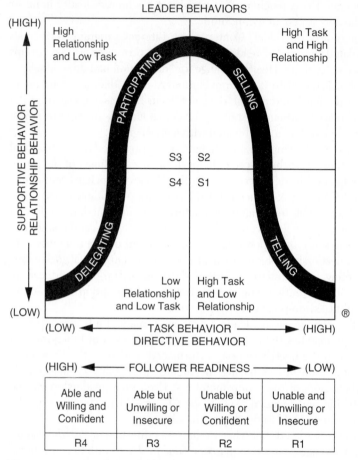

Figure 14.1 Matching on the Hersey-Blanchard Situational Leadership® Model

teachers. Thus, there is a real need in the field for informal advocacy for Content Area Literacy. Three routes to developing this include the following:

1. Have on-site or internal specialist(s) providing daily information and guidance.
2. Develop a leadership committee.
3. Arrange for external consultants and reviews.

▶ COMPONENTS OF CONTENT AREA LITERACY PROGRAMS

The term *program* as used here means any plan targeted at a stated goal or objective, as opposed to a "commercial program." Programs are necessary because day-to-day events can become random and even fragmented when unfolding in quasi-isolated classrooms. For this reason alone, it can be satisfying to get and have a place to refer back to the big picture. Another reason to try to gain a top-down perspective is its value in giving the professional educator an opportunity to exercise a more assertive role in defining, refining, and aligning classroom practices with larger school goals and objectives.

Successful Content Area Literacy programs, typically, are built around five key components that together equal the big picture:

- Vision
- Roles and Responsibilities
- Program Design
- Staff Development
- Program Evaluation

The following sections show how some of these components might be or are being implemented in actual school programs. The examples and discussions include some optional as well as essential components.

▶ VISION

The term *vision* is used here not in the sense of some impractical ideal, but as an agreed-upon set of professionally accepted *ideas* and proven practices. It usually is expressed in the form of a unifying theme or focus that serves as the conceptual basis for all other aspects of the Content Area Literacy program.

Several philosophies have held sway in recent years. Most notable among these has been the mastery learning perspective, which emphasizes heavy doses of direct instruction, a strong dose of testing for transmission of knowledge, and a skills-based orientation. In counterpoint is the *whole-language* orientation, which emphasizes indirect teaching; transactional, or constructionist, subjectivity in reading; virtually no testing; and the integration of content mastery, reading, writing, and speaking largely through literature-based learning.

In recent years, there has been a return to an eclectic philosophy of picking whatever parts, principles, and practices seem to fit a need from a variety of philosophies. A refinement of this fallback position is *Informed Eclecticism* (Manzo & Manzo, 1997b), which has three distinguishing characteristics:

- Every effort must be made to reconcile (seemingly) competing ideas.
- Instructional decisions should be guided not merely by subjective judgments but also by assessment of student needs and reference to research findings that support or fail to support given practices and their degrees of value.
- There must be an emphasis on critical-constructive or inquiry-based learning, since this is the fundamental purpose of schooling.

The chief value of these simple guidelines is that they encourage attention to innovation but help schools resist fads and buzzwords.

Objectives and Goals

The first step in implementing a vision for a Content Area Literacy program is the development of specific *goals* and *objectives*. These become the basis for the development of strategic planning and allocations of resources. Since resources are almost always limited, this is where priorities and compromises should be negotiated.

Here are some examples of sentences and phrases that align with the themes in this text and that can be combined into descriptive statements to guide Content Area Literacy programs and curricula:

- Promoting progress toward reading-language-thinking-content-social/emotional maturity as opposed to mere reading competence.
- Promoting higher-order literacy, or working to assess and remedy shortfalls in critical-constructive thinking, among the academically proficient as well as those reading below age-grade expectations.
- The improvement of reading, writing, speaking, listening, and thinking.
- Promoting multiple literacies, including knowledge of diverse cultures and backgrounds.
- Fusing literacy, content teaching, internet technology, and diverse cultures.
- Creating an inquiry-based, multiple-literacy and learning curriculum.

Realistically, goals such as these may not play well in a particular school or community. For example, it might be fairly easy to get a faculty committee to say that the school literacy program should include attention to the higher literacy needs of the three subtypes of "proficient" readers identified previously in Chapter 8; in practice, however, there likely would be several objections. Objections might range from limited resources to lack of knowledge about what to do. In such situations, it is more practical first to express the focus for the school program in more traditional terms, such as the following:

- Advancing comprehension and vocabulary.
- Promoting efficient reading and study habits.
- Increasing reading and writing to learn.
- Preparing for standardized tests.

Ironically, the most concrete-looking item, "preparing for standardized tests," may best open the door for attention to higher literacy since questions on such tests can tend to be of a more abstract nature than on conventional classroom tests. As such, the standardized test will show which students have been receiving good grades in class despite serious weakness in abstract thinking. In most cases, school goals and objectives will be expressed in a combination of the preceding terms with some locally recognized need. Examples of specific local needs might include functional literacy for job flexibility, college preparation, or effective reading and use of technology.

▶ ROLES AND RESPONSIBILITIES

The chief element in translating program ideals into practice is the assignment of roles and responsibilities. Following are the most commonly acknowledged responsibilities of the school administrator, reading specialist, and classroom teacher.

The School Principal

The school principal has the primary responsibility for initiating and supporting the development and implementation of the goals, objectives, curriculum, and design of the literacy program. In this capacity, the principal is the one who needs to know enough to initiate schoolwide survey testing, program evaluation, and ongoing literacy-related faculty development programs. It also is the principal's responsibility to cultivate a positive school climate. It is important to note, however, that "a poor climate can inhibit learning, but a positive climate does not guarantee success" (Hoffman, 1991, p. 926). In other words, "team building," while truly important to faculty morale, should not become a primary goal since it is not easily translated into improved student performance. A "mature" faculty, as illustrated in the discussion of Figure 14.1 earlier in this chapter, is not only willing and motivated; it also has the knowledge and experience related to the accomplishment of a given goal. Administrative leadership is like glue on a chair—largely unrecognized or appreciated when working, but evident and faulted when it is not (Glickman, 1985).

The Reading Specialist

The term *reading education* as the name of this field of study is being replaced with the term *literacy education* for a variety of reasons. However, in this discussion of the role of the "reading specialist," we are retaining the traditional terminology, primarily because this term still is more widely used in practice. Additionally, there is an increasing use of the term *literacy coach* for a role that is significantly different from the traditional role of the reading specialist.

The reading specialist traditionally holds a masters degree in Reading Education (now often renamed Literacy Education). This degree, according to national standards, qualifies its holders to develop, administer, evaluate, and/or teach in instructional reading programs for pre-kindergarten through adult levels, in public and private school settings, and, increasingly, in business and industry. (This latter segment of the field, referred to as *workplace literacy*, has a great deal of overlap [60% to 70%] with Content Area literacy.)

In middle and high school Content Area Literacy programs, reading specialists are liaisons between and among individuals serving in various roles at the district level, at the school administration level, and on the school literacy committee, as well as the content area teachers. In many schools, the most important role of the reading specialist, initially, is to raise teachers' (and often administrators') awareness of the fundamental precepts of Content Area Literacy, thereby dispelling common misconceptions about reading, such as those discussed in Chapter 1:

- Students learn to read in elementary school.
- Students get better at reading by reading.

- At higher levels, "reading" becomes a function of IQ.
- Reading, if needed, should be taught in a separate pull-out class.
- Content teachers already are held accountable for more curriculum objectives than they can cover, without adding reading to their responsibilities.
- Some subjects don't involve reading at all.
- Most students read more or less on grade level.
- If students have difficulty learning from their textbooks, the textbooks must be too difficult.

Middle and high schools vary greatly in maturity, as defined by the Hersey-Blanchard model discussed earlier, with respect to implementing an effective Content Area Reading program. Thus, the best leadership style for the reading specialist may vary from highly informational and supervisory with immature faculty groups, to a much higher degree of delegation with mature groups. Some general aspects of the reading specialist's role include the following:

- Serving as resource person in the development of Content Area Literacy goals and objectives, and overall design of the program.
- Reviewing and interpreting student reading achievement test data, to assist in ongoing evaluation of the Content Area Literacy program.
- Providing ongoing assistance to teachers, individually and in groups, including demonstrating Content Area Literacy teaching methods in classrooms or small or large group in-service sessions, evaluating and/or preparing instructional materials, and helping teachers evaluate the reading levels of their students. (With some teacher groups, the reading specialist may need to begin with inservices to present basic information about the study-reading process, as discussed in Chapter 2, and an instructional Framework for text-based instruction, as shown in Chapter 3.)
- Providing references, as appropriate, to support services such as librarians, counselors, district-level and community services, and outside consultants.

The Literacy Leadership Committee

Everything about newer concepts of leadership suggests the importance of building a bottom-up consensus for the Content Area Literacy program. Leadership today is based on consensus building. The "chapters" on how to build consensus and get it pointed in the best direction are still being written. The idea of a *literacy leadership committee*, however, is looking like one fairly sound way to proceed. The confounding nature of group dynamics notwithstanding, a literacy leadership committee has merit for several reasons:

- It creates an advocacy group for an area of programming that otherwise tends to be underrepresented within the organizational structure of most schools.
- It allows leadership to emerge from within the organization.

- It provides a means of building consensus and systemic support over time.
- It creates responsible parties but is not vested in one individual and hence likely to rise and fall with that person's social influence.
- It tells faculty, students, community, and central administration that literacy is a valued goal, *a cause beyond oneself.*
- It almost always leads to seeking higher levels of expertise as issues are refined and important implementation decisions are pending.

The Content Area Teacher

The ultimate power and responsibility for the overall Content Area Literacy program rests with classroom teachers. A vital Content Area Literacy program enlists teachers' participation in the identification and development of the goals, objectives, curriculum, design, and evaluation procedures for the schoolwide literacy program. This participation helps ensure whole-hearted implementation of the program.

There is a growing belief that teachers may be the chief agents for change in literacy programming. For a *source* book on supporting this movement, see Lawrence G. Erickson's (1995) *Supervision of Literacy Programs—Teachers as Grass-Roots Change Agents.* It is important to note that durable results are not possible without scheduled time for classroom teachers to make their contribution (Glickman, 1985).

▶ PROGRAM DESIGN

The core of any effective Content Area Literacy program is every content area teacher's classroom use of research-based methods and approaches to implement text-based instruction that aligns with the nature of the study-reading process. In addition, a number of special services can be made available.

Special Services

Programs for students with special needs that cannot easily be met in a regular classroom setting may be in the form of pull-out programs, elective or mini-courses, resource rooms, and drop-in help. It now also can include e-mail and phone "hot-line" help.

Pull-Out Services

In *pull-out services,* a reading specialist or other teacher offers diagnostic and/or remedial/corrective tutoring for students who cannot be adequately provided for in regular classes. This component is intended to ensure that:

1. No remedial-level reader falls through the cracks and leaves school quasi-literate after 13 years in our charge.
2. Students whose first language is not English and language-handicapped students receive special attention when this appears necessary.

3. Assessment and treatment are provided for other difficult, different, or sometimes overlooked problems (e.g., higher-order literacy needs, cultural differences, study skills deficiencies, and reading-related writing, grammar, and spelling).

In general, pull-out programs create a safety net, in which a member of the faculty becomes responsible for the subject that no one seems to think that he or she can teach. Typically, the reading specialist also holds conferences with parents and seeks additional resources, both within the school and district and in the community, for those students at risk of becoming school dropouts or social graduates.

Elective Courses

Content Area Literacy specialists in middle and high schools frequently offer exploratory mini-courses or full elective courses in remedial reading, and on topics such as study strategies, reading rate, critical reading, and vocabulary enrichment. This type of short-term, focused instruction reinforces and builds on the ongoing Content Area Reading instruction provided daily in content classrooms. It also extends the services of the literacy specialist and committee to a fuller complement of the student body.

Learning Centers

The learning center usually is the hub out of which a reading specialist operates. Bernice Bragstad (1985), an International Reading Association award-winning Content Area Literacy specialist, says that her former high school's learning center provided these three services:

1. Individualized or small-group tutoring in any subject or skill, provided by a select cadre of proficient student-tutors or the reading specialist
2. Individualized help with writing, provided by several English teachers who served their duty periods in this way
3. A preventative biweekly summer tutoring program conducted by high school students for middle school students

In addition to these services, learning centers can offer walk-in assistance with almost any pressing homework or academic problem. Many districts extend this concept to the offer of homework hotlines and websites.

▶ STAFF DEVELOPMENT

A well-planned staff development schedule is an important means of ensuring that programs mature and endure over time in an institutional setting that undergoes frequent changes in administration, staff, and faculty. An effective plan for staff development should include four basic components:

- Regular review of the research on the study-reading process, even if this is brief: Continuing teachers' understandings will be reinforced, and new teachers may recognize that they need to seek additional guidance in this crucial knowledge base.

- Regular review of instructional methods and techniques that are working, and presentation of new ones.
- Regular review of schoolwide reading achievement data, including analysis of trends and implications of these for instruction.
- Regular review of techniques for assessing student reading level in specific course textbooks.

Marzano (1977) suggests that the first question that should be asked when planning staff development is, "What part of the learning process needs to be improved?" See mcrel.org, a federal teaching-learning laboratory, for Marzano's "Framework for Planning Staff Development."

At the upper end of faculty 'maturity,' a generative means of enhancing staff development is support for action research. Action research is conducted by teachers in their own classrooms. It is a proven way to improve instruction. Teachers who plan, conduct, and report their own classroom research show a significant increase in their sense of ownership of ideas, while demonstrating the value of basic Content Area Literacy methodology (Santa, Isaacson, & Manning, 1987).

The process of involving teachers in action research projects is more manageable today than ever before. Assistance with research design and statistics usually can be had for a small fee or even free from a school district's own office of research, from advanced degree-seeking teachers, and/or from nearby university campuses.

Consultants: Look for Certified Experts

External literacy consultants are a logical progression for most schools. It is unrealistic to expect school administrators and leaders, and even on-site literacy specialists and advocates, to know all they need to about this area of school programming. But this need for external assistance always raises the specter of who is an "expert" and "don't experts often disagree?" There are a lot of predicaments inherent in this scenario, and they are not of leadership but of competent stewardship, attention to details, and lack of professional knowledge.

Although schools of education are not blameless for such lapses in effective teacher education and training, they are most likely the best hope for fixing such problems in the near term. *Certified* (that is, college and university educated) *experts* tend to disagree much less than one would think and on fewer matters. Most of the seeming dilemmas of conflicting "experts" come from failure to establish who is certified and who is somehow self-proclaimed.

A meta-analysis of staff developments of many studies (Wade, 1984–1985) and our own more recent research (Manzo & Manzo, 1995) support the following conclusions:

- Regardless of who conducts in-service sessions (trainers come under many different job classifications), teachers are more likely to benefit when they use methods that permit learning by doing.

1. Make informal textbook diagnostic tests.
2. Create a reading-study-thinking guide.
3. Identify key questions that underlie a course's content.
4. Search for instructional paradigms that virtually define the most complete way to teach something that is fundamental. Three such paradigms include the Directed Reading–Thinking Activity (a design for teaching a complete content literacy lesson), the Frayer model (for teaching vocabulary and concepts), and the "writing process" (for teaching all phases of effective writing).
5. To further ensure that teachers are becoming investors in a school program, invite them to participate in identifying and solving instructional problems. (See Chapter 8 on critical-constructive teaching and learning for relevant ideas.)
6. Recommend the Listen-Read-Discuss method from Chapter 1 as an initial offering. This *time-release* method was designed to stimulate professional discussion and to invite increasingly more sophisticated discussion among the professional staff.
7. Administer instruments that tend to uncover areas of suboptimal literacy development, for example, *The Informal Reading–Thinking Inventory* (Manzo, Manzo, & McKenna, 1995), for middle grades.

Figure 14.2 Suggested in-service heuristic/discovery workshop activities

- Move beyond *doing* to discovery-learning workshops that are built around *heuristic* tasks, actions, and activities that result in penetrating insights. See Figure 14.2 for suggested in-service discovery workshop activities.
- There is no magical combination of methods for successful in-service education. Nevertheless, in-service programs that use observation, microteaching, auditory and visual feedback, and practice, either individually or in some combination, are more effective than programs that do not use these methods.

▶ PROGRAM EVALUATION

Information about students' reading status and about the effects of the school program on this basic school obligation is essential to determining what needs to be done and how best to do it. Literacy leaders in their various roles—principal, reading specialist, and teacher—should keep these questions in the forefront of all aspects of program planning:

- Are students making expected progress in *reading*?
- If not, why not?
- How can program lapses be strengthened?

Sustained attention to these questions will tend to lead to extending assessment beyond the basic annual standardized testing to look at more specific aspects of instruction and "process variables" that support reading achievement, such as "engaged time on task." There needs to be clear evidence that sufficient time (we estimate, no less than 30% to 40% of the total school day) be spent on "basics" such as these:

- Organized presentation of information
- Frontloading, or preparation for Guided Silent Reading
- Discussion and supervised study
- Frequent, brief periods of additional help to students with special needs

Chapter 10 on assessment offers several techniques for content teachers to use in evaluating their own students' ability to read and understand their own specific content textbooks.

▶ CONCEPT SUMMARY

There are many levels of leadership in an effective Content Area Literacy program. In the best programs, all content area teachers are literacy leaders in their classrooms. It might even be said that in the best classrooms, students become literacy leaders. A literacy leadership committee can maintain essential channels of communication among participants to plan, implement, and maintain program components. If a visitor to the school inquires about the "literacy" or "reading" program, any member of the school community should be ready and willing to explain that reading is taught in every class every day. They should know what special provisions are made for students with severe reading needs but also that this is but a part of the schoolwide literacy program.

APPENDIX

MODEL PROFESSIONAL PORTFOLIO RECORDER AND PLANNER

A professional portfolio, begun early in your career, can be an invaluable lifelong resource. To construct a model portfolio, you will need the following materials:

- A three-ring binder (you may want to begin with a one-inch binder and transfer materials to a larger-size binder as your collection grows).
- Nine 3-hole notebook pockets for storing materials in various sections of the portfolio (see later sections).
- Attachable index tabs to mark each section (attach these to the pockets, since these extend farther than regular-sized sheets).
- Section titles (described next), copied onto separate sheets for insertion into the notebook, between pockets.

With these simple materials, and a bit of reflection on your past, present, and future, you are ready to assemble a model portfolio that will grow with you through your professional career.

Section I: Guiding Thoughts

In this section, record relevant quotations you run across that strike you as worth remembering and that can serve to keep your thinking and instructional decision making on track.

A. Thoughts and perspectives on careers in general

Examples

- Successful careers don't just happen; they are the result of vision, planning, and effort.
- Most successful careers are beset by occasional setbacks. Expect these, and be ready to push on.
- When truth stands in your way, you are headed in the wrong direction.

B. Thoughts and perspectives on teachers and teaching

Examples

- The art of teaching is the art of assisting discovery.
- The enthusiastic teacher is a lifelong student.
- The finer the instruction, the more it invites; the poorer it is, the more it compels.

C. Thoughts and perspectives on schools and schooling

Examples

- Nowadays, school heads are chosen to run a school rather than lead it.
- The school's task is to take a lot of live wires and see that they get well grounded.

Section II: Employment Record

In this section, keep a running record of both teaching and nonteaching experiences, and store an updated resume.

A. Nonteaching job experiences

B. Educational job experiences

C. Other

(Pocket: current resume)

Section III: Personal History (Birth to High School)

In this section, make relevant notes about your family and early school background, and store related documents.

A. Family background

B. Medical/health factors

C. Social, athletic affiliations

D. Academic record, K–12

E. Hobbies and interests

F. Significant memories

(Pocket: birth certificate, passport, school records, early photos, letters, memorabilia)

Section IV: Personal History (Postsecondary)

In this section, make notes about your college life and education, and store related documents.

A. Academic record (degrees, majors, minors)

B. Activities (extracurricular; organizations, religious, athletic)

C. Social life (personal and family)
D. Intellectual development (books, magazines, ideas)

(Pocket: transcripts, letters of reference, other records)

Section V: Material Accounting

In this section, keep notes about your financial standing and store related documents.

A. Gifts, trusts, support
B. Income history
C. Loan history
D. Assets (stocks, car, furniture, property)
E. Approximate net worth
F. Prospects (likely legacies and/or opportunities)

(Pocket: financial records, photos, memorabilia)

Section VI: Professional History

In this section, make notes about your teaching career, and store related documents.

A. Certificates
B. Evaluations/recommendations
C. Memorable teachers and colleagues
D. Teaching experiences: subjects, grade levels, situations
E. Related nonteaching roles and experiences
F. Memorable in-service sessions, conferences, sabbaticals
G. Memorable articles, books, papers
H. Membership and roles in committees and professional organizations
I. Grants, travel, awards
J. Summer activities and employment

(Pocket: teaching certificates, letters, articles or summaries)

Section VII: Self-Appraisals

In this section, keep notes on an ongoing self-assessment, and store related records.

A. Attitudes
B. Interests and abilities
C. Temperament/personality

D. Teaching/learning style

E. Personal assessment of strengths and weaknesses as a person and as a teacher

(Pocket: records)

Section VIII: Occasional Notes

In this section, make additional notes of memorable events and experiences, and store related records.

A. Notes on memorable personal events (marriage, deaths, births, friendships)

B. Notes on memorable professional experiences (significant mentor relationships, special students)

(Pocket: records)

Section IX: Blueprints

In this section, keep notes about long-term career plans, and store related documents.

A. Personal career goals

B. Objectives that might contribute to your professional education

(Pocket: related articles, notes, and documents)

Section X: Teaching Competence

In this section, keep notes about your experiences in using various teaching approaches and methods, and store related materials.

A. Teaching methods you have mastered

B. Teaching methods you intend to try

(Pocket: related articles and notes on each method)

REFERENCES

Aaronson, E., Blaney, N., Sikes, J., Stevan, C., & Snapp, N. (1975, February). The jigsaw route to learning and liking. *Psychology Today*, 43–50.

Aaronson, E., Stephan, C., Sikes, J., Blaney, N., & Snapp, M. (1978). *The jigsaw classroom.* Beverly Hills, CA: Sage.

Adams, E. K. (1982). What research says to the disciplinarian. In G. H. McNinch (Ed.), *Readings in the disciplines, Second yearbook of the American Reading Forum* (pp. 109–111). Athens, GA: American Reading Forum.

Adler, M. J. (1982). *The paideia proposal.* New York: Macmillan.

Alexander, P.A., & Fox, E. (2004). A historical perspective on reading research and practice. In R.B. Ruddell & N.J. Unrau (Eds.), *Theoretical models and processes of reading* (5th ed., pp. 33–68). Newark, DE: International Reading Association.

Allen, K., & Ingulsrud, J. E. (2003). Manga literacy: Popular culture and the reading habits of Japanese college students. *Journal of Adolescent & Adult Literacy 46*(8), 674–683.

Alley, G., & Deshler, D. (1980). *Teaching the learning disabled adolescent: Strategies and methods.* Denver, CO: Love.

Alvermann, D. E., & Boothby, P. R. (1983). A preliminary investigation of the differences in children's retention of "inconsiderate" text. *Reading Psychology, 4,* 237–246.

Alvermann, D. E., Dillon, D. R., & O'Brien, D. G. (1987). *Using discussion to promote reading comprehension.* Newark, DE: International Reading Association.

Alvermann, D. E., Moon, J. S., & Hagood, M. C. (1999). *Popular Culture in the Classroom: Teaching and Researching Critical Media Literacy,* Newark, DE: International Reading Association.

Anders, P. L., Bos, C. S., & Filip, D. (1984). The effect of semantic feature analysis on the reading comprehension of learning-disabled students. In J. A. Niles & L. A. Harris (Eds.), *Changing perspectives on research in reading/language processing and instruction. Thirty-third yearbook of the National Reading Conference* (pp. 162–166). Rochester, NY: National Reading Conference.

Anderson, R. C., & Nagy, W. E. (1989). *Word meanings* (Tech. Rep. No. 485). Cambridge, MA: Bolt, Beranek and Newman.

Ankney, P., & McClurg, E. (1981). Testing Manzo's Guided Reading Procedure. *The Reading Teacher, 34,* 681–685.

Applebee, A. N. (1981). *Writing in the secondary school.* Urbana, IL: National Council of Teachers of English.

Applebee, A., Langer, J., Mullis, I., Lathan, A., & Gentile, C. (1994). *NAEP 1992 Writing Report Card.* Washington, DC: U.S. Department of Education, Office of Educational Research and Improvement.

Artley, A. S. (1944). A study of certain relationships existing between general reading comprehension and reading comprehension in a specific subject-matter area. *Journal of Educational Research, 37,* 464–473.

Athanses, S. (1988). Developing a classroom community of interpreters. *English Journal, 77,* 45–48.

Ausubel, D. P. (1960). The use of advance organizers in the learning and retention of meaningful verbal material. *Journal of Educational Psychology, 51*, 267–272.

Bacon, E. (1963). *Notes on the piano.* Syracuse, NY: Syracuse University Press.

Baines, L. (1998). The future of the written word. In J. S. Simmons & L. Baines (Eds.) *Language study in middle school, high school and beyond: Views on enhancing the study of language.* (pp. 190–214). Newark, DE: International Reading Association.

Baker, L., & Brown, A. L. (1984). Metacognitive skills and reading. In P. D. Pearson (Ed.), *Handbook of reading research* (pp. 333–394). New York: Longman.

Baker, R. L., & Schutz, R. E. (Eds). (1972). *Instructional product research.* New York: Van Nostrand.

Baldwin, R. S., & Kaufman, R. K. (1979). A concurrent validity study of the Raygor readability estimate. *Journal of Reading, 23*, 148–153.

Baloche, L., Mauger, M. L., Willis, T. M., Filinuk, J. R., & Michalsky, B. V. (1993). Fishbowls, creative controversy, talking chips: Exploring literature cooperatively. *English Journal, 82*, 43–48.

Bandura, A., & Walters, R. (1963). *Social learning and personality development.* New York: Hold, Rinehart & Winston.

Barton, J. (1995). Conducting effective classroom discussions. *Journal of Reading. 38*, 346–350.

Baumann, J. F., & Kameenui, E. J. (1991). Research on vocabulary instruction. In J. Flood, J. M. Jensen, D. Lapp, & J. Squire (Eds.), *Handbook of research on teaching the English language arts* (pp. 604–631). Upper Saddle River, NJ: Prentice Hall.

Bean, T. W. (1981). Matching materials and strategies for comprehension. In V. Pesqueira & C. Boling (Eds). *Reading: A Foundation for Success.* Fourth Yearbook of the Arizona State University Reading Conference, (pp. 210–211). Tempe, Arizona.

Bean, T. W. (2000). Reading in the content areas: Social constructivist dimensions. In M. L., Kamil, P. B., Mosenthal, P. D., Pearson, & R. Barr, (Eds.), *Handbook of reading research, volume III.* (pp. 629–644). Mahwah, NJ: Erlbaum.

Bean, T. W., & Bishop, A. (1992). Polar opposites: A strategy for guiding students' critical reading and discussion. In E. Dischner et. al (Eds.) *Reading in the Content Areas.* (pp. 247–254). Dubuque, IA: Kendall/ Hunt.

Bean T. W., Bean, S. K., & Bean, K. F., (1999). Intergenerational conversations and two adolescents' multiple literacies: Implications for redefining content area literacy. *Journal of Adolescent and Adult Literacy, 42*, 438–448.

Bean, T. W., & Moni, K. (2003). Developing students' critical literacy: Exploring identity construction in young adult fiction. *Journal of Adolescent & Adult Literacy, 46*(8), 638–648.

Bean, T. W., & Pardi, R. (1979). A field test of a guided reading strategy. *Journal of Reading, 23*, 144–147.

Bereiter, C. & Scardamalia, M. (1985). Cognitive coping strategies and the problem of inert knowledge. In S. F. Chipman, J. W. Segal, & R. Glazer, (Eds.) *Thinking and learning skills, Vol. 2: Current research and open questions* (pp. 65–80). Hillsdale, NJ: Erlbaum.

Bintz, W. (1997). Exploring reading nightmares of middle and secondary school teachers. *Journal of Adolescent & Adult Literacy, 41*, 12–24.

Bishop, A. (2003). Course supplement for Reading 508. (Available from School of Education, P.O. Box 6868, California State University—Fullerton, Fullerton, CA 92834).

Blanc, R. A. (1977). Cloze-plus as an alternative to "guides" for understanding and appreciating poetry. *Journal of Reading, 21*, 215–218.

Bloom, B. S. (1976). *Human characteristics and school learning.* New York: McGraw-Hill.

Bormuth, J. R. (1965). Validities of grammatical and semantic classifications of cloze test scores. In J. A. Figurel (Ed.), *Reading and inquiry. International Reading Association Conference Proceedings* (Vol. *10*, pp. 283–286). Newark, DE: International Reading Association.

Bradley, A. (1999). Science group finds middle school textbooks inadequate. *Education Week, 19*(6), 5.

Bragstad, B. (1985, March). *Mapping: Using both sides of the brain.* Lecture handout, International Reading Association State Council Meeting. Orlando, FL.

Bromley, K. D. (1985). Precis writing and outlining enhance content learning. *The Reading Teacher, 38*, 406–411.

Brown, A. L. (1980). Metacognition development and reading. In R. J. Spiro, B. C. Bruce, & W. F. Brewer (Eds.), *Theoretical issues in reading comprehension* (pp. 453–481). Hillsdale, NJ: Erlbaum Associates.

Brown, H. & Cambourne, B. (1987). *Read and retell.* Portsmouth: Heinemann.

Brozo, W.G. (1990). Hiding out in secondary classrooms: Coping strategies of unsuccessful readers. *Journal of Reading, 33*, 324–328.

Bruer, J. T. (1993). *Schools for thought: A science of learning in the classroom.* Cambridge, MA: A Bradford Book of MIT Press.

Bruner, J. S. (1966). *Toward a theory of instruction.* Cambridge, MA: Harvard University Press.

Burke, K. (1950/1969). *A rhetoric of motives.* Berkeley, CA: University of California Press.

Bush, V. (1945). *Science—the endless frontier: a report to the President by Vannevar Bush, Director of the Office of Scientific Research and Development, July 1945.* Washington, DC: U.S. Government Printing Office.

Calfee, R. C., Dunlap, K. L., & Wat, A. Y. (1994). Authentic discussion of texts in middle school. *Journal of Reading, 37*(7), 546–556.

Campbell, J., Donahue, P., Reese, C., & Phillips, G. (1996). *NAEP 1994 reading report card for the nation and the states.* Washington, DC: U.S. Department of Education, OERI, 1996.

Camperell, K. (1982). Vygotsky's theory of intellectual development: The effect of subject matter instruction on self-regulated cognitive processes. In G. H. McNich (Ed.), *Reading in the disciplines. Second yearbook of the American Reading Forum* (pp. 33–35). Athens: University of Georgia.

Carr, E. M., & Ogle, D. M. (1987). K-W-L Plus: A strategy for comprehension and summarization. *Journal of Reading, 30*, 626–631.

Casale, U. P. (1985). Motor imaging: A reading-vocabulary strategy. *Journal of Reading, 28*, 619–621.

Casale, U. P., & Kelly, B. W. (1980). Problem-solving approach to study skills (PASS) for students in professional schools. *Journal of Reading, 24*, 232–238.

Casale, U. P., & Manzo, A. V. (1983). Differential effects of cognitive, affective, and proprioceptive approaches on vocabulary acquisition. In G. H. McNinch (Ed.), *Reading research to reading practice. Third yearbook of the American Reading Forum* (pp. 71–73). Athens, GA: American Reading Forum.

Cerullo, M. (1997). *Reading the environment: Children's literature in the science classroom.* Portsmouth, NH: Heinemann.

Chandler-Olcott, K., Mahar, D. (2003). Adolescents' anime-inspired "fanfictions": An exploration of multiliteracies. *Journal of Adolescent & Adult Literacy, 46*(7), 556–566.

Chase, R. H. (1926). *The ungeared mind.* Philadelphia: F.A. Davis Company, Publishers.

Ciardiello, A. V. (1998). Did you ask a good question today? Alternative cognitive and metacognitive strategies. *Journal of Adolescent and Adult Literacy. 42,* 210–219.

Ciardiello, A. V., & Cicchelli, T. (1994). The effects of instructional training models and content knowledge on student questioning in social studies. *The Journal of Social Studies Research, 19,* 30–37.

Clewell, S. E., & Haidemos, J. (1983). Organizational strategies to increase comprehension. *Reading World, 22,* 314–321.

Cloer, T., Jr., & Denton, G. R. (1995). The effects of read-along tapes on the comprehension of middle school students. In K. Camparell, B. L. Hayes, & R. Telfer (Eds.), *Linking literacy: past, present, and future. American Reading Forum Yearbook* (Vol. 15, pp. 85–92). Logan, Utah: American Reading Forum Yearbook.

Collins, C. (1987). Content mastery strategies aid classroom discussion. *The Reading Teacher, 40,* 816–818.

Condus, M. M., Marshall, K. J., & Miller, S. R. (1986). Effect of the key-word mnemonic strategy on vocabulary acquisition and maintenance by learning disabled children. *Journal of Learning Disabilities, 19,* 609–613.

Crafton, L. K. (1983). Learning from reading: What happens when students generate their own background information? *Journal of Reading, 26,* 586–592.

Culver, V. I., Godfrey, H. C., & Manzo, A. V. (1972). A partial reanalysis of the validity of the cloze procedure as an appropriate measure of reading comprehension [Research report summary]. *Journal of Reading, 16,* 256–257.

Cummins, J. (2001). *Language, power, and pedagogy: Bilingual children in the crossfire.* Clevedon, UK: Multilingual Matters.

Cunningham, D., & Shablak, S. L. (1975). Selective Reading Guide-O-Rama: The content teacher's best friend. *Journal of Reading, 18,* 380–382.

Cunningham, J. W., Cunningham, P. M., & Arthur, S. V. (1981). *Middle and secondary school reading.* New York: Longman.

Cunningham, P. M., & Cunningham, J. W. (1976). SSSW, better content-writing. *The Clearing House, 49,* 237–238.

Cunningham, P. M., Moore, S. A., Cunningham, J. W., & Moore, D. W. (1983). *Reading in elementary classrooms: Strategies and observations.* New York: Longman.

Dahmus, M. E. (1970). How to teach verbal problems. *School Science and Mathematics, 70,* 121–138.

Davey, B. (1983). Think aloud—Modeling the cognitive processes of reading comprehension. *Journal of Reading, 27,* 44–47.

DeBlase, G. (2003). Acknowledging agency while accommodating romance: Girls negotiating meaning in literacy transactions. *Journal of Adolescent & Adult Literacy, 46*(8), 624–635.

Derby, T. (1987). Reading instruction and course related materials for vocational high school students. *Journal of Reading, 30,* 308–316.

Desmond, R. (1997). Media literacy in the home: Acquisition vs. deficit models. In R. Kubey (ed.). *Media literacy in the information age* (pp. 323–343). New Brunswick, N.J.: Transaction Books.

Diehl, W. A., & Mikulecky, L. (1980). The nature of reading as work. *Journal of Reading, 24,* 221–227.

Diggs, V. M. (1973). The relative effectiveness of the SQ3R method, a mechanized approach, and a combination method for training remedial reading to college freshmen (Doctoral dissertation, West Virginia University, Morgantown, 1972). *Dissertation Abstracts International, 33,* 5964A. (University Microfilms No. 74-4, 786)

Doctorow, M., Wittrock, M. C., & Marks, C. (1978). Generative processes in reading comprehension. *Journal of Educational Psychology, 70,* 109–118.

Dodson, S. (1997). *The mother daughter book club.* New York: Harper Perennial.

Donald, M., Sr. (1967). The SQ3R method in grade seven. *Journal of Reading, 11,* 33–35, 43.

Dortch, S. (1995, April). Talking with fewer words. *American Demographics.* (April) http://www.demographics.com/publications/.

Duckworth, S., & Taylor, R. (1995). Creating and assessing literacy in at-risk students through hypermedia portfolios. *Reading Improvement, 32*(1), 26–31.

Duffelmeyer, F. (1994). Effective anticipation guide statements for learning from expository prose. *Journal of Reading, 37,* 452–457.

Duffelmeyer, F., Baum, D., & Merkley, D. (1987). Maximizing reader-text confrontation with an extended anticipation guide. *Journal of Reading, 31,* 146–151.

Duke, C. R. (1987). Integrating reading, writing, and thinking skills into the music class. *Journal of Reading, 31,* 152–157.

Duke, N. K. (2000). 3.6 minutes per day: The scarcity of informational texts in first grade. *Reading Research Quarterly, 35*(2), 202–224.

Durkin, D. (1978–1979). What classroom observations reveal about comprehension instruction. *Reading Research Quarterly, 14,* 481–533.

Eanet, M. G., & Manzo, A. V. (1976). REAP—A strategy for improving reading/writing/study skills. *Journal of Reading, 19,* 647–652.

Echevarria, J., Vogt, M. E., & Short, D. (2004). *Making content comprehensible for English learners: The SIOP model* (2nd ed.). (Ch. 5, pp. 92–93). Boston: Allyn & Bacon.

Ediger, M. (1992). The middle school student and interest in reading. *Journal of Affective Reading Education, 10*(2), 9–13.

Edwards, P. A., & Simpson, L. (1986). Bibliotherapy: A strategy for communication between parents and their children. *Journal of Reading, 30,* 110–118.

El-Hindi, A. E. (2003). Integrating literacy and science in the classroom: From ecomysteries to readers theatre. *The Reading Teacher, 56*(6), 536–539.

El-Koumy, A.S.A. (1996). Effects of Three Questioning Strategies on EFL Reading Comprehension. Paper presented at the Annual Meeting of the Teachers of English to Speakers of Other Languages (30th, Chicago, IL, March 1996). (ERIC Document Reproduction Service No. ED411696).

Ennis, R. H. (1962). The concept of critical thinking. *Harvard Educational Review, 32,* 81–111.

Erickson, L. G. (1995). *Supervision of literacy programs: teachers as grass-roots change agents.* Boston: Allyn & Bacon.

Ericson, B., Hubler, M., Bean, T. W., Smith, C. C., & McKenzie, J. V. (1987). Increasing critical reading in junior high classrooms. *Journal of Reading, 30,* 430–439.

Fairclough, N. (1989). *Language and Power.* London: Longman.

Farr, R. (1992). Putting it all together: Solving the reading assessment puzzle. *The Reading Teacher, 46*(1), 26–37.

Farris, P. J., & Kaczmarski, D. (1988). Whole language: A closer look. *Contemporary Education, 59*(2), 77–81.

Feathers, K. M., & Smith, F. R. (1987). Meeting the reading demands of the real world: Literacy based content instruction. *Journal of Reading, 30,* 506–511.

Flower, L., & Hayes, J. R. (1981). A cognitive process theory of writing. *College Composition and Communication, 32,* 365–387.

Frager, A. M., & Thompson, L. C. (1985). Conflict: The key to critical reading instruction. *Journal of Reading, 28,* 676–683.

Fry, E. (1968). A readability formula that saves time. *Journal of Reading, 11,* 513–516, 575–578.

Fry, E. (1977). Fry's readability graph: Clarification, validity, and extension to level 17. *Journal of Reading, 21,* 242–252.

Galbraith, J. K. (1996, May). *Interview on CNBC [Television broadcast].* New York: NBC.

Garber, K. S. (1995). *The effects of transmissional, transactional, and transformational reader-response strategies on middle school students' thinking complexity and social development.* (Unpublished doctoral dissertation, Kansas City, MO: University of Missouri–Kansas City.)

Gardner, H. (1983). *Frames of mind: The theory of multiple intelligences.* New York: Harper and Row.

Gardner, H. (1985). *The mind's new science.* New York: Basic Books.

Gauthier, L. R. (1996). Using guided conversation to increase students' content area comprehension. *Journal of Adolescent & Adult Literacy, 39,* 310–312.

Gee, T. C., & Rakow, S. J. (1987). Content reading specialists evaluate teaching practices. *Journal of Reading, 31,* 234–237.

Gentile, L. M. (1980). *Using sports and physical education to strengthen content area reading skills.* Newark, DE: International Reading Association.

Gipe, J. P. (1978–1979). Investigating techniques for teaching word meanings. *Reading Research Quarterly, 14,* 624–644.

Gipe, J.P. (1998). *Multiple paths to literacy: Corrective reading techniques for classroom teachers.* Upper Saddle River, NJ: Prentice Hall.

Glickman, C. D. (1985). *Supervision of instruction: A developmental approach.* Newton, MA: Allyn & Bacon.

Glass, G. G. (1973). *Teaching decoding as separate from reading.* Garden City, NY: Adelphi University Press.

Godin, S. (1999). *Permission Marketing: Turning strangers into friends, and friends into customers.* New York: Simon & Schuster.

Gomez, M. L., Graue, M. E., & Bloch, M. N. (1991). Reassessing portfolio assessment: Rhetoric and reality. *Language Arts, 68*(8), 620–628.

Gough, E. B., & Cosky, M. J. (1977). One second of reading again. In N. J. Castellan, Jr., D. Pisoni, & G. Potts (Eds.), *Cognitive theory* (Vol. 2, pp. 271–288). Hillsdale, NJ: Erlbaum.

Gray, D. (1988, Summer). *Socratic seminars: Basic education and reformation. Basic Education: Issues, Answers, and Facts, 3, 14.* Washington, DC: Council for Basic Education.

Gray, W. S. (1946). *On their own in reading.* Chicago: Scott, Foresman.

Greenewald, M. J., & Wolf, A. E. (1980). Professional journals in secondary education: Which ones do teachers recommend most? *The Clearing House, 53,* 349–350.

Greenhoe, M. L. (1972). Parameters of creativity in music education: An exploratory study (Doctoral dissertation, The University of Tennessee, Knoxville). *Dissertation Abstracts International, 33,* 1766A.

Guinier, L., Fine, M., & Balin, J. (1997). *Becoming gentlemen: Women, law school, and institutional change.* Boston: Beacon Press.

Gurian, M. (1998). *A fine young man: What parents, mentors and educators can do to shape adolescent boys into exceptional men.* New York: Jeremy P. Tarcher/Putnam.

Gurrola, S. (1975). Determination of the relative effectiveness and efficiency of selected combinations of SQ3R study method components (Doctoral dissertation, New Mexico State University, 1974). *Dissertation Abstracts International, 35,* 6938A. (University Microfilms No. 75-10, 822)

Guthrie, J. T. (1984). Lexical learning. *The Reading Teacher, 37,* 660–662.

Haggard, M. R. (1978). The effect of creative thinking-reading activities (CT-RA) on reading comprehension. In P. D. Pearson & J. Hansen (Eds.), *Reading: Disciplined inquiry in process and practice. Twenty-seventh Yearbook of the National Reading Conference* (pp. 233–236). Clemson, SC: National Reading Conference.

Haggard, M. R. (1982). The vocabulary self-collection strategy: An active approach to word learning. *Journal of Reading, 27,* 203–207.

Haggard, M. R. (1986). The vocabulary self-collection strategy: Using student interest and world knowledge to enhance vocabulary growth. *Journal of Reading, 29,* 634–642.

Harmon, J. M. (2002). Teaching independent word learning strategies to struggling readers. *Journal of Adolescent & Adult Literacy, 45*(7), 606–616.

Harste, J. (1978). Instructional implications of Rumelhart's model. In W. A. Diehi (Ed.), *Secondary reading: Theory and application. The 1978 Lilly conference on secondary reading* (Monographs in Teaching and Learning No. 1, pp. 21–23). Bloomington: Indiana University, School of Education.

Harste, J. C. (1994). Whole-language assessment. In A. Purves (Ed.), *Encyclopedia of English studies and language arts* (Vol. 2, pp. 1262–1263). New York: Scholastic.

Haven, K. (1999). "Good to the last drop": Making the most of stories to enhance language arts learning. *The California Reader, 32:2,* 5–9.

Heaton, M. M., & Lewis, H. B. (1955). *Reading ladders for human relations* (3rd ed.). Washington, DC: American Council on Education.

Henry, G. H. (1974). *Teaching reading as concept development: Emphasis on affective thinking.* Newark, DE: International Reading Association.

Herber, H. L. (1978). *Teaching reading in content areas* (2nd ed.). Englewood Cliffs, NJ: Prentice Hall.

Hersey, P., & Blanchard, K. H. (1997). *Management of organizational behavior: Utilizing human resources.* Englewood Cliffs, NJ: Prentice Hall.

Hirsch, E. D. (1987). *Cultural literacy: What every American needs to know.* Boston: Houghton Mifflin.

Hittleman, D. K. (1978). Readability, readability formulas, and cloze: Selecting instructional materials. *Journal of Reading, 22,* 117–122.

Hoffman, J. V. (1977). Intra-Act: A languaging in the content areas teaching procedure (Doctoral dissertation, University of Missouri-Kansas City). *Dissertation Abstracts International, 38,* 3248A.

Hoffman, J. V. (1991). Teacher and school effects in learning to read. In R. Barr, M. Kamil, P. Mosenthal, & D. P.

Pearson (Eds.), *Handbook of reading research* (Vol. *11*, pp. 911–950). White Plains, NY: Longman.

Hori, A. K. O. (1977). *An investigation of the efficacy of a questioning training procedure on increasing the reading comprehension performance of junior high school learning disabled students.* (Unpublished master's thesis) Lawrence. University of Kansas.

Indrisano, R., & Paratore, J. R. (1992). Using literature with readers at risk. In B. E. Cullinan (Ed.), *Invitation to read: More children's literature in the reading program* (pp. 139–149). Newark, DE: International Reading Association.

Jackson-Albee, J. A. (2000). *The effect of Read-Encode-Annotate-Ponder annotation exchange (REAP AnX) on the complex thinking of undergraduate students in children's literature courses.* (Unpublished doctoral dissertation, Kansas City, MO: University of Missouri–Kansas City.)

Jamar, D., & Morrow, J. (1991). A literature-based interdisciplinary approach to the teaching of reading, writing, and mathematics. *The Ohio Reading Teacher, 25*(3), 28–35.

Johnson, A. P. (1995). Science in reading: A harmonic convergence. *Iowa Reading Journal, 8*(1), 12–13.

Johnson, S. (2005). *Everything bad is good for you: How today's popular culture is actually making us smarter.* New York: Riverhead Books/Penguin Group (USA).

Johnson, D. D., & Pearson, P. D. (1984). *Teaching reading vocabulary* (2nd ed.). New York: Holt, Rinehart & Winston.

Johnson, D. D., Toms-Bronowski, S., & Pittelman, S. D. (1982). *An investigation of the effectiveness of semantic mapping and semantic feature analysis with intermediate grade students* (Program Report 83–3). Madison: University of Wisconsin, Wisconsin Center for Education Research.

Jonassen, D. H. (Ed.). (1982). *The technology of text: Principles for structuring, designing, and displaying text* (Vol. *1*). Englewood Cliffs, NJ: Educational Technology Publications.

Jonassen, D. H. (1985a). Generative learning vs. mathemagenic control of text processing. In D. H. Jonassen (Ed.), *The technology of text: Principles for structuring, designing, and displaying text* (Vol. *2*, pp. 9–45). Englewood Cliffs, NJ: Educational Technology Publications.

Jonassen, D. H. (Ed.). (1985b). *The technology of text: Principles for structuring, designing, and displaying text* (Vol. *2*). Englewood Cliffs, NJ: Educational Technology Publications.

Kagan, S. (1994). *Cooperative learning.* San Clemente, CA: Kagan Publishing.

Kay, L., Young, J. L., & Mottley, R. R. (1986). Using Manzo's ReQuest model with delinquent adolescents. *Journal of Reading, 29*, 506–510.

Kelly, B. W., & Holmes, J. (1979). The Guided Lecture Procedure. *Journal of Reading, 22*, 602–604.

Kibby, M. W. (1995). The organization and teaching of things and the words that signify them. *Journal of Adolescent and Adult Literacy, 39*, 208–223.

King, C. M., & Parent Johnson, L. M. (1999). Constructing meaning via reciprocal teaching. *Reading Research and Instruction, 38*(3), 169–186.

King, A., & Rosenshine, B. (1993). Effects of guided cooperative questioning on children's knowledge construction. *Journal of Experimental Education, 61*(2), 127–148.

Kirby, D., & Liner, T. (1981). *Inside out: Developmental strategies for teaching.* Montclair, NJ: Boynton/Cook.

Kirshner, D., & Whitson, J. A., Eds. (1997). *Situated cognition: Social, semiotic, and psychological perspectives.* Mahwah,

NJ: Lawrence Erlbaum Associates, Publishers.

Kobrin B. (1988). *Eyeopeners! How to choose and use children's books about real people, places, and things.* New York: Penguin.

Koskinen, P. S., Wilson, R. M., Gambrell, L. B., & Jensema, C. J. (1987). *Using the technology of closed-captioned television to teach reading to handicapped students.* (Performance Report, U.S. Department of Education Grant No. G-00-84-30067). Falls Church, VA: National Captioning Institute.

Kress, G. (2003). *Literacy in the new age media.* London: Routledge.

Lambert, L. (2005). *Leadership capacity for lasting school improvement.* Alexandria, VA: Association for Supervision & Curriculum Development.

Lee, D. M., Bingham, A., & Woelfel, S. (1968). *Critical reading develops early.* Newark, DE: International Reading Association.

Legenza, A. (1978). Inquiry training for reading and learning improvement. *Reading Improvement, 15,* 309–316.

Lenski, S. D., Wham, M. A., & Johns, J. L. (1999). *Reading and learning strategies for middle and high school students.* Dubuque, IA: Kendall/Hunt Publishing Company.

Leu, D. J. (2001). Internet Project: Preparing students for new literacies in a global village. *The Reading Teacher* (*54*) 6, 568–572.

Levin, J. R., Morrison, C. R., McGivern, J. E., Mastropieri, M. A., & Scruggs, T. E. (1986). Mnemonic facilitation of text-embedded science facts. *American Educational Research Journal, 23,* 489–506.

Lewis, C. (1999). Forward to *Popular culture in the classroom: Teaching and researching critical media literacy* (Alvermann, Moon, & Hagood, authors). Newark, DE: International Reading Association.

Lipson, M. Y., & Wixson, K. K. (1997). *Assessment and instruction of reading and writing disability: an interactive approach* (2nd ed.)., New York: Longman.

Luce-Kapler, R. (2004). *Writing with, through, and beyond text: An ecology of language.* Mahwah, NJ: Lawrence Erlbaum Associates, Inc.

Luce-Kapler, R. (2007). Radical change and wikis: Teaching new literacies. *Journal of Adolescent & Adult Literacy, 51*(3), 214–223.

Luke, A., & Freebody, P. (1997). The social practices of reading. In S. Muspratt, A. Luke, & P. Freebody (Eds.), *Constructing critical literacies: Teaching and learning textual practices* (pp. 185–225). Cresskill, NJ: Hampton Press.

Maier, N. R. E. (1963). *Problem solving discussions and conferences: Leadership methods and skills.* New York: McGraw-Hill.

MacNeal, E. (1994). *Mathsemantics: Making numbers talk sense.* New York: Viking.

Maggart, Z. D., & Zintz, M. V. (1992). *The reading process: The teacher and the learner* (6th ed.). Dubuque, IA: W. C. Brown & Benchmark.

Maloney, W. H. (2003). Connecting the texts of their lives to academic literacy: Creating success for at-risk first-year college students. *Journal of Adolescent & Adult Literacy, 46*(8), 664–673.

Manzo, A. V. (1969a). Improving reading comprehension through reciprocal questioning (Doctoral dissertation, Syracuse University, Syracuse, NY, 1968). *Dissertation Abstracts International, 30,* 5344A.

Manzo, A. V. (1969b). The ReQuest procedure. *Journal of Reading, 13,* 123–126.

Manzo, A. V. (1973). CONPASS English: A demonstration project. *Journal of Reading, 16,* 539–545.

Manzo, A. V. (1974). The group reading activity. *Forum for Reading, 3,* 26–33.

Manzo, A. V. (1975). Guided reading procedure. *Journal of Reading, 18,* 287–291.

Manzo, A. V. (1977). *Recent developments in content area reading.* Keynote address, Missouri Council of Teachers of English, Springfield, MO.

Manzo, A. V. (1980). Three "universal" strategies in content area reading and languaging. *Journal of Reading, 24,* 146–149.

Manzo, A. V. (1983). "Subjective approach to vocabulary" acquisition (Or ". . . I think my brother is arboreal!"). *Reading Psychology, 3,* 155–160.

Manzo, A. V. (1985). Expansion modules for the ReQuest, CAT, GRP, and REAP reading/study procedures. *Journal of Reading, 28,* 498–502.

Manzo, A. V. (1998). Teaching for creative outcomes: Why we don't, how we all can. *The Clearinghouse,* (5), 287–290.

Manzo, A. V. (2003). Literacy crisis or Cambrian Period? Theory, practice, and public policy implications. *Journal of Adolescent & Adult Literacy, 46*(8), 654–661.

Manzo, A. V., & Casale, U. P. (1980). The five C's: A problem-solving approach to study skills. *Reading Horizons, 20,* 281–284.

Manzo, A. V., & Casale, U. P. (1985). Listen-read-discuss: A content reading heuristic. *Journal of Reading, 28,* 732–734.

Manzo, A. V., Garber, K., & Warm, J. (1992). *Dialectical thinking: A generative approach to critical/creative reading.* Paper presented at the National Reading Conference, San Antonio, TX, 1992.

Manzo, A. V., Garber, K., Manzo, U. C., & Kahn, R. (1994). *Transmission, transaction, and transformation: Response to text perspectives.* Paper presented at the National Developmental Educators Conference, Kansas City, MO.

Manzo, A. V., & Garber, K. (1995). Study guides. In A. Purves (Ed.), *Encyclopedia of English studies and language arts* (pp. 1124–1125). New York: Scholastic.

Manzo, A. V., & Legenza, A. (1975). Inquiry training for kindergarten children. *Journal of Educational Leadership, 32,* 479–483.

Manzo, A. V., & Manzo, U. C. (1987). *Asking, answering, commenting: A participation training strategy.* Paper presented at the annual meeting of the International Reading Association, Anaheim, CA.

Manzo, A. V., & Manzo U. C. (1990a). *Content area reading: A heuristic approach.* Upper Saddle River, NJ: Merrill/Prentice Hall.

Manzo, A. V., & Manzo, U. C. (1990b). Note Cue: A comprehension and participation training strategy. *Journal of Reading, 33,* 608–611.

Manzo, A. V., & Manzo, U. C. (1995). *Teaching children to be literate: A reflective approach.* Fort Worth, TX: Harcourt Brace College Publishers.

Manzo, A. V., & Manzo, U. C. (1997a). *Content area literacy: Interactive teaching for active learning,* (2nd ed.). Upper Saddle River, NJ: Merrill.

Manzo, A. V., & Manzo, U. C. (1997b). A new eclecticism for literacy education. *Journal of Reading Research and Instruction, 37:2,* 94–100.

Manzo, A. V., & Manzo, U. C. (2002). Mental modeling. In B. Guzzetti (Ed.) *Literacy in America: An encyclopedia of history, theory, and practice.* Santa Barbara, CA: ABC CLIO.

Manzo, A. V., Manzo, U. C., & Albee, J. J. (2004). *Reading assessment for diagnostic-prescriptive teaching* (2nd Ed.). Belmont, CA: Wadsworth/Thompson Learning.

Manzo, A. V., Manzo, U. C., Barnhill, A., & Thomas, M. M. (2000). Of different minds: Possible proficient reader subtypes—implications for literacy and gendered theory and practice. *Reading Psychology, 21,* 217–225.

Manzo, A.V., Manzo, U.C., & Estes, T.H. (2001). *Content area literacy: Interactive teaching for active learning,* 3rd edition. New York: John Wiley & Sons.

Manzo, A. V. & Martin, D. C. (1974). Writing communal poetry. *Journal of Reading, 17,* 638–643.

Manzo, A. V., & Sherk, J. K. (1971–1972). Some generalizations and strategies for guiding vocabulary acquisition. *Journal of Reading Behavior, 4,* 78–89.

Manzo, A. V., & Sherk, J. K. (1978). Reading and "languaging in the content areas": A third generation approach. *The New England Reading Association Journal, 13*(1), 28–32.

Maor, E. (1979). A unification of two famous theorems from classical geometry. *Mathematics Teacher, 72,* 363–367.

Maring, G. H., & Furman, G. (1985). Seven "whole class" strategies to help mainstreamed young people read and listen better in content area classes. *Journal of Reading, 28,* 694–700.

Maring, G. H., & Ritson, R. (1980). Reading improvement in the gymnasium. *Journal of Reading, 24,* 27–31.

Martin, D. C., Lorton, M., Blanc, R. A., & Evans, C. (1977). *The learning center: A comprehensive model for colleges and universities.* Grand Rapids, MI: Central Trade Plant.

Marzano, R. J. (1997). *Designing standards-based districts, schools, and classrooms.* Alexandria, VA: ASCD.

Marzano, R. J., & Marzano, J. S. (1988). *A cluster approach to elementary vocabulary instruction.* Newark, DE: International Reading Association.

Mason, L.H. (2004). Explicit self-regulated strategy development versus reciprocal questioning: Effects on expository reading comprehension among struggling readers. *Journal of Educational Psychology, 96*(2), 283–296.

Matza, N. (2009–10). *Health science for teachers.* Long Beach, CA: Copy Pro.

McEneaney, J. E. (2002). Prologue to an object-agent theory of literacy. In D. Schallert, C. Fairbanks, J. Worthy, B. Maloch, & J. Hoffman (Eds.), *51st Yearbook of the National Reading Conference* (pp 321–332). Oak Creek, WI: National Reading Conference.

McKenzie, J. V., Ericson, B., & Hunter, L. (1988). *Questions may be an answer.* (Unpublished manuscript, California State University at Northridge.)

McKeon, R. (Ed.). (1947). *Introduction to Aristotle.* New York: The Modern Library.

McKeough, A., Lupart, J., & Marini, A. (Eds.) (1995). *Teaching for transfer: Fostering generalization in learning.* Mahway, NJ: Lawrence Erlbaum Associates, Publishers.

McNamara, L. P. (1977). A study of the cloze procedure as an alternate group instructional strategy in secondary school American government classes. (Doctoral dissertation, Northern Illinois University, DeKalb). *Dissertation Abstracts International, 39,* 216A.

Meichenbaum, D., & Asarnow, J. (1979). Cognitive-behavioral modifications and metacognitive development. In P. C. Kendall & S. D. Hollan (Eds.), *Cognitive-behavioral interventions: Theory, research and procedures* (pp. 11–35). New York: Academic Press.

Metzger, M. (1998). Teaching reading: Beyond the plot. *Phi Delta Kappan, 80*(3), 240.

Meyer, B. J. E. (1975). *The organization of prose and its effect on memory.* Amsterdam: North-Holland.

Michener, J. A. (1976). *Sports in America,* 1st edition. New York: Random House.

Mikulecky, L. (1982). Job literacy: The relationship between school preparation and workplace actuality. *Reading Research Quarterly, 17,* 400–419.

Miller, W. E., & Dollard, J. (1941). *Social learning and imitation.* New Haven, CT: Yale University Press.

Moffett, J. (1989). *Storm in the mountains: A case study of censorship, conflict, and consciousness.* Carbondale, IL: Southern Illinois University Press.

Moore, D. W., Readence, J. E., & Rickelmam, R. J. (1983). An historical exploration of content area reading instruction. *Reading Research Quarterly, 18,* 419–438.

Moss, B. (1991). Children's nonfiction trade books: A complement to content area texts. *The Reading Teacher, 45*(1), 26–32.

Mountain, L. (2002). Flip-a-chip to build vocabulary. *Journal of Adolescent & Adult Literacy, 46*(1), 62–69.

Mulliken, C. N., & Henk, W. A. (1985). Using music as a background for reading: An exploratory study. *Journal of Reading, 28,* 353–358.

Murry, C. (2003, April). Tablet computing: The "next big thing" in school computing has arrived. *ESchool News, eSN Special Report.* Retrieved from http://www.eschoolnews.com/resources/reports/TabletSpec403/.

NCES (2001). U.S. Department of Education, National Center for Education Statistics. *Outcomes of Learning: Results From the 2000 Program for International Student Assessment of 15-Year-Olds in Reading, Mathematics, and Science Literacy,* NCES 2002-115, by Mariann Lemke, Christopher Calsyn, Laura Lippman, Leslie Jocelyn, David Kastberg, Yan Yun Liu, Stephen Rocy, Trevor Williams, Thea Kruger, and Ghedam Bairu. Washington, DC: NCES.

Newby, T., Stepich, D., Lehman, J., & Russel, J. (1996). *Instructional technology for teaching and learning.* Englewood Cliffs, NJ: Prentice Hall.

New London Group (1996). A pedagogy of multiliteracies: Designing social futures. *Harvard Educational Review, 66,* 60–92.

Nilsen, A. P., & Nilsen, D. L. F. (2003). Lessons in the teaching of vocabulary from September 11 and Harry Potter. *Journal of Adolescent & Adult Literacy, 46*(3), 254–261.

NSES (1998). *National Science Education Standards.* Washington, DC: National Academy Press.

Ogle, D. M. (1989). Study techniques that ensure content area reading success. In D. Lapp, J. Flood, & N. Farnam (Eds.), *Content area reading and learning* (2nd ed.). Boston: Allyn & Bacon.

Ogle, D. M. (1996). Study techniques that ensure content area reading success. In D. Lapp, J. Flood, & N. Farnan (Eds.), *Content area reading and learning* (2nd ed.). Boston: Allyn & Bacon.

Ollmann, H. E. (1996). Creating higher level thinking with reading response. *Journal of Adolescent and Adult Literacy, 39,* 576–581.

Ordonz-Jasis, R. (2002) *Latino families and schools: Tensions, transitions and transformations.* Unpublished Doctoral Dissertation, University of California-Berkeley.

Otto, W., & Hayes, B. (1982). Glossing for improved comprehension: Progress and prospect. In G. H. McNinch (Ed.), *Reading in the disciplines. Second yearbook of the American Reading*

Forum (pp. 16–18). Athens, GA: American Reading Forum.

Padak, N. D. (1986). Teachers' verbal behaviors: A window to the teaching process. In J. A. Niles & R. V. Lalik (Eds.), *Solving problems in literacy: Learners, teachers, and researchers. Thirty-fifth Yearbook of the National Reading Conference* (pp. 185–191). Rochester, NY: National Reading Conference.

Paley, V. G. (1986, May). On listening to what the children say. *Harvard Educational Review, 56*(2), 122–131.

Palincsar, A. S., & Brown, A. L. (1984). Reciprocal teaching of comprehension monitoring activities. *Cognition and Instruction, 1,* 117–175.

Palmatier, R. A. (1971). Comparison of four note-taking procedures. *Journal of Reading, 14,* 235–258.

Palmatier, R. A. (1973). A notetaking system for learning. *Journal of Reading, 17,* 36–39.

Palmatier, R. A., & Bennett, J. M. (1974). Notetaking habits of college students. *Journal of Reading, 18,* 215–218.

Pauk, W. (1989). *How to study in college* (4th ed.). Boston: Houghton Mifflin.

Paul, R. W. (1993). *Critical thinking: How to prepare students for a rapidly changing world.* Santa Rosa, CA: Foundation for Critical Thinking.

Pauler, S., & Bodevin, D. (1990). Book-specific response activities: Satisfaction guaranteed. *George Journal of Reading, 16*(2), 30–35.

Perry, M. (1971). *Man's unfinished journey.* Boston: Houghton Mifflin.

Peters, C. W. (1982). The content processing model: A new approach to conceptualizing content reading. In J. P. Palberg (Ed.), *Reading in the content areas: Application of a concept* (pp. 100–109). Toledo, OH: University of Toledo, College of Education.

Piercy, D. (1976). *Reading activities in content areas.* Boston: Allyn & Bacon.

Pond, M., & Hoch, L. (1992). Linking children's literature and science activities. *Ohio Reading Teacher, 25*(2), 13–15.

Post, A. R. (1992). The camel caper: An integrated language arts lesson. *Michigan Reading Journal, 25*(2), 29–35.

Pressley, M. (2000). What should comprehension instruction be the instruction of? In M. L., Kamil, P. B., Mosenthal, P. D., Pearson, & R. Barr, (Eds.), *Handbook of reading research, volume III.* (pp. 545–561). Mahwah, NJ: Erlbaum.

Pressley, M., Johnson, C. J., & Symons, S. (1987). Elaborating to learn and learning to elaborate. *Journal of Learning Disabilities, 20,* 76–91.

Pressley, M., Levin, J. R., & MacDaniel, M. A. (1987). Remembering versus inferring what a word means: Mnemonic and contextual approaches. In M. C. McKeown & M. E. Curtis (Eds.), *The nature of vocabulary acquisition* (pp. 107–129). Hillsdale, NJ: Erlbaum.

Pressley, M., Levin, J. R., & Miller, G. E. (1981). How does the keyword method affect vocabulary comprehension and usage? *Reading Research Quarterly, 16,* 213–225.

Putnam, L., Bader, L., & Bean, R. (1988). Clinic directors share insights into effective strategies. *Journal of Clinical Reading, 3,* 16–20.

Rakes, S. K., & Smith, L. J. (1987). Strengthening comprehension and recall through the principle of recitation. *Journal of Reading, 31,* 260–263.

Ratekin, N., Simpson, M. L., Alvermann, D. E., & Dishner, E. K. (1985). Why teachers resist content area reading instruction. *Journal of Reading, 28,* 432–437.

Raths, L. E., Harmon, M., & Simon, S. B. (1978). *Values and teaching* (2nd ed.). Columbus, OH: Merrill.

Reeve, R. A., Palincsar, A. S., & Brown, A. L. (1985). *Everyday and academic thinking: Implications for learning and problem solving* (Journal of Curriculum Studies Technical Report No. 349). Champaign: University of Illinois, Center for the Study of Reading.

Rhoder, C., & Huerster, P. (2002). Use dictionaries for word learning with caution. *Journal of Adolescent & Adult Literacy, 45*(8), 730–736.

Robinson, F. (1946). *Effective study.* New York: Harper Brothers.

Roby, T. (1983, April). *The other side of the question: Controversial turns, the devil's advocate, and reflective responses.* Paper presented at the annual meeting of the American Educational Research Association, Montreal.

Rogoff, B. (1990). *Apprenticeship in thinking: Cognitive development in social context.* New York: Oxford University Press.

Rosenblatt, L. (1938). *Literature as exploration.* New York: Appleton-Century.

Rosenshine, B. V. (1984). Content, time, and direct instruction. In P. L. Peterson & H. J. Walberg (Eds.), *Research on teaching: Concepts, findings, and implications* (pp. 102–106). Berkeley, CA: McCutchan.

Rowe, M. B. (1974). Wait time and rewards as instructional variables, their influences on language, logic, and fate control: Part One—Wait time. *Journal of Research in Science Teaching, 11,* 81–94.

Rowe, M. B. (1986). Wait time: Slowing down may be a way of speeding up! *Journal of Teacher Education, 37,* 43–50.

Ruddell, M. R. (1997). *Teaching content reading and writing,* (2nd ed). Boston: Allyn & Bacon.

Ruddell, M. R., & Shearer, B. A. (2002). "Extraordinary," "tremendous," "exhilarating." "magnificent": Middle school at-risk students become avid word learners with the vocabulary self-collection strategy (VSS). *Journal of Adolescent & Adult Literacy, 45*(5), 352–364.

Rush, T., Moe, A., & Storlie, R. (1986). *Occupational literacy education.* Newark, DE: International Reading Association.

Russell, D. (1961). *Children learn to read* (2nd ed.). New York: Ginn.

Santa, C. M., Dailey, S. C., & Nelson, M. (1985). Free-response and opinion proof: A reading and writing strategy for middle grade and secondary teachers. *Journal of Reading, 28,* 346–352.

Santa, C. M., Isaacson, L., & Manning, G. (1987). Changing content instruction through action research. *The Reading Teacher, 40,* 434–438.

Schumm, J. S., & Mangrum, C. T., II (1991). FLIP: A framework for content area reading. *Journal of Reading, 35,* 120–123.

Simmons, J. (2003). Responders are taught, not born. *Journal of Adolescent & Adult Literacy, 46*(8), 684–693.

Simpson, M. (1986). PORPE: A writing strategy for studying and learning in the content areas. *Journal of Reading, 29,* 407–414.

Simpson, M. L., Hayes, C. G., Stahl, N. A., Connor R. T., & Weaver, D. (1988). An initial validation of a study strategy system. *Journal of Reading Behavior, 20,* 149–180.

Singer, H., & Dolan, D. (1980). *Reading and learning from text.* Boston: Little, Brown.

Sizer, T. R. (1984). *Horace's compromise: The dilemma of the American high school.* Boston: Houghton Mifflin.

Smith, R. J., & Dauer, V. L. (1984). A comprehension-monitoring strategy for reading content area materials. *Journal of Reading, 28,* 144–147.

Smyth, J. (2003, January 23). Study says boys do read, they just don't read books. *National Post.* Retrieved January 23, 2003 from http://www.nationalpost.com and now available for order from the archive at http://www.infomart.ca.

Spiegel, D. L. (1980). Adaptations of Manzo's guided reading procedure. *Reading Horizons, 20,* 188–192.

Spor, M. W. & Schneider, B. K. (1999). Content reading strategies: What teachers know, use, and want to learn. *Reading Research and Instruction, 38:*(3), 221–231.

Stahl, S. A., & Fairbanks, M. M. (1986). The effects of vocabulary instruction: A model-based meta-analysis. *Review of Educational Research, 56,* 72–110.

Stahl, N. A., & Henk, W. A. (1986). Tracing the roots of textbook study systems: An extended historical perspective. In J. A. Niles & R. V. Lalik (Eds.), *Solving problems in literacy: Learners, teachers, and researchers. Thirty-fifth yearbook of the National Reading Conference* (pp. 366–374). Rochester, NY: National Reading Conference.

Stanovich, K. E. (1986). Matthew effects in reading: Some consequences of individual differences in the acquisition of literacy. *Reading Research Quarterly,* (21) *4,* 360–407.

Stauffer, R. (1969). *Directing reading maturity as a cognitive process.* New York: Harper & Row.

Stenger, C. (1999). *A characterization of undergraduate mathematical thinking.* Paper presented at the Fourth Annual Conference on Undergraduate Mathematics Education. Chicago, IL.

Stevens, K. C. (1982). Can we improve reading by teaching background information? *Journal of Reading, 25,* 326–329.

Stieglitz, E. L., & Stieglitz, V. S. (1981). SAVOR the word to reinforce vocabulary in the content areas. *Journal of Reading, 25,* 48.

Tan, A., & Nicholson, T. (1997). Flashcards revisited: Training poor readers to read words faster improves their comprehension of text. *Journal of Educational Psychology, 89*(2), 276–288.

Taylor, G. C. (1980). Music in language arts instruction. *Language Arts, 58,* 363–367.

Technology counts 2007: A digital decade (published March 29, 2007). *Education Week. 26*:30 Retrieved September 5, 2008 from http://www.edweek.org/ew/toc/2007/03/29/index.html

Tchudi, S. (1988). Invisible thinking and the hypertext. *English Journal, 77*(1), 22–30.

Tharp, R. G., & Gallimore, R. (1989). *Rousing minds to life: Teaching, learning, and schooling in social context.* New York: Cambridge University Press.

Thomas, M. M. (1998, May). *Furthering higher-order literacy using the internet.* Paper presented as part of a full-day seminar with others entitled "Higher-Order Literacy: Redefining Remedial, Developmental, and Proficient Readers" at the 43rd Annual Convention of the International Reading Association, Orlando, Florida.

Thomas, M. M. (2001). *Proficient reader characteristics: Relationships among text-dependent and higher-order literacy variables with reference to stage theories of intellectual development. Dissertation Abstracts International* (UMI No. 3010626).

Thomas, M. M., & Hofmeister, D. (2003). Moving content area literacy into the digital age: Using online discussion board interactions. *Journal of Content Area Reading, 2*(1), 61–80.

Thomas, M. M., King, A., & Cetinguc, T. (2004). My first year with a Tablet PC: Has literacy found a means to ubiquitous computing at last? *Proceedings of the 2004 Society for Information Technology in Teacher Education Conference*, Atlanta, Georgia.

Thorndike, E. L. (1917). Reading as reasoning: A study of mistakes in paragraph reading. *Journal of Educational Psychology, 8*, 323–332.

Tierney, R. J., Readence, J. E., & Dishner, E. K. (1990). *Reading strategies and practices* (3rd ed.). Needham Heights, MA: Allyn & Bacon.

Tierney, R. J., Soter, A., O'Flahavan, J. F., & McGinley, W. (1989). The effects of reading and writing upon thinking critically. *Reading Research Quarterly, 24*, 134–137. *Time* (March 22, 1993). 54.

Tuchman, B.W. (1982). *Practicing history: Selected essays.* Ballantine Books.

Unrau, N. J. (1997). *Thoughtful teachers, thoughtful learners: A guide to helping adolescents think critically.* Scarborough, Ont: Pippin Publishing.

Vacca, R. T., & Alvermann, D. E. (1998). The crisis in adolescent literacy: Is it real or imagined? *NASSP Bulletin, 82*(600), 4–9.

Vogt, M. E. (2002). *SQP2RS: Increasing students' understandings of expository text through cognitive and metacognitive strategy application.* Paper presented at the 52nd Annual Meeting of the National Reading Conference, Miami, FL.

Vygotsky, L. S. (1978). *Mind in society: The development of higher psychological process.* Cambridge, MA: Harvard University Press.

Wade, R. K. (1984–1985). What makes a difference in inservice teacher education? A meta-analysis of research. *Educational Leadership, 42*(4), 48–54.

Walker, A., & Parkman, M. (1924). *The study readers: Fifth year.* New York: Merrill.

Watkins, J., McKenna, M., Manzo, A., & Manzo, U. (1995). *The effects of the listen-read-discuss procedure on the content learning of high school students.* (Unpublished manuscript.)

Weaver, W. W., & Kingston, A. J. (1963). A factor analysis of cloze procedure and other measures of reading and language ability. *Journal of Communication, 13*, 252–261.

Welker, W. A. (1987). Going from typical to technical meaning. *Journal of Reading, 31*, 275–276.

Wilkins, G., & Miller S. (1983). *Strategies for success: An effective guide for teachers of secondary-level slow learners.* New York: Teachers College Press.

Willmore, D. J. (1967). *A comparison of four methods of studying a college textbook.* (Doctoral dissertation, University of Minnesota, 1966). *Dissertation Abstracts, 27*, 2413A.

Wilson, E. O. (1998). *Consilience: The unity of knowledge.* New York: Knopf.

Wood, K. D. (1992). Fostering collaborative reading and writing experiences in mathematics. *Journal of Reading, 36*(2), 96–103.

Wood, K. D. (2000). Asset building in the classroom: An instructional perspective, research into practice. *Middle School Journal, 31*(3), 53–56.

Wood, K. D. (2002). Aiding comprehension with the imagine, elaborate, predict, and confirm (IEPC) strategy: Research into practice. *Middle School Journal, 33*(3), 47–54.

Wooster, G. E. (1958). Teaching the SQ3R method of study: An investigation of the instructional approach (Doctoral dissertation, The Ohio State University, 1953). *Dissertation Abstracts International, 18*, 2067–2068.

Wooten, D. A. (1992). The magic of Martin. In B. E. Cullinan (Ed.), *Invitation to read: More children's literature in the reading program* (pp. 73–79). Newark, DE: International Reading Association.

Worthy, J. (1998). On every page someone gets killed! Book conversations you don't hear in school. *Journal of Adolescent and Adult Literacy, 41*, 508–517.

Zola, J. (Host). (1998). *How to conduct successful Socratic seminars [Video recording]*. Alexandria, VA: Association for Supervision and Curriculum Development.

CHILDREN'S BOOKS CITED

Adamson, J. (1960). *Born Free.* New York: Pantheon.

Bahr, R. (1982). *Blizzard at the Zoo.* New York: Lothrop.

Barton, B. (1986). *Planes* New York: Crowell.

Barton, B. (1986). *Trucks.* New York: Crowell.

Bash, B. (1989). *Desert Giant: The World of the Saguano Cactus.* Boston: Little Brown.

Brown, M. W. (1988). *Goodnight Moon.* New York: Harper & Row.

Burton, V. L. (1939). *Mike Mulligan and His Steam Shovel.* Boston: Houghton Mifflin.

Caselli, G. (1992). *Life Through the Ages.* New York: Darling Kindersley.

Cavanah, F. (1978). *Abe Lincoln Gets His Chance.* New York: Scholastic.

Cohen, B. (1983). *The Carp in the Bathtub.* Illustrated by Joan Halpern. New York: Lothrop.

Curtis, C. (1978). *Panda.* New York: Delacorte.

dePaola, T. (1975). *The Cloud Book.* New York: Holiday.

Freedman, R. (1984). *Animal Superstars: Biggest, Strongest, Fastest, Smartest.* New York: Prentice Hall.

Gemming, E. (1974). *Born in a Barn.* New York: Coward, McCann, & Geoghegan.

Gibbons, G. (1982). *The Post Office Book: Mail and How It Moves.* New York: Crowell.

Goudey, A. (1961). *Here Come the Dolphins.* New York: Scribner's.

Graham, A., & Graham, F. (1978). *Whale Watch.* New York: Delacorte.

Herge. (1975). *Tintin in Tibet.* New York: Little Brown.

Hughes, S. (1985). *An Evening at Alfie's.* New York: Lothrop.

Keats, E. J. (1967). *The Snowy Day.* New York: Viking.

The Kids' Question and Answer Book, by the editors of *Owl* magazine. (1988). New York: Putnam.

Lilly, K. (1982). *Animals in the Country.* New York: Simon & Schuster.

Lobel, A. (1970). *Frog and Toad Are Friends.* New York: Harper & Row.

Marshall, J. (1987). *The Cut-Ups Cut Loose.* New York: Viking.

Martin, B., Jr., & Archambault, J. (1985). *Chicka Chicka Boom Boom.* Illustrated by T. Rand. New York: Simon & Schuster.

Martin, B., Jr., & Archambault, J. (1988). *Listen to the Rain.* New York: Henry Holt.

Macaulay, D. (1988), *The way things work: An illustrated encyclopedia of technology.* Boston: Houghton Mifflin.

McMillan, B. (1983). *Here a Chick, There a Chick.* New York: Lothrop, Lee & Shepard.

Momaday, N. S. (1975). *Owl in the Cedar Tree.* Flagstaff, AZ: Northland Press.

Noble, T.H. (1984). *The Day Jimmy's Boa Ate the Wash.* New York: Dial Press.

Parish, P. (1989). *Amelia Bedelia.* Illustrated by Fritz Seibel. New York: Harper & Row.

Pope, J. (1986). *Do Animals Dream?* New York: Viking.

Rey, H. A. (1973). *Curious George.* Boston: Houghton Mifflin.

Schwartz, D. M. (1985). *How Much Is a Million?* Illustrated by Steven Kellogg. New York: Lothrop, Lee & Shepard.

Sendak, M. (1985). *Where the Wild Things Are.* New York: HarperCollins.

Silverstein, S. (1987). *The Giving Tree.* New York: HarperCollins.

Viorst, J. (1987). *Alexander and the Terrible, Horrible, No Good, Very Bad Day.* Illustrated by Ray Cruz. New York: Macmillan.

Waber, B. (1973). *Ira Sleeps Over.* Boston: Houghton Mifflin.

Wilder, L.I. & Williams, G. (1994). *The complete little house nine-book set.* New York: HarperTrophy.

Williams, V. (1982). *A Chair for My Mother.* New York: Greenwillow.

Wong, J. S. (1963). *Fifth Chinese Daughter.* New York: Scholastic.

Wood, A. (1984). *The Napping House.* Illustrated by D. Wood. San Diego: Harcourt Brace Jovanovich.

PHOTO CREDITS

Chapter 1
Page 3: Photodisc Red./Getty Images.

Chapter 2
Page 21: PhotoDisc, Inc./Getty Images.

Chapter 3
Page 39: Photodisc Green/Getty Images.

Chapter 4
Page 61: Digital Vision.

Chapter 5
Page 93: Photodisc Green/Getty Images.

Chapter 6
Page 117: PhotoDisc, Inc./Getty Images.

Chapter 7
Page 147: PhotoDisc, Inc./Getty Images.

Chapter 8
Page 175: Digital Vision.

Chapter 9
Page 223: Image 100 Ltd./Corbis Images.

Chapter 10
Page 251: Photodisc Red/Getty Images.

Chapter 11
Page 273: Photodisc Blue/Getty Images.

Chapter 12
Page 289: Royalty-free/Corbis Images.
Page 310: Bettmann/Corbis Images.

Chapter 13
Page 325: Thinkstock/Getty Images.

Chapter 14
Page 345: Brand X Pictures/Getty Images.

INDEX